PELICA

# PREHISTO

Grahame Clark was Master
1973 until 1980 and Fellow
was Disney Professor of Archaeology from 1952 to 1974 and Head of the Department of Archaeology and Anthropology from 1956 to 1971 at the University of Cambridge. He was awarded the C.B.E. in 1971 and has received many other awards. He has travelled widely in many parts of Europe, North America, the Middle and Far East and Australasia. He has served as visiting professor in different parts of the world and is an honorary member of academies and other learned bodies in many countries and his pupils hold many posts in archaeology, not only in this country but notably in different parts of Africa, the United States, Australia, New Zealand and the Middle East. His excavations have mainly been in England. Professor Clark has published many papers and books, some of which have been widely translated, including *World Prehistory* (a new and almost entirely re-written edition of which was published in 1969). He edited the *Proceedings of the Prehistoric Society* (1935–70) and his publications include *The Earlier Stone Age Settlement of Scandinavia*, *Mesolithic Prelude* and *The Identity of Man*.

Stuart Piggott was born in 1910 and from 1949 until 1977 held the Abercromby Chair for Prehistoric Archaelogy in the University of Edinburgh. He was awarded the C.B.E. in 1972. While his studies have mainly been concerned with prehistoric Europe, he was able, in the intervals between Military Intelligence duties during the last war, to work on the archaeology of prehistoric India and the Near East. He has travelled extensively in Europe and Asia. In addition to numerous papers in archaeological journals, he has also published *Prehistoric India*, *Ancient Europe*, *The Druids* (published in Penguins), *France Before the Romans*, of which he is joint editor, *Antiquity Depicted* and *The Earliest Wheeled Transport*.

# PREHISTORIC SOCIETIES

*Grahame Clark and*
*Stuart Piggott*

PENGUIN BOOKS

*by arrangement with Hutchinson of London*

Penguin Books Ltd, Harmondsworth, Middlesex, England
Viking Penguin Inc., 40 West 23rd Street, New York, New York 10010, U.S.A.
Penguin Books Australia Ltd, Ringwood, Victoria, Australia
Penguin Books Canada Ltd, 2801 John Street, Markham, Ontario, Canada L3R 1B4
Penguin Books (N.Z.) Ltd, 182–190 Wairau Road, Auckland 10, New Zealand

First published by Hutchinson 1965
Published in Pelican Books 1970
Reprinted 1976, 1985



Made and printed in Great Britain by
Richard Clay (The Chaucer Press) Ltd.,
Bungay, Suffolk
Set in Bembo

# Contents

# *List of Illustrations and Maps*

PLATES



ILLUSTRATIONS IN THE TEXT

MAPS

# *Prefatory Note*

The present edition incorporates a number of emendations and corrections to the text as originally published in 1965.

The Carbon 14 dates quoted must be taken in the knowledge that they represent the expression of a statistical probability that the true date of the specimen tested lies within the range of one standard deviation (usually ± 150 years or less) of which the figure given represents the median point. It was felt, however, that in a book of this nature it would be irritating and perhaps misleading to the general reader to quote the standard deviation in each instance.

Although chapter 6 has been written in the present tense, it unhappily relates almost entirely to the recent past.

Chapters 1–7 and the first half of chapter 11 were written by Grahame Clark; and chapters 8–10, the latter half of 11 and 12, 13 by Stuart Piggott.

The authors are grateful to Messrs Faber & Faber, Cambridge University Press and Methuen, for supplying illustrations.

# CHAPTER ONE

# *Man's Place in Nature*

It is important to realize that man is an animal, but it is even more important to realize that the essence of his unique nature lies precisely in those characteristics that are not shared with any other animal. His place in nature and its supreme significance to man are not defined by his animality but by his humanity.

GEORGE GAYLORD SIMPSON

MANY of the leading problems of universal history are now recognized to fall within the competence of men of science rather than of letters: we look to mathematicians and physicists to decide whether the universe was born and will die or whether through some process of continuous evolution it will run on for ever; and to biochemists, biophysicists and palaeontologists for information on the origins of life and the course of organic evolution. Yet the beings who frame such questions are, after all, human, and it is to men alone that their answers have relevance: man's concern with his place in nature and with his own history are in themselves outstanding attributes and symbols of his unique character, a character which in essentials was moulded long before he began to maintain written records. It is of the essence of man that, while being an animal, he is more than an animal, and it is one of the main tasks of prehistory to trace the emergence of characteristics of a peculiarly human order, characteristics without which human society could hardly have arisen.

Yet the characteristics we regard as human, whether physical, psychological or behavioural, have necessarily emerged from animal antecedents, and it is well to begin by considering, even if perfunctorily, man's position in the genealogy of life. The geological record (Table 1) shows that to begin with, and for a period to be measured in many tens of millions of years, living organisms were confined to the ocean. It was not until the middle of the Palaeozoic era that geographical conditions favoured the appearance of the first terrestrial plants and of animals capable of living directly or indirectly upon them. The first land animals were, not surprisingly, amphibious and it was only towards the end of Palaeozoic times that these yielded their dominant place to reptiles. The earliest evidence for mammals dates from mid-Mesozoic times; and the primates, the most recently evolved of the mammalian orders and the one that includes man and his immediate forbears, appeared for the first time at the dawn of the Tertiary period.

| *Millions of years* | *Eras* | *Periods* | *Epochs* | *Life* |
|---|---|---|---|---|
| 0.01–Present | | Quaternary | Recent | Hominids |
| 1–0.01 | | | Pleistocene | |
| 12–1 | CENOZOIC | Tertiary | Pliocene | |
| 28–12 | | | Miocene | Anthropoid apes |
| 39–28 | | | Oligocene | Monkeys |
| 58–39 | | | Eocene | Prosimian primates |
| 75–58 | | | Palaeocene | spread and radiate |
| 135–75 | MESOZOIC | Cretaceous | | Mammals and birds |
| 165–135 | | Jurassic | | appear |
| 205–165 | | Triassic | | Reptiles predominant |
| 230–205 | | Permian | | |
| 280–230 | PALAEOZOIC | Carboniferous | | Amphibians predominant |
| 325–280 | | Devonian | | Terrestrial vegetation |
| 360–325 | | Silurian | | Many marine forms, |
| 425–360 | | Ordovician | | including vertebrates |
| 505–425 | | Cambrian | | Earliest fossils |
| *c.* 2000 | | | Conditions become possible for life | |
| *c.* 4000 | | | Birth of the planet Earth | |

Table 1. Landmarks in the evolution of life

It is possible to arrange the existing primates in a graded evolutionary series (Table 2); first, the Prosimians (tree-shrews, lemurs and tarsiers) (Figure 1); next, the New World (Platyrrhine) and Old World (Catarrhine) monkeys; and, lastly, the Hominoids, comprising Anthropoid Apes and Hominids (including man). Yet it has to be remembered that we are really dealing not so much with stages in evolution as with fruits that have ripened on branches, which diverged long ages past from the parent stem. In this respect the biological history of the primates conforms to a general pattern: in the course of geological time the tree of life has constantly thrown out side-branches, some to wither and die, others still sending out blossoms.

| *Sub-orders* | *Infra-orders* | *Super-families* | *Families* |
|---|---|---|---|
| ANTHROPOIDEA | | *Hominoidea* | *Hominidea* (Hominids) |
| | | | *Pongidae* (Apes) |
| | | *Cercopithecoidea* (Catarrhine or Old World monkeys) | |
| | | *Ceboidea* (Platyrrhine or New World monkeys) | |
| PROSIMII | TARSIIFORMES | *Tarsioidea* (Tarsiers) (Figure 1) | |
| | LORISIFORMES | *Daubentonioidea* (Aye-aye) | |
| | LEMURIFORMES | *Lemuriodea* (Lemurs) | |
| | | *Tupaioidea* (Tree-shrews) | |

Table 2. The order PRIMATES

One of the most important facts about the primates is that throughout all but the final phase of their history they spent most of their time in the trees. This not merely preserved them from many of their predators; it also enabled them on the one hand to retain a number of primitive unspecialized traits, and on the other to develop characteristics of immense significance for the future. Thus, by overemphasizing the need for specialized locomotion on four feet and by necessitating versatile and agile grasping, life in the trees encouraged the survival of a generalized structure of the limbs adapted to prehensile functions, with mobile digits and flattened nails in place of claws. Again, arboreal existence reduced the importance of smell and increased that of vision, while at the same time putting a premium on the coordination of muscular activity. This in turn led, initially, to a diminution in the size of the muzzle and snout, and a forward movement of the eyes from the side of the head so that they looked directly ahead, making it possible to achieve stereoscopy by focusing vision on both retinae simultaneously; and, in due course, to a progressive expansion and elaboration of the cerebral cortex of the brain.

Yet it was the adoption by certain primates of an exclusively terrestrial existence that caused them to take the decisive steps that led to the emergence of hominids and ultimately of men. From a purely physical point of view the most important change associated with existence on the ground was the assumption of an upright carriage, which had the effect of freeing the hands, already adapted to prehensile functions, for the manipulation and ultimately the fabrication of tools. No less important must have been the psychological effect of having to compete with predators, from which an arboreal existence had granted them

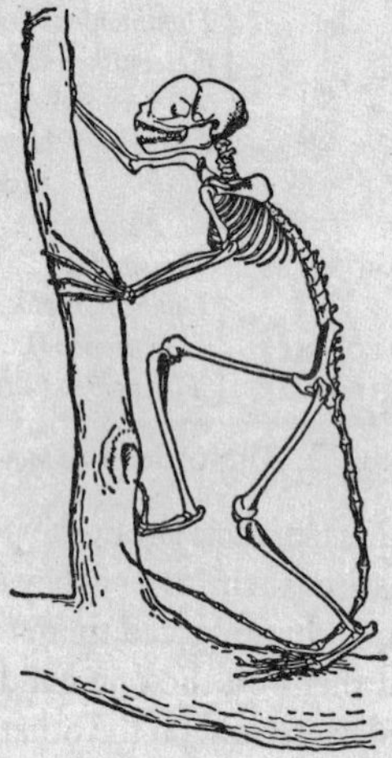

1. Skeleton of tarsier in characteristic Prosimian attitude

asylum. One may regard it as certain that the descent from the trees gave an effective impulse to the history both of material culture and of social relations. Conversely cultural developments progressively modified the hominid environment. Increasingly effective tools decreased the need for powerful teeth and at the same time stimulated the use of the brain, as did the practice of articulate speech and the increasingly cultural pattern of behaviour. The successive types of hominid were in a very real sense social artefacts.

Although, as T. H. Huxley stated long ago, the hominids and the anthropoid apes stand closer together anatomically than either of them does to any other primate group, their lines of ascent had almost certainly diverged in the course of Miocene times, possibly as much as twenty million years ago. A main factor in their differentiation seems to have been that, whereas the Pongidae held largely to their arboreal habits, the immediate predecessors of man incurred the risk, but enjoyed the stimulus, of life on the ground.

It is, however, only during the Pleistocene that we can recognize in

| *Families* | *Sub-families* | *Genera* | *Species* |
|---|---|---|---|
| *Hominidae* | | *Homo* | *H. sapiens sapiens* |
| | | | *H. sapiens* |
| | | *Australopithecus* | *H. erectus* |
| *Pongidae* | *Ponginae* | *Gorilla* | |
| | | *Pan* (Chimpanzee) | |
| | | *Pongo* (Orang-utan) | |
| | *Hylobatinae* | *Hylobates* (Gibbon) | |

Table 3. The Super-family *Hominoidea*

The fossils formerly classified under the genus *Pithecanthropus* are now included within the genus *Homo* as *Homo erectus*. Similarly, the Neanderthal and other forms of 'palæoanthropic' man are now accepted as members of *Homo sapiens*. Fossils of 'neoanthropic' type are assigned to the species *Homo sapiens sapiens*, to which the recent races of man belong.

the manufacture of tools to standard patterns the first evidence of human society. Although expert opinion differs within wide limits about the duration of the Pleistocene and its several phases, there can be no doubt whatever that in human terms it lasted an immensely long time; and that by comparison with this the period covered by historical records, even in the earliest centres of civilization, has been brief indeed. In temperate Europe, where the Pleistocene period was first closely studied, it has for some time been customary to subdivide it according to a series of glacial and interglacial stages. In the following table, which shows sequences established for the Alps and for north-western Europe respectively, only the main periods are shown, leaving out of account the minor sub-phases within each glacial episode. The dates shown for the main divisions of the Pleistocene agree broadly with those given by Zeuner for major fluctuations of solar radiation and by Emiliani on the basis of palaeotemperature curves taken from ocean cores. On the other hand it must be pointed out that the dates obtained by Evernden on the basis of the rate of decay of potassium argon in volcanic rocks for an early phase of the Mindel-Riss interglacial (*c.* 270,000) and for an interstadial of the Mindel glaciation (*c.* 370,000) are substantially longer. Equally, there is a broad range of estimates for the transition from the Pliocene to the Pleistocene.

| | | *Glacial and Interglacial phases* *Alps* | *N.W. Europe* | *Dates before present* |
|---|---|---|---|---|
| HOLOCENE | | Postglacial | | 10,000 |
| PLEISTOCENE | LATE | Würm Gl. | Weichsel Gl. | 65,000 |
| | | Riss–Würm Igl. | Eemian Igl. | |
| | MIDDLE | Riss Gl. | Saale Gl. | 130,000 |
| | | Mindel–Riss Igl. | Hoxnian Igl. | |
| | | Mindel Gl. | Elster Gl. | |
| | EARLY | Günz–Mindel Igl. | Cromerian Igl. | 275,000 |
| | | Günz and Donau Gl. | | |
| PLIOCENE–PLEISTOCENE BOUNDARY | | | | *c.* 1 to 2,000,000 |

Table 4. Major divisions of the European Pleistocene

There is no doubt that the Lower Pleistocene lasted considerably longer than the Middle and Upper Pleistocene combined. Traces of at least three glaciations antedating the Günz have been noted in Central Europe, and their existence has been confirmed by the evidence obtained by deep-sea cores obtained from the bed of the Caribbean and from the Pacific Ocean. In the palaeontological record the Lower Pleistocene is broadly equivalent to the period during which the Villafranchian fauna flourished (so named after a locality in the valley of the Arno in Tuscany). This fauna is marked by early forms of elephant (*Elephas meridionalis*), rhinoceros (*Rhinoceros etruscus*), horse (*Equus stenosis*) and beaver (*Trogontherium*).

The broad areas of uncertainty that surround the duration and subdivision of the Lower Pleistocene, a period that witnessed developments vital to the evolution of mankind, are in themselves enough to counsel caution at the present stage of the subject. Other reasons for caution are the rarity and fragmentary condition of the fossils at present available and the expectation that, as greater resources are engaged, new discoveries are likely to be made at an increasing tempo. It follows that argument from negative evidence is more than usually hazardous, and existing finds afford no more than a tentative basis for historical reconstruction: it is only to be expected that, as a glance at the periodical literature shows, wide areas of disagreement should exist on almost every aspect of early hominid evolution.

One of the great clarifications of recent years has been the recognition of a distinct form that flourished already during the Lower Pleistocene. This owes its importance to the fact that it helps to bridge the gap between man and the still largely hypothetical forms that stemmed many millions of years ago from the main trunk of primate life. Fossils of this genus were first recognized in South Africa, but finds of great importance have since been made in East Africa by Lake Eyasi and in the Olduvai Gorge, on the southern margin of the Sahara north of Lake Chad, at Al Ubeidiya in the Jordan valley, Palestine, and as far afield as Java. Although the Australopithecines seem to have survived in South Africa down to Middle Pleistocene times, as witnessed by the fossils from the Sterkfontein Extension Site, Swartkrans and Kromdrai, most palaeontologists agree that those from Makapansgat, the Sterkfontein Type Site and Taungs date from the Lower Pleistocene. Similarly, Bed I at Olduvai in northern Tanganyika which yielded Australopithecine fossils in the form of *Zinjanthropus boisei* and its precursor, though formerly assigned to the Middle Pleistocene, is now generally attributed to the Lower Pleistocene. Whatever the precise age of individual fossils, there is widespread agreement among palaeontologists that the Australopithecines help to illustrate a stage in primate evolution leading on from fossil pongids to the earliest men.

From an anatomical point of view, the most interesting fact about the Australopithecines is that they had evidently adopted an upright posture. The significant point about walking erect on two feet is, as we have already noted, that it sets the forelimbs free for such functions as coping with food and manipulating extraneous objects like tools. Interesting confirmation of this is afforded by the teeth of the Australopithecines which are characteristically arranged in hominid style on a rounded arcade; and the much reduced size of the canine is, of course, consistent with circumstances under which much of the work done by them in a previous phase of evolution was transferred to the hands. Within this general category several varieties can already be distinguished. From South Africa we have two well-documented forms, namely *A. australopithecus* and *A. paranthropus*, adapted respectively to open conditions and a forested environment, the one lightly built and omnivorous, the other more robust, but vegetarian;

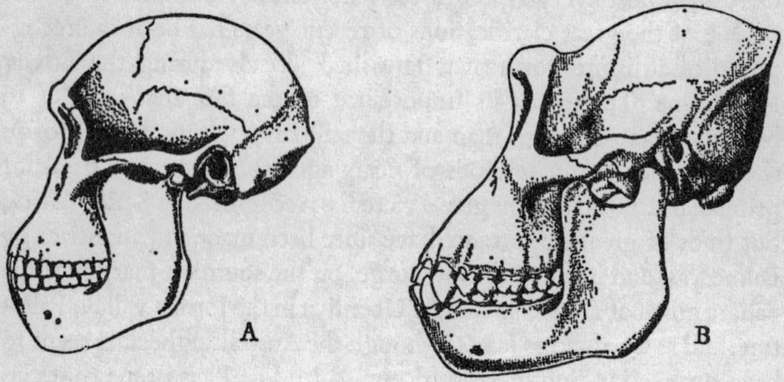


2. Skulls of (A) *Australopithecus* and (B) adult female gorilla

and the indications are that these have close analogues in the fossils from Bed I at Olduvai, *Zinjanthropus* comparing more with *Paranthropus* and his predecessor with *Australopithecus*. In addition to these well-established forms a few jaw fragments from Swartkrans have been held by some, though not by all, authorities to represent a distinct form, *Telanthropus*, standing rather closer to *Homo*. A point which needs to be emphasized is the relatively small brain capacity of the Australopithecines known to us; indeed the brain capacity of the two main South African varieties (*c.* 450–550 c.c.) falls short of the maximum for present-day gorillas (Figure 2). Expressing this in another way, we may say that it was only about half that of *Homo erectus* existing during the early phase of the Middle Pleistocene. This strongly suggests the possibility that fossils remain to be found in Lower Pleistocene deposits having brain capacities of intermediate size.

Although, as we have seen, Australopithecines seem to have survived in the isolated territory of South Africa into the Middle Pleistocene, it is evident even from the existing finds that before the end of an early phase of this period much larger-brained hominids existed over a broad territory from north-west Africa to the Far East. The fossil once known as *Pithecanthropus,* now as *Homo erectus* came from the Middle Pleistocene Trinil beds of Java and the same island has since yielded a child's skull from the underlying Djetis beds. Much the most extensive group of fossils from this phase of hominid evolution is that from the limestone fissures of Choukoutein near

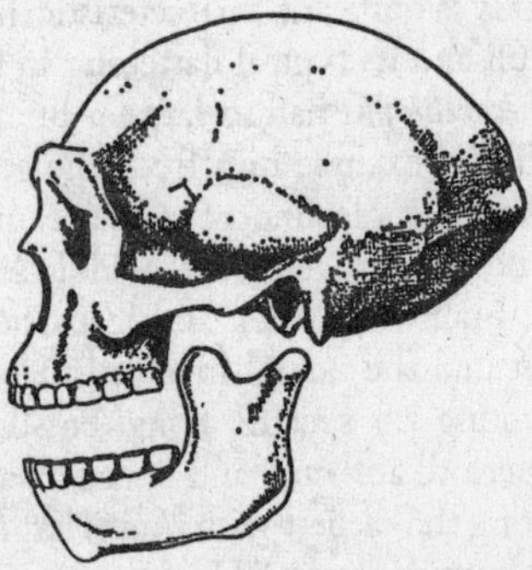

3. Skull of tool-making *Homo erectus pekinensis*

Pekin, the earliest of which have recently been shown to be of approximately the same age as Trinil. Although once accorded the status of a distinct genus (*Sinanthropus*), the Pekin fossils are now generally regarded as a variety of man (*Homo erectus pekinensis*) (Figure 3). Despite the fact that fossils of *Homo erectus* are still very sparse in Africa, most palaeontologists believe that the east-central part of this continent is likely to have been a main focus of its evolution. The most complete fossil of this group from Africa is the newly found and still not fully described skull from Bed II at Olduvai Gorge. Other fossils of this group come from north-west Africa, about the same distance as the crow flies from Olduvai as that locality is from Java. The most important of these, three mandibles and an isolated parietal bone from Ternifine in Algeria, date from about the same period as the fossils from the Trinil beds and from Locality I at Choukoutien; mandibles from the Littorina cave at Sidi Abderrahman and from Rabat, both in Morocco, are rather younger in age but help to confirm the presence of *Homo erectus* in this part of Africa. The only hominid fossils of comparable age from Europe comprise the occipital bone of an adult and the teeth of an infant from deposits of Mindel age at Vertesszöllös in Hungary; and a massive mandible from sands at Mauer near Heidelberg in south-west Germany. The massive character of the mandible, going with large teeth and a marked projection of the lower part of the face, is, together with a matching development of the brow-ridges, one of the main features of the type. Another highly significant characteristic is that, despite the low vault of his skull and its typical flattening in front, the hominid once known as *Pithecanthropus* had so large a brain that palaeontologists now feel unable to exclude him from the genus *Homo*.

The most important single line of advance in the evolution of hominids during the latter part of the Middle Pleistocene was the enlargement of the brain (Figure 4), and in particular of the frontal lobes in which is seated the neural mechanism concerned with the power of concentrating on specific tasks. Fossils attributable with certainty to this period are rare and incomplete, but two skulls may be cited as among the earliest with brains large enough to qualify beyond any doubt as members of Homo sapiens. These come from gravels of Great Interglacial age, respectively from the valley of a tributary of the Neckar at Steinheim and from the Lower Thames valley at Swanscombe. Although the frontal region was missing from the latter, it is evident that both skulls belong essentially to the same type. Neither was very large and each had rather thick walls, but the capacity of the Steinheim skull has recently been reassessed at 1150–75 c.c. and that from Swanscombe at 1250–1300 c.c. In a number of respects, including the moderate height of the vault and in the case of the Steinheim skull the prominent brow-ridges, they agree most closely with the large-brained early Neanderthaloid skulls of early Late Pleistocene times.

The customary picture of the Neanderthaler, short and stocky, the head set rather far forward instead of being balanced on the spinal column, large-faced, with prominent brow-ridges and heavy chinless jaws set with robust teeth (Figure 5), is based on fossil material from

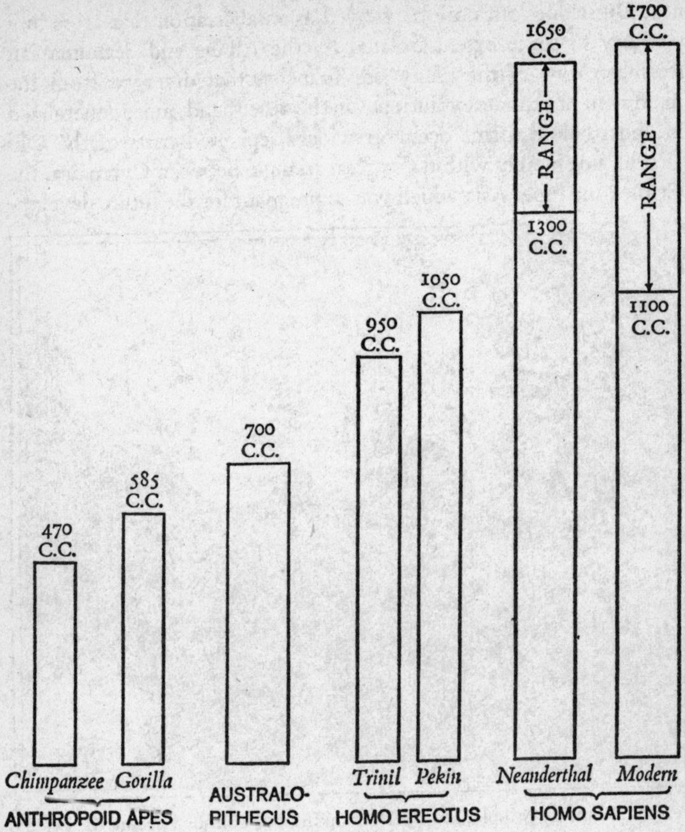


4. The enlargement of the brain in Primate evolution

western Europe, notably the skeletons from La Ferrassie and La Chapelle-aux-Saints in south-west France which date from an early part of the last glaciation. Neanderthaloid remains from the preceding warm phase, such as the skulls from Saccopastore near Rome or the assemblage from Ehringsdorf near Weimar, were less specialized in character; and the same applies to many of the fossils brought to light as the search was extended to eastern Europe, Africa and Asia. The 'classic' form of the type named after the locality of Neanderthal near Düsseldorf can now be viewed as an aberration that arose in a territory to some extent isolated by the Alpine and Scandinavian ice-sheets, one of the many side-branches that diverged from the main stem of primate evolution. On the other hand, more generalized Neanderthaloid forms occur in widely separated parts of the Old World, not merely within the great triangle between Cyrenaica, the Crimea and inner Asia which was so pregnant for the future develop-

Map 1. Territory (stippled) to which mankind was confined during the Middle Pleistocene

ment of civilization, but far to the south at Eyasi in northern Tanganyika, Broken Hill in Northern Rhodesia, Hopefield in Cape Province, and away to the east at Ngandong on the Solo river of Java. The widespread distribution of the generalized Neanderthaloids suggests that they represent a veritable stage in the physical evolution of mankind. The men of this phase combined primitive with advanced traits. Whereas they retained the pronounced brow-ridges of Steinheim and of *Homo erectus*, the size of their brains pointed ahead to modern man: indeed, it is a striking fact that the cranial capacity of male Neanderthalers from western Europe (*c.* 1540 cc) was well above the average of today. It appears that *Homo sapiens sapiens* first emerged nearly 40,000 years ago among Neanderthaloid groups somewhere between the east Mediterranean and the mountains of inner Asia. This does not mean that evolutionary change was

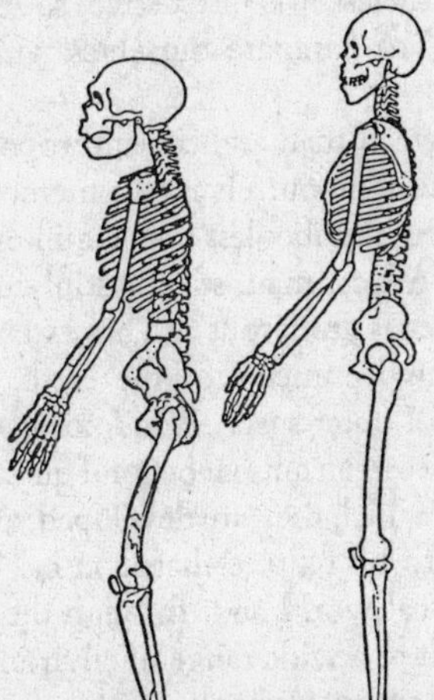

5. Comparison of the stance of Neanderthal (*Homo sapiens*) and Cromagnon man (*Homo sapiens sapiens*)

confined to this zone, important though it proved to be in the history of mankind. The assumption is rather that the transition was merely a regional aspect of the widespread evolutionary change that brought modern man into being.

*

Although man is admittedly an animal from a biological standpoint, the fact remains that none of the other primates living today are more than very remote relatives. The advance of modern palaeontological research suggests that great progress is likely to be made during the next few years in tracing the lineage of modern man. What we can already be sure of is that the forms through which he has evolved have long since become extinct: indeed there are already indications that the lines leading to men and apes diverged many millions of years ago. Were it only possible to study these primitive ancestors as living organisms we might expect to gain the most fruitful insights into the behaviour of the earliest men. The surviving great apes may well be almost as far removed from the primitive primates as is modern man himself. Nevertheless it is instructive, so long as we remember what we are doing, to compare ourselves with our nearest living relatives.

The disparity between man and the anthropoid apes is impressive enough even if we confine ourselves to a merely demographic level. Whereas the great apes number less than a million and are confined to a restricted zone of Africa, man, still multiplying rapidly, is already more than 3,000 times as numerous and has extended his domain over the most extreme environments of the earth, not to mention his current exploration of outer space. Paradoxical as it may sound, man owes his pre-eminence as an animal beyond question to characteristics that, in the degree to which they are developed, are peculiarly human: it is, above all, due to his culture that man has been able to survive changes in the physical world and, through the ability it confers on him, to adapt himself to a wide range of environments, to extend his geographical range; and it is thanks to this same factor that he has been able to win mastery over, and ultimately to tame and domesticate, animals and plants, and so make possible far denser populations than could subsist under wild conditions.

The overriding importance of social evolution in the history of man will be a constant theme in this work, but one ought not to overlook the fact that human society is rooted in biological circumstances. The most powerful force making for its cohesion is beyond doubt the mutual attraction of the sexes. It is an outstanding characteristic of the surviving primates as an Order that the males are potent continuously and the females receptive for a high proportion of the reproductive cycle. Again, the period of nurture, both pre-natal and parental, tends to increase as one ascends the scale of evolution. Among the mountain gorillas of eastern Congo the normal group might well include several females and their offspring, who formed a comparatively stable element, by contrast with the males, liable to move quite often from one group to another. In human society it seems likely that from a very early stage the normal group was composed of a monogamous pair and their offspring. This characteristic was strengthened by the need for paternal help in transmitting and inculcating cultural patterns of behaviour: the father plays a much more important role in this respect among men than among apes. One reason for this may lie in a highly significant difference in food habits. Whereas in general the apes depend on plant food, supplemented only occasionally from other sources, man, adapted to a terrestrial rather than an arboreal existence, availed himself much more freely of animal food. Since hunting put a premium on masculine qualities, this activity became the special province of males, and a sexual division of labour was instituted under which women continued to gather plant, insect and comparable foods while men developed the skills required for tracking down and killing game. This heightened the need for a partnership of the sexes, both in winning subsistence and in training the young. Moreover it would hardly have been possible, under conditions which must often have required his absence for lengthy periods, for a successful hunter to have retained a harem in the face of unsatisfied males or, for that matter, to have obtained meat enough to support a polygamous family.

The possession of culture, by which one implies patterns of behaviour inherited by virtue of belonging to social rather than genetic groups, while by no means confined to man – it has, for instance, been studied in some detail in relation to birdsong – is in human society carried to a point at which it constitutes a unique endowment. Human infants are born to traditions incomparably richer than those prevailing in communities of birds or apes, and altogether unique in their apparently unlimited capacity for growth. So much is this the case that one may speak of human society being subject to a new kind of evolution, social evolution, which makes possible advances far beyond those open to the mere breeding groups through which biological evolution must necessarily operate.

The most important medium through which social evolution has proceeded is probably articulate speech employing verbal symbols, since this has provided the mechanism by which man has ordered his experience and transmitted his cultural inheritance. By comparison with the noises, gestures, postures and expressions by which apes express their emotions and desires, language is an instrument of marvellous flexibility and power, even among the most backward groups of humanity. Verbal and, later, mathematical symbols not merely provided shortcuts to learning and communication, but afforded mental tools every bit as valuable to man in his struggle with nature as the material ones on which the reconstruction of prehistory has to so large an extent to depend. This makes it the more unfortunate that no evidence survives for the development of speech during the formative period of human prehistory. Present indications are that articulate speech came into use early in the Middle Pleistocene period, at a time when the brain underwent what may have been a rapid development and when tools began to be made skilfully and to standard patterns.

There can be no question that tools (extra-corporeal limbs, as they have sometimes been termed) constitute the mechanism by which mankind has utilized and progressively gained control over his external environment up to the moment when it can be shaped to correspond more or less closely with his expanding and ever more discriminating desires. The use by organisms of extraneous objects or parts of such objects to further their own ends is a quite widespread phenomenon in nature. What is so distinctively human is the fabrication of progressively more effective tools conforming to types traditional to established cultures: indeed, it is primarily as an artificer than man can in practice be distinguished most easily from the non-human primates, and it is largely through a study of his artifacts that archaeologists have been able to piece together the main outlines of prehistory. The level of technology has always been both limited by and reflected in the materials used for artifacts: only the youngest societies discussed in this book, for example, attained the use of metals, and most were compelled to rely on flint, stone, clay, and organic materials like wood, plant fibres and stems, antler, bone, ivory, skins and shells. No less significant are the techniques and procedures used in shaping raw materials, and a study of these throws important light on cultural groupings, movements and progress. Again, improvement in the techniques of production of artifacts had widespread repercussions over a broad field of culture, ranging from the mode of subsistence to the nature of such important things as dwellings, clothing, transport and warfare.

The manufacture of artifacts to well-defined and socially accepted patterns presupposes an attitude to time as well as to environment quite different from that prevailing among apes. Whereas even chimpanzees live almost entirely in the present and seek to attain only those ends which appear more or less immediately within reach, the most backward of living men are conditioned by their prevailing social climate to forgo immediate satisfactions in the furtherance of more long-term aims. Even though tools may on occasion be intended primarily to satisfy a need already manifest, the act of fabrication, frequently involving previous collection and selection of the raw material, betrays a certain measure of foresight. No evidence for similar foresight exists in the manipulation of sticks or strings by captive apes, intent on bringing within immediate reach food or other visible objects. Foresight and planning were destined to play an ever-increasing role in human affairs, and a readiness to take risks in the hope of a profit in the more or less distant future is a distinctive mark of more advanced humanity.

There are many other ways in which an appreciation of time has affected the outlook of men. Anyone who has attempted to train animals knows that they have certain powers of memory, but in men this power is enormously enhanced by the possession of articulate language. It was, indeed, through their oral traditions, tales of how things came about in the more or less remote past, that human societies were able to develop a consciousness of separate identity. One might even say that human societies differ from animal ones, in the final resort, through their consciousness of history.

Another and highly significant way in which man shows an awareness of time lies in his appreciation of his own individual mortality. Doubtless it was a realization of the transitoriness of personal existence – a realization which seems first to have been betrayed by Neanderthal man in his careful attention to burial – that led men to meditate on the existence of powers underlying surface appearances, powers creative and immortal on which his own well-being depended. From this sprang some of the main impulses towards magic and religion, each of them in its different way characteristic of man.

Finally, it needs to be emphasized that social evolution differed from biological evolution in allowing for the first time an element of conscious choice both to social groups and to individuals. Whereas organisms in a state of nature are confronted directly by their environment, culture as it develops imposes a cushion, a cushion which enables men to resist up to a point the immediate external pressures and so to be in a position to exercise choice between alternate courses of action. With this element of choice goes a range of variability and individualization at the level both of the group and of the individual that transcends anything attained by non-human primates. So far from weakening social cohesion or biological effectiveness, the exercise of moral choice, the basis of ethics, is capable of enhancing the resilience and power of human societies, which in this way acquired a marked adaptive advantage over life at the purely biological level.

CHAPTER TWO

# *The Beginnings of Culture: Lower Palaeolithic Man*

MAN'S earliest essays in culture are best traced through his artifacts of flint or other kinds of stone. These were not only the most effective tools available to primitive man, controlling what he was able to achieve in shaping materials like bone or wood, but, being abundant and almost imperishable, they provide the only continuous series of cultural fossils. With individual specimens, it may not be possible to distinguish primitive artifacts from natural products because many such agencies as soil creep, storm waves, waterfalls and the movement under pressure caused by the solution of underlying formations are capable of splitting and detaching flakes from pebbles or boulders. It requires systematic collecting under controlled conditions, followed by detailed analysis of assemblages from successive deposits, for prehistorians to be able to reconstruct with any confidence the earliest, long-drawn-out Lower Palaeolithic phases of human industry.

One of the guiding clues has been that artifacts, from the mere fact that they are cultural products, conform in general to traditional patterns, and it is of the nature of these patterns to undergo change in time; whereas natural processes might be expected to operate in a uniform manner under a given set of conditions. It follows that where identical forms recur throughout a succession of deposits of widely varying age, as many of the flint 'eoliths' were found to do, natural agencies may be suspected or even inferred; but where the pattern can be shown to undergo a consistent change in time, it is reasonable to interpret successive assemblages as the products of an evolving social tradition.

This is precisely what has been found to apply to assemblages from successive beds in French Morocco containing traces of a Villafranchian fauna. No clear-cut assemblage can yet be attributed to the earliest Villafranchian deposits in this area, but those from successive levels in the middle and upper zones show a gradual but definite trend of evolution. The earliest assemblage comprises pebbles flaked into the form of choppers from one direction. In the second phase uni-directional flaking is still predominant, but this is supplemented by work from two directions and applied to a wider range of shapes. Phase three is marked, above all, by the predominance of bi-directional flaking. Finally, the primitive pebble forms are supplemented by others flaked on both faces, precursors of the bifacially flaked tools of the succeeding Middle Pleistocene. From this brief account it is plain that evolution was extremely slow, since on any of the accepted chronologies it was spaced out over a period running into hundreds of thousands of years. Yet, though it proceeded by hardly perceptible gradations, the evolution we can observe had a logic of its own, covering the development of the most primitive pebble-tools to a point at which we can envisage the appearance of the most characteristic fossil of man's next phase in social evolution, the Middle Pleistocene hand-axe.

Primitive pebble industries of the kind obtained from successive levels of the Middle and Late Villafranchian of Morocco have been found in deposits of comparable age in east-central and southern Africa; they also mark the earliest spread of human culture in northern India, Burma and north-west China. The conclusion seems inescapable that they represent the most primitive level of hominid industry yet recognized. Recent excavations in Bed I at Olduvai have brought to light assemblages of chopper-tools, which include bifacially flaked forms of the type characteristic of the third phase in the Moroccan series. The importance of the Olduvai site is that here we have undoubted living-floors which in Early Pleistocene times rested directly on mud-flats bordering a lake. Of special interest is the evidence of food debris provided by animal bones broken open for the extraction of marrow. Among the animals represented were pig, antelope, horse and baboon, as well as birds, rodents, snakes and frogs. It seems a fair assumption that a main purpose of the stone tools was the dismemberment of game. If this is indeed so, then here we have proof of a direct connexion between the adoption of an omnivorous diet and the fabrications of at least the earliest stone industry.

The discovery of actual living-floors gives rise to the hope that remains may be identified of the craftsmen of the Oldowan industry.

As we have already indicated, Bed I at Olduvai has already yielded representatives of each of the main forms of Australopithecine in *Zinjanthropus boisei* and his predecessor. The question inevitably arises whether these hominids made the stone tools or whether they were victims of some more advanced being. So far no traces of any such form have come to light at this level in the Olduvai beds and it remains true that the only hominid remains associated with the Oldowan industry are of Australopithecine type. Again, Australopithecine remains have recently been found with a Villafranchian fauna and stone implements of primitive type at Al Ubeidiya in the Jordan valley some three kilometres south-south-west of Lake Tiberias in Palestine. Yet the number of associations is still very small and the only site in South Africa to yield remains of Australopithecines with a stone industry – the pebbles and relatively advanced chopping-tools from the Sterkfontein Extension Site – is of Middle Pleistocene age, when more advanced hominids are in any case known to have existed. Conversely, traces of stone artifacts are conspicuously absent from the several sites of Lower Pleistocene age in South Africa known to have yielded Australopithecine remains. This is generally explained by attributing the concentrations of bones, including those of Australopithecines and numerous baboons, to the activities of carnivores. On the other hand, the mere fact that Australopithecines were fellow victims with baboons makes one doubt whether, in this part of Africa at least, they were tool-users. Another reason for caution is the huge disparity in brain capacity between at any rate the South African Australopithecines and members of *Homo erectus*, the first hominids proved beyond reasonable doubt, at least in their Far Eastern form, to have been tool-makers. What is certain is that, so long as we define man as the tool-making animal, whoever ultimately proves to have been responsible for the pebble-tools from Olduvai will qualify as man. In this sense the very taxonomy of the higher primates waits on the progress of research on the Villafranchian deposits of Africa, and of the Olduvai Gorge in particular.

At the present time the earliest cultural assemblage we can link with absolute certainty with its maker comes from the early Middle Pleistocene in-fill of limestone fissures at Choukoutien near Pekin in northern China. Doubts were at one time expressed, just as they had earlier been about Neanderthal man, whether *Homo erectus pekinensis* was the responsible agent or whether he was not himself the victim of some higher form of hominid. As we have just seen, the same problem awaits decision with the different groups of Australopithecines. At Pekin the question has been answered with reasonable finality by the scale of the excavations. Whereas remains of some forty specimens had been found even before the 1939–45 war, not one single tooth of any more advanced hominid has yet been recovered from the thousands of cubic metres of Middle Pleistocene deposits excavated. In complete contrast, no artifacts have yet been recovered from deposits yielding traces of *Homo erectus javanensis*. This, and the fact that the Java form had a noticeably smaller brain capacity, has suggested that in this area at least the threshold of tool-making may have been crossed by some intermediate form. On the other hand, definite flake-tools have been recovered from the upper part of the Trinil beds and renewed search may well produce artifacts from the same levels as *Homo erectus*.

The fissures at Choukoutien yielded abundant traces of food debris. We have already stressed the importance in primate evolution of the shift from a primarily vegetarian to an omnivorous diet in which animal food played an important part. In this respect the discarded meat bones from Choukoutien are as eloquent of the status of *Homo erectus pekinensis* as the remains of his material culture. Numerous carnivores are represented, including sabre-toothed tiger, leopard and hyenas, and there are indications of animal gnawing on the bones of numerous ruminants. On the other hand, there seems little doubt that many of the latter, which include a broad range from elephant and rhinoceros to horse, bison, water-buffalo, camel, wild boar, sheep, antelope and several species of deer, provided meat for Pekin man, since many bones have been broken open, presumably for the extraction of marrow.

Examination of the remains of *Homo erectus pekinensis* himself shows that he was apparently a cannibal as well as a hunter. Some of the long bones have clearly been bitten open by carnivores, but others have been split lengthwise, in the same way as those of wild animals, presumably for extracting marrow. Again the skulls of *Homo erectus pekinensis* show precisely the enlargement of the foramen magnum, the hole at the base of the skull through which the spinal column connects with the brain, that would be necessary for extracting this delicacy without splitting open the cranium. Was this cannibalism purely utilitarian or did it partake in any way of ritual? There is no means of knowing this. One can only say that Pekin man has given no other sign that he was aware of considerations other than the satisfaction of his appetites, and that animal brain is good to eat.

The stone artifacts from the earlier locations at Choukoutien (Figure 6) were largely made from greenstone pebbles found in a nearby stream-bed, but quartz crystals must have been brought from granite hills some miles away. Rough choppers were made by striking flakes

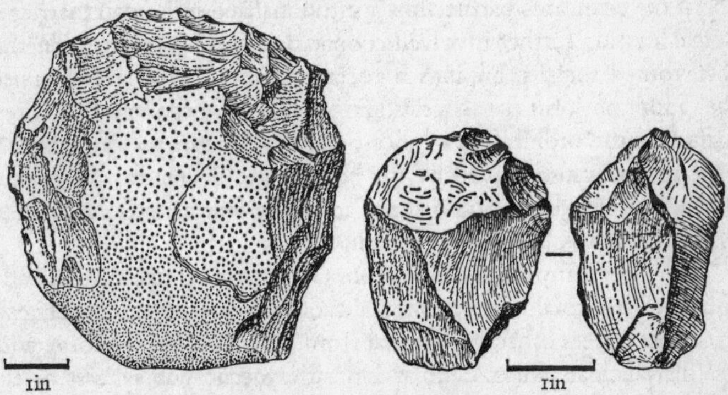


6. Crude stone implements made by *Homo erectus pekinensis*

from pebbles by blows from alternate directions. Flakes, sometimes of considerable size, were struck either by single blows or by crushing between two boulders, but in neither case were they converted into standardized shapes by secondary flaking, so that the overall impression of the early material leaves one with an impression of crudity. It has been argued that Pekin man supplemented his lithic industry by detaching and utilizing various parts of the skeletons of the animals on which he lived, but this, though plausible and even likely, is difficult to prove.

One important asset he did have was fire, the possession of which is suggested by the presence of ash and charcoal fragments as well as carbonized antlers and bones. Whether it was produced artificially or merely collected from natural outbreaks and carefully maintained is an open question. What is quite sure is its value under primitive conditions, not only for providing warmth and making it possible to roast meat, but also as a protection against wild animals. This makes it all the more strange that there seems to be no evidence for its use in Africa until the final stage of the Middle Pleistocene or in Europe before the Great Interglacial.

Even though he seems, on present evidence, to have been among the first to utilize fire, the resources open to Pekin man were sufficiently meagre. His success as a hunter can only be explained in social terms. Hunting in itself implied as it developed an increasing differential between the economic role of the sexes and in this way brought about the economic partnership institutionalized in human marriage. Social hunting further involved cooperation among several men and so favoured social groupings transcending the family. This implied the adoption of rules conditioning relations between the sexes, including the prohibition of incest and the practice of exogamy. A vital role was also played by the home base, shelter for the young during the lengthy period spent in acquiring culture and the place to which food was brought for sharing.

Technologically the industry from Choukoutien, like that recently found with animal bones and remains of *Homo erectus* at Chenchiawo in Shensi, agrees broadly with that from Bed I at Olduvai Gorge with a Villafranchian fauna. Similar industries occur widely east of the hand-axe province. One may point to the Anyathian of Burma, the industry from Kota Tampan in Malaysia and to others from the present islands of Java, Palawan and Formosa, not to mention the Australian continent. To the west others occur on the northern margin of the hand-axe world, notably the Soan of Pakistan, the Biharian of Hungary and the industries first recovered from Mindel-Riss deposits at Clacton, England (Figure 8).

Beyond question, Africa continued to lead in cultural development during much of the Middle Pleistocene. As we have seen, there is good reason for believing that the hand-axe, flaked on either face to form a more or less even working edge – the dominant tool of the period – developed by gradual stages from the Oldowan chopper (Figure 7). As is only to be expected of a tool that played a leading part for around a quarter of a million years, the hand-axe underwent considerable development in the course of its history. Because the hand-axe industries were first systematically worked out in the Somme valley of northern France they are sometimes called after localities there, Abbeville being used to designate the earlier, cruder stage and St Acheul the more evolved one. Probably the most carefully studied sequence is that obtained from successive levels through Beds II–IV in the Olduvai Gorge. The sequence shows clearly how by insensible gradations handier, and incidentally more beautiful, tools with smoother working edges were produced from a smaller amount of raw material. Up to a point, improvement could be made by acquiring greater skill in the use of a hammerstone, but no marked or rapid advance was possible

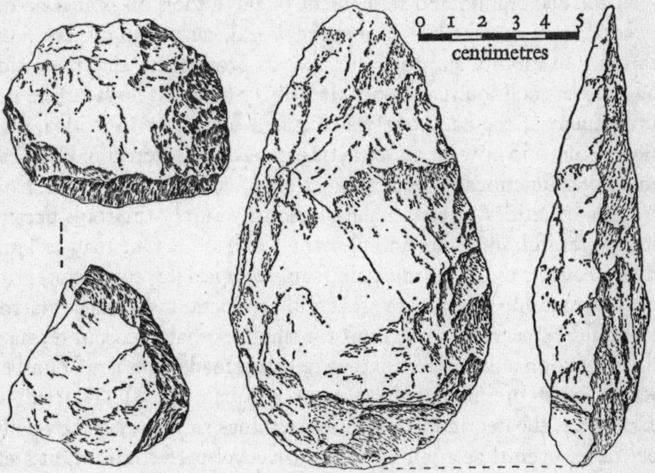


7. Oldowan chopper-tool and Acheulian hand-axe compared

until someone had the idea of using a punch of wood or bone and striking this sharply at right-angles. By this means it was possible to detach thinner flakes having shallower bulbs of percussion than those removed by hammerstones; and the intersection of shallower flakes produced a more regular working edge. The first hand-axes to appear alongside chopping tools in the Olduvai sequence had one thick end, easy to grasp in the hand, and another more or less pointed by means of bifacial flaking. At later levels these primitive hand-axes with irregular flaking at one end were supplemented by others with working edges, which, though still irregular, were now carried all the way round the tool instead of being confined to the pointed end. At a certain stage the effect of the adoption of the punch technique was manifested in the appearance of slimmer tools having more regular working edges all the way round. Soon after this a variant form appeared in the cleaver, in which the point was replaced by a sharp, knife-like edge formed by the intersection of a few large flake-scars. Meanwhile the hand-axes themselves began to be made smaller and in some cases they were flaked in such a way as to produce a working edge which when viewed from the side had an S-shaped twist or profile.

In the elaboration and refinement of these tools on which he depended so largely for his place in the world, early man displayed the capacity to modify and to accumulate improvements that possession of cultural tradition made possible. It may be asked how far the improvement of the hand-axe was dictated by purely functional considerations, and how far an aesthetic element had entered in. Certainly there was functional advance; more effective tools were made from smaller quantities of raw material. Equally surely the tools became more graceful, smoother and pleasanter to handle. One may feel sure that whatever the economic gain from technical improvement, pride of craftsmanship in the mere process of production was a major factor. It would be perverse to account for the finest hand-axes in terms of their function alone, since they were better made than large numbers which must presumably have been adequate (pl. 1). The cult of excellence, the determination to make things as perfect as they could be made, even if at a purely utilitarian level perfection might seem excessive, is something which began thus early in the history of man.

Although local varieties of hand-axe appeared in different localities, particularly during later times, a feature of the Middle Pleistocene was the similarity of the main types over the whole extent of the hand-axe province. This included the greater part of Africa from the Atlantic coast to the Nile valley and south through Kenya, Uganda and the Rhodesias to the Union of South Africa, Angola and the Congo. Outside Africa, hand-axe industries occurred over the greater part of the territories first occupied by makers of flake- and chopping-tool cultures, even as far east as north-eastern India, where the frontier is marked by finds in the Singrauli district of Mirzapur in southern Bihar and in the Mayurbhanj district of northern Orissa. Although it cannot be excluded that hand-axes were developed locally from the chopper-tool basis, the geographical distribution of hand-axes in Europe and Asia is certainly consistent with the idea that they emanated from the northern parts of Africa*: thus it is reasonable to suppose that the hand-axe industries of south-western Europe, which extended as far as southern England, and eastward to the Rhine, spread from north-west Africa; and those of Jordan, Palestine, Syria and Mesopotamia from Egypt or at least from north-east Africa. Even the Indian province could be accounted for in terms of a geographical spread, perhaps during a period of lower sea-level, along the northern coast of the Gulf of Oman.

The hand-axe industries thus extended from the Bay of Bengal to the Atlantic coast of Mauritania, and from the region of the North Sea to the Cape of Good Hope, a territory not quite so extensive as that ultimately attained by the chopper-tool and flake tradition, but still sufficient to involve the use of a wide range of materials. Some of these were homogeneous, fissile and easily flaked, like the flint of parts of Europe, north Africa and south-west Asia, the obsidian of Kenya or some of the finer-grained quartzites of Africa and India; others, coarse-grained lavas, quartz and even granite, presented much greater difficulties to the craftsmen. While the finish of the implements was certainly affected by the properties of the raw material, the same fundamental forms were achieved. Despite all difficulties the idea consistently triumphed over matter. We may well admire the tenacity with which ideas were adhered to and transmitted through countless generations; the modifications traced in a sequence like that studied at Olduvai were spread over periods tens of thousands of years long.

As a general rule the makers of the hand-axe industries seem to have lived in the open, so that the vast majority of their encampments have been eroded away. Only their stone implements survive in the gravels of the ancient rivers, which themselves often had complex histories resulting in all manner of sorting and admixture. The most promising sources of information come from the beds of the ancient lakes on the

* Since there is no evidence for any movement round the east Mediterranean or for any land-bridge linking Tunisia with Sicily and south Italy during the Pleistocene period, the most likely route for any migration would have been from Africa to Spain, a distance of under ten miles and during periods of lowest sea-level of hardly more than six.

shores of which they encamped, because here we sometimes find remains of their food refuse in the form of animal bones as well as their lithic industries in a fresh state. Evidence, gathered from such lacustrine sites as Torralba in north-central Spain, Hoxne in eastern England and Olorgesailie in Kenya leaves us in no doubt that the hand-axe makers were hunters as redoubtable as those of Choukoutien. The fauna included many large species and the way in which the long-bones were split for marrow and the skulls broken open for the brain makes it plain that they lived largely on animal flesh. It was doubtless their concern with game animals that led them to camp by lakes and river courses. One may imagine, for instance, that the hunters who dismembered their game by the lake of Torralba, over ten thousand feet up in the mountains, were accustomed to follow herds of elephants migrating during the heat of an interglacial summer to the cooler mountain uplands. Lower Palaeolithic man had not yet learnt to fashion stone heads for his weapons, but the forepart of a strong stem of yew-wood, the point hardened in the fire, from an interglacial deposit at Clacton in Essex, shows that he used a form of primitive lance. To judge from the more complete, though rather later, find from the marl of a lake dating from the last interglacial period at Lehringen in Lower Saxony, this was none the less effective for its simple character: this spear, again made from yew hardened in the fire at the tip, was nearly eight feet long and lay between the ribs of an extinct elephant *Hesproloxodon antiquus*. One is forcibly reminded of the pygmies of the Cameroons who hunt elephants by stalking, thrust a spear into the body with both hands and follow the trail of blood to the point where the victim sinks down to die. It may well be, though no proof survives, that pit-traps were dug by the help of sticks and hand-axes to disable big-game on trails or by watering-places. The presence of rounded balls of stone, sometimes improved by man, at sites such as Olorgesailie suggests that smaller game may have been brought down by the use of a device like the Patagonian *bolas*. The stone would have been attached in leather bags to the ends of thongs, several of these joined together, and the whole assembly hurled at the legs of a running animal. Modern studies of Bushmen suggest that, in the case of larger game at any rate, the kill would have been dismembered, often many days after it was first disabled, at the point where it finally died. In the work of butchery one may believe that hand-axes, in all probability freshly made for the occasion, were effective tools, as they doubtless were also for grubbing up roots and tubers, cutting down trees and vegetation and digging holes.

As to the hand-axe makers themselves, the fossil record, defective though it remains, is now beginning to tell a consistent story. The massive chinless mandibles from Ternifine and Sidi Abderrahman in Algeria and Morocco respectively and the skull recently discovered, but not yet described, from Bed II at Olduvai, all found with early hand-axe industries, agree in conforming broadly to the *Homo erectus* type. In other words both the early hand-axe industries and the industries of Choukoutien seem to have been made by hominids belonging to the same phase in the evolution of man. This is very important because it shows that, even at this early stage, men of the same broad physical type and at the same level of economic development could be responsible for stone industries of quite distinct type in different parts of the Lower Palaeolithic world.

At a later stage of the Middle Pleistocene, at a period corresponding to the Great Interglacial, when implements of Middle Acheulian type were being made, we find evidence for men of a more highly evolved physical type. The most reliable fossils for this phase, the incomplete skulls from Steinheim and Swanscombe, while retaining primitive features reminiscent of *Homo erectus*, display a definite advance, notably in the size of their brains. Even though they both belong to women, the skulls comfortably exceed in capacity the average for *Homo erectus* and in the case of Swanscombe approach that of a modern individual. The interaction between cultural advance and growth in the size of brain seems likely at this time to have been in some measure reciprocal. When the authorship of the Oldowan industries has been satisfactorily cleared up we shall be in a better position to determine at what stage in the evolution of the brain tool-making became possible, but clearly a certain minimum capacity was needed. On the other hand, it is easy to appreciate that once cultural growth got under way it would favour mental activity. The manufacture of tools would in itself have demanded coordination of hand, eye and brain, which must have been of immense value in exercising man's neural apparatus. The men responsible for the magnificent hand-axes of the Middle and Late Acheulian phase of culture had already achieved the status of *Homo sapiens*.

CHAPTER THREE

# *The Middle Palaeolithic*

THE close of the Middle Pleistocene ushered in a new phase of prehistory associated with Neanderthal man and his near cousins. Whereas for hundreds of thousands of years tropical Africa had played the dominant role, the most significant areas of change during the final hundred thousand were to lie in a broad belt extending from the Atlantic to inner Asia, mainly between latitudes 30°–50° north of the equator. A widespread archaeological symbol of the Middle Palaeolithic period (with which this phase began) was the rise to predominance of flint industries based on the production of flakes. This technical change was, in the most general sense, progressive. Even the most perfectly finished hand-axe represented no more than the culmination of a process of refining on the primitive chopper-tool. By contrast, the production of complete implements at a single blow from cores previously prepared so as to ensure that flakes when detached conformed to desired patterns was something new, something which marked a further extension of human foresight. Moreover, since it was possible to strike off a series of flakes by rejuvenating the same core, the technique was economical both of labour and of raw material. Even more important, the flakes so formed could easily be shaped by a simple retouch into a variety of forms, so that in place of the all-purpose hand-axe it was a simple matter to fabricate a whole range of tools adapted to specific functions.

The replacement of hand-axes by flake-tools was neither sudden nor complete; and it needs emphasizing that in reality no hard-and-fast line can be drawn between flake and core industries or traditions. The manufacture of hand-axes, and still more perhaps of chopping-tools, led inevitably to the production of flakes, some of which were large enough to serve for tools. This has often been overlooked in the past, in all probability owing to limitations in most of the evidence available to archaeologists: many of the lithic assemblages of Middle Pleistocene age have been sorted by river action and weathering of various kinds, and a large proportion of the lithic material in museums has been abstracted from geological deposits on a highly selective basis by collectors intent on securing well-worked specimens.

It looks as though industries based primarily on the production of flake tools struck from carefully prepared cores first developed in the northern zone of the then inhabited world from north Africa and south-west Asia to western, central and eastern Europe. The most easily recognized fossil of this new mode of working flint, the tortoise shaped core from the under surface of which a flake tool could be struck by a single blow (Figure 9), was first recognized from sites in the locality of Levallois, a suburb of Paris.

The technique was already being practised in northern France and southern England at the time of the Riss glaciation, that is before the end of the Middle Pleistocene. By an early stage of the Late Pleistocene the technique was widely diffused throughout large areas of the hand-axe province. Even in Africa south of the Sahara, flake-tools struck from prepared cores and having faceted butts formed an integral part of more or less specialized hand-axe cultures: for example, they occurred alongside small hand-axes and well-made cleavers in the culture named from the locality of Fauresmith in the Orange Free State and distributed with intervals down the eastern part of the continent from the Horn down through Kenya to the Union of South Africa; and, again, in the geographically complementary culture known as the Sangoan (named from Sango Bay in south-west Uganda), which was centred on the Rift and the forest areas of the Congo and Angola, and in which the early stages were marked by large picks and the middle ones by lanceolate hand-axes. On the other hand, there is no doubt that it was in the northern parts of the old Palaeolithic world that the flake technique rose to predominance over the core-tool tradition.

There is no particular reason for thinking that this happened in any one part of the northern zone. More probably it was the product of a general trend. Well-defined Levalloisian industries appeared during a period equivalent to the last interglacial period as far afield as the Somme and Nile valleys. Information about these Levalloisian industries is unhappily confined almost entirely to the flints themselves. A much fuller picture is available for Middle Palaeolithic industries occurring in caves or under rock-shelters. One of these, named after

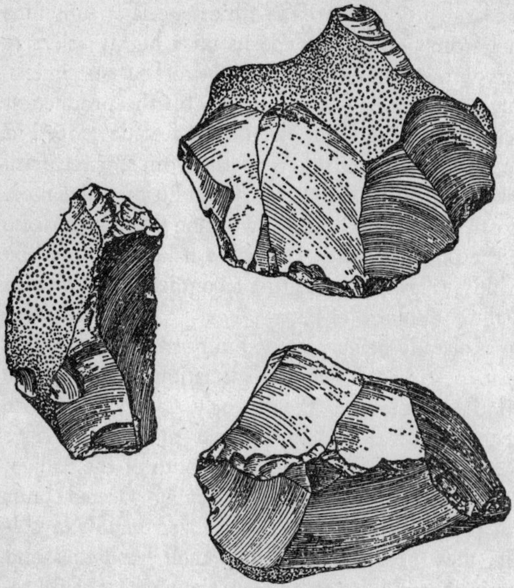

8. Chopper-core and flake-tool from interglacial deposits at Clacton, south-east England

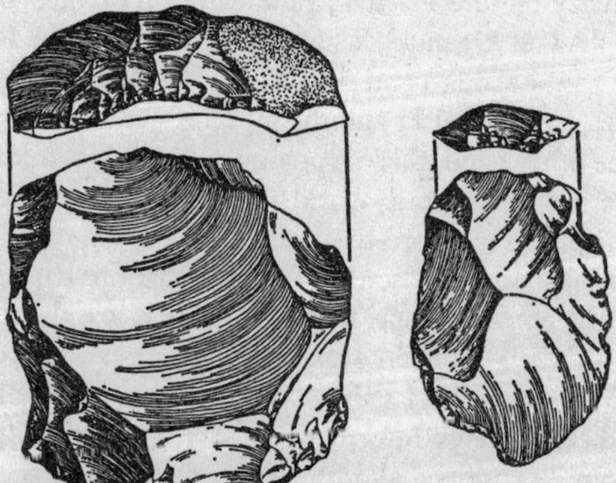

9. Flake-tool and tortoise-core of Levalloisian type

the French rock-shelter of Le Moustier, is closely allied to the Levalloisian but differs in that the cores were small and disc-like, and designed so that a series of flakes could be detached without the need to rejuvenate the core. The caves of western Asia and Libya, on the other hand, yielded Levalloiso-Mousterian industries sharing elements from each.

Mousterian industries first began to appear in the last interglacial, but persisted well into the last or Würm glaciation. Over the wide territory occupied by makers of the Mousterian industry one may distinguish between a western group, which extended from the Pyrenees to Belgium and southern England and included in its repertoire an appreciable proportion of small triangular and cordiform (heart-shaped) hand-axes, and an eastern one, stretching from the Alps and the Rhine to the Volga and having a westward extension to Italy and the Riviera, in which hand-axes are absent or rare and special forms of flake-tool are present. Nevertheless certain broad characteristics are common to both in addition to the disc-core technique already mentioned. Particular instances are the leading forms shaped from selected primary flakes, the side-scraper with convex working edge, and the point trimmed on either edge at one end, or more rarely at each end. The same technique of secondary flaking was used to achieve both these forms, namely step-flaking: this consisted in striking off numerous small flakes and spalls in such a manner that, instead of emerging evenly at the angle at which the blow was applied, the force set up by the impact of the hammer bent back on itself to form a smoothly rounded or hinge fracture. The great majority of Mousterian flake-tools from the west were trimmed on only one face, retaining the primary flake surface intact on the other; in this respect the removal of bulbs of percussion from many of the side-scrapers from La Quina (in the Charente district of south-west France) by means of flat flaking is an exception which helps to prove the rule, since it can plausibly be explained by the exceptional size of the raw material available there and by the consequently exceptional prominence of the bulbs on the primary flakes. In the eastern group, on the other hand, bifacial flaking was much more widespread, though never abundant and seldom more than very shallow on the original under-flake surface: from sites like Kiik-Koba in the Crimea and Ilskaya in the Caucasus come particularly fine triangular points, some retaining the striking platform, but others trimmed at the base, a few so as to form a shallow concavity; there were, in addition, a few double-ended leaf-shaped points with flaking on either face such as are also known from central Europe and from the newly discovered site of Kokkinopolis in north Greece. The side-scraper and point were again the leading forms of flake-tool in the Levalloiso-Mousterian industries of south-west Asia and North Africa, but the rich industries of Mount Carmel included a number of burins. These are made by removing flakes that so to speak bite into the blade to produce a chisel-like edge; useful for cutting into materials like antler and bone and in other contexts for engraving designs on the limestone roofs or walls of caves.

From a material point of view the advances made by Neanderthal man were of a relatively unspectacular kind, but the adoption of skin clothing, which can reasonably be inferred from the abundance and ubiquity of the flint scrapers, is significant because it increased the possibility of occupying territories having more rigorous climates. It has already been pointed out that flake-tools first rose to predominance in the northern parts of the old hand-axe province. What needs stressing now is that the makers of flake industries significantly extended the range of human settlement north of the warmer territories to which the hand-axe people were confined and that they did so despite the onset of the last glaciation. By the beginning of the Würm period the northern frontier of this settlement seems to have run from southern England along the northern foot-hills of the central European upland zone from the Ardennes, by way of the Sauerland, the Harz and the Sudeten, to the headwaters of the Vistula; and thence from the middle Dniester to the Dnieper, at the point where it turned south in the neighbourhood of Dniepropetovsk, and to the Donetz near Vorochilovgrad. Further east the precise frontier is still vague, but it is worthy of special comment that, unlike the hand-axe makers, the flake-tool people not merely penetrated the Zagros mountains of south-west Persia but expanded north of the Iranian plateau to the neighbourhood of Krasnovodsk, east of the Caspian, in western Turkmenia, and further still to the regions of Samarkand and Baisun in eastern Uzbekistan. To judge from the character of the flint industry of the Advanced Palaeolithic settlers of the Irkutsk region, near the southern end of lake Baikal, Mousterian impulses must at some time or another have penetrated inner Siberia; indeed, flint assemblages from the Ordos in the northern loop of the Huangho suggest that they reached as far as north China. Thus the Middle Palaeolithic phase witnessed the beginning of that process of geographical expansion into climatically more difficult territories, in which man could not exist without some form of clothing, that has been completed in our own day. The success of the Mousterian and Levalloiso-Mousterian people as hunters is shown by the abundance of discarded animal bones on their sites, evidence which has survived with particular fullness owing to their habit of occupying caves and rock-shelters. Confirmation that their diet consisted to a great extent of meat is provided by the condition of their surviving teeth which show an absence of caries and a comparative lack of wear. On the other hand, there is no evidence that they made any significant advance in the technique of hunting. Careful study of the hip region of one of the men buried at the Mount Carmel cave of es-Skhūl has shown that at death, or only shortly after, this individual had received a dreadful wound from what must have been a wooden spear like those described from a previous age (p. 42); the weapon had been driven in with such force that the head penetrated the head of the femur and emerged into the pelvic cavity. However, with the possible exception of certain bifacially flaked objects from eastern Europe, none of the flint artifacts of these industries seems to have been especially adapted for mounting as the heads of projectiles and there is no certain evidence of any other weapon than the wooden lance or spear.

Study of the quantities of animal remains from the cave deposits makes it plain that bones and similar materials were only used to the most limited extent for making artifacts. Thus, of the 6,000 or so fragments of long-bones of asses from Mousterian levels at Staroselie in the Crimea the vast majority had been broken open for the extraction of marrow, but hardly more than 250 showed any signs of use and none had been artificially shaped into tools. The main purpose for which bone was utilized – and this applies generally to Mousterian and Levalloiso-Mousterian assemblages – was for anvils or more likely compressors for trimming flake-tools; the material chiefly used included splinters from fairly stout long-bones and complete phalanges. Although a few simple tools have been claimed from time to time, it seems that there was as yet no established tradition of working, as distinct from utilizing, animal skeletal material; presumably any skin clothing must have been of the most rudimentary character, something in the nature of a kaross that did not need sewing.

Some insight into the limitations of Neanderthal man and that of his associates is given by his apparent lack of concern with personal decoration or art. The absence of even a single perforated animal tooth, the commonest of all the ornaments worn by hunters, must be significant when account is taken of the number of burials found and the good state of preservation of bone. Equally diagnostic, since he so often lived in caves, is the absence of any trace of decorative or graphic art. The only evidence we have for any aesthetic quality lies in his work as a craftsman: like the hand-axe makers, he often endowed his tools with a perfection of form beyond that dictated by their function.

Yet Neanderthal man certainly displayed signs of spirituality, the earliest for which we have certain evidence, both in his treatment of the dead and, if one may accept slight but suggestive clues, in his behaviour to his fellows. The discovery in the Croatian cave of Krapina of fragmentary remains of over ten Neanderthalers broken open and in some cases burnt, like the remains of animals eaten for food, suggests the practice of cannibalism, a practice which we have already encountered in the Middle Pleistocene deposits at Choukoutien; it is especially significant in this respect that the skull from the Italian locality of Monte Circeo had been broken open for the removal of the brain in the way characteristic of Pekin man.

The evidence for careful burial, on the other hand, is even more abundant and widespread: indeed it was precisely to this practice of burying his dead in caves that we owe the survival of such relatively complete traces of Neanderthal man. One of the most illuminating of the earlier finds is that of two adults and two children in a cave near La Ferrassie in the Dordogne. The burials were made in shallow trenches. The head of the man had been protected by stone slabs and it was noticed that the woman had been tightly flexed before burial, the arms being folded and the legs pressed against the trunk, an attitude that can only have been brought about by binding tightly with thongs before the corpse stiffened. Flexing of the lower limbs seems to have been a widespread Neanderthal practice, since it has been observed as far afield as Kiik-Koba in the Crimea and Mount Carmel in Palestine.

The practice admits of a prosaic explanation in that it would economize the chore of grave-digging, which frequently involved excavation of rock; but the possibility cannot be excluded that it was intended to prevent the dead man from coming back to haunt the living.

The most numerous burials found in one cave, enough to warrant the term cemetery, were the ten uncovered on the terrace of the Mugaret-es-Skhūl, Mount Carmel (Figure 10). The bodies were laid in shallow hollows scooped out of the floor and the legs were flexed. There was no sign that the bodies had been protected by stones or

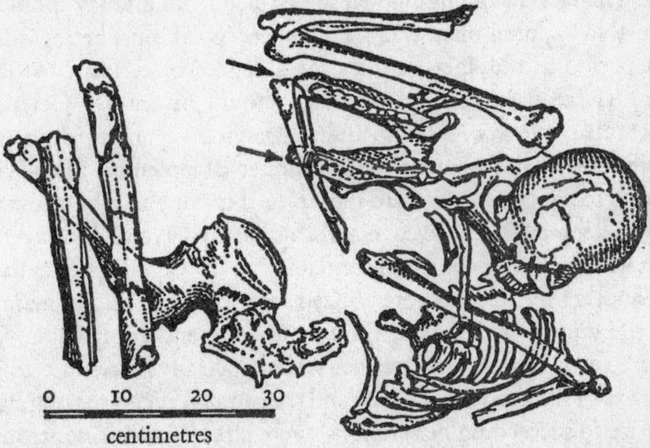


10. Neanderthal burial, Mugaret-es-Skhūl, Mount Carmel, Palestine

other means, nor were they, any more than their analogues from Europe, accompanied by ochre or by personal ornaments. The only objects buried with the Mount Carmel people were the two mandibles of the lower jaw of a very large wild boar, each broken off at the angle and clasped in the arms of a forty-five-year-old man in such a way that the jaw lay parallel with his right upper arm-bone. A particularly remarkable piece of ritual has recently been reported from the cave of Teshik-Tash in eastern Uzbekistan, where a buried child was closely surrounded by a ring of five or six pairs of goat horns still attached to their parent skulls and pushed points downward into the floor.

A hardly less penetrating insight into the psychology of Neanderthal man is provided by one of three skeletons from the cave of

Shanidar situated at a height of 2,500 feet in the Zagros mountains. The subject, thought to have been killed by a fall of stone from the roof of the cave, was a man, an arthritic one-armed cripple, who had attained the age of around forty years. Careful study of the skeletal remains has shown that the right arm and shoulder had never fully developed and that the arm had indeed been amputated below the elbow. Furthermore, examination of the condition of the teeth confirms that, unlike those of other Neanderthalers, they show signs of marked wear, as if they had been used to remedy the lack of a right arm. The fact that an individual so disabled from infancy should have been able to attain manhood – and indeed what must be regarded for that period as old age – argues for a degree of concern for the individual far transcending anything shown in animal societies for others than the very young. Indeed, having regard to the rigorous conditions of life and the small number of potential meat-winners in each social group, the care shown to this cripple, who presumably had to keep close to the cave and can hardly have shared in hunting activities, reflects a degree of humanity not always displayed towards one another by members of civilized societies. The concern manifested for the cripple of Shanidar shows that love and compassion, which as we have emphasized earlier were especially necessary for men because of the need to inculcate and transmit an ever-growing body of culture to succeeding generations, were already operating strongly in Neanderthal society. It was solidarity based on ethical considerations that in the last resort made possible the future achievements of man, even in the field of material endeavour.

CHAPTER FOUR

# *Advanced Palaeolithic Hunters and Artists*

THE first great climax of human achievement was attained by the Advanced Palaeolithic peoples who flourished in parts of Europe and south-west Asia during the later stages of the Upper Pleistocene between *c.* 35,000–10,000 B.C. At an economic level these peoples carried to a higher pitch than had previously been known the arts of hunting and catching, by means of which man had established himself as a biologically dominant species. From this secure base, the foundations of which had been laid by forbears of the earliest men, whether Australopithecines or more mature cousins of these, the Advanced Palaeolithic peoples were free to explore avenues of feeling and self-expression which foreshadowed unmistakably the achievements of civilized man. It is indeed no coincidence that the original centres of food production and urban civilization in the Old World grew up precisely within the territories of these Advanced Palaeolithic peoples.

It must be stressed at the outset that traces of Advanced Palaeolithic culture are consistently associated with men whose skeletal remains show them to have been without doubt members of *Homo sapiens.* The earliest human remains from Advanced Palaeolithic deposits, the burial of a man from Combe-Capelle in the Dordogne, conform in general to the type first revealed at Cromagnon in the same department of France. Cromagnon man was tall, erect and well built. His head was long and, though the vault was relatively low, the anterior and median portions of the cranium were notably full and presented a smooth profile. The brain was strikingly above the modern average in capacity, that of the Combe-Capelle man being *c.* 1590 cc. The prominence of the parietal bones on either side of the skull gave it a characteristically pentagonal cross-section. The face was large, but the brow ridges were only slight, the nose narrow and the chin notably prominent.

It has already been suggested that modern man is likely to have emerged more than once in different parts of the world from human stocks at a Neanderthaloid stage. Cromagnon man and his cousins in Europe and western Asia thus represent only one of a number of groups of modern man to appear during the latter part of the Upper Pleistocene. The special claim they have on our attention is that they alone supported the Advanced Palaeolithic culture on which the future of western civilization was to depend. In seeking the precise origins of this particular group of men we are confronted by the usual difficulties, the scarcity of fossil traces and the imprecise dating of several of these.

The 'classic' Neanderthal stock as it appeared in western and southern Europe at the onset of the last glaciation is by common consent a by-product of the evolutionary process, one that can be excluded from the ancestry of modern man. The most promising sources are the less specialized Neanderthaloid stocks which both preceded and coexisted with the 'classic' or extreme form. One of the interesting facts about these is that they show a wide range of variation within which individual populations may display an apparent mixture of traits. One may take as an example the fossil type represented at es-Skhūl: certain parts of the skeleton, notably the limb bones, posterior part of the skull and lower jaw, exhibit so modern an appearance that they might well, if found together or singly, have been classified as belonging to a prototype of Cromagnon man; whereas the anterior part of the skull, recovered alone, would have qualified as Neanderthal. There is much discussion how this ought to be interpreted: does it mean that we have to do with the product of admixture between Neanderthal and modern strains; or are we in the presence of an unstable group, showing a comparatively wide range of variation, a group from which *Homo sapiens sapiens* could conceivably have emerged? On the face of it this seems much the more likely hypothesis. It is reasonable to think of *Homo sapiens sapiens*, as we encounter him in his Advanced Palaeolithic setting, as the outcome of a progressive development through an unspecialized Neanderthaloid stage from primitive antecedents.

One of the most evident characteristics of Advanced Palaeolithic culture is its much greater dynamism. This shows itself in a much more rapid tempo of change, in a greater variability as between one group and another and in a greater complexity of material equipment. This latter is reflected both in the greater degree to which artifacts were specialized to suit particular functions and in the use of composite tools and weapons made up of items from different materials. Thus, whereas Neanderthal man made do with plain wooden lances, his successors invented a wide range of spears, harpoons and arrows, as well as fishing tackle, and commonly made these with separate heads of antler, bone, ivory or flint. Even more pervasive in some respects

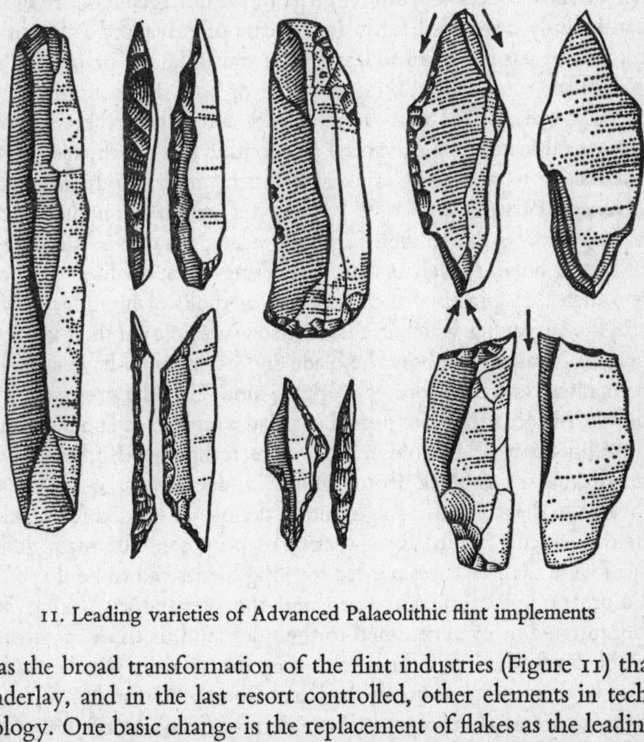

11. Leading varieties of Advanced Palaeolithic flint implements

was the broad transformation of the flint industries (Figure 11) that underlay, and in the last resort controlled, other elements in technology. One basic change is the replacement of flakes as the leading primary product by blades having more or less parallel flake-scars. A second innovation was the employment of a steep, almost vertical, retouch for shaping such products as knife-blades, projectile heads or insets for composite tools, the twin objects of which were to concentrate on the strongest, thickest part of the blade and to blunt edges, either for ease of mounting or as a protection to the finger. A third major change was the emergence in a great variety of forms of the graving-tool or burin, its sharp working edge formed by a blow or blows struck at varying angles into the main axis of the blade, a type of tool especially important for the working of antler and bone as well as for engraving ornamental designs and graphic art.

In considering origins it is important to bear consistently in mind that we have to seek a primitive stage of the emergent culture rather than its fully developed form. In the case of Advanced Palaeolithic culture one has therefore to leave aside traits like the practice of art or even the extensive working of antler or bone and concentrate on the basic traits of the flint-work. Blades and burins, the two most widespread features of Advanced Palaeolithic flint-work, are known sporadically from earlier, sometimes much earlier, industries. If the Advanced Palaeolithic people laid greater emphasis on these techniques, this was due to their particular needs, notably in their use of antler and bone, as well as flint, in making the specialized weapons by which they practised their superior methods of hunting, as well as in the engraving which in due course was to crown their achievement. It is easy to see how the blade and burin could have emerged from antecedent traditions of working flint. Thus the preparation of the kind of core needed for producing blades represented no more than a modification of the old tortoise-core technique. Both involved the shaping of a block from which in due course it would be possible to detach with a single action the blanks needed for making the implements needed for a variety of purposes. The main differences were that the cores needed for long blades had to be shaped to a more or less cylindrical form and the preparatory flaking was concentrated or even confined to the sides; and that in consequence the blades themselves, which were now detached by punches rather than by hammers, normally had plain butts. As for burins, their manufacture might easily have been derived from observation of the fortuitous blows liable to occur in flint industries generally, and especially so in ones in which hand-axes were a prominent feature.

If the blade and burin techniques were both, so to say, immanent in earlier traditions of flint-working, it follows that they might well have emerged independently at different times and places, a conclusion which must greatly complicate any discussion of origins. Thus the discovery of industries exhibiting these basic techniques at various caves in Syria and Palestine, notably Adlun, Jabrud and et-Tabun, in deposits underlying the Levalloiso-Mousterian of the region does not necessarily indicate priority for this particular area. Yet it does provide a suggestive pointer, for here, in layers dating from the last interpluvial period and containing advanced types of hand-axe, we find not merely blades but most of the principal types of burin, as well as various knife-blades and points which have a nibbling retouch on one edge or a battered back of a kind characteristic of Advanced Palaeolithic industries. Again, it is in this area that the Levalloiso-Mousterian industries show the strongest proportion of types characteristic of Advanced Palaeolithic assemblages: in the case of et-Tabun it might be argued that the blade and burin element obtruded from the underlying hand-axe layer mentioned earlier, but this can hardly be said of es-Skhūl where no such layer existed. Does this combination of Advanced and Lower Palaeolithic types in the Levalloiso-Mousterian of the Mount Carmel caves indicate admixture, or does it not point to cultural evolution in or close to this area? The parallelism between the cultural and palaeontological problems is further underlined by the fact that similar combinations are found as far afield as Teshik-Tash, in Uzbekistan, where a few burins, prismatic cores and flakes with steep retouch occur with Neanderthaloid remains and a flint industry of predominantly Mousterian type. Once again one is left with an extensive region within which there remain wide gaps awaiting field-investigation.

Radio-carbon dates for early occurrences of Advanced Palaeolithic culture (from localities as widely separated as Arcy-sur-Cure in the French department of Yonne, Haua Fteah in Cyrenaica, Shanidar in the Zagros mountains of northern Iraq and Kara Kamar in Afghanistan) all bunch closely around the time-span 35,000–30,000 B.C. Unless this pattern is radically altered, the prospects of being able to use this method of defining some original locus of Advanced Palaeolithic culture are not good, particularly if we allow for the margin of error inherent in radio-carbon analysis and for the possibility that movement may have been rapid during an initial expansive phase.

When considering the relationships of different parts of the Advanced Palaeolithic world, it is indeed important to remember that during much at least of the last glaciation the area was more of a unity and allowed much greater freedom of overland movement than it does today. Lower sea-levels meant among other things that Anatolia, and thus the west Asiatic hinterland, was joined by dry land to the Balkans and so to central and western Europe; that the Crimea formed part of a continuous unindented plain from the Caucasus to central Europe; that the head of the present Adriatic was dry land, affording easier access from the Danubian area to Italy and south France; and that the ice-free parts of Britain were joined to the continental mainland.

The earliest manifestation of Advanced Palaeolithic culture in France where the sequence is most complete, namely the Châtelperronian, is sparsely represented and too poorly characterized to give much clue to its origin. Bone work is confined to point tools, art is still absent, and the flint-work is without marked peculiarities, though including knife-blades backed along one edge by a steep retouch. Some prehistorians, it is true, have stressed the Mousterian elements in Châtelperronian assemblages from early excavations, and the suggestion has even been made of an indigenous origin in the local Mousterian. Since the Mousterian in this part of Europe is associated with the 'classic' or extreme Neanderthal physical type, the implications of this, if accepted, would indeed be revolutionary and sufficient to jeopardize the whole notion of the separateness of this physical type. However, the fact that Châtelperronian deposits almost invariably overlie Mousterian ones, taken in conjunction with the recovery by modern excavators of Châtelperronian assemblages without Mousterian elements, suggests very strongly the presence of contamination and admixture.

The earliest Advanced Palaeolithic cultures sufficiently well defined and widely distributed to make it profitable to discuss their origin are the Aurignacian and Gravettian, each, like the Châtelperronian, named after type stations in France. Although sharing certain basic characteristics and equally associated with modern types of men, the two cultures display marked differences. Aurignacian flint-work is characterized by a strong predominance of flake-scrapers, among them numerous *rostrate* or beaked-forms as well as a large number steeply flaked, sometimes to a keel; by numerous burins, including a number of beaked forms; and by a skilful form of retouch, involving the removal of delicate micro-flakes, which was applied particularly to steep scrapers and beaked burins. One of the few well-defined types of point commonly found in Aurignacian industries was that named after the French site of Font-Yves, comprising a thin narrow blade with the tip pointed by a nibbling retouch applied to one or both edges. Conspicuously absent were points and knife-blades shaped by the steep blunting retouch which was to be such a feature of the Gravettian.

Aurignacian industries appeared in south-west France with an abruptness that suggests the spread of ideas, if not of groups of people from a distance. The wealth and apparent duration of similar industries in the Mount Carmel caves and their high antiquity as far afield as Iran and Afghanistan argue that the main impulse, whatever its precise character, may have come from the east by way of the Balkans and central Europe. Some confirmation that this route may in fact have been followed is provided by the distribution of a type of bone point split at the base to engage the shaft that was characteristic of the earliest Aurignacian industries in western Europe. Such split-bone points are significant as the earliest well-defined type of detachable weaponhead. Although they have yet to be discovered in western Asia, it is particularly interesting to find them in caves in the Balkan mountains of northern Bulgaria, in the Bükk mountains of Hungary and in the middle and upper Danubian area. For what they are worth, these bone points certainly suggest an intrusion from the east through central Europe to the west.

Some of the Hungarian finds are additionally significant for the light they throw on the relations between the intrusive representatives of modern man and the indigenous Neanderthaloid inhabitants of central Europe. Typical split-base bone points occur in the context of the well-defined Szeletian culture which seems to have developed in the north-west Carpathian basin as an outcome of the impact of Aurignacian on Mousterian culture. The culture has been found to extend from the Bükk mountains of northern Hungary through Slovakia to Moravia and possibly Bohemia. The flint-work combines certain Aurignacian traits, notably keeled scrapers and certain types of burin, with Mousterian elements, including disc-cores, side-scrapers and bifacially flaked points with one face flatter and less completely worked. The bone-work, in addition to characteristic split-base points, includes elongated lozenge forms known as Lautsch and Mladec points. There can hardly be any doubt that we are in the presence of a hybrid culture, one that implies contact between the intrusive and indigenous populations of central Europe. The easy relationship this seems to imply between modern men and the indigenous population is presumably to be explained by the fact that the Neanderthaloid people of central Europe were relatively less specialized than the 'classic' Neanderthal population of western and southern Europe. Some confirmation of this comes from south Russia where the Neanderthaloid population was also of the less specialized type, because traditions of flint-making of Mousterian ancestry played a definite part in some of the Advanced Palaeolithic industries of this area.

The Gravettian, which overlay the Aurignacian in western and central Europe, differed profoundly from it at a technical level and was in several respects more richly endowed. Although extending far to the west, its main focus lay in central and eastern Europe. The number of sites with evidence of prolonged settlement in the zone of south Russia between the rivers Don (Figures 12–13) and Dniester and within latitudes 50° and 55° north suggests that this was a key area, but rich and important finds on the loess of Moravia and contiguous areas suggest that central Europe was also of special significance in the life of the Gravettian culture. There are still important gaps in the record of radio-carbon dates, especially in south Russia, but (for what they are worth) they seem to indicate that Gravettian culture appeared earlier in central than in western Europe and so support the idea of an east-west movement. Although there is evidence for some movement north of the Alps, the main drive to the west seems to have passed through Italy (where we find in the Grimaldian a long-lived regional variety of the basic Gravettian culture) to southern France and so to Spain.

The sequence observed in the French caves would thus reflect that arrival of impulses from different directions rather than an indigenous evolution. The view held by some French prehistorians that the Gravettian developed directly from the Châtelperronian tradition, the two forming part of a continuing Perigordian indigenous to France is difficult to sustain in the light of modern knowledge. For one thing, if we can rely on a growing body of radio-carbon age determinations from south Russia and from Czechoslovakia, it seems that industries of Gravettian type appeared in eastern and central Europe before they did in France, just as the Châtelperronian itself has been shown to be relatively retarded in relation to the Dabban of Cyrenaica or industries as far afield as Afghanistan. Again, recent critical assessment of the evidence from the French caves has, to say the least, cast doubt on the hypothesis of a continuing Perigordian tradition preceding, running alongside and surviving the Aurignacian intrusion.

Gravettian flint-work included narrow asymmetric penknife blades backed by steep retouch and a variety of backed bladelets and points, some of microlithic proportions (Figure 13). On the south Russian sites there is an interesting suggestion of delayed Mousterian tradition. From the lower levels at Kostienki we find, alongside burins and end-scrapers on blades, bifacially flaked points resembling forms from Mousterian sites in the Crimea and the Caucasus; for instance, laurel-leaf forms and triangular points with a slightly concave base (Figure 12) recall examples from the Caucasian site of Ilskaya. This suggests that we have here in south Russia evidence that Mousterian traditions blended with Gravettian ones, just as in Hungary and Slovakia they did with the Aurignacian. This makes it all the more significant that the bifacial technique should have reappeared at intervals during the Gravettian succession, notably in the upper layer at Telmanskaya (Figure 13) in the same region as Kostienki, where shallow flaking is found either on both faces or, more often, mainly on one face of small leaf-shaped or larger elongated points. From a later period, most likely contemporary with the Magdalenian of western Europe, one finds at the site of Mezine on the upper Desna quite a different blade industry with burins, end-scrapers, awls, pronged implements and a few battered-backs.

Although their technology depended mainly on flint-working, the Gravettians made considerable use of bone and, notably in east and central Europe, of mammoth ivory for making a variety of artifacts, including implements and weapons as well as ornaments and works of art. Among the techniques used in working these materials were the ringing of antlers to divide them into sections and of long-bones to remove their articular ends; the cutting of parallel grooves in the surfaces of antler and large bones, probably by means of burins, to make available the blanks required for working into the smaller forms of artifact; edge-flaking; perforation by means of awls; and finishing by means of rubbing or polishing on some such material as sandstone. Among the articles made were items of hunting-gear, including long biconical lance-heads, frequently of bone, but sometimes, as at Gontzi on the upper Desna, of ivory grooved on either face; perforated objects meant for straightening shafts or possibly for softening thongs, from Gontzi and Mezine; and various club-like objects made from reindeer antler, having hammer-like heads, like those from the same sites, or with the stump of one of the tines bevelled to form an adze-like blade as at Pavlov in south Moravia. Pointed awls made by

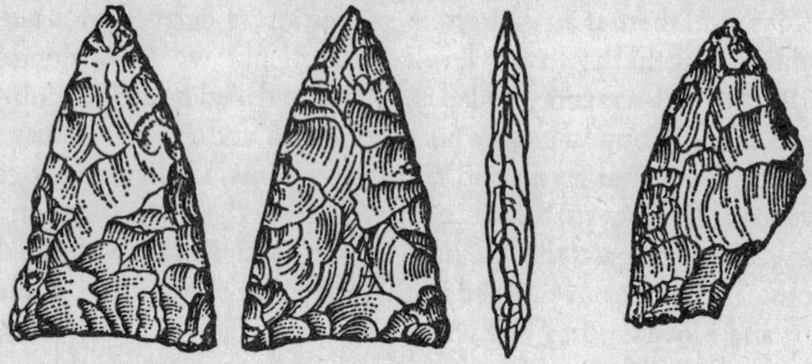

12. Bifacially flaked points from the base of Kostienki I, on the Don, south Russia

sharpening a splinter or reducing one end of a small long-bone occur over the whole Gravettian territory and may have served any of a number of purposes. Eyed needles like those from Gontzi and Mezine are important for the hints they give of skin clothing. Spatulate tools of bone or ivory may have been employed in working leather or skins. Shovels or scoops made from lengths of mammoth rib from Ardeevo and Kostienki, having one end rounded and the other converted into a handle constricted for gripping and provided with a thickened pommel, resemble in some respects the beaters used by some Eskimos for removing the snow from skin clothing. Lastly, one might mention the spoons from Pavlov with narrow handles and oval ladles cut out of mammoth ivory, smoothly finished and presumably for eating.

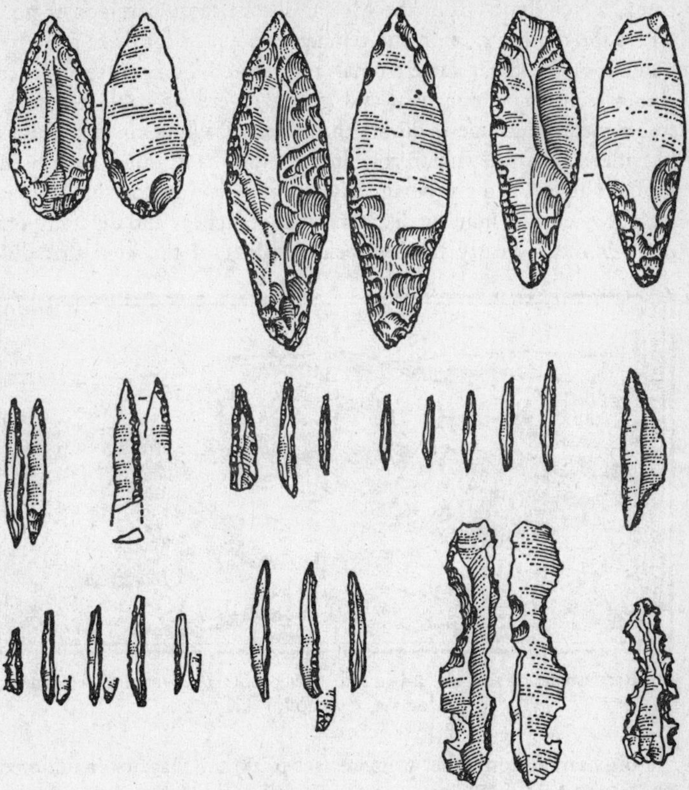

13. Points with bifacial retouch (*top row*) from the upper layer and Gravettian flints from the middle layer at Telmanskaya, on the Don, south Russia

Extensive and sometimes thick middens in close association with settlements, both in south Russia and central Europe, reinforce the impression that mammoth-hunting was particularly significant in the economy of peoples who deployed a Gravettian technology in eastern Europe. At Mezhirich, a site recently excavated near Cherkassy in the Ukraine, mammoths formed well over nine tenths of the larger game animals by number and even more by weight, showing that certainly at one time of the year they provided the main source of animal protein. Yet, seasonally at least, hunting was more broadly based, as we know from the Mezine site in the Chernigov region where the musk-ox, bison and reindeer accounted for three fifths by number of the larger game animals represented. Some of the smaller game, including arctic hare and grouse, were probably taken in snares made from sinews during the season of winter cover. Animals like mammoth and rhinoceros, on the other hand, must have been brought to a stand by being driven over pit-traps or some other such device: their hunting, like their mere butchery and the transport of their meat, clearly implies social hunting of the kind that dis-

14. Reconstruction of an Advanced Palaeolithic (Gravettian) settlement, Moravia, Czechoslovakia

tinguishes men from other primates (see p. 38) and was first manifested during the Middle Pleistocene. On the other hand the presence, as at Kostienki IV, of pestle-rubbers and grinding-slabs points to the gathering and preparation of plant food, no doubt on the part of the women members of the group.

In western and parts of central Europe the Gravettians were able to occupy caves and rock-shelters, but over most of south Russia these were not available and they had to camp in the open. In this wide territory they settled on the banks of the large rivers that flowed into the Black Sea or on those of their tributaries. Here, as on the loess of Moravia, they constructed artificial dwellings as shelter against the cold conditions that prevailed during most of the late glacial period (Figure 14). As we have already seen, earlier types of man made artificial dwellings, even though traces have only rarely survived.

Although the palaeolithic dwellings of south Russia have been the subject of a good deal of sociological speculation based in some cases on dubious interpretations, the discovery and excavation of these sites has been one of the major contributions of Soviet archaeology to prehistoric research.

Even where the footings of walls or the post-holes or wall-slots of frame-built structures survive, it is notoriously difficult to make definite reconstructions of buildings from their ground plans alone. This difficulty is greatly enhanced where no such traces exist: all that remain, apart from a row of post-holes suggesting a pitched roof at the Moravian site of Dolní Věstonice, are the floor, sunk to some extent into the sub-soil; deeper hollows used possibly for storage; fireplaces; and rocks and mammoth-tusks that may in certain instances have been used to weigh down some form of covering. Even such features may be difficult to interpret when it is unknown whether they all relate to one period of occupation. For the same reason, and because it has seldom been possible to uncover more than a portion of a single settlement, it is difficult to assess how many dwellings existed or were occupied at any one time within a single settlement. Where exploration has been anything like complete, as at Mezine or Kirilovsky, Kiev, several dwellings have been found, indicating cohesive groups of hunters and their respective families. In their general form the south Russian dwellings have been compared with the roundish houses of *yaranga* type built by the modern Chukot, which have low walls of dry stones set with timber uprights that, together with a central post, carried the roof. On the other hand the palaeolithic hunters used different materials, making extensive use of skeletons of mammoths. This was carried to extreme lengths in the case of the dwelling excavated at Mezhirich. This had an internal area of some 23 square metres and was built from the skeletal remains of no less than 95 mammoths: the walls were made of skulls and long bones and the roof, presumed to have been of animal skins, was supported on a frame of mammoth tusks, and probably of tree branches, and kept in place by the weight of tusks and reindeer antlers, with mammoth shoulder-blades arranged like tiles on the skull foundation holding down the perimeter.

During the closing stages of the Ice Age the reindeer hunters of the north European plain made tent-like structures supported on wooden poles and held down by glacial boulders in round or pear-shaped settings. These remind one of Eskimo tents, the great advantage of which resides in their mobility. Skin coverings could be rolled up on the poles and carried to another encampment, leaving only traces of fire-places and of the stone weights so necessary on frozen ground. The probability is that, even when the Gravettians and other Advanced Palaeolithic peoples occupied territories where caves and rock-shelters were available, they supplemented the draughty cover with artificial screens; camping in the mouths of deep caves would hardly have been possible under more or less glacial conditions without some form of shelter, and if appropriate methods of excavation were more generally adopted there is little doubt that traces of this would be found.

Another feature of the Gravettian culture, whether in eastern, central or western Europe, is the elaborate way in which the dead were buried. The practice of careful burial was, as we have already seen, initiated by Neanderthal man and his close relatives. The main innovations of the Advanced Palaeolithic rite are that the dead were commonly decked in the finery worn in life and sprinkled with red ochre, a symbol, it may be, of blood and so of life; and, more rarely, that they were protected to some extent by stones or heavy bones, roofed over perhaps with branches. There are no signs of any attempt to separate the dead from the living symbolically by burying them away from settlements: on the contrary, it was normal in limestone country to dispose of corpses by digging graves in deposits previously accumulated on the cave floor and to continue occupying the site; even on the open sites of south Russia and the Moravian loess, graves are brought to light in the course of excavating settlements.

As a rule, the body of the dead person would be contracted, with the knees drawn up to the stomach, in order perhaps to economize on the size of the grave; but that this was by no means invariable is proved by burials in a fully extended position from the Grottes des Enfants and La Barma at Grimaldi on the Riviera frontier of France and Italy. Most individuals were buried singly, but in several instances two, three or more corpses were buried in the same grave. In the case of the well-known double burial from the Grottes des Enfants, it appears certain that the old woman crouched right up against a youth was buried subsequently and pushed into the same grave; but there is no clear evidence whether the three fully extended burials at La Barma Grande, a young woman flanked on one side by a man and on the other by a youth, were buried strictly at one and the same time or successively. The mass burial found under the Gravettian deposit at Predmost in Moravia and comprising remains of twenty individuals, surrounded by a stone ring, must surely be interpreted as in part at least an ossuary, since six of the individuals were represented by no more than a few bones each: indeed it seems difficult to accept the fourteen complete skeletons as the result of more or less simultaneous deaths, unless the hunting bands were much bigger than we have any reason for believing. When the dead were buried in caves occupied by their relatives, there was no real need to give them physical protection against wild animals, and one is entitled to doubt whether the protective stones noted by some early excavators as intentionally placed were not in fact accidental. There can be no doubt, on the other hand, that artificial protection was sometimes provided on open sites, though even here but rarely; apart from the stone rampart at Predmost, which may well have been roofed over with branches, one may cite the oval chamber constructed of mammoth bones at Kostienki II and the covering of a contracted burial at Dolní Věstonice by two shoulder-blades of mammoth. The presence of personal ornaments and in certain instances the suggestive disposition of perforated mollusc shells, as for example at the Grottes des Enfants, where they were found to cover the hips and thighs of two child skeletons, makes it likely that Advanced Palaeolithic people buried their dead fully clothed.

It is thanks to this practice that we have such a good idea of what the Gravettians chose to wear in the way of jewellery. A point to notice is that the men wore quite as much finery as the women; indeed, in the triple burial at La Barma Grande the woman was noticeably less well provided for than the man and the youth buried beside her. The materials used were natural substances perforated or otherwise only slightly modified, but fired clay was sometimes used for pendants, and beads might be carved from ivory, in at least one case reproducing the form of deer teeth. Among animal substances, teeth, particularly deer canines, and snail-shells were chiefly favoured, but *Dentalium* shells, mother-of-pearl discs and fish vertebrae were also used. The most popular form of ornament was the necklace, which might on occasion be quite complex, as with one from a burial in La Barma Grande made up from incised deer teeth, snail-shells and salmon vertebrae; but beads might also be threaded to make bracelets or sewn on to hair-nets or garments. Pendants were made of stone lumps or discs, fired clay and carved ivory, the latter taking the form at Pavlov of a tapered necklet engraved on the outer face and perforated at either end. Bracelets were made up of threaded beads or

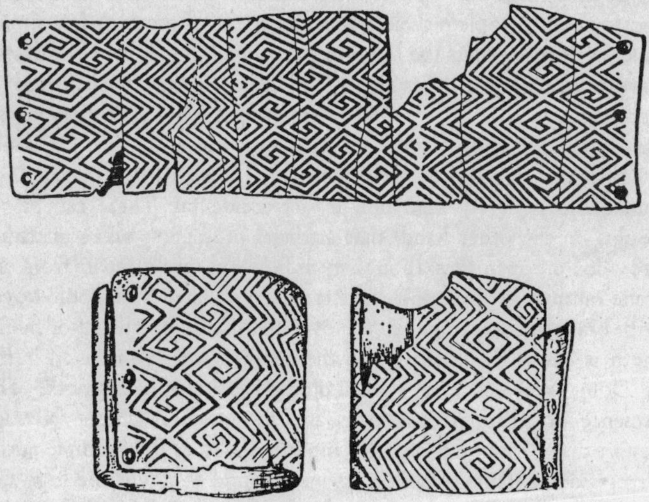

15. Mammoth-ivory bracelet from Mezine, on the Desna, south Russia

cut from a single piece of ivory like the splendid decorated piece from Mezine (Figure 15). An ivory pin from Kostienki IV with flattened disc-head perforated in the middle and milled along the edge deserves special mention (Figure 16). As a rule ornaments like other artifacts were made from local materials, but the salmon vertebrae from Grimaldi on the Riviera must have been obtained, either by exchange or in the course of seasonal movement, from a river flowing into the Atlantic.

The custom of wearing personal ornaments in itself indicates the awakening of an aesthetic sense for which even more conclusive proofs are available, both in decorative patterns applied to bone and ivory implements and ornaments and above all in relatively complex designs and in graphic and sculptural representations of animals and women. The commonest technique used for decorating bone and ivory was incision, presumably by means of a sharp flint. This might take the form of short strokes defining or even milling the edge of implements or perforated teeth, of fine lines built up into simple patterns, or of small pits bored into the surface of the object concerned (a technique at present only known from this time in eastern Europe where it is well seen at Kostienki IV: Figure 17). The commonest geometrical patterns used were zones of short parallel strokes like those on ivory pendants from La Barma Grande, Predmost and

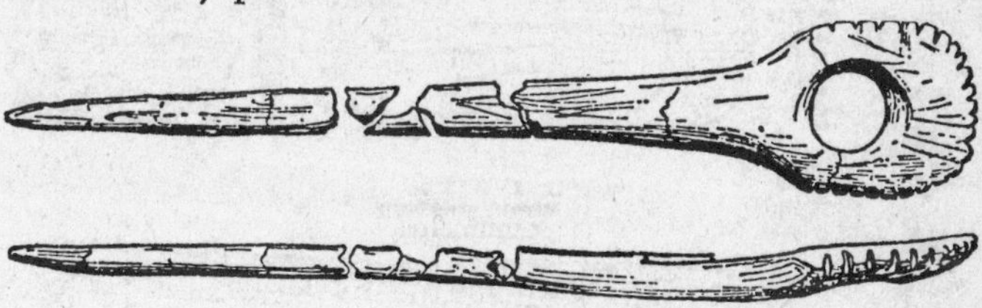

16. Ivory pin from Kostienki IV, south Russia

Pavlov; finely barbed lines, seen on objects from the Grotta Polesini near Tivoli within fifteen miles of Rome; criss-cross patterns as displayed at La Barma Grande and from the upper level at Kostienki I; herring-bone patterns, lacking median lines, from Predmost and from the Ukrainan site of Mezine on the Upper Desna; and linear chevrons, sometimes multiple, incised on objects from Kostienki and Mezine in the east to the Grotta Polesini and La Barma Grande in the west. The most complex patterns in Gravettian art are the meanders engraved often in combination with multiple chevrons on ivory figurines and, in particular, on an ivory bracelet of astonishing finish and sophistication from Mezine. The linear chevron designs applied in red paint to the jaws and skulls of mammoths from Mezine and Mezhirich repectively betray a special and hardly unexpected concern for the animals that bulked so largely in diet.

The most oustanding products of Gravettian art were beyond doubt figurines of animals and women. Most of these were carved from natural substances, notably mammoth ivory, and the spongy tissue of mammoth bone, as well as a variety of mineral substances including calcite, coal, haematite, limestone, sandstone, serpentine and steatite. Others, notably from Dolní-Věstonice and Pavlov but rarely also from south Russia, were modelled from clay and hardened in the fire like pottery; some of these plastic figurines were evidently made with care and deliberation, but most of those found in and around a hearth at Pavlov might almost have been produced by a hunter squatting by the fire and idly kneading clay into the shapes of his intended victims. It is significant that in central and eastern Europe, where the mammoth was a principal victim of the hunter, this was

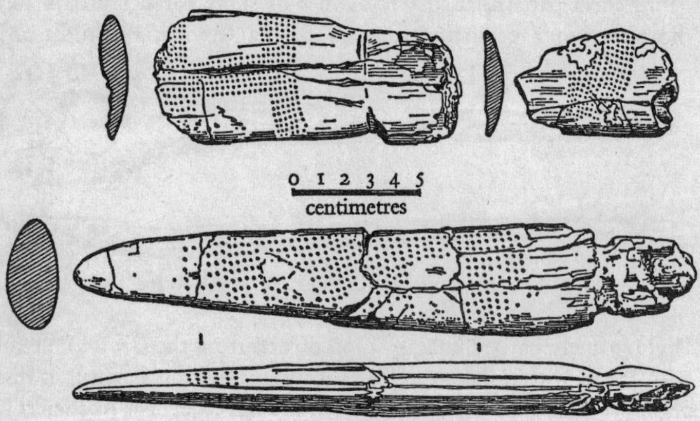


17. Decorative patterns made by small pits on ivory plaques, Kostienki IV, south Russia

the animal most widely represented; and the similarity in its treatment, whether in ivory (Plate IIb) or clay, only goes to underline the strong community of culture between the two areas. Yet mammoths were by no means the only animals represented: the Pavlov modellers also turned out bear, wolf, ibex-like animals and rhinoceros (Figure 18), and those of Dolní Věstonice contributed felines to the repertoire; again, the hunters of the Vogelherd, an open station in the neighbourhood of Ulm, carved mammoth, horse and felines of similar style from mammoth ivory. Animal figurines were also carved by the Magdalenians (Plate IIIb).

Leaving aside the remarkable but unique doll-like figure of a man carved from ivory and accompanying a ceremonial male-burial under

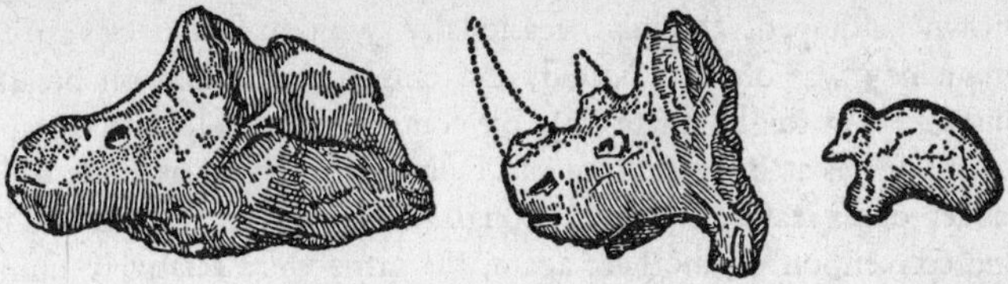

18. Clay figurines of rhinoceros and mammoth from Gravettian site at Pavlov, Moravia, Czechoslovakia

a thick loess deposit at Brno, the human figurines made by the Gravettians were all female. Some of these, notably examples from Mezine in the Ukraine and from the Moravian sites of Pavlov and Pekarna, were highly symbolic (Figure 19), but the majority, whether carved or modelled, were naturalistic at least so far as the trunk was concerned. The emphasis was undeniably sexual: the figures were

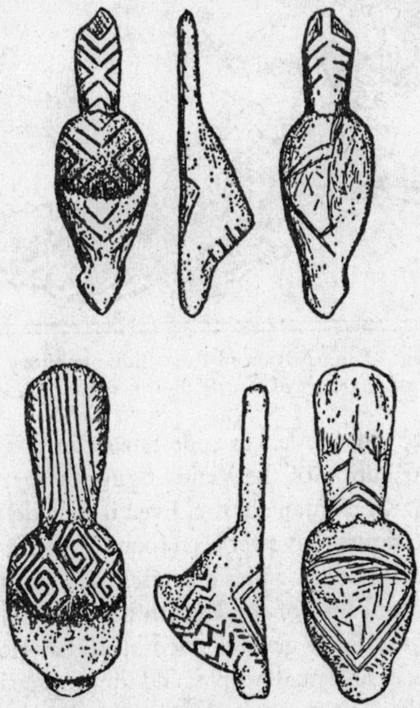

19. Symbolic female figurines in mammoth ivory, Mezine, south Russia

shown undraped, though occasionally with a fringe or girdle; pregnancy was often indicated; and emphasis was laid on breasts, buttocks and thighs (Plate IIa). By contrast the head, with notable exceptions as at Brassempouy and Dolní Věstonice, was liable to be rendered as a featureless knob, though the hair might be indicated by one convention or another; again, the arms were relatively unimportant; the legs tapered and the feet were barely suggested, if shown

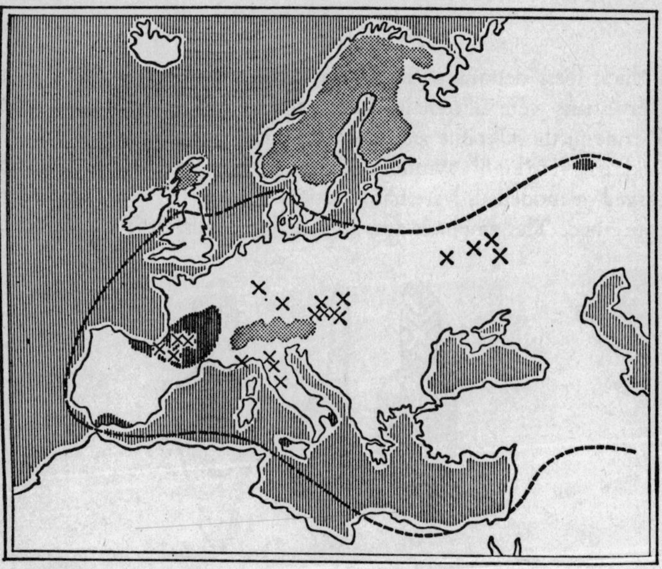

Map 2. Extent of the Advanced Palaeolithic territory, and the main occurrences of female figurines and cave art

at all (Figure 20). If one leaves aside Siberia in this context (but see p. 91), the distribution of the Venus figurines agrees fairly closely with that of the Gravettian culture. Even if they do not extend quite so far west – no figures have yet been found in Iberia – they still occur over a distance as the crow flies of some 2,000 miles: over this great distance from the banks of the Don to the foot-hills of the western Pyrenees they display a general resemblance so close as to suggest the movements of an actual people; and this impression is heightened by agreements in flint-work, in decorative art and, so far as east and central Europe are concerned, in the representations of mammoths.

Enough has been said to make it plain that the Gravettians were keenly aware of the possibility of decorating both their persons and many of the objects they used and wore; and further that they were responsible for sculptures which in their own way are as eloquent as the works of Graeco-Roman or Renaissance art. In respect of art the Gravettians lived in a different world from the Levalloiso-Mousterians and even, it would appear, though to a lesser degree and with some

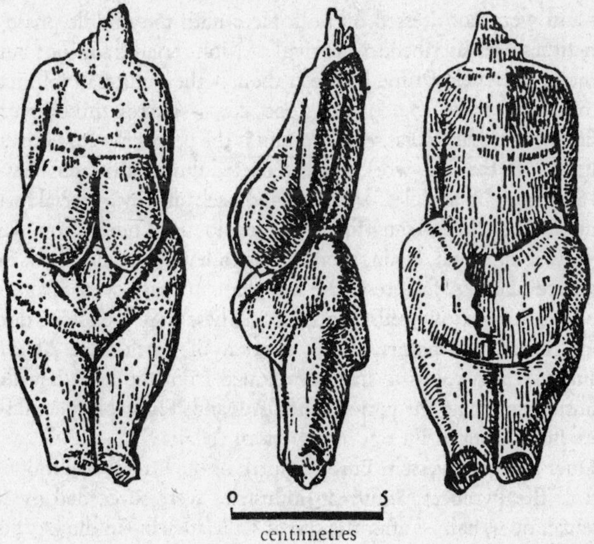


20. Mammoth-ivory figurine of woman from Kostienki I, south Russia

possible exceptions, from their immediate predecessors the Aurignacians. Over by far the greater part of their territories the Aurignacians left no evidence that they practised art at all; and where, as in the Dordogne, works of art have been found in Aurignacian contexts, it is difficult to know, especially in view of the character of many early excavations, if such works were not really due to Gravettian influence. Whether or not the Gravettians were the sole begetters of Advanced Palaeolithic art, it seems reasonably sure that France was the principal hearth as it was certainly the most important theatre of cave art in the sense of engraving, painting and relief-carving on the walls or ceilings of caves and shelters.

Before looking more closely at this, it may be useful to consider the chief Advanced Palaeolithic groups which carried the art to its ultimate stage of development. Immediately overlying Gravettian layers in the French caves are industries featuring leaf-shaped points flaked on one or both faces and named after the site of Solutré in the department of Saône-et-Loire. The origin of the Solutrean points, which to begin with were flaked only on one face and often on only part of this and were not dressed on both faces until the middle phase, has sometimes been ascribed to a revival of Mousterian tradition; but the immense interval of time between them – the Solutrean fell mainly within the period 17,000 to 15,000 B.C. – makes this hypothesis difficult to sustain. What seems certain is the persistence of Gravettian influence. In the flint-work this is reflected during the later phases of the Solutrean by bladelets with battered backs and by a special form of point having a lateral tang formed by removing a notch from part of the lower end; and, again, there seems to have been no break in the sequence of art. A feature of the last phase in south-west Spain is the appearance of arrowheads (Figure 21). These may well have derived from the tanged points of the Aterian of north-west Africa, an industry which seems to have developed from the local Levalloiso-Mousterian during the period when Advanced Palaeolithic industries were flourishing in Europe and western Asia.

Over much of western Europe, north of the Cantabrian mountains and of the Pyrenees, Solutrean industries were succeeded by Magdalenian ones, named after the site of La Madeleine in the Dordogne. The character of Magdalenian flint-work suggests that it was rooted in the Gravettian, and indeed Proto-Magdalenian industries have in fact been recognized underlying Solutrean levels. The Magdalenian knappers were capable of striking fine blades which they knapped into end-scrapers and, above all, into the burins needed for engraving antler and bone. During the earlier phases of the Magdalenian, before the emergence of barbed harpoon-heads of antler, battered-back bladelets and triangles, often of microlithic proportions, were in common use and presumably served as elements in composite tools and weapons. Much greater emphasis than ever before was laid on antler and bone, particularly for hunting-gear. To begin with the leading forms of projectile head were lances with bone heads of flattened or oval section and pointed or bevelled bases. It may be significant that a markedly different form, the harpoon-head of reindeer antler, at first barbed on one edge, and later on both, with a basal swelling for attaching the line, came into use at a time when the climate became markedly colder and the Magdalenian hunter concentrated on reindeer as a main quarry. Many of these harpoon-heads were not only beautifully finished but were incised to emphasize the lines of stem and barbs (Figure 22). The spear-thrower cut

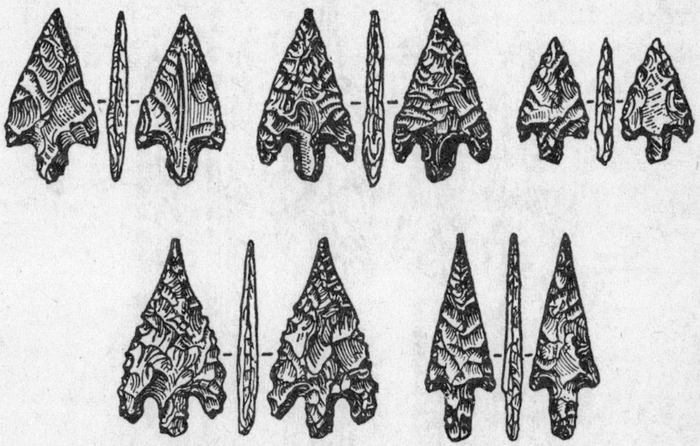

21. Barbed and tanged flint arrowheads from Advanced Palaeolithic (Upper Solutrean) layer at Parpalló, Valencia, Spain

from a length of reindeer antler and having one end hooked to engage the base of a shaft was another item of equipment – which to judge from the decoration lavished upon it was much favoured during phase IV – at the time, that is, before fully barbed harpoon-heads had come into use. Horses were the animals most often carved on these throwers, but ibex, bison, deer, reindeer, musk-ox, mammoth, a feline and various birds and fishes were also shown. They were apparently made to throw lances or spears of two distinct weights and those intended for lighter ones were weighted at the hooked end. The thicker weighted end of this type of thrower provided an opportunity of which the Magdalenian carver was not slow to take advantage. Some of these, notably those showing an ibex evacuating while standing with four feet together as though on a rocky pinnacle, display a certain rustic wit as well as the keen observation one would expect of people who lived largely by hunting wild animals.

Although centring on the region between the Cantabric mountains and the Alps, the Magdalenian culture extended at different times over a much wider area: for instance, during the earlier phases of

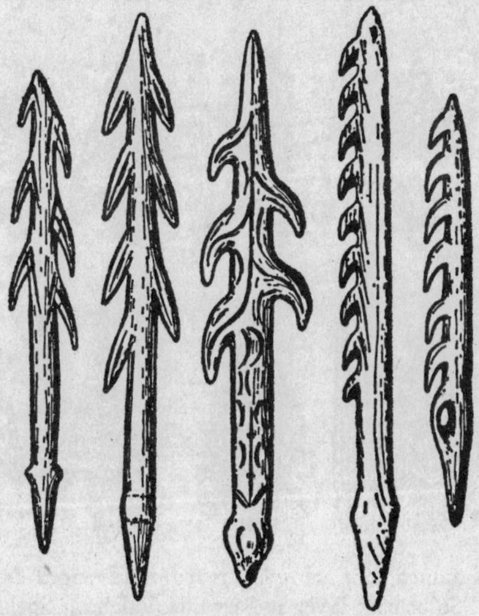

22. Advanced Palaeolithic (Magdalenian) harpoon-heads of reindeer antler

their culture (I-IV), the Magdalenians reached as far south as Parpalló in Valencia; and in the opposite direction they seem to have entered south Poland during phases III–IV and to have penetrated Hungary and Moravia by way of the Upper Danube during phases V and VI. Over the whole of this territory they left behind unmistakable traces in the form of antler and bone equipment, some of it richly decorated by carving and incision (Figure 23).

In many parts of Europe, notably in Iberia and Italy, as well as in central Europe and south Russia, the Gravettian tradition persisted, but, apart from the distinctive school of cave art in southern Italy, it is difficult to point to any advance on earlier Gravettian achievement. No more productive from the point of view of world prehistory were the Advanced Palaeolithic cultures of North Africa. On the other hand, although far too little is yet known about them, the younger Advanced Palaeolithic peoples of south-west Asia were obviously significant as forbears of the Mesolithic innovators who began the processes of domestication that led ultimately to a vast transformation in human life.

If it is to the Advanced Palaeolithic peoples of south-west Asia or their immediate successors that we have to look for the next main advance in human history, it was their close relatives in western Europe who created the most eloquent memorial of the great age of hunting. The distinction between cave art, in the sense of engravings,

23. Magdalenian decorative art: spiral ornament on antler rods from Isturitz, Basses Pyrénées, France

paintings and carvings on walls and ceilings, and chattel art, that is, art applied to movable possessions like ornaments or hunting-gear, is from some points of view artificial. This becomes obvious enough when we recall that the same people were often responsible for both and that some of the engravings on loose stone plaques have the appearance of trials for larger representations on the solid rock. Yet the very scale on which it was often possible to execute cave art lends it a certain monumental character and invites a separate treatment.

The geographical distribution of cave art is more uneven than that of chattel art, and it is even more markedly concentrated in the west. If its absence from the south Russian plains is understandable enough, this hardly applies to Czechoslovakia, Hungary, Austria and south Germany where plenty of caves are known to have been occupied by

Advanced Palaeolithic man. This gap is emphasized by recent discoveries in the South Ural district of Russia, a notable centre of Advanced Palaeolithic occupation. Here, in the Kapova cave near the south bend of the Bielaya river, an impressive group of paintings has been found, featuring stag, wild steppe-horse, mammoth and cave bear. The significance of this find of cave art, comparable in style with some of those from the Dordogne something like 2,500 miles to the west, is that it emphasizes both the broad homogeneity of the Gravettian culture and its essentially creative character.

The fact remains that by far the greater number of occurrences of cave art are in parts of France south of the Loire and west of the Lower Rhône, notably Charente, Dordogne, Languedoc and the northern slopes of the Pyrenees; north of the Loire one can only point to Arcy-sur-Cure in the department of Yonne. In Spain the most numerous

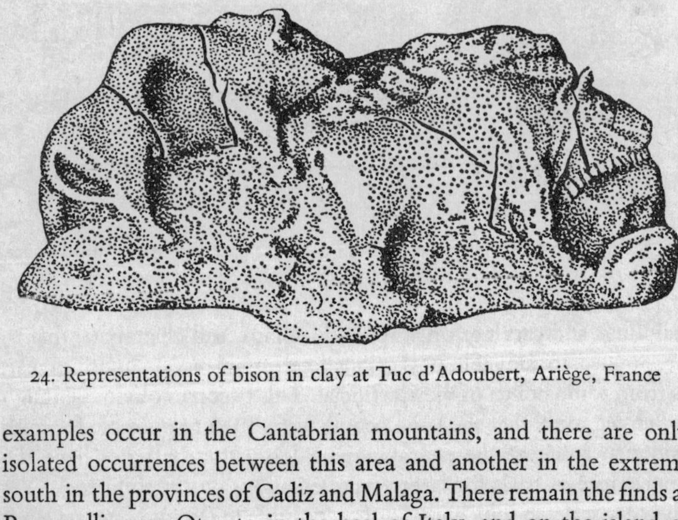

24. Representations of bison in clay at Tuc d'Adoubert, Ariège, France

examples occur in the Cantabrian mountains, and there are only isolated occurrences between this area and another in the extreme south in the provinces of Cadiz and Malaga. There remain the finds at Romanelli, near Otranto in the heel of Italy, and on the island of Levanzo to the west of Sicily (see Figure 28), which belong to a Mediterranean group in some respects distinct from the Franco-Cantabric one.

The men responsible for cave art were subject to all the tensions of the hunter's life under conditions which evidently allowed a certain leisure without rendering the winning of food in any sense easy or secure. The content of the art itself leaves us in no doubt that it was conceived in and intimately bound up with the hopes and desires of hunters; and its essentially masculine character is emphasized by the extreme rarity of plant forms. The use of rock-surfaces as receptacles of art, surfaces frequently far from the light of day and sometimes difficult of access, must surely owe something to the mystery and suggestibility of the caves themselves. That this was so is hinted at in the way the prehistoric artists utilized bosses, stalagmitic formations and even drip-marks as elements in animal shapes, natural irregularities which may nevertheless have proved suggestive when viewed by the flickering light of a primitive lamp.

For obvious reasons it is more difficult to date the art on cave walls than chattel art, which is normally found mixed with other cultural material in archaeological layers. It happens only occasionally that occupational rubbish gets heaped up against rock engravings or other forms of cave art, or that portions of the rock-surface bearing traces of art flake off and become incorporated in the underlying deposits: when either of these accidents occurs, however, it is safe to assume that the art is at least as old as the deposits in question. The recovery of engraved and painted slabs from successive Aurignacian deposits at La Ferrassie makes it certain, therefore, that cave art was already being practised in the Dordogne by around 25,000 years B.C., even though the work was still rudimentary, comprising crudely incised representations of the female organ and outlines, engraved and painted in black, of the fore-parts of animals. During the time the Dordogne caves and shelters were occupied by Gravettians (*c.* 22,000–18,000 B.C.), on the other hand, cave art underwent rapid progress and seems indeed to have reached a certain climax: meanders and various crude linear patterns were traced by hand in the clay adhering to rock surfaces or applied in paint to the rock itself; human hands, sometimes shown mutilated or with some of the fingers bent back, were stencilled or reproduced in flat wash; animals were engraved or painted in outline in a naturalistic but often rather stiff style with horns shown singly or full-face, and others painted in a blotted technique or in a flat wash; and animals and human beings were carved in relief on the rock-face. Among the latter is the Venus of Laussel, a figure comparing in most important respects with the smaller and fully sculptured examples found in contemporary deposits over the greater part of the Gravettian territory. To a substantial degree the art of the Solutreans (*c.* 18,000–15,000 B.C.) and Magdalenians (*c.* 15,000–8,300 B.C.) either carried forward the tradition of the Gravettians, as in the relief sculptures of the Roc de Sers, Cap Blanc and Angles-sur-Anglin, or recapitulated in outline, blotted line and flat-wash an analogous sequence of paintings. In certain respects, however, for instance in the development of polychrome painting and in the use of fine-line engraving to suggest convexity, it showed definite advances on its predecessor. The end of cave art, at a time when it had reached a high standard of technique, came as suddenly as that of the Magdalenian culture itself, and for that matter of the whole way of life founded on the hunting of reindeer, coinciding with the end of the Pleistocene ice age and the final onset of temperate conditions not much more than 10,000 years ago.

Technically the cave artists displayed considerable versatility, and considering the crude means at their disposal they achieved results of which we can only gauge the effect at the comparatively few sites, Lascaux outstanding among them, where they have survived in something approaching their pristine state. As to the actual methods employed, engravings varying greatly in depth and strength were presumably cut by flint burins or engraving tools. The figures in sculptured friezes were thrown into relief by cutting into the limestone and finished off by being rubbed smooth and, in some instances at least, painted. A distinct group of plastic representations comprises figures of animals modelled in clay and standing on the floors of caves, like the bison at Tuc d'Adoubert (Figure 24) and the bears of Montespan; one of the latter had evidently been treated as a dummy with an original bear's head mounted in position, presumably with the skin still attached and hanging over the back. Painting was carried out by means of the finger dipped in pigment; by the use of some kind of brush; by means of a pad of feathers or fur; or by blowing from the mouth or through a pipe. The only pigments to survive are minerals, including ferruginous ochres for reds, browns and yellows and manganese for black.

No one who has contemplated the art of Altamira or Lascaux (Plate IIIa) can doubt that the artists shared a delight in capturing and even dramatizing the animal forms with which they were so familiar in daily life, and it is difficult not to believe that some element of decoration entered into the great sculptural friezes executed on the walls of certain rock-shelters. There is even some suggestion of idle doodling in the meanders and arabesques described on the slimy clay of rock-faces, as there was also in many of the unfinished clay models hardened, probably accidentally, in one of the fireplaces at Věstonice; one can almost sense the pleasure gained from kneading soft clay or from tracing the fingers over slime. Indeed, one might go further and suggest that play and activities of a purposeless character, such as one can observe so well among primates in captivity, played a

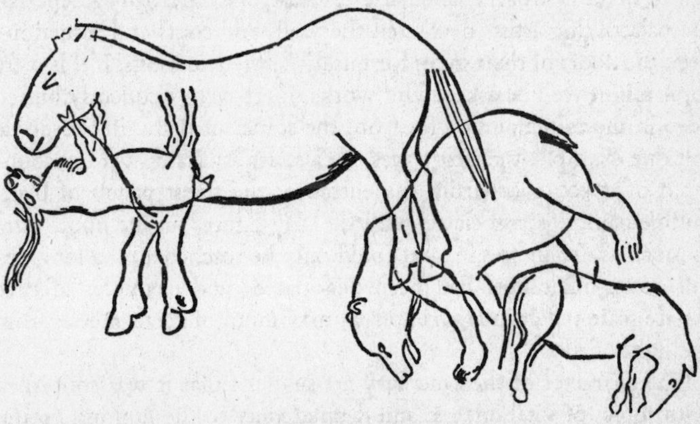

25. Magdalenian cave art: engravings of bear, horses and reindeer at Teyjat in the Dordogne, France

part in cultural evolution in all probability as influential as mutations did in the evolution of life: it is not indeed impossible that the existence of slimy rock-surfaces such as those in the Dordogne caves may have provided just the opportunity needed to trigger off the whole development of cave art.

So much emphasis has often been placed on the magical interpretation of cave art that it is sometimes overlooked that supporting evidence is confined to the great sanctuaries like Altamira, Combarelles, Font-de-Gaume and Lascaux, which belong to the more recent of the two main cycles of artistic activity. If we take the art of the earlier cycle, developed by the Gravettians and continuing into the time of the Early Magdalenian culture, we find the deep engravings and reliefs of animals and humans exposed to full daylight or at least lit by it indirectly; and representations of wounds or weapons are conspicuously absent. It would be quite wrong to regard cave art as though it was merely an aid in the eternal quest for food. However much it may later have been turned to magical use, in origin the art must have served aesthetic or psychological rather than economic needs: it is significant precisely because it was a disinterested activity, a vehicle for projecting symbols, a means of attuning individuals to their surroundings.

Yet, in the case of the sanctuaries, at least, one can hardly accept that the palaeolithic artists decorated the walls and roofs and sometimes even the floors of their caves for purely aesthetic reasons. If this were so, it might well be asked why works of art were frequently buried deep in the mountainside far from the scenes of daily life: to quote but one example, the first traces of cave art at Niaux were encountered over 500 paces from the entrance; the finest panels of black outline paintings, associated with the clay figures on the floor, were as much as 612 metres in, and could only be reached after a long up-hill down-hill tunnel had been negotiated; and examples of cave art are scattered at intervals up to a maximum of 1,114 metres from the light of day.

The character of the sanctuary art suggests that it was concerned with topics of vital interest and deep anxiety to the hunting groups responsible for them: they were, after all, preoccupied beyond all else with catching and killing the animals on whose meat they depended for very life and with the continual replenishment both of themselves and of the animals on which they lived. The representations may have played a part in the rites by which young men were initiated as fully adult members of society (see p. 106). To judge by analogy with what is known, for example, of Australian aboriginal art, it seems highly unlikely that rock-paintings or -engravings were sufficient in themselves. A much more likely probability is that they formed part of a complex of activities which certainly included dancing and may also have included miming. Yet indications are not lacking that the very act of delineation was regarded as possessing in itself a certain value, whether by conferring some element of magical control or by enhancing the solidarity of those sharing in the rites. In marked contrast to the rock-paintings found in eastern Spain and dating in all probability from the post-glacial period, those made by Advanced Palaeolithic hunters in the Franco-Cantabric region were concerned with single individuals or pairs to the general exclusion of organized scenes; and there are even cases where representations were superimposed on pre-existing ones. Yet there is also evidence, as we shall see (p. 87), that the disposition of different categories of representation and sign within a cave was in itself symbolic and helps to provide a key to the meaning of the art.

The content of sanctuary art reflects on the one hand preoccupation with the chase. The vast majority of the engravings, paintings, reliefs and plastic figures represents animals hunted for food, mainly rum-

26. Cave painting of bison with weapon-heads pointed at 'wounds', Niaux, Ariège, France

inants ranging in size from mammoths down to ibex, but including also birds, fish and snakes; and the small minority of carnivores depicted, notably bears and lions, comprise animals with which early man had to dispute his home, if not on occasion his prey. Again, quite a number of representations have been modified in a manner that might suggest a belief in the efficacy of hunting magic. One of the commonest ways in which this was done was to superimpose missile weapons on the representations of game animals: thus at Lascaux six 'arrow-marks' can be seen on the flank of a horse and seven on that of a bison, while feathered projectiles are depicted in close conjunction with another horse; and at Niaux 'arrow-marks' have been added to outlines of bison painted on the wall (Figure 26) and in one case incised on the mud floor, the tips of the arrows in the latter pointing into 'wounds' formed by cup-like drip-marks from the roof. Even more striking signs of 'killing' are such features as the thirty or more javelin thrusts in the sides of a bear modelled in clay on the floor of Montespan, the small circular to oval marks on what appears to be an engraved representation of just such a model on the cave wall at Trois Frères, and the deep holes pushed into the body of a horse incised in clay at Montespan. A particularly dramatic scene featuring a wounded animal is the painting at Lascaux depicting a bison with its entrails falling out of its side and a great single-barbed spear lying across its hind-quarters and almost touching what must either be a spear-thrower or the broken head of another spear: before the beast and fronted by it lies the prostrate body of a man with arms outstretched and a bird-like head; and close beneath is a shaft surmounted by a bird in similar style. Lastly, there are the enigmatic signs, such as the pentagonal signs superimposed at Bernifal and Font de Gaume on representations of mammoths, signs which though variously interpreted as huts or traps, may well have been symbols of sexual meaning.

If we turn to the not very common representations of human figures in cave art, we find similar preoccupation with hunting, notably in the symbolically masked figures of dancing men apparently engaged in identifying themselves with the animals they sought to kill. Particularly fine examples are known from Trois Frères in the Ariège: in one case, the man wears the horned mask of a bison from which the skin hangs with the tail swinging to the rhythm of the dance (Figure 27); in another, rendered all the more impressive by its position dominating the Sanctuary, with its panels of engraved bears, bison, horses and reindeer, a larger engraved figure picked out by black paint is shown wearing the tail of a wolf or horse and a mask consisting basically of the antlered head of a deer or reindeer, modified by the removal of the brow tines and the addition of rosette-like eyes and a long beard. Among hunting peoples in many parts of the world masks are worn for stalking quarry, a method particularly effective during the breeding season when the males are easily attracted within range of the hunter; but in the context of cave art there seems no reasonable doubt that the masked figures were performing a ritual or a symbolical function.

The interpretation of the masked figures may be a useful reminder that in primitive society no clear distinction is drawn between econo-

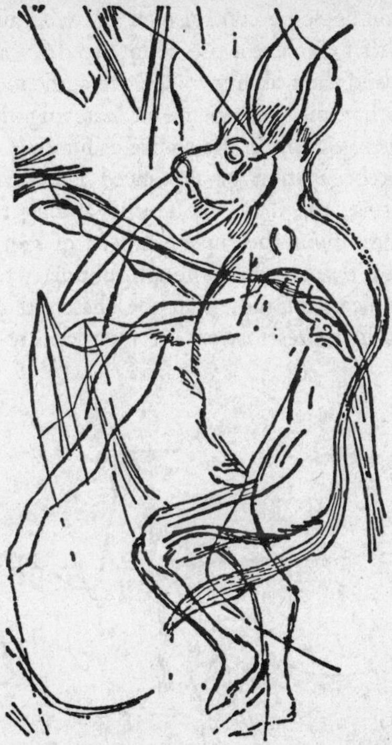

27. Rock-engraving of dancer with bison mask, Trois Frères, Ariège, France

mic, religious or magical activities, or, to put it in more abstract terms, between ritual and what we would regard as practical activities. This same consideration applies with more or less force to cave art as a whole, and, if the psychological effect of the ritual (including the production of cave art) is taken into account, who is to say that the ice age hunters were wrong? When as much depended on luck as it did in hunting, an activity in which man was matched with only primitive weapons directly against the beasts, magical rites that had the effect of increasing confidence and heightening solidarity were evidently of the utmost practical value. The value of a rite, or rather its efficacy, depends after all on the response it evokes. By the same token, there is no essential conflict between the aesthetic and magical aspects of cave art: it is precisely as a means of identifying themselves with and so gaining some control over the wild animals on which they depended that the cave artists set out to delineate them with so much passion; and their ability to achieve authentic representations was based on a lifetime's experience of watching the attitudes and behaviour of their victims in the course of hunting.

If a main preoccupation of Advanced Palaeolithic people was success in hunting, the more thoughtful among them must have worried at times about the replenishment of game and the continuation of their own stock. Although subsidiary to the overriding and immediate need for success in the chase, concern for fertility seems manifest in representations of bulls closely following their

28. Rock-engraving of bull following cow, Levanzo I., Sicily

cows at Levanzo (Figure 28) and Teyjat and of numerous cows and mares carrying their young at Lascaux. A more explicitly sexual interest seems to be present in a number of representations of the human form. Engravings of female organs on stone blocks from Aurignacian deposits at La Ferrassie were indeed among the very earliest manifestations of cave art. The same kind of interest appears in relief sculptures of both the Gravettian and Magdalenian cultures. The earlier group, that from Laussel, includes representations of four women: of the two most informative, one is that of an obese undraped figure painted red with a knob-like head, carrying in the right hand a bison's horn, an object in itself significant as symbolic of growth and replenishment; and the other depicts what is commonly interpreted as an actual birth scene. Again, the Magdalenian frieze at Angles-sur-Anglin includes the middle portions of three women standing side by side, the thigh, organs and stomach lovingly reproduced, but apparently stopping short at the waist. The fulsome representation of breasts and thighs at Laussel, in striking contrast to the summary treatment of the head, reminds us irresistibly of the small Venus figures so widely distributed over the Gravettian territory.

Palaeolithic man realized intuitively, what modern artists proclaim as doctrine, that the power of symbols does not depend on any close correspondence with the appearance of what they aim to symbolize; and, again, that in so far as they do utilize natural forms, the part is as effective, often more effective, than the whole, a point exemplified in widespread representations of sex organs or of the hand, the organ that reaches furthest, commands, supplicates and warns, as well as shaping and utilizing the tools and weapons on which human society depends. Indeed, much greater weight is now placed on the symbolic element in cave art and increasing doubts are expressed about some of the interpretations placed on it by the abbé Breuil. It is argued by Leroi-Gourhan and his followers that so far from being an adjunct of hunting magic the art was fundamentally religious, being centred first and foremost on the opposite yet complementary nature of the male and female principles. The animals themselves can, according to this school, be divided into 'male' and 'female' moieties, and the signs, previously in some cases thought to represent weapons or structures, are instead considered to symbolize the male or female sex. Even some of the details most eagerly seized upon as evidence of hunting magic can be explained in similar terms, the arrows or darts on the Niaux bison symbolizing the male and the wounds the female sex. Similarly the disposition of representations and signs on the cave walls can, when systematically studied with symbolism in mind, be seen to reflect the same basic theme.

We take leave of the Advanced Palaeolithic hunters of western Europe when at the peak of attainment their whole world was about to disintegrate with brutal suddenness before the impact of environmental change. In their art, applied to small objects and to the walls and roofs of their caves and shelters alike, they left behind a legacy widely recognized as one of the supreme achievements of mankind, superior in significance to the more parochial attainments of the civilized peoples of antiquity, because more universal in its relevance. Both conceptually and physically the Advanced Palaeolithic peoples were true representatives of modern man, representatives who tried out as it were for the first time the faculties by which during the astonishingly brief period of 10,000 years were shaped all the diversities and intricacies of civilization itself.

## CHAPTER FIVE

# *The Expansion of Human Settlement*

THROUGHOUT the earlier phases of his evolution, for a period to be measured in hundreds of thousands of years, early man was confined to the frost-free zone of the continental portion of the Old World to which his distant cousins the great apes are still restricted. As we have seen previously, it was not until well into Late Pleistocene times that Neanderthal men penetrated the Zagros mountains, traversed the Iranian plateau to inner Asia and spread as far east as north China; or, to the west, crossed the Caucasus and settled in the Crimea. Again it has been noted how their successors, the Advanced Palaeolithic peoples, settled the banks of the great rivers of south Russia up to latitude 55° and expanded from the south over the north European plain to Schleswig-Holstein, penetrating at the time of the Alleröd oscillation as far north as Denmark.

It is in such a context that we may now view the even more northerly extension of human settlement along the rivers that flow across Siberia to the Arctic Ocean. Even at the height of the last glaciation, ice-sheets in this great territory were restricted to mountain ranges and to the extreme northern regions, but much of the lowland of the northern part of the country between the Urals and the Yenisei was covered by extensive lakes and marshes. Accordingly, human occupation in western Siberia was confined during the Late Glacial period to the upper Ob and Yenisei valleys, where traces have been reported from the areas of Biisk and of Minusinsk and Krasnoyarsk respectively. But the most important focus of Advanced Palaeolithic settlement in Siberia was in the Angara and Selenga valleys of the south Baikal region, and it is even likely that the west Siberian colonization may have proceeded from there. Certainly it is in the Angara valley that the earliest Advanced Palaeolithic sites in Siberia occur, notably Mal'ta and Buret'. In several respects, above all in their sculptured figurines, their use of personal ornaments and their bone and ivory industries, the inhabitants of these Siberian sites display features characteristic of the Advanced Palaeolithic stage of south Russia. On the other hand, their flint-work exhibits a combination of Advanced Palaeolithic and Mousterian traits. The flint industry from Mal'ta included side-scrapers, awls, burins and leaf-shaped points flaked over both faces, of a type known from south Russia, central Europe and north-western Greece and which even more significantly appeared in the territory of the north-west Altai, notably in the cave of Ust' Kanskaia where it occurred together with side-scrapers and points of Mousterian character. Yet a well-defined Advanced Palaeolithic technique was used to detach pieces of bone for working up into artifacts, a technique that involved the use of flint burins for cutting out the necessary splinters.

The early hunters of the Angara valley depended for their food very largely on characteristically glacial animals, such as mammoth, woolly rhinoceros, musk-ox and glutton, and the severity of the climate is farther reflected in the measures they took to protect themselves against it. Both in Mal'ta and Buret' they lived in oblong or oval houses scooped out of the ground along the river-banks. The roofs were covered with earth and apparently supported by rafters made of long-bones. Entry was effected by narrow passages that sloped down into the interior, from which they were doubtless sealed off by hanging skins, a form of entrance well adapted to a cold climate and still widespread in Arctic territories today. To judge from Eskimo practice, the earliest Siberians probably lived more or less naked indoors, but during their prolonged periods of hunting in the cold outer air they evidently wore some skin clothing of a kind once again paralleled in the present Arctic territories of northern Siberia and North America. Evidence for this is provided by the eyed bone needles from Mal'ta, and still more eloquently by a figurine from Buret' (Figure 29), carved out of mammoth tusk and from all appearances wearing skin clothing that covered the head and shoulders as well as the rest of the body and limbs. This contrasts markedly with a score of ivory ones from Mal'ta, some naturalistic, others highly stylized, but all of nude women, comparable with those from south Russia and central and western Europe.

A vivid impression of the wealth of personal ornaments worn by the earliest Siberians is conveyed by the objects associated with the ceremonial burial of a child from Mal'ta; although disarrayed by subsequent disturbance, it could be seen that the child wore a circlet round its head and a necklace strung at intervals with pendant beads ornamented by small pits, as well as being accompanied by flint implements and a pointed bone object. Among the wealth of ornaments from the site may be mentioned oblong plaques of ivory perforated through the middle and decorated by incised lines or by numerous small pits arranged in concentric circles and spirals.

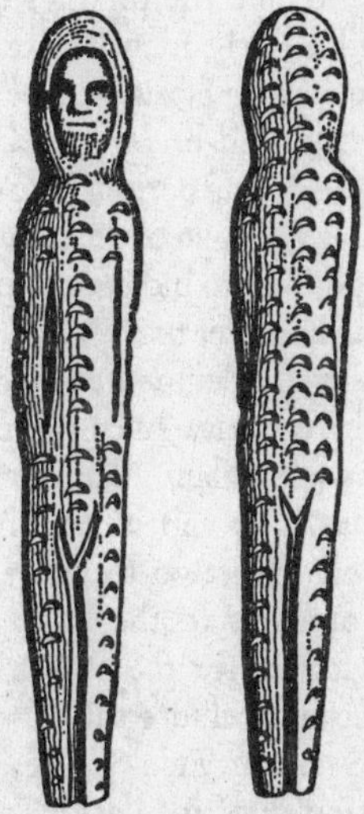

29. Ivory figurine of fur-clad individual, Buret', Siberia

The importance of fish in the lives of these river-bank dwellers is reflected in a carving of a fish, also ornamented by pits, and in the use of fish vertebrae for beads.

The animal remains from Afontova Gora, near Krasnoyarsk, the earliest site so far found in the Yenisei valley, show that the inhabitants depended mainly on hunting reindeer, mammoth, arctic hare and fox. The flint industry combines Mousterian features, such as side-scrapers and points, with burins, small round scrapers and bladelets with battered backs, all of Advanced Palaeolithic type. The rich industry of antler and bone included perforated reindeer antlers, eyed needles, handles slotted to receive flint insets, and a variety of beads, including sections of the long-bones of birds and perforated animal teeth.

To the north-east of lake Baikal, occupation has so far only been found in the basin of the Lena river, and no traces of Advanced Palaeolithic man have yet been found beyond the confluence with the Aldan river in the neighbourhood of latitude 61° north. This is at first sight disconcerting, since north-east Siberia lies on the most obvious route to the New World, and the findings of radio-carbon analysis leave us in no doubt that early man had traversed the land-bridge across what is now the Bering Strait well before the end of the Late Glacial period. The Bering land-bridge could easily have been crossed by hunters pursuing game during periods of low ocean levels. One such occurred between about 21,000–26,000 B.C., twenty-eight and twenty-three thousand years ago, but no indications of man's existence in the New World at this time have yet been validated. On the other hand a substantial number of well-documented finds suggest that men had certainly been active in America since the period between thirteen and ten thousand years ago when a land-bridge existed for the last time between the continents; and it was then also that the North American ice-sheets split into two to allow a passage from Alaska east of the Rocky Mountains to the High Plains. The continuing absence of positive evidence for the earlier presence of man in the New World by no means excludes the possibility, though it is fair to add that exhaustive tests at Tule Springs not merely showed the claim for the high antiquity of man at this site to be erroneous, but more significantly illustrated the manner in which error can so easily arise.

The route followed by the first colonizers of the American continents is not the only problem raised by them. It may be asked why the movement took place at all. Why was it that bands of hunter-fishers should have traversed great distances of what may appear to us most unattractive territory and in the course of a few thousand years have spread down to the Strait of Magellan and across to the Atlantic seaboard? Yet, in a sense, the mere framing of such questions shows a defective appreciation of historical reality. Deliberate, purposeful exploration is a product of the modern age of science. What we are concerned with is surely an unwitting process, having more in common with the spread of animal or even plant species than with planned exploration or colonization. It must be remembered that the hunter-fisher way of life, more especially in a difficult environment, depended above all on an intensive and often far-ranging quest for food and was in itself conducive to movement; the actual occasion for the crossing may have been a temporary fluctuation of climate such as we have envisaged, a fluctuation causing some ecological displacement that could well have provided the decisive impulse.

Although our knowledge of the Palaeoindian stage of New World prehistory is still rudimentary, the general pattern is becoming clearer. The evidence suggests that the original settlers pressed rapidly through the inhospitable territory of Alaska and headed south through the gap between the Laurentide ice-sheets centred on Hudson Bay and the glaciated Rocky Mountains to the High Plains, which during the pluvial period and its aftermath afforded rich grazing for herds of bison and mammoth. Most of what we know of these people is derived from kill-sites, where skeletons, frequently in anatomical articulation, suggest that the victims had been hunted in herds and stripped and skinned as they lay. Among the bones, stone knives and scraping-tools bear witness to the process of butchery, and every now and then the discovery of carefully made projectile heads in significant positions testifies to methods used in hunting. The open nature of the country, and the fact that their forbears apparently left Siberia before the adoption of the bow and arrow, may help to explain why the Palaeoindians relied upon the spear as their principal weapon. They lavished immense care on the flaking of their spearheads, which they worked on both faces to a variety of shapes (Figure 30). Although many of these were of indigenous New World origin, the basic notion of a bifacially flaked point presumably formed part of the equipment brought in during the original colonization from Siberia, where, as we have seen, this formed an element in the local Advanced Palaeolithic culture and one which stemmed ultimately from Mousterian sources. No useful purpose would be served by retailing the manifold variants of projectile point manufactured in different parts of America: no doubt fashion played an important part, but there are indications that functional differences may sometimes have operated. For instance, the form named after the locality of Folsom, in New Mexico, obtusely pointed and fluted on either face by punching long flakes from their concave bases so as to facilitate hafting, seems to have sufficed for bison, whereas the larger, heavier and more tapered Clovis points, fluted for only part of their length, seem to be associated rather frequently with remains of mammoth.

From the High Plains the Palaeoindians spread out far and wide, as if to confirm the teaching of the animal behaviourists that exploration of the environment is a drive as basic in its way as the desire for food or reproduction. To the south, their trail is marked in the valley of

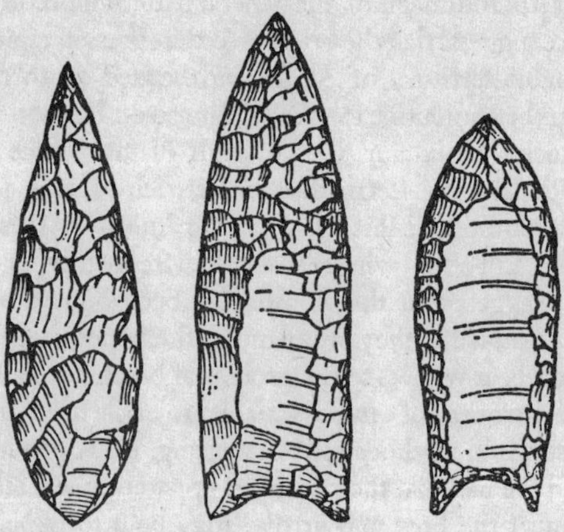

30. Palaeoindian projectile points of Lerma, Clovis and Folsom types

Mexico by the skeletons of butchered mammoths from an old lake bed at Santa Isabel Iztapan, accompanied by finely made projectile points of laurel-leaf shape, known as Lerma points, at a period which to judge by radio-carbon dates was as early as the tenth millennium before Christ. The spread of the Palaeoindians to South America, a much more remarkable phenomenon, involving the traverse of the entire tropical zone, is marked by finds of laurel-leaf points in Venezuela and the Argentine; the radio-carbon dates suggest that middens had begun to form on the northern shore of the Strait of Magellan by the ninth millennium B.C. The movement from the High Plains of North America to the extremity of the southern continent is even more surprising for the range of habitats through which the Palaeoindians had to pass than for the very considerable distances involved. When more is known about the earliest phases of South America's prehistory, it will probably be found that the Palaeoindians reacted to varying environments by developing a variety of economies. The middens of south Patagonia point to a very early adaptation to coastal life; and from around the middle of the third millennium B.C. we have evidence from the middens of Huaco Prieta, in the Chicama valley of Peru, for quite an elaborate culture based primarily on net-fishing and the collection of shellfish, but supported also by the gathering of wild plant food and by the cultivation of such plants as beans and gourds.

About the expansion of settlement in North America we are already rather better informed, and it is possible to see in more detail how the Palaeoindians adapted themselves to differing environments. The culture of the High Plains was evidently a highly specialized one based on hunting big game that moved over open country in large herds. When the Palaeoindians moved west and penetrated the Great Basin region between the Rocky Mountains and the Pacific, they found themselves in a less hospitable territory that called for a much more diversified food quest. Hunting was still possible, but it is noticeable that antelope, mountain sheep and occasionally bison had to be supplemented by a wide range of rodents and even of carnivores like desert fox, coyote or skunk. Desert folk, whose culture seems to have taken its form as early as 7000 B.C., occupied rock-shelters and caves, a practice which, combined with the dryness of the deposits, means that we are remarkably well informed about their mode of subsistence and their technology. Their hunting gear survived with more than usual completeness. We can see that they propelled their darts, tipped with carefully flaked stone heads, by means of wooden throwers (atlatls) and that they used a variety of snares and nets to take their diverse victims. For the same reason, we know that they drew widely on wild plants, which they gathered by means of digging-sticks and baskets and prepared for eating as a kind of mush by abrading on grinding-stones. The intermittent nature of the occupation of the caves suggests that the Desert people had to move diligently over their territory in search of food. Their stone projectile points, bone and wooden artifacts, nets, baskets, matting and grinding equipment were admirably adapted to their way of life, so well adapted in fact that their culture seems to have lasted with little change over prolonged periods of time and even to have survived in some degree in parts of California down to the nineteenth century A.D. Nevertheless it seems likely that the domestication of maize, on the cultivation of which the great indigenous cultures of Mesoamerica (Maya, Aztec) and of the highlands of Peru (Inca) ultimately rested, was first achieved by plant foragers on the southern fringe of the Desert culture, possibly in the region of New Mexico and north-east Mexico, where primitive types of the domesticated plant have been dated to the fourth millennium B.C.

On the other hand, the distribution of fluted projectile points shows that the Palaeoindians spread east to Florida and New England and even as far as Nova Scotia in the north, entering tracts of forested country and ultimately reaching the Atlantic on a broad front. In the new habitat, bounded by the Mississippi valley, the St Lawrence and the Atlantic, alternative sources of food became more numerous and inevitably new forms of cultural life developed. The Archaic culture that grew up in the eastern United States was based on a combination of hunting, fishing, plant-gathering and, where possible, the collection of shellfish. The Archaic people were true hunter-fishers – their only domestic animal was the dog, which presumably reached them from the Old World. Their settlements were of the simplest kind and they apparently lived in small groups. Equally simple was their material equipment. They had no pottery and made do with containers made from organic materials. For tools they depended on flint and stone and on the organic substances they could shape with these. The only exception to this, the use of copper for awls, knives, spuds, projectile heads and ornaments, was more apparent than real, since the metal, obtained from outcrops in the southern part of Lake Superior and from floats carried by glacial action over a number of contiguous states, was not subjected to metallurgical processes, but merely treated as a malleable form of stone, that could be shaped into simple flat and flanged forms. Their use of antler and bone for such things as barbed spearheads, harpoon-heads and fish-hooks admirably reflects their mode of life, and their flaked stone projectile heads include fluted forms of clear Palaeoindian ancestry. On the other hand, the barbed spearheads, harpoon-heads and fish-hooks they made from antler and bone display close Eurasian affinities; these, together with the introduction of dogs and of polished stone woodworking tools, remind us that contacts between the Old World and the New across the Bering Strait by no means ceased with the passage of the first pioneers.

Indeed, the peopling of the Arctic territories of the North American continent, of the great islands north of Hudson Bay and of the Greenland coasts proceeded mainly by successive east–west migrations from Siberia, though with a certain backwash in the opposite direction. The first culture to spread over this territory, named after the Denbigh river in Alaska, where it first appeared around 4,000 B.C., flourished as far west as the Lena valley. Although the Siberian and North American appearances were probably largely parallel in time, there can be no doubt that the culture as a whole drew its inspiration from the south Baikal region. Particularly noteworthy indicators are various forms of slotted bone tool, micro-blades and bifacially flaked side-blades designed to inset into these, and miniature burins used in bone and antler work. Elements of Denbigh equipment occur as far east as Greenland and may even prove to indicate a spread anterior to the growth in the Hudson Bay region of the well-defined regional culture named after Cape Dorset on Baffin Island. Settlement of the Arctic territories of the New World can hardly be said to have contributed materially to the course of universal history. Yet it exemplifies two of its major motive forces: on the one hand, the strength of the drive to explore the environment, which we have seen to be one of the basic impulses of animals in general; on the other, the capacity to adapt to extreme conditions, especially characteristic of man and closely linked both with his lack of biological specialization and with his possession in culture of an apparatus to store up the experience gained by individuals and indeed by whole generations.

Already, before the end of the Ice Age, man had spread over much of the Old World and had penetrated the New. Most of this he was able to do on foot. We have already seen that during periods when sea-levels were at their lowest the Asiatic mainland extended much further to the south-east, making possible the human occupation of much of Indonesia as early as the Middle Pleistocene; also how at times a land-bridge across the present Bering Strait gave ready access from Siberia to the New World. It is now evident that Japan was occupied by palaeolithic man at a time when the country was joined to the Asiatic mainland; radiocarbon dates from each of the three main islands extend human occupation back to eleven or twelve thousand years B.C. and the lithic industries of this period belong plainly to the blade and battered back tradition dating from late in the Upper Pleistocene of Eurasia and parts of North Africa, even though they display such idiosyncratic elements as the Kiridashi knife.

Radiocarbon analysis makes it certain that Australia was first occupied during the late Pleistocene, more than twenty thousand years ago. It is still too early to fix the precise date, but it is fair to assume that the first immigration took place at a time when sea-levels were relatively low. At a time when Borneo and much of Indonesia were joined to south-east Asia and New Guinea was linked by the Sahul shelf to the Australian continent, it would have been possible to go nearly the whole way on foot. Yet several gaps would still have remained between island and island and these could only have been crossed by using floats or rafts if boats were not yet available. Once arrived in Australia it would have been possible to reach Tasmania on dry land, since the Bass Strait was not formed until ocean levels rose in response to the world-wide reduction in ice-sheets at the close of the glacial period. As yet extremely little is known about details of the climatic and floristic history of Australia since it has been occupied by man. It seems inherently unlikely that the conditions encountered by man in Australia during his long prehistory remained constant, and there are indeed signs of considerable shifts in ecological zones. When man arrived, northern Australia, including the now submerged Sahul shelf, may have been more welcoming than it is today; it may have supported grassland easy of access and well stocked with food; and the interior may have received more rainfall than it does today. By contrast, at the climax of Neothermal times, zones of tropical rain forest and aridity were probably established a good deal further south than at present.

The earliest human skeletal remains at present known from Australia, those from Keilor and Green Gulley near Melbourne, are more modern in type than those from Talgai and Cohuna, which compare closely with those of recent aborigines, having rather sloping foreheads, prominent brow-ridges, large canines and molars in almost parallel sets. In the general character of their hair, pigmentation and skull form, the Australian aborigines resemble the pre-

Dravidians of south India and there can hardly be any question that their prototypes came by way of south-east Asia: this is confirmed in the fossil record by the discovery of skulls of men and women from the locality of Wadjak in Java which closely resemble that already mentioned for Talgai in Queensland. The status of the Tasmanians, who failed to stand up for long to the impact of European colonizers and have been extinct for a hundred years or so, has been the subject of much speculation. As against those who have sought to account for certain peculiarities – notably their woolly hair – by presupposing a negroid strain, recent opinion is readier to accept that they could have arisen genetically during the period of isolation since the formation of the Bass Strait, eight or nine thousand years ago.

The immense size of Australia and the comparatively brief span of human settlement, coupled with the isolation and the lack of stimulus that went with this, make it more than usually difficult to discern any clear line of progress. Yet it is possible to detect three main stages. The only stone industry known for the first ten thousand years or so of Australian prehistory resembles closely that collected from Tasmania and confirms the impression that Tasmania was settled during the continental period. Around 3000 B.C. we find evidence in the Lower Murray valley for much more highly differentiated industries (Figure 31) marked by small tools, notably backed blades, microliths and *pirri* points flaked by pressure over one face, which must have been inset into wooden hafts. Sporadic and partial analogies exist for these in Java, the Celebes and as far afield as Ceylon and southern India. During this phase pebble tools, flaked as a rule from one surface, together with edge-ground stone axes that seem to date from a remote period of Australian prehistory, continued in use, as indeed they did down to the 19th century. During the Recent Stone Age lithic technology continued at a high level in parts of northern Australia and in particular in the Kimberley region, focus of spear-heads finished by fine pressure-flaking on either face; on the other hand in the south the lithic industry was reduced to the edge-ground stone axe and flakes mounted as adze-scrapers or used directly in the hand for shaping wooden tools and weapons. Microliths dropped completely out of use and may well have been rendered superfluous by the finely barbed spearheads made of wood that characterized the recent material culture of the Australian aborigines.

The prehistoric Australians had no domesticated animals or plants. They depended entirely on hunting, fishing and gathering, including where possible the gathering of shellfish. The dingo, it is true, was brought to Australia by man at an unknown date, though certainly as far back as the second millennium B.C., but like the pariah of south Asia it remained essentially a wild animal. Some of their microlithic flints resemble forms used in Europe to barb and tip arrows, but, since the bow is absent from Australian aboriginal culture, and is unlikely to have been completely lost, it is probable that they were

31. Microlithic implements and *pirri* point, current in south-east Australia by the fourth millennium B.C.

used in this context to arm spearheads, the universal weapon of the Australian hunter. Various kinds of marsupial, including kangaroo and wallaby, provided meat, as well as smaller game, lizards and, as occasion allowed, turtles and fish. To judge from the habits of the recent aborigines, the prehistoric Australians depended to an important extent on a wide range of plant and insect food, collected by the women and children; the simplest equipment was used and, in the complete absence of pottery, containers were made from a variety of natural substances such as bark. During the course of the year the people moved systematically over their habitat, taking the natural harvest as it ripened. Where caves or rock-shelters were available these were occupied, a fact to which we owe the main possibility of discovering the prehistoric sequence. Elsewhere, and at other times, the simplest form of shelter would have been used, and the only trace left by a prehistoric settlement would be the sites of fireplaces and such artifacts and food debris as survived under the prevailing local conditions. Yet we know that surviving representatives of these people, with an equally primitive economy and technical apparatus, possess highly complex social institutions; have cultivated totemism, the nexus of ideas and beliefs concerning the relationships between classes of men and specific natural phenomena, to a degree unknown anywhere else; and have built up an intricate mythology. Tangible traces of the social, intellectual and emotional aspects of the lives of the prehistoric Australians, the complication and elaboration of which contrast strikingly with their material poverty, are mainly comprised in their graphic art or at least in those aspects of it which commonly survive. Rock-engravings, mainly pecked into the surface, are known from many widely separated localities of the continent. That some of these are of substantial antiquity is suggested by the ignorance of the recent aborigines about them, by the fact that some of them depict animals no longer existing locally and by the evidence of weathering and the occurrence of surface films on the rock. Other hints include the occurrence of engraved rocks in Tasmania and of worn lumps of ochre in early levels at a site like Kenniff Cave.

The prehistoric aboriginal art of Australia took the forms of rock-engraving (Figure 32) and rock-painting, and, to judge from recent manifestations, of carvings on cult objects, ornaments, weapons and even the trunks of living trees. Although they remain enigmatic as we see them across the distance of time, it can be assumed, again in the light of recent usage, that much of the art was designed to illustrate myths and legends of tribal ancestors and totems, to which the attention of the group would be specially drawn on such occasions as the initiation of young people into the mysteries and responsibilities of adult society. The prehistoric art of Australia has several features in common with the much older art of the Advanced Palaeolithic people of Europe, even though there is of course no direct historical connexion. It is interesting to observe how the early Australians, like the artists of Altamira or Lascaux, seized on natural features or irregularities of the rock-surface, like holes, crevices or concretions, and incorporated them in their designs. Again, the commonest things depicted are those concerned with man himself or with his main activity, the getting of food: human figures and

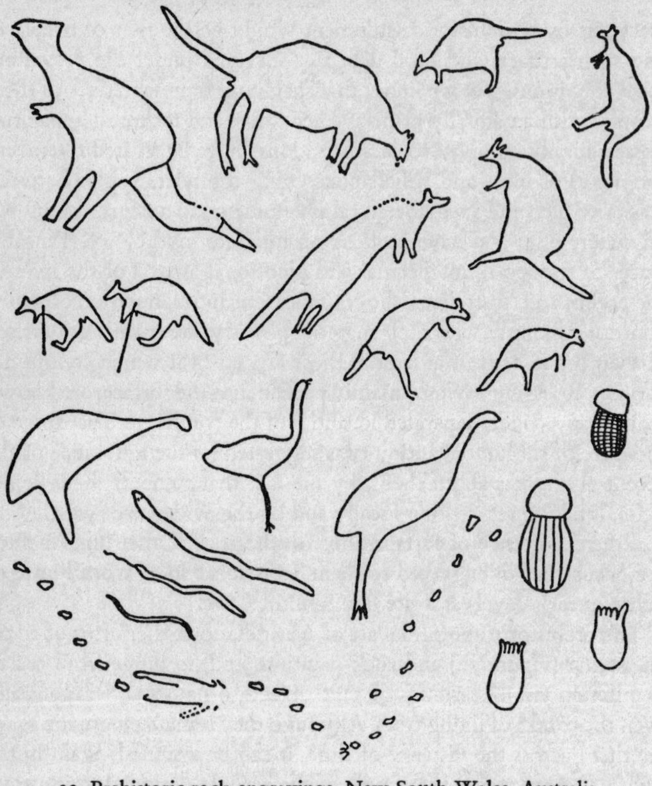

32. Prehistoric rock-engravings, New South Wales, Australia

hands; lizards, spiny ant-eaters, duck-billed platypus, kangaroo, turtles and fish; tracks of emu, kangaroo and men; and weapons like boomerangs and spear-throwers. In depicting these the Australians, like many other prehistoric artists, ignored any work already existing on the rock-surface, so that palimpsests are frequent, a sure sign that the act of delineation, or the observances that accompanied this, was considered as being in some way efficacious.

The occupation of Australia and Tasmania reminds us that it was as a hunter-fisher that man inherited almost the whole earth. For the greater part of his history he was confined to the warmer lands in which his biological forbears had emerged from earlier forms of life.

The first stage of expansion, begun by Neanderthal man and extended by early representatives of modern man equipped with at any rate some elements of Advanced Palaeolithic culture, was restricted to territories capable of being reached on foot or which did not require the passage of channels so wide that land could not be seen on the far side from mid-point, territories which included large tracts of northern Eurasia, Australia and the New World. The only territories remaining to be brought within the range of human settlement were those that required means of transport available only to peoples possessed of economic and technical resources beyond those available to the hunter-fishers.

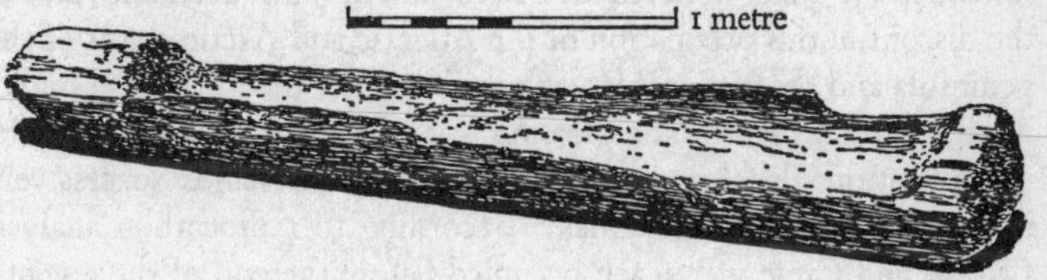


33. Dug-out boat from Pesse, Drenthe, north Holland

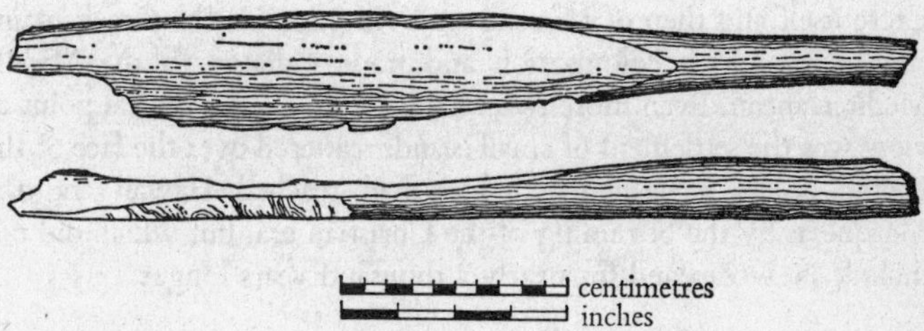


34. Wooden paddle (damaged) from Star Carr, Yorkshire, England

It is probably no coincidence that the first palpable evidence for navigation dates from early post-Glacial times when ocean levels rose, causing the sea to flood over and sever former land-connexions. The oldest well-documented finds indicating that man had learnt to move over water comprise a dug-out boat, formed by hollowing out a section of tree-trunk (Figure 33), from Pesse in north Holland, dating from around 6400 B.C., and a carefully shaped paddle (Figure 34) from the English site, Star Carr, a thousand years or so earlier; but it must be remembered that the only evidence likely to survive would be that relating to inland navigation. It may well be that skin boats, such as we know from representations on rock-engravings from west Norway which probably date from the end of the third millennium B.C., were already employed in earlier times. However this may be, the possession of navigable craft, as distinct from the mere floats that were probably used from a much earlier period, must have been a potent force in opening up new territories for settlement.

Some indication that this was indeed so is available from north-western Europe. The contraction of ice-sheets and the consequent recovery of land between them made available extensive new areas for settlement, notably in northern Britain and in south Scandinavia; but the discontinuous occupation of the Atlantic and Arctic coasts of the peninsula and the intractable nature of much of the hinterland makes it fairly certain that the colonization was achieved by the use of boats.

Navigation also brought the Mediterranean islands successively into reach of human settlement. According to radiocarbon analysis Cyprus and Crete were each occupied before the end of the seventh millennium B.C. Moreover, navigation, by linking Crete with Egypt and Syria, stimulated the rise first of Minoan civilization on Crete itself and then of Mycenaean civilization on the Greek mainland from which colonization and trade radiated to the Middle Mediterranean. Even more remarkable from a geographical point of view was the settlement of small islands scattered over the face of the Pacific ocean, a settlement which had reached Hawaii and the Marquesas by the beginning of the Christian era, but which did not include New Zealand for nearly a thousand years longer.

CHAPTER SIX

# *Hunter-fishers of the Recent Past and Their Limitations*

THE colonization of almost the whole of the habitable world was, as we have just seen, accomplished by peoples who subsisted entirely on various forms of hunting, fishing, gathering and collecting, peoples who were subject to the same kind of limitations as the men of the Old Stone Age, but who in this, as in so many other respects, made possible the future progress of mankind. When outlying parts of the world were opened up by European explorers, many of them had still not been colonized by peoples with more productive economies and remained in the sparse and as a rule shifting occupation of hunter-fishers and collectors. A brief examination of these may serve to bring out the limitations of the old way of life and emphasize the importance of the economic changes which enabled mankind in certain favoured regions to enter on an ampler stage.

The greater part of the Old World was appropriated by food-producers: broadly speaking the subtropical and temperate zones of the northern hemisphere were occupied, sometimes intensively enough to support urban life, by mixed farmers who combined plough-agriculture with stock-raising; extensive zones of the tropical forests of west and central Africa, south-east Asia and Indonesia were cultivated by peoples who used a variety of hand-tools; and vast areas of desert, steppe, grassland and tundra were, in so far as they were inhabited at all, sparsely occupied by nomadic or semi-nomadic pastoralists. The main territories in which the older forms of economy persisted in the Old World were those too remote or too unfavourable from a climatic point of view even for the poorest cultivators or pastoralists: indeed it would seem that certain territories, like the Kalahari desert, were refuge areas into which hunters and collectors retreated in the face of more formidable competitors, and it may well be that the culture of these hunter-gatherer groups may even have suffered some impoverishment.

By far the most extensive territory in which the old way of life has persisted on account of geographical isolation is the Australian continent, and more particularly the central and northern regions which were last to feel the impact of white settlement: here aboriginal culture, if no longer untouched, survives sufficiently intact to show how complex may be the institutions of people whose culture on a material plane must appear to us strictly limited. At the time of the colonization by white men the aboriginal Australian still practised, as they do today in remote areas, a stone age economy, and one based exclusively on hunting and gathering. Study by modern ethnologists has shown that they possess a remarkably complete knowledge of their environment as well as the skills needed to fashion and manipulate their simple but effective tools and weapons: although compelled to move more or less widely over their traditional territories, their seasonal wanderings are anything but haphazard, being based on a remarkably exact understanding of the life-cycles of the various plants, insects and animals on which they depend. Furthermore, it is evident that these people are accustomed to look behind and beyond material, outward appearances to a hidden, timeless world: the very limitations of their understanding of their environment and the slightness of the material means at their disposal make them more keenly aware of the need to establish relations with the uncontrolled forces of nature and with the ancestors from whom they inherited their land and their traditions. The insecurity of their parasitic mode of life causes them to devote much of their time and energy to ritual activities, in which chanting, acting and dancing are combined with representational and decorative art, activities which serve to enhance group solidarity and confidence and enlist the help of unseen but creative forces. The Australian aborigines have no generalized nature religion: rather they seek to establish direct relations between particular individuals or groups, whether sexes, moieties or clans, and the specific classes of natural objects or species that serve as totems (Figure 35). At the time of his initiation – for only men participate in totemic ceremonies – the young man enters upon a rich inheritance of lore and ritual observance; it is by means of this that he seeks to integrate himself, not merely into contemporary society but into the company of his ancestral spirits, and at the same time to enter into close communion with the underlying realities of his physical environment.

In the rest of the Old World, cultivators and pastoralists have between them occupied all but a few isolated or climatically extreme territories. No food-gatherers survive in Europe, and even in northern Asia the domestication of the reindeer has made it possible for almost all hunter-fishers to adopt a pastoral mode of life. It is only the very coldest parts of eastern Siberia, north of the Verkhoyansk and Stanovoi mountains, that the hunter-fisher way of life has persisted down to modern times among the mongoloid Yukaghir. Seasonal changes are especially marked. The winter is long and severe, with water

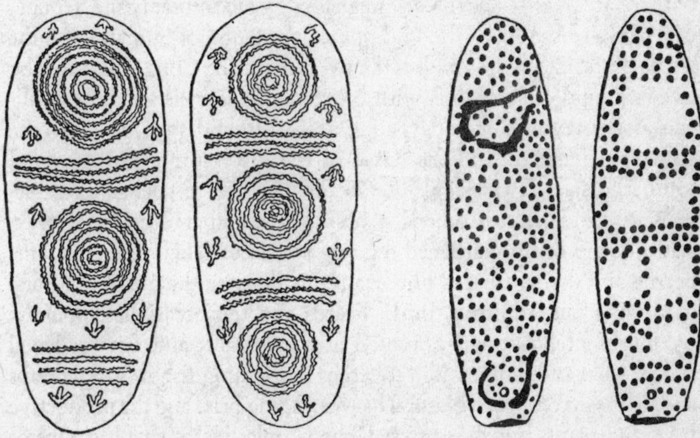

35. Aboriginal Australia: stone churinga and bullroarer

surfaces frozen for some two-thirds of the year and a mean January temperature as low as −70°F. The brief, hot summer witnesses a sudden flowering of sedge-grasses, mosses, lichens and dwarf bushes on the open tundra. During the summer fish can be taken in nets and on line as they move upstream, ptarmigan and water-birds snared, and berries and other plant food gathered. Most serious hunting is done in the autumn or spring when the reindeer seek and leave the shelter of the forests to the south; the hunters drive them into ambush or even run them down by sheer persistence. At all times of the year the people inhabit conical skin-covered tents, easily dismantled and re-erected. During the summer they use dug-out boats and in the winter dog-drawn sledges. In such an environment, great application is needed to maintain life at this level of technology, but in the summer the people find time to hold games, in which young men conduct trials of strength and rival shamans or magicians (on whose ability to cajole the spirits that protect animals the hunter feels himself to depend) engage in contests.

Far to the south, a number of interesting groups of food-gatherers still exist in those parts of the equatorial rain-forests of Africa and south-east Asia not taken up by cultivators. Most live primarily on plant food, supplemented to a greater or lesser degree by hunting. Many of them are pygmy negroids or negritoes by race, notably the Semang of Malaya, the Aeta of the Philippines, the Kubu of Sumatra and the Toala of the Celebes, as well as the pygmies of the Congo forests who live in a kind of symbiosis with Negro agriculturalists; but in south-east Asia they also include people of Australoid type, notably the Andaman islanders and the Sakai of the lower mountain slopes of southern Malaya. The staple diet of the Semang, to take an example, consists principally of tubers, mainly yams, gathered by the women with the aid of fire-hardened digging sticks; but such things as nuts, berries and shoots are also important. In addition, the men hunt small game like rats, squirrels, birds, lizards and the occasional monkey, by means of bows and poisoned arrows, snares and fire-hardened stakes. Men and women join together in catching fish in simple traps and by means of spears. Natural harvests being brief and the productive trees and plants widely scattered, the people live in small groups of up to twenty or thirty people and have to keep perpetually on the move, seldom remaining more than three or four days on the same spot in their rapidly improvised palm-leaf shelters (Figure 36). Yet it is worth noting that, however widely they range over the forest, individual groups enjoy exclusive rights to the fruits of certain trees over well-recognized territories.

The only people in the whole African continent to maintain themselves exclusively by hunting and gathering, without maintaining the close relations with agriculturalists characteristic of the Congo pygmies, are the Bushmen (Figure 37), at present confined to the Kalahari desert, but once occupying a territory extending from southern Rhodesia to the Cape and east to Basutoland and Natal. The pressures which confined them to their present habitat were exerted by Hottentot pastoralists (a closely related stock), Bantu cultivators and

36. Interior of Semang hut shelter with collecting basket

finally Boer farmers who over great tracts exterminated the Bushmen by the use of organized commando raids. Even though in their restricted territories they have been compelled to adapt themselves to extreme aridity, as well as being subjected to the effects of culture-contact, the Bushmen still preserve a way of life comparable in many respects with that of their stone age forbears.

The Bushmen depend above all on hunting. It is true that the

37. A Bushman camp

women, armed with digging-sticks tipped with horn and weighted by bored stones, collect roots, fruits, grubs, insects and small animals like lizards and tortoises; but the sources of food are essentially subsidiary to the hunting of the herbivorous game in which the country abounds, above all the large and small antelope, elephant, giraffe, hippopotamus, ostrich, quagga and zebra, as well as the carnivores that prey on these. The hunters use great resource. They commonly stalk their intended victims wearing masks and on occasion simulating their cries. Then, having got within range and shot them with poisoned arrows, they track them and finally bring them to their deaths. Alternatively, animals may be driven into pit-falls arranged close to tracks leading to water-holes. At the height of the drought when hoofs are shed, animals are even run down and disabled with knobbed throwing-sticks. Until they borrowed iron and glass, the Bushmen depended exclusively on stone and various organic materials for their material equipment, stone being used particularly for making scrapers and drill-points as well as the microliths mounted in resin that served to tip their arrows. They still rely on wood for bows, spears, throwing-sticks and fire-drills; reeds for arrow-shafts; sinews for bow-strings; bones for foreshafts and arrow-tips; shredded bark for cords; skins for clothing and containers; and ostrich-egg shells for beads and containers. Scarcity of water plays an important part in their lives, and during the dry season they have to suck it up from old stream-beds through reed tubes stuck into grass filters. During the dry season, also, when they gather closely round the water-holes, between twenty and a hundred individuals may live together in single bands, but at other times they split up into family groups over the wide communal territories. Since they change their place of settlement several times a year, their small dome-shaped huts, each sheltering a single biological family, are lightly made of grass and sticks, quickly erected and readily abandoned. Poor as they have always been, in an economic sense, the Bushmen executed rock-engravings and paintings of abounding vitality until well into the latter half of the nineteenth century, even though at the present day they do no more than scratch designs with the points of metal knives on ostrich egg-shells or pots. An important element in the drive to execute this art was almost certainly the hope of exercising some degree of control over the game animals on which the lives of the people mainly depended. Yet there was also a strong historical element, a desire to record or recall events that strongly influenced the life of the community, well seen in pictures of fights with the Bantu or of Boer commando raids. Whatever the motive behind them, the best representations reflect in the sharpest fashion the powers of observation and the joy of life of born hunters who glory in matching their skill against the keen senses and speed of the wild animals of the open scrub and desert.

Much more of the New World than of the Old – more particularly of North America – was still occupied by food-gatherers and hunter-fishers down to the time of white colonization. Among the reasons for this were that settled civilization had a much shorter history in the New World and less time to expand its influence, and that outside the Andean and Arctic regions there were no animals capable of being domesticated so as to allow the rise of pastoral economies.

In South America, agriculture based on the use of hand-tools spread over almost the whole continent apart from the extreme south. Within the tropical zone, food-gatherers only survive in areas of comparative isolation: in the north-west, around the western head-waters of the Orinoco; in the interior of Guiana, along the southern head-waters of the same river and the northern ones of the Río Negro; and in patches round the southern rim of the Amazon basin. Although several marginal tribes have borrowed culture-traits from economically more advanced neighbours – the Shirianá of Guiana, for instance, have evidently acquired a knowledge of basketry and potting as well as of agriculture – it is still possible to recognize down to the present day the elements of a simple and very limited way of life. The people depend, wholly or in part, on gathering and hunting, mainly by means of the bow. They live a nomadic life in small groups, wear little or no clothing, and shelter in flimsy huts, round or annular in plan with sloping walls open to the sky.

Beyond the southern limit set to agriculture by climate, the inhabitants of South America had no choice, before the introduction of pastoralism by European colonists, but to live by various forms of hunting, fishing and gathering. Even today, they survive by this way of life in the most extreme environments. In the case of the Patagonian hunter-fishers we can be quite sure that we are dealing with lineal descendants of prehistoric peoples of high antiquity: archaeological excavation of caves and shelters on the north shore of the Strait of Magellan and of shell-middens on the coasts of the Beagle Channel shows a continuing development since the region was first settled probably around 8,000 or 9,000 years ago.

The southern hunters have a number of broad characteristics in common: they all depend on a hunting and collecting economy; rely for tools and weapons on stone and organic materials, such as wood, vegetable fibres and animal bones and skin; are organized in small family bands; lead a nomadic life; and occupy natural shelters or light movable structures. On the other hand, there is room for wide divergencies of culture between the Canoe Indians, who occupy the islands and coastal inlets of the Chilean coast south of latitude 43°, and the

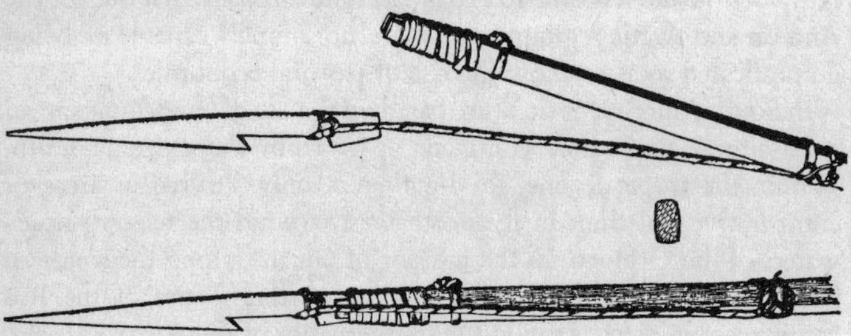

38. Yaghan harpoon, South America

Foot Indians of the south Argentinian mainland and eastern Tierra del Fuego. The former, among whom the Chrono, Alacaluf and Yahgan are the principal groups (from north to south), are largely pelagic: they depend mainly on hunting sea-lions, fishing, taking sea-birds and collecting shellfish; spend much of their time in boats, and camp by sheltered anchorages; wear very little clothing; use harpoons (Figure 38), spears, slings and clubs for weapons; and for containers rely on coiled baskets. The Foot Indians on the other hand – the Puelche, Poya, Tehuelche and Ona – are essentially land people who hunt guanaco by the bow and arrow and make clothing and containers from animal skins.

Describing the way of life of the Canoe Indians in the journal he kept while aboard H.M.S. *Beagle* during her voyage round the world, Charles Darwin wrote:

At night five or six human beings, naked and scarcely protected from the wind and rain of this tempestuous climate, sleep on the wet ground, coiled up like animals. Whenever it is low water, winter or summer, night or day, they must rise to pick shell-fish from the rocks; and the women either dive to collect sea-eggs, or sit patiently in their canoes, and with a baited hair-line without any hook jerk out little fish. If a seal is killed, or the floating carcass of a putrid whale discovered, it is a feast; and such miserable food is assisted by a few tasteless berries and fungi.

So depressed was the great Victorian naturalist by the apparent misery and squalor of these people that he went so far as to exclaim that 'viewing such men, one can hardly make oneself believe that they are fellow-creatures, and inhabitants of the same world'. Yet we do well to remember that they were living representatives of the original settlers of the region, men who after all shared in the great pioneering colonization of the world and whose way of life was well adapted to a physical environment into which a more productive economy was unable to penetrate.

Agriculture only spread north of Mesoamerica during prehistoric times over two main regions, the south-west, including most of Arizona and New Mexico and parts of Utah and Colorado, and the eastern United States from the Mississippi basin to the Atlantic seaboard. Elsewhere, direct successors of hunting and gathering cultures, some of them of high antiquity, persisted, and in part continue down to the present day, modified to a greater or lesser degree by outside contacts. The high grasslands, that run east of the mountain zone from Canada almost to the Gulf of Mexico, supported vigorous Palaeo-indian hunting cultures at least as far back as the tenth millennium B.C.; they continued to provide in their herds of bison the basis of life for Plains Indians down to the 1880s, when, largely as a result of the use of horses first acquired from Spanish colonists in the seventeenth century, these were brought to the point of extinction. Although not neglecting plant food, as long as the herds remained the Indians of this region depended, first and foremost, on bison: the meat and fat provided their main source of food, whether fresh or dried in the sun, slightly roasted, pulverized and mixed with fat, in the form of pemmican that could be kept for lengthy periods in bags sealed in tallow; the hides served for clothing, bags and tent-covers; the sinews for threads; the hair for stuffing pillows and for decoration; the horns for spoons and ladles; and the bones for making leather-working tools. Although individual hunting was carried on, the most important kind was communal. For this purpose great camps were set up during the summer, comprising rings or penannular settings of tents, three or four deep, in an area some half mile or so in diameter. The main idea was to drive the herds of bison down converging lanes of stone-heaps or bushes into pounds or enclosures formed of earth, stone or logs; or, where the topography made this possible, the herds would be driven over steep cliffs, as the Advanced Palaeolithic hunters of France did with herds of wild horses at La Solutré nearly 20,000 years ago. Although the abundance of food, and the comparative ease with which this could be obtained, provided the Plains Indians with plenty of leisure, the nomadic life meant that they could hardly find an outlet for this in ostentatious building or lavish material equipment. Instead, they found satisfaction in the activities of the men's societies, which at the time of the great hunting camps indulged in elaborate ceremonial and dances. Interest in these social activities was enhanced by the elaborate way in which the societies were graded by seniority, and also by the status accorded to individuals by virtue of their prowess in hunting or through the potency of their medicine, which, though consisting of no more than ritual apparatus wrapped in strips of animal skin, was deemed all-important for ensuring health and success.

By contrast, but likewise carrying forward a tradition going back for many thousands of years, the Indians of the Great Basin, survivors of the ancient Desert Culture, gain their living to a large extent by gathering wild plants, having been little affected by modern civilization until late in the nineteenth century. They are omnivorous and, when they get the chance, hunt game or take small animals and insects; but their most important food comprises seeds, berries, nuts, roots and bulbs, which they gather and prepare as systematically as if they had been cultivated. Indeed, in a real sense they regard them as crops; and it is particularly interesting to note that they encourage growth by means of a primitive form of irrigation, damming and diverting streams, though it cannot be excluded that this notion was derived from agricultural groups. The seeds of tall grasses are particularly important to them: these they beat into collecting baskets, winnow and parch by shaking them up with live coals; crush and grind between mullers and grindstones; make into cakes; dry and store. The lack of vegetation in the late winter and spring makes it especially important to build up supplies by storing food at the winter settlements, and this they do in grass-lined pits. Among plant foods most favoured for storing are roots and pine-nuts, and among neighbouring tribes in central California, where the climate is mild enough for the oak, acorns. Even grasshoppers, caught in great numbers by being swept into pits, can be stored after being pounded into a paste and dried.

A third group of hunter-fishers, this time adapted to river and sea fishing and to the capture of sea-mammals, maintained their culture intact down to the present century in the coastal zone of British Columbia, a territory indented by fiords and fringed by islands, some of them quite large. Although elk and deer abound in the forests of the hinterland, the Indians take little stock of the resources of the dry land except for the harvests of roots and berries gathered by the women at the close of the summer. Salmon, halibut and cod are taken in coastal waters, the first two on hook and line, the latter by spearing. Other important sources of food yielded by the sea are seals, sea-lions, sea-otters and porpoises; and whales, when stranded on the shore, are eagerly appropriated. Most assured and abundant of all are the salmon that ascend the rivers in vast numbers to spawn: at the right time of the year the fish can be taken in traps, netted, speared or even pulled out by gaffs. At the time of the salmon-run, immense numbers are split and dried over fires so as to form a reserve of food comparable in its way with cereal crops.

Under such conditions it is possible for communities comparable in size with those of early agriculturalists to live together on the sea-coast at permanent sites, even if not always remaining in residence throughout the year. Permanent villages, at which several hundred people might live together, commonly consist of rows of houses set end on to the shore (Figure 39). The houses themselves are substantial in size, sometimes several hundred feet in length. They are built on a massive timber framework that normally lasts for generations, though the outer planking has to be renewed at shorter intervals and may even be dismantled from time to time for use during seasonal migrations in quest of food. The comparative ease with which cedar

39. Kwakuitl village, British Columbia, Canada

trunks can be made to split must lessen the amount of labour required, but it is nevertheless salutary to reflect what vast structures can be erected by people ignorant of metallurgy and having to depend for lumbering and wood-working on tools made of bone, shell or stone. The houses are not merely large but carefully finished and embellished by carved or painted designs over the entrance. Equally impressive in their way are the great canoes needed for hunting and travel. The main portions of the hulls are hollowed out from the split halves of cedar trunks by the use of fire, chisels and mallets, and then worked smooth by adzing, before being softened by means of hot water and forced open with cross pieces inserted to retain the expanded shape. Prows and sterns are made separately and sewn on by means of cords threaded through holes carefully bored into the thickness of the wood. Like the houses, canoes are completed by the addition of the heraldic devices of their owners.

The nucleus of north-west coast communities is formed as a rule by noble families and their retainers and supporters, and considerations of personal prestige play an immensely important part in community life. Although nobles inherit their titles and many of their rights, they have constantly to justify their privileges by gifts and by lavish feasts or *potlaches* held at the various crises of life: indeed the prestige of the donor depends to a great extent on the extravagance of his display, the acme of which is reached in the ostentatious destruction of possessions, whether (as formerly) slaves, accumulations of valuable commodities, such as fish-oil, or symbols of wealth like coppers, great shield-shaped objects hammered out of native copper and decorated with stylized animal motives. Quite apart from the interest and excitement centring on the displays themselves, the striving for prestige on the part of rival nobles and their adherents serves as an important stimulus for the production of the wealth destroyed or redistributed in this way. If abundance of food has made the institution possible, the *potlache* itself stimulates the efforts needed to win the maximum surplus over and above what would otherwise have been deemed adequate, so that, as in the case of advertising in our own society, what might appear on the face of it wasteful is, in fact, given the potency of social emulation, a major stimulus to production.

Another reflection of social emulation, which likewise presupposes a certain surplus, is the application of carving and painting on a considerable scale to major possessions such as houses, canoes and chests, as well as to the great totem poles planted in some communities immediately in front of the house. Yet the art of this region also gives expression to even deeper feelings, namely the basic desire that we saw at work among the aboriginal Australians to establish continuity with previous generations and with the community of living things. While there is undoubtedly a strong heraldic element in the art, it gives the impression of being charged with emotions that spring from a deeper level of consciousness.

The representations themselves are highly conventionalized, and the artists have seized on particular characteristics of the creatures whose attributes they commonly seek to combine with human features, as for example the fins of cetaceans or the beaks of birds of prey. The overall impression given by the art is a concern with mythological representations in which human and animal characteristics are inextricably combined; and in the case of the great totem poles there is even a suggestion of genealogical record, so that one might conclude that the art is essentially concerned with a kind of mythological genealogy in which men and beasts are intimately combined.

The last, and in certain respects the most remarkable, surviving hunter-fishers of the New World are the Eskimos. As is only to be expected of a people inhabiting a territory some 6,000 miles across from the Aleutian Islands to the east coast of Greenland and ranging over more than 25° of latitude from the northernmost settlements of mankind to the fringes of the forest zone, the Eskimos encountered considerable variations in the natural conditions to which they had to adapt themselves. Nevertheless, the first impression conveyed by their culture is that of substantial homogeneity, a homogeneity explained in part by the underlying ecological similarity of their environment over wide tracts, and in part by the ready means of transport available to them in the dog-drawn sledge and the skin-covered frame-boat.

The main energies of the Eskimos are occupied in winning food and securing shelter under conditions so extreme that civilized men can only penetrate them, as a rule, at great expense and with the resources of a much more evolved economy. The way in which they secure their livelihood is, of course, affected to some degree by regional conditions. The most typical Eskimo culture is an essentially maritime one. Under Arctic conditions their way of life necessarily differs markedly as between the months of fast ice and those in which there are inlets and ultimately broad expanses of open water. During the summer, the Arctic Eskimos disperse in family groups, shelter in tents of caribou or seal-skin, and hunt sea-mammals from boats, whales from the heavier *umiak*, and seals (bladdernose and Greenland) from the more manoeuvrable *kayak*. With the approach of autumn the hunters in many areas turn to caribou before settling down to hunting and fishing through the solid ice. During the two darkest months of the winter life is more or less confined to the permanent settlements, where several families live together and draw on stores of food accumulated during previous months; but during the opening and closing months of this season the hunter is able to move over frozen surfaces by dog-drawn sledges. At this time of the year he depends to a great extent on the *maupoq* method of taking ringed seals, in which the hunter stations himself by a breathing-hole and patiently waits his chance to strike with a harpoon. Fish are also taken through the ice by jigging with baited but barbless hooks, by harpooning, or by lowering net-traps to intercept moving shoals. In the High Arctic territories occupied by the Polar Eskimos of the Thule district of north-west Greenland fast ice exists almost throughout the year, and under these conditions it is hardly surprising that ice-hunting prevails to the virtual exclusion of activities on the open water. On the other hand, in more southerly regions, such as west Greenland south of the Arctic

Circle or, again, among the Pacific Eskimos of the south Alaskan coast or the Aleutian islanders, the culture acquires a sub-Arctic character and the emphasis rests on hunting and fishing from skin-boats rather than from sledges.

If the importance of the sea as a source of food has been stressed, this is not to overlook the part played by the hunting of land-mammals and birds. Quite apart from the trapping of foxes (greatly increased on account of the Hudson's Bay Company) and the snaring of ptarmigan, caribou are hunted both for their meat and their hide, even if in Greenland this activity is confined to the autumn. It is only on the barren grounds west of Hudson's Bay that land hunting, and more specifically caribou hunting, plays a role of main importance – so important, in fact, as to earn the local people the title of Caribou Eskimos. In this region, most of the caribou, who spend the summer grazing on the tundra, migrate south to the shelter of the forest. During the winter, the Eskimos exist by taking a few caribou in pit-falls, snaring ptarmigan, trapping foxes and fishing; but they depend mainly on the spring migration of the caribou and on the return movement in the autumn. At the height of summer, between these migrations, the Caribou Eskimos will make for the coastal ice margin to hunt seals and walruses, but they soon have to turn back if they are to catch the return movement of the caribou.

The more one looks at the culture of the Eskimos, the more clearly one sees how closely it depends on an exact knowledge both of seasonal changes and of the lives and habits of the various animals on which they directly depend for their very lives. Again, their tools and equipment, from boats and sledges to highly ingenious harpoons, though made from the simplest materials – mainly stone and animal substances, helped out by driftwood and only latterly by iron – are perfectly adapted for the purpose in hand under the very special environmental conditions of the Arctic zone. No less noteworthy are the steps taken by the Eskimos to survive the prolonged cold of their homeland. Great attention is paid to clothing, which has Advanced Palaeolithic antecedents. Their garments, made for preference from caribou hides, are finely sewn but loose-fitting, to hold an insulating layer of air and at the same time permit the free evaporation of sweat (Figure 40). They include hoods, fur stockings and boots, and mittens or gloves. Care is reflected, not only in the careful sewing but in the matching of skins and the way in which garments are decorated by hair-embroidery, patterns and fringes. Great attention is paid to preventing moisture from getting into garments, and snow is carefully removed by specially made beaters. To safeguard the eyes from snow-glare, wooden goggles are made with narrow slits.

40. Eskimo man's summer skin clothing

Houses are no less important than clothing, and indeed Eskimos commonly remove their main garments when indoors. During the summer, the standard shelter is a tent made of caribou or seal-skin, stretched over a frame with ridge-roof, and having the end opposite the entrance rounded. The permanent winter villages, on the other hand, are made up of earth-houses refurbished from year to year or of snow structures that need more or less frequent renewal. The former, stemming ultimately from the semi-subterranean structures made by the Advanced Palaeolithic Siberians and widely spread over the circumpolar zone during later prehistoric times, are characteristically subrectangular or oval in plan. The central area is excavated into the subsoil, and the spoil is used to build walls at a slight distance in such a way as to leave a bench for sleeping and the storing of gear. The entrance passage is long and narrow, to reduce the cold of the outer air, and avoids draughts by entering the chamber from a slightly lower level. The roofing of layers of seal-skin and moss is laid over rafters that were formerly of whale-ribs but are now of stone or drift-wood, and is renewed from year to year as the owner returns to winter quarters. Light is admitted by a small gut window immediately over the point where the passage enters the chamber. Even more ingenious is the dome-shaped snow-house. In parts of Alaska this is built over a frame of willow branches, but elsewhere it has no support, being fashioned entirely from rectangular blocks of hard snow cut by knives of antler or whalebone. The hollow left by the removal of the blocks forms the main floor of the interior, and the low bench surrounding this within the dome serves for sleeping and storing gear. Because of its speed of construction – it can be erected in an hour or so – the snow-house is widely used for winter hunting or travel, but among the central Eskimos it has even displaced the earth-house in the permanent winter settlements. When intended for lengthy use, the house is enlarged by building out a series of store-houses and dog-kennels in front. This arrangement, by forming a series of air-locks, helps to keep draughts from the interior, though for obvious reasons the temperature inside such houses, which are lit by means of small panes of ice, cannot be allowed to reach too high a level. Perhaps more dramatically than any other feature of their culture, the snow-house symbolizes the way in which the Eskimos have turned even the severities of their climate to their own advantage.

Although the cultures of the various peoples surveyed in this chapter display a considerable diversity of expression, they are all subject to the same broad limitations, limitations which arise primarily from the parasitic nature of their economy. So long as men have to depend exclusively on what they can divert from wild nature, whether by hunting, catching, or various forms of collecting and gathering, narrow boundaries are set to their development. The pressure of the food quest does not rest equally heavily upon all such groups, and in fact we find a wide range of cultural attainment among them. For some peoples, the southernmost inhabitants of South America among them, the effort of maintaining life has absorbed so much of their energy and time that they have little over for elaborating other aspects of social life. Others are able to live more fully at certain times of the year, like the Plains Indians who used to congregate during the summer for the communal hunting of buffalo herds, and had the opportunity of fostering the activities and ceremonies of the men's societies which form in some respects the outstanding element in their culture. In yet others, exceptionally rich and easily harvested supplies of food, like the salmon of the British Columbian rivers, make possible greater fixity of settlement, larger and more elaborate dwellings, and a society in which the ceremonial destruction of wealth is an accepted mode of winning and retaining prestige. The indications are that it was among some such hunter-fisher group or groups with exceptional sources of food that the take-off to a more productive form of economy in many different parts of the Old and New Worlds.

It remains to review in brief outline the factors which have restricted and still restrict the possibilities of cultural advance for societies depending for subsistence exclusively on hunting, fishing and food-gathering. First and foremost are the demographic facts. It is characteristic of hunter-fishers that, unless special local circumstances exist, such as a prolific and easily won source of food, they live, at any rate for most of the year, in small groups, as a rule comprising a few or even single families; and, further, that each group requires an extensive, often a very extensive, territory to provide it with its basic requirements of food. This means that men are thinly scattered, so that for instance the Eskimos number hardly more than 50,000 souls scattered over a territory some 6,000 miles across. Even so, it is only possible to survive by gathering wild harvests and hunting and trapping wild animals wherever they happen to be available at different times of the year. There is, of course, a wide variation in the degree of mobility required. Among some communities movement is perpetual, so that the same settlement may hardly ever be occupied for more than a few days at a time. Among the Caribou Eskimos, on the other hand, there are only two main seasonal migrations, corresponding to the northward and southward movement of the caribou herds on which their culture is mainly based. Even where, as in British Columbia, there are fixed settlements with substantial dwellings, seasonal movements are generally made to collect roots and berries or harvest the salmon that move upstream to spawn. The necessity of movement, particularly among peoples for whom this involved frequent changes of settlement, in itself set a close limit to their movable possessions as well as to their actual dwellings.

One of the most important effects of living in small and often widely separated groups is that they allow little scope for the subdivision of functions. Among communities of hunter-fishers, it is normal to find that adult members discharge all the functions open to their sex. In other words, there was little or no possibility of the degree of specialization needed for rapid or significant advances in technology. Moreover, the groups in which hunter-fishers live are not only as a rule small but commonly isolated, so that the number of contacts either between groups or individuals is narrowly restricted and with it the kind of stimulus normally involved in cultural change. The effect of these circumstances is to make for conservatism, so that progress is inhibited or at best greatly retarded, unless the equilibrium is drastically disturbed either by environmental change or by the impact of a more advanced culture.

Because of these facts, the technology of surviving hunter-fishers is everywhere simple. The various weapons and devices used in securing prey, though often ingenious and closely adapted to the habits of the animals concerned, are made from the simplest materials by comparatively elementary processes. For gathering plant food and for household purposes, receptacles of eggshell, leaves, bark, skin or basketry are widely used. Unless extreme cold makes it necessary, clothing is often dispensed with entirely, save for a few bands and fringes, and where it is used extensively, as among the Yukaghir or the Eskimos of the far north, it is made by sewing together the skins of wild animals; weaving, like potting, when practised by hunter-fishers, betrays contact, direct or indirect, with peoples having a productive economy. Equally, houses, if we except the great timber structures of the north-west coast of North America and the earth houses of the winter settlements of the circumpolar zone, are liable to be flimsy and made from light organic materials like grass, reeds, leaves, branches and skins. To aid them in the movements they have to make, nearly all existing hunter-fishers possess some kind of boats, and the northernmost ones also have sledges for travelling over winter snow; but all these devices are made by simple methods from readily accessible organic materials.

The social life of the hunter-fisher peoples, although as we know from the Australian aborigines it may be regulated in a highly complex fashion, revolves around the interrelation of comparatively small numbers of people. Among many groups, indeed, the biological family is for much of the year the normal unit, and even where larger numbers are united for certain periods these involve no more than the equivalent of a village. Again, if we leave aside exceptional cases like the British Columbian Indians, with their 'nobles' and highly developed cult of social emulation, hunter-fisher societies are normally devoid of classes beyond the basic ones of sex and age-grades. The social roles of individual adults are as undifferentiated, each in their proper sex category, as are their economic functions, a conclusion by no means invalidated by the appearance of leaders who in any form of society are likely to emerge by virtue of their personality or special insights or skills. In a broad sense it is true that the most primitive surviving peoples, if this term be understood in a purely descriptive sense, are organized on a pre-class basis. The concept of property is nevertheless important as a means of ensuring both the more effective use and conservation of resources. Thus among hunting peoples the group ownership of game and their territories imposes a restraint on over-hunting by individuals, as well as eliminating a main source of intergroup conflict. The scale of groups exercising ownership varies according to ecological circumstances: thus, in Labrador, the herds of migratory caribou are vested in bands, since the tundra called for cooperation by large numbers of hunters; whereas the woodland caribou, beavers and other animals of the forest zone are more effectively hunted by the smaller family groups in which ownership is in this case vested. Again, where resources are strictly local, as in stone quarries or particular stands of wild nut-trees, ownership is likely to be exercised by individual families. Group ownership often extends also to the bulkier gear employed in the food-quest, such as boats or weirs. Private or individual ownership, on the other hand, is generally restricted to personal possessions like weapons and ornaments, the precise things in fact that we find buried with individual hunter-fishers from the prehistoric period.

Spiritually, the surviving hunter-fishers share with primitive peoples having a more developed economy, and indeed in a certain sense with all human beings, a desire to enter into some form of communion with past generations through genealogy and myths. More or less closely allied with this is their sense of kinship with the animals and plants upon which they directly depend, and even of outstanding features of their habitat, an awareness which finds one of its most elaborate expressions in the Australian institution of totemism. Both the concern with ancestors and heroes and the sense of identification with natural forces are reflected in the representational art which, though by no means universal, is yet in itself an outstanding expression of the hunter-fisher way of life.

Appreciation of the character and limitations of the hunter-fishers available for study today, or in the recent past, is important for the insight it affords into the lives of the analogous peoples of the more or less remote past, peoples whose very existence can only be inferred from the archaeological evidence. Yet the surviving exponents of ancient modes of existence merit attention in their own right. After all, it is still impracticable to introduce food-producing economies to extensive parts of the world over which hunter-fisher economies prevail; indeed, it is sometimes only possible to penetrate the remoter areas by deploying the resources of modern technology for reasons of military expediency, national prestige or scientific research. Neither Eskimos, Patagonians, Arunta, Bushmen or Semang are likely to influence world affairs or even to provide new markets large enough to attract the concern of modern business. Yet such peoples as these, few in number as they may be and primitive though they are in relation to ourselves, are fellow citizens of the world and in their institutions contribute to the diversity of man.

CHAPTER SEVEN

# *Setting the Stage for Economic Change*

As we have already seen, the indications of climatic change enshrined in the geological record are sufficiently clear to provide a chronological framework without which it would hardly have been possible to interpret in historical terms any but the more recent traces of prehistoric man and his culture. Further, the ecological stresses of the Pleistocene period played an important role in prehistory by their often renewed impact on existing ways of life, an impact which enhanced the adaptive value of responsiveness to change. So long as the tool-making primates were confined to the same territories as the apes and monkeys it is true that the impact of climatic change was muffled: prolonged periods of greater or lesser rainfall must have affected the distribution of vegetation, but in tropical territories these were by no means sudden or compulsive. For immense periods of time, man lived in territories where climatic stresses were least insistent, during a phase in his history, moreover, when his cultural endowment was at its weakest. The wonder is less that he made slow progress than that he made any at all. It was not until his cultural endowment had grown enough during Late Pleistocene times that he was able to break out of the old primate habitat and colonize territories where for the first time he was exposed to the full stimulus of pronounced variations in the environment. The Advanced Palaeolithic hunting cultures were, as we have seen, distinguished above all by their dynamism and responsiveness to change.

It can hardly be an accident that the next great break-through in human awareness and technical prowess took place precisely in those territories where ecological changes were most clearly marked. The transformation of temperate Europe and of south-west Asia which occurred at the close of the Ice Age and the onset of the Neothermal period was no more far-reaching or severe, indeed rather less so, than many that had gone before. It owes its outstanding significance to the fact that it came at a time when the Advanced Palaeolithic peoples of the regions in question were fitted, as never before, to take advantage of changes in their external environment.

The sweeping nature of the changes implied in the close of the Ice Age can best be estimated by reference to the natural conditions under which the most advanced Palaeolithic hunters pursued their game. To obtain anything like a full picture of environmental history, one needs a concerted effort by each of the various disciplines open to modern Quaternary Research, and this has only been put forth effectively in north-western and central Europe and locally in North America. Much has been learned about the setting in which the way of life of the most advanced Palaeolithic hunters developed into that of their Mesolithic successors; and, further, about the transformation of the European continent into a state in which it was capable of being settled by Neolithic peasants spreading from the south-east during the middle of Post-glacial times. Much less is known about the ecological transformation of the more northerly parts of the north subtropical zone from North Africa across south-west Asia to the Iranian plateau, and we have at present to rest content with rather generalized knowledge about the setting in which the domestication of animals and plants was first accomplished and mixed farming first took shape as a way of life.

By comparison with their size at the peak of the last glaciation, the European ice-sheets, though still extensive, were much reduced during Late Glacial times. Thus the margin of the Scandinavian ice-sheet, which during the full Würm glaciation had reached south of Berlin and almost as far as Hamburg and Warsaw, had withdrawn from Scania by the Late Glacial period, though still covering most of the Scandinavian peninsula north of Oslo and Stockholm and all but the southern strip of Finland. Again, the much smaller British ice-sheets, which at the peak of the Würm glaciation covered the whole of Scotland, nearly three-quarters of Ireland and much of Wales and northern England, had greatly shrunk by Late Glacial times, and by the beginning of the Post-glacial occupied only isolated mountain areas.

The fact that so much ice had already melted by Late Glacial times means that sea-levels were by no means as low as they had been at the peak of the glaciation. On the other hand, the still substantial size of the Scandinavian ice-sheet and of the very much larger North American one means that even at the close of Late Glacial times sea-levels were still substantially lower than they are today. Conversely and for the same reason, emphasized in this case by the fact that it took some time for the earth's crust to respond to the removal of the weight of ice, most of Scandinavia and the northern parts of Britain were still depressed at the beginning of the Post-glacial period. In regions where the two factors were evenly balanced no great shift in the relations of land and sea occurred, but outside the range of isostatic depression, in areas which after all were the important ones from the point of view of prehistoric settlement, very important geographical changes occurred.

Sea-levels were something like thirty fathoms (*c.* 55 m.) lower in the North Sea area than they are today: this meant that Britain was joined to the continent along a broad front from the neighbourhood of Beachy Head to the coast of northern Yorkshire; and that as the Scandinavian ice-sheet withdrew, the water occupying the basin of the present Baltic sea was an ice-dammed lake cut off from the open sea by a broad barrier of land incorporating Jutland, the Danish islands, south Sweden, the intervening belts and the surrounding shallows. With the retreat of the ice from the Late Glacial moraines, the ice-dammed lake was converted into a branch of the open sea taking its name from *Yoldia arctica*, a mollusc indicative of the still low temperatures. Further contraction of the ice, by bringing about an isostatic recovery of land in middle Sweden, temporarily reconverted the Baltic into a lake, this time named after *Ancylus fluviatilis*. Meanwhile the eustatic rise of sea-level proceeded until it breached the land-barrier and re-connected the Baltic with the sea, resulting in the formation of the Litorina Sea, which locally even inundated land at present above sea-level, a transgression repeated on four separate occasions in the northern parts of Denmark.

The climate of the Late Glacial period underwent fluctuations corresponding with the vicissitudes of the Scandinavian ice-sheet. Thus, over a territory extending from the Pyrenees to the margins of the ice, and from Ireland to eastern Europe, there are clear traces in the geological sequence of a relatively warm phase interrupting the predominantly cold conditions of the Late Glacial period. Corresponding to the pauses in the glacial retreat are clay deposits formed of material brought down by alternate freezing and thawing and containing traces of a cold *Dryas* flora; whereas the rapid contraction of the ice preceding the final halt in Middle Sweden is represented in the sequence by organic muds of the type first recognized between *Dryas* clays at Allerød in Zealand, muds formed under more temperate conditions with a continuous vegetation cover.

| *Radio carbon dates B.C.* | *Vegetation zones* | *Climate* | *Glacial episodes* Scandinavia | N. America |
|---|---|---|---|---|
| 8800–8300 | III | Younger *Dryas*: cold | Last moraines: Norwegian Raa Middle Swedish Finnish Salpasselka | Valders re-advance |
| 10000–8800 | II | Allerød: temperate | Gotiglacial retreat: from south Scania to Middle Sweden | Two Creeks stage |
| –10000 | I | Older *Dryas*: cold | Scanian moraines | Cary sub-stage |

Table 5. The Late Glacial Sequence in the Northern Hemisphere

Our knowledge of the vegetation prevailing during the period represented by these deposits depends more than anything else on the systematic application of the technique of pollen-analysis; by means of this method it is possible both to measure the progress of floristic change, by noting variations in the proportion of fossil pollen from successive samples in the same locality, and to establish the type of vegetation existing in different regions at the same period of time. It is known that during the *Dryas* periods the landscape prevailing over most of the ice-free area of the present temperate zone was of a curiously open character for which no precise parallel exists today. The predominance of grasses and sedges, the fact that birch and willow were represented by their dwarf varieties, and the presence of a whole series of arctic-montane plants, including Mountain Avens (*Dryas octopetala*), Crowberry (*Empetrum nigrum*), Mountain Sorrel (*Oxyria digyna*), Thrift or Sea-Pink (*Armeria maritima*) and Link (*Selaginella selaginoides*), suggests tundra vegetation like that found today in the circumpolar zone; on the other hand, plants like Sea Buckthorn (*Hippaphaë rhamnoides*) and the genera *Artemesia* and *Helianthemum* are more characteristic of the alpine zone of central Europe; and there is evidence, for instance in the distribution of *Ephedra distachya*, that elements of steppe vegetation penetrated much further west than they do today. The extent to which forest trees entered the picture varied according to time and place, but in north-west Europe as a whole they appeared only during the Allerød phase; during this time a kind of park tundra prevailed in marginal territories like north Jutland, most of the British Isles and Ireland, with small islands of trees, particularly birch, in an otherwise open landscape; whereas closed woodlands of birch and pine managed to establish themselves even as far north as Holstein. Little exact information is available about the situation in south-west France, but the indications are that here, too, though woodland almost certainly played a rather more important part, especially during interstadial phases, the landscape was still predominantly an open one.

It is only to be expected that many of the ruminants depicted in cave art, on whose flesh the Advanced Palaeolithic peoples of the present temperate zone lived, were those adapted to tundra, steppe and arctic conditions, even if these were supplemented at times by sylvan creatures like red deer and wild pig. During the final cold phase of the Late Glacial period, the reindeer ranged as far south as the eastern part of the Cantabrian mountains; the Pyrenees; the south of France, where for the first and only time they penetrated the Riviera; and the northern foot-hills of the Alps. What makes this all the more impressive is that the reindeer antlers from a number of sites have been identified as of the barren-ground variety. Although the late Magdalenian hunters, whose type fossils were barbed harpoon-heads made from reindeer antler, depended very greatly on reindeer, they also caught many other animals. On the southern periphery of their distribution, on the Cantabrian coast and in Catalonia, for example, the Magdalenians frequently took red deer: equally, north of the Pyrenees, horse and bison provided important alternative sources of meat, as well as smaller game of arctic-alpine character, such as arctic fox, arctic hare and white grouse. Even so, among cave-dwellers of Switzerland and south Germany, reindeer might form anything up to three-quarters of the larger mammals taken for food. An even greater concentration on reindeer, verging on 100 per cent, was characteristic of the Advanced Palaeolithic hunters of the North European Plain. Peoples like the Hamburgians and the Ahrensburgians took advantage of the gregarious character of the reindeer and of its propensity to undertake seasonal migrations: the masses of discarded reindeer antlers and bones found in the tunnel-valleys of Holstein bear witness to a dependence on this one animal that suggests a relationship of a very particular kind between hunting bands and reindeer herds.

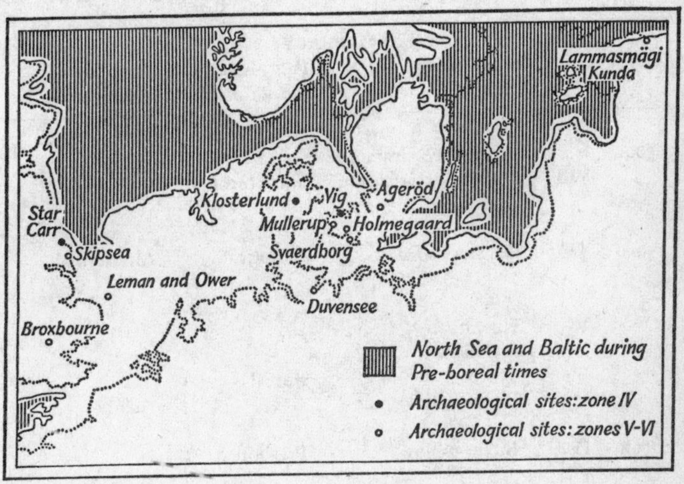


Map 3. The North Sea and Baltic areas at the beginning of Post-glacial times

Note the combination of low ocean level, with Britain still joined to the Continent, and the depressed state of Scandinavia, not yet recovered from the weight of the retreating ice-sheet. The archaeological sites shown are those of the Mesolithic Maglemosian Culture. Those belonging to zones V and VI in the forest sequence relate to a subsequent stage in geographical evolution in the course of which Britain was insulated.

The end of the Pleistocene Ice Age seems to have been as sudden as the thawing of a frozen pond. Its date can already be fixed to within a few hundred years. According to counts of the clay varves (annual sedimentary layers) deposited in glacial melt-water, counts which should be regarded as minimal owing to the difficulty of recognizing loss by erosion, the Scandinavian ice-sheet began its final retreat before 7900 B.C. On the other hand radio-carbon analyses of samples from the end of the Late Glacial period suggest a date of 8300 B.C.

The most significant ways in which the Late Glacial environment changed as it gave place to the temperate conditions of the Post-glacial period can be summarized quite briefly. Temperatures rose during an initial Anathermal period from levels prevailing under sub-arctic conditions to ones approaching those of today, before attaining a peak some $2\frac{1}{2}$°C. higher by the middle of the Altithermal period (corresponding to the Climatic Optimum), from which during Medithermal times they declined to present levels. One of the most obvious effects of the rise in temperature was a further pronounced retreat of ice-sheets, a withdrawal which laid open extensive territories for human occupation. The rapid melting of ice-sheets carried a stage farther the general rise of sea-levels and the local recovery of land-masses formerly depressed by the weights of ice-sheets. One of the most striking implications of this was the flooding-over of the North Sea bed and the insulation of Britain, probably some time in the

| *Dates B.C.* | | NORTH-WESTERN EUROPE *Forest history* | *Post-glacial climatic phases* | NORTH AMERICA *Neothermal climatic phases* |
|---|---|---|---|---|
| | IX | | Sub-atlantic | Medithermal |
| 500 | | Progressive clearance | | |
| | VIII | (livestock cultivation) | Sub-boreal | |
| | a | | | |
| 3000 | VII | Deciduous forest | Atlantic | Altithermal |
| | a | | | |
| | VI | Pine, hazel, deciduous | | |
| | | | Boreal | |
| | V | Birch, willow pine | | Anathermal |
| *c.* 8300 | IV | Birch, willow | Pre-boreal | |

Table 6. The Post-glacial or Neothermal sequence in the North Temperate Zone

seventh millennium B.C. The rise of temperature also resulted in a dramatic change in the plant cover, open vegetation being rapidly replaced by forests except on high ground and marshes: at first, the forests were composed of trees able to tolerate relatively cold conditions, notably birch and willow and, in due course, pine; but, as the climate warmed up, hazel and then the deciduous trees, oak, elm, lime and alder, spread in and at the peak of Altithermal times, when Post-glacial climate reached its optimum, finally dominated the forests. Lastly, the radical changes in grazing implied by the transformation of an open into a closed forest landscape had a profound effect on the kind of animals available for hunting, so that reindeer, horse and bison gave place to such sylvan forms as red and roe deer, elk, aurochs and wild pig.

The impact of ecological change varied regionally just as did the changes themselves. In the more southerly territories of the present temperate zone, where some tree cover was probably already present during the Late Glacial period, the change was less marked than in more northerly ones. It is in these latter, on the North European Plain, that we can observe the most marked cultural change, notably in the new dynamic attitude towards the spreading forests. Indeed, over much of western Europe, and also of central Europe and south Russia, the onset of Neothermal climate, however favourable it may appear to us, was one of cultural stress down to the time of the spread of Neolithic economy. This can be illustrated by the situation in south-western France, the centre of the most highly developed culture during Late Glacial times. The Azilian culture, named after the site of Mas d'Azil in the Ariège, was in almost every respect inferior to that of the Late Magdalenian which it immediately succeeded and from which it almost certainly sprang. The flint workers developed no new ideas of importance, and their small thumb-nail scrapers compared ill with the splendid blade scrapers of their predecessors. The antler and bone industry was greatly diminished. The only significant form to survive was the barbed harpoon-head, made from stag – rather than reindeer – antler and no longer picked out by vigorous incision. A few traces of incised lines and zig-zags on pointed bone objects and the rather pathetic lines and dots painted on river-worn pebbles, the most expressive of which suggest highly devolved anthropomorphic forms, are the only sad remnants of the splendours of Magdalenian chattel art. Again, and even more revealingly, though the Azilians almost without exception occupied the self-same caves, they apparently gave up blazoning their walls and roofs with representations of their prey.

The cultures that flourished as vegetation approached and attained its Post-glacial climax were even more impoverished. As an example, one may take the assemblage immediately overlying an Azilian level at Sauveterre-la-Lémance, Lot-et-Garonne, a French representative of an industry stemming from advanced Gravettian sources over a

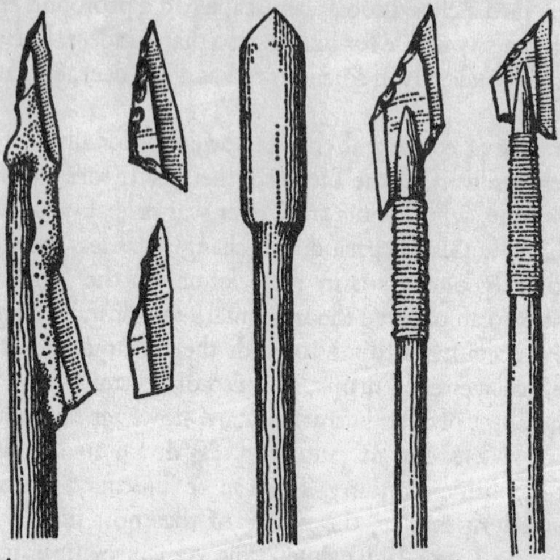

41. Mesolithic arrows set with flint microliths, and wooden bolt, from north-west Europe

territory that extended from Iberia across France and Italy to central Europe. The Sauveterrian flint-worker made scraping tools, awls and burins, but concentrated on the production from narrow micro-flakes of numerous microliths, some of them geometric in form and of minute size, presumably intended in most instances for arming wooden arrows (Figure 41); all of which can be paralleled from Advanced Palaeolithic industries. The Sauveterrians seem to have been limited in their use of bone to such elementary forms as awls or bodkins; and there is no sign that they practised art. The Tardenoisian industries, named after Fère-en-Tardenois, Aisne, which succeeded the Sauveterrian in south-west France and ran parallel with or at least overlapped the earliest peasant cultures of the area, were similarly impoverished, though belonging to a distinct tradition of flint-work, the leading feature of which was the manufacture of arrowheads and barbs of trapeze or triangular form from sections of blades. Caves and rock-shelters continued in use, but open settlements in the form of clusters of huts began to spring up, for example, round the lakes of south Germany and Switzerland. Equally, hunting remained the main source of food, though the Tardenoisians began to acquire domestic animals, and in the Atlantic zone, both on the coast of Finistère and in the Tagus estuary, they supplemented their diet with shellfish.

The picture of cultural decline sketched for the heart of the Advanced Palaeolithic world could be matched over a wide extent of the west Mediterranean, central Europe and south Russia. The leading feature of the Mesolithic industries of this extensive territory – and one, indeed, that was common to those of northern Europe and western Asia – was an abundance of microliths suggesting widespread and general use of the bow and arrow in hunting. On the other hand, though in south-west France, as in other parts of temperate Europe, the forest reached its climax during the Mesolithic settlement, no specific equipment was developed to fell and work trees except on the North European Plain. In all essentials the Post-glacial hunter-fishers of the more southerly parts of Europe were Epi-palaeolithic in character down to the time at which they came under Neolithic influence.

A much more dynamic response to changing ecological conditions was made in the low-lying territory, which up to the sixth millenium B.C. formed an unbroken plain from eastern England to Poland and Esthonia and from Brandenburg in the south to Scania and Blekinge in the north. Only the southern parts of this broad territory had been occupied, at any rate seasonally, during Late Glacial times by bands of hunters who pursued the reindeer cropping the rich grazing of the open terrain. To judge from the results of pollen-analysis, the transformation of this landscape into one of forest began as soon as the ice-sheet entered on its final major retreat. Conversely, archaeology has shown that by around the middle of the eighth millennium, if not earlier, the cultural pattern was already distinctively Mesolithic.

As the forests closed in, settlement concentrated on river-courses and around the numerous lakes left behind by the Pleistocene ice-sheet. Most of what we know about the Mesolithic people of northern Europe has been preserved in the muds and peats which have since formed over the margins and sometimes over the entire beds of these lakes, a circumstance to which we owe the survival of an unusually wide range of organic materials. Incidentally, it was the character of these finding-places that led to the name Maglemosian (Danish *magle mose*=great bog) being applied to the archaeological material from them. In the classic form in which it was first discovered, the Maglemosian culture flourished during Boreal times, but its prototype had already appeared in Yorkshire, Jutland and Scania during the Pre-boreal phase of the Post-glacial period.

There are manifest signs, both in the forms and techniques of flint, antler and bone tools and in the designs sometimes engraved on the latter two, that the Maglemosians stemmed from Advanced Palaeolithic sources. On the other hand, there are indications of radical adaptations and even innovations that, in some cases at least, relate clearly enough to the large-scale ecological changes of Post-glacial times. In this respect the settlers of the North European Plain showed themselves far more enterprising than their neighbours to the south and south-west; indeed, the Maglemosians displayed something of the cultural vigour that characterized the Advanced Palaeolithic peoples of an earlier age. One of the most striking ways in which they adapted themselves to the spread of forest was to devise means for felling and utilizing trees. For this purpose they made axes and adzes with wooden handles and stag antler hafts (Figure 42). The blades were flaked down from flint nodules and sharpened by blows, struck transversely to the main axis and differing only in their angle from burin blows. There can be no question that such tools were effective, because trees apparently felled by their use have been found at Star Carr and these date from the closing stages of the Pre-boreal period: the pointed or obliquely truncated bases of the trunks of these suggest that they were felled by oblique strokes directed downwards to a previously cut ring. One of the uses to which timber and tree branches were put was to consolidate patches of swamp by the lake margins for settlement. Larger timbers were split for making huts. Main trunks were hollowed out for dug-out canoes – one such from Pesse in Holland has been dated to the seventh millennium B.C. by radio-carbon analysis (Figure 31) – and smaller pieces were shaped to form paddles. In a landscape of lakes and rivers the Maglemosians were thus able to move about, as well as to fish, by propelling small boats, and it was doubtless partly for this reason that lake margins were favoured for settlement.

The Maglemosians gained their living mainly by hunting elk, aurochs, red deer, roe deer and wild pig, but they also took smaller animals, including some fur-bearing ones as well as wild-fowl. One of their most important weapons was the bow and arrow, both of which sometimes survive in the northern bogs more or less complete

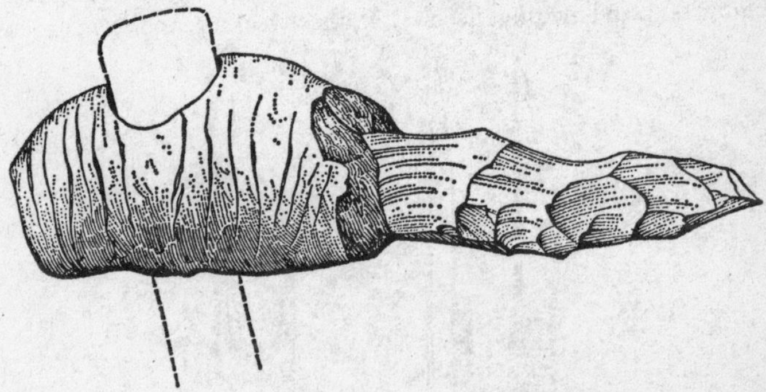

42. Maglemosian flint adze-head set in wooden holder, perforated for handle, from the Elbe-Trave canal, Schleswig-Holstein

(Figure 43). The bows were made from single pieces of timber shaped in the middle for the hand-grip and notched at either end for the bow-string, and the arrows were armed with microliths held in position by resin. Spears with heads of antler or bone, barbed on one edge, were probably used for hunting as they certainly were for fishing. Indeed, fishing for pike in the numerous lakes and rivers was an important ancillary source of food, and this activity was carried on most often from boats by means of hook and line and seine net, as well as by fish spears. In addition, nuts and various kinds of plant-food were gathered in season. Like other Mesolithic groups the Maglemosians kept dogs, whose forbears had almost certainly been domesticated from wolves. Their relationship, however, was quite

43. Maglemosian elm bow from Holmegaard IV, Denmark

different from that established between farmers and their livestock, which was based on subservience and profit: theirs was one in which convenience was more nearly mutual, the dog providing companionship, watch-keeping and scavenging in return for food and protection.

Like the Magdalenians, but unlike the Sauveterrians and other Epi-gravettian groups, the Maglemosians made great use of antler and bone for hunting- and fishing-gear, including spearheads, fish-hooks (Figure 44) and netting needles; leather-working tools; mattock-

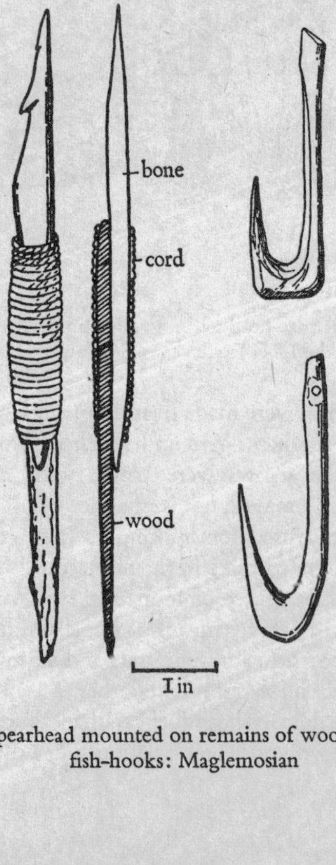


44. Barbed bone spearhead mounted on remains of wooden handle, and bone fish-hooks: Maglemosian

heads; axe and adze hafts; perforated batons and the like. Similarly, they were fond of personal ornaments and used beads and pendants of amber, stone and perforated animal teeth. Again, they ornamented some of their favourite implements with designs finely engraved by a sharp flint or formed by pits drilled into the surface. A favourite design took the form of a net-like pattern, with parallel lines formed by zig-zags or barbed lines tied together by oblique strokes at either end; but stylized animals were occasionally depicted, and anthropomorphic designs (Figure 45), some of them presenting analogies with those on Azilian painted pebbles, were rather common. At the heart of the culture area, in Denmark, the Maglemosians occasionally

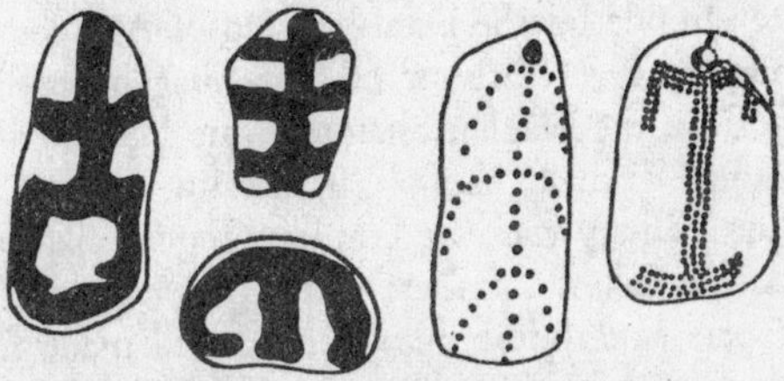

45. Mesolithic anthropomorphic patterns on amber pendants (Maglemosian) and painted pebbles (Azilian)

carved figurines from lumps of amber; often these are too generalized for identification, but they include a head of an elk, which from the holes at the bottom of the neck may have been secured to a model made from some substance that has perished, and also a water-bird and a possible bear. The Maglemosians were no mere survivors of an outworn tradition, hanging on in a territory soon to be colonized by the bearers of a new way of life: they were innovators and, over much of their territory, pioneers; and, particularly at the centre of their culture-area, they displayed in their artifacts the exuberance of men who lived as well as they reasonably could as hunter-fishers in their day and age.

During the later stages of the Maglemosian culture, the sea, replenished by water from the rapidly melting ice-sheets as temperatures mounted towards the Post-glacial peak, flooded over large areas of the low-lying ground to which the hunter-fishers were so well adapted. Geographically, this rise of sea-level cut off Britain from the continent and, by forming narrow belts between the Danish islands, Jutland and south Sweden, turned the Ancylus lake into the Litorina Sea, immediate precursor of the Baltic. Since the Late Glacial and early Post-glacial shores of the North Sea and Baltic areas are now deeply submerged, it is hardly possible to tell at what stage coastal settlement began there. However, it seems certain that, by reducing the territories for inland hunting and fishing and extending the length of sea-coasts, the rise of sea-level must have helped to focus attention on the sea-shore as a source of food as well as providing a stimulus to migration. The material equipment of the early coastal settlers of the West Baltic area, dating from the transition from Boreal to Atlantic times, is well represented at the submerged site of Carstensminde off the Danish island of Amager and in finds dredged from the Free Harbour of Copenhagen nearby. It differs so markedly from the Maglemosian that one can imagine it to have developed along distinct, though in certain respects convergent, lines. The flint industry was based on long regular blades rather than on narrow micro-flakes; and these were converted into burins, end-of-blade scrapers and rhombic arrowheads, all made from oblique sections with the breaks blunted by steep flaking and the edges of the present blade left sharp. Bone and antler forms included points slotted on either edge for the reception of sharp flint flakes, and perforated mattock-heads, decorated in some cases by deeply incised zig-zag patterns of distinctive character. Axe and adze-blades of Maglemosian pattern were chipped out of flint nodules; but stump-butted greenstone blades, pecked into shape and having the working-edge ground and polished, introduced a new and highly significant form, widely distributed among early agriculturalists.

During the later phases of the Atlantic period, Neolithic economy made a much greater impact on the inhabitants of Denmark without breaking the continuity of coastal settlement. When by the time of the third transgression of the Litorina Sea the coastal culture had taken the form named after the midden of Ertebølle (on the shore of a former fiord in northern Jutland), its economy was still based to an important extent on hunting, fishing and shell-gathering, even though cereal crops were cultivated and livestock kept in stalls. Moreover, although pottery was now made in the form both of coarse jars with pointed bases and of finer beakers of funnel-neck form, and changes occurred in the forms of flint, bone and antler tools, the basic techniques and many of the products quite evidently carried on traditions already formed in the Carstenminde culture. The indications are that the Ertebølle culture persisted on the Danish coasts until Middle Neolithic times when it was replaced by another one with Norwegian and Swedish connexions in which seal-hunting played a special part.

If the present temperate zone was brought into very existence as a result of wide-ranging environmental change, the transition seems to have been much less clearly defined in the Mediterranean zone, in parts of which indeed prehistorians have been hard put to it to distinguish between deposits of Late Pleistocene and Early Neothermal date. It is difficult to know how far this is due to lack of intensive Quaternary Research in the Mediterranean lands and how far it corresponds with fact. One of the few investigations to combine pollen-analysis with study of animal remains from a vertical sequence of deposits, undertaken at the Cueva del Toll near Moyà in the province of Barcelona, shows that in the north-west of the Mediterranean area climate oscillated between humid-temperate and arid-warm, corresponding with glacial and interstadial phases in the temperate zone: during humid phases pine forests existed in the area and accounted for eighty per cent of the pollen; whereas in arid phases pine contributed only some thirty per cent and vegetation was predominantly open. In this way pollen analysis confirms the expectation that during glacial periods high pressure over expanded glaciated territories would have deflected Atlantic rainstorms south of their present track: and conversely that a rapid withdrawal of ice-sheets would be likely in the absence of countervailing influences, to bring desiccation to some parts of the Mediterranean area formerly better supplied with rainfall.

At the Cueva del Toll it was possible to see that increases in the proportion of animals of sylvan habitat were, in fact, matched by an increase in forest trees, and so to infer climatic change with some show of confidence. At the opposite end of the Mediterranean we have to depend almost entirely on incomplete studies of the animal remains brought into caves mainly by prehistoric man himself. Far too little is known about the vegetational history and climate of the Near East during the last ten or twelve thousand years to establish with any precision the natural context in which the domestication of animals and plants was first achieved, still less to provide any satisfactory explanation in ecological terms of the economic changes which made possible the emergence of new forms of society between, say 9000 and 6000 B.C. Meanwhile, the most reasonable hypothesis is that the apparent temporal correlation between climatic and economic change in this key area implies some causative link, whether this be found directly in the challenge of desiccation or in some recondite complexities of ecological readjustment. It is, of course, possible that the marked decline at the crucial level of the Mount Carmel caves of remains of *Dama mesopotamica*, a woodland deer, and the corresponding rise of *Gazella gazella*, a form adapted to grassland conditions, was due merely to a changed preference on the part of the Mesolithic hunters. Yet, since the change from *Dama* to *Gazella* merely repeated a cycle observed from earlier levels in the same caves, it seems more reasonable to assume that it reflected altered conditions in nature rather than the whims of human beings; and, without proof to the contrary, one has surely to accept that stone age hunters would be most likely to hunt the game most readily available.

The best defined and most fully studied of the early Neothermal hunting cultures of the East Mediterranean is the Natufian, named after the Wady en-Natuf in Palestine, a culture confined to a zone within some forty miles of the coast of south-west Syria, Lebanon and Palestine, and having an extension to Lower Egypt and possibly further west. The Natufians, like all Mesolithic groups, had much in common with their Advanced Palaeolithic predecessors: they commonly occupied the mouths of caves; they practised a naturalistic art which occasionally reached a standard comparable with that of the Magdalenians; their flint-work included the production of blades and burins and the use of a steep blunting retouch; they were adept at working bone and antler; they accorded ceremonial burial to their dead; and they were fond of wearing personal ornaments made of perforated shells, animal teeth, the ends of gazelle phalanges and artificially shaped bone-forms like the twin pendants from el-Wad. On the other hand, there are signs that the Natufians were adopting a more settled mode of life and enlarging the basis of their food-supply. For one thing, their settlements began to show signs of structural activity, such as the paving and walling on the platform in front of the el-Wad. Again, the size of the cemeteries – eighty-seven burials were found at el-Wad and forty-five at Shouqbah – suggests either larger groups or more prolonged settlement; and at Eynam a circular stone-walled structure having a stone-paved floor served as a tomb for at least seven individuals buried in their personal finery and covered with red ochre. Indications of an intensified quest for food

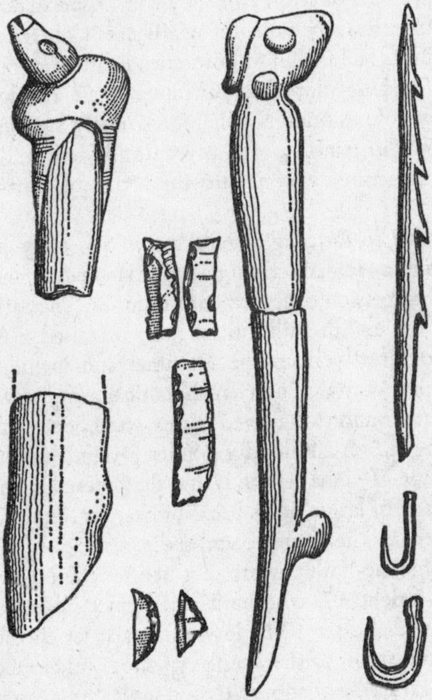

46. Natufian reaping-knife, pestle, spearhead, arrow-armature and fish-hook from Palestine

include presumptive evidence for the use of the bow in the crescent-shaped microliths that served as armatures for arrows, and the appearance of bone fish-hooks (Figure 46). No signs of domesticated animals have so far been found in Natufian deposits; even the 'dog' from Mugharet el-Wad has turned out to be a small Asian wolf. On the other hand, the appearance of carefully made stone pestles and of mortars made on small blocks of stone or hollowed out of living rock shows that plant food was prepared on a considerable scale. Again, reaping-knives and their flint insets indicate that crops were systematically harvested. The diffuse gloss on some of the insets is consistent with cereals but tells nothing of their status: at the 8th millennium B.C. Syrian site of Mureybit they were associated with einkorn and barley of exclusively wild forms. There is indeed no evidence that the Natufians had begun to domesticate either animals or plants, even if they had developed significantly close relationships with gazelles. Their role as hunter-gatherers is neatly symbolized by the fact that even the handles of the reaping-knives and their stone pestles were sometimes carved into the forms of animal heads and hoofs.

The transition to farming is reflected in the early levels at Tell es-Sultan, Jericho. Here, overlying a Natufian encampment, we have evidence of a succession of settled communities. The earliest of these, dating from the eighth millennium B.C., practised a flint industry that stemmed directly from the Natufian and included numerous insets for reaping-knives. Sufficient botanical samples were taken to show that emmer and two-rowed barley were being cultivated; and it has been argued on admittedly slender grounds that domesticated goats were kept. What is certain is that they were able not merely to build huts made of large 'hog's back' bricks, but, more impressively, to cut a ditch in the living rock and construct a defensive wall reinforced by stone-built towers. Yet neither these people nor their successors of Jericho III, who built rectangular houses and plastered their floors, made pottery. The lower levels at Jericho show an early stage in the transition of the peoples of the southern Levant from a hunting and gathering economy to one sufficiently based on farming to permit the construction of apparently extensive defended settlements. Yet the inhabitants of Jericho II–III were not yet formally neolithic in the sense this term has been applied for over a century to peoples whose economy was based on farming, whose technology was still founded on the use of flint and stone, and who manufactured pots.

The Natufian culture, restricted though it is in geographical range, rightly claims attention because we know so much more about it than any other of its kind in western Asia. Much more widespread is a

Mesolithic industry – one can hardly call it a culture yet – characterized by blades and by the production of microliths including some of trapeze shape. Industries of this kind occur over a territory from Greece and the Crimea to eastern Iran and Turkmenia, with extensions westward over the Mediterranean basin and central and western Europe, in a variety of economies, from ones based on hunting and gathering to others depending significantly on farming. Among the former one might first quote the assemblage from the lower level at Palegawra, north-east of Kirkuk in the Kurdish foot-hills of northern Iraq: here we have a flint industry with trapeziform, triangular and crescentic microliths, battered-backs, burins and end-scrapers, together with simple bone tools, and beads and pendants made of stone, shell and animal bones of exclusively wild species such as equids, gazelles, wild goat or sheep, bovids and red deer. Again, one could cite similar industries associated with Mesolithic hunters from the lower levels of the Belt Cave near the south-eastern shore of the Caspian, dated by radio-carbon to the period from the tenth to the seventh millennia B.C.; or from the initial occupations of shelters like Shan-Koba and Tash Air in the Crimea.

Essentially, the same flint industry is also found in Kurdistan in incipient Neolithic contexts, that is, on settlements occupied by people who had begun to farm but had not yet started to make pottery. Not very far to the west of Palegawra, the lower level in the mound at Jarmo yielded traces of farmers who lived in mud huts with matted floors, cultivated cereals and beans, and maintained domestic cattle, but who had not yet begun to make pottery: these people made flint blades for their reaping-knives, axes of polished flint, and stone pestles and mortars, but they also fabricated flint microliths of triangular, crescentic and trapeziform shape. Based as they were on mixed farming, the Jarmo people were not formally speaking Neolithic, since they did not make pottery. They were farmers but not yet potters: their technology was truly transitional. Just as the lithic tradition of Jericho II was basically Natufian, so that of early Jarmo was Palegawran. The cultures of south-west Asia and north-west Europe from the beginning of the Neothermal down to the establishment of pottery-making farming communities were equally transitional or Mesolithic in character; and the archaeological fossils from the two extremes share many leading traits, among them a microlithic flint technology, bone-work including barbed points, handles and shafts slotted for flint insets and barbless fish-hooks, personal ornaments of perforated animal teeth, shells and stone discs and, more sporadically, indications of a cult of human skulls.

Modern research has already made it plain that even in relation to a territory as restricted as that which lies between the Atlantic and the Zagros it is hardly meaningful to speak of the 'invention' of farming. What we are concerned with is a process of transformation from one basis of subsistence to another, and it must be evident that this process must have been related to the ecological circumstances prevailing in distinct territories. A good case can be made out for supposing that the cereals that played a leading role in this territory were first taken into domestication in territories where they flourished in the wild state; and it is likely enough that other plants were systematically sown and even cultivated over ever more extensive territories including those into which cereal agriculture spread comparatively late. Again, in relation to animals the evidence points strongly to the possibility that cattle were first domesticated in south-east Europe; horses must have been tamed either in south Russia or inner Asia; and on present evidence dogs may well have been domesticated from wolves among the hunter-fishers of northern Europe. Mesolithic man was indeed far from passive even in parts of Europe remote from the home of early cereal cultivation. He not only occupied territories previously covered by ice-sheets or too inclement for settlement, such as northern Britain, Ireland and much of Scandinavia and northern Russia, but discovered many of their resources and even initiated the process of forest clearance that farming was so greatly to extend. If his role was less dynamic in some territories than in others, Mesolithic man even in temperate Europe was far from a mere time-filler passively awaiting a new way of life. He not only prepared the ground, but in appropriating elements of the Neolithic way of life to his own needs and circumstances he enriched the pattern of culture as this unfolded in the new age.

CHAPTER EIGHT

# *The Origins of Farming in the Old and New Worlds*

## *1. The Beginnings of Animal Domestication and Plant Cultivation in the Old World*

THE existence of the wild ancestors of sheep and goats, and the archaeological evidence, at least demonstrate within which area of the Old World the first agricultural communities in fact emerged. This occurred as early as the ninth millennium B.C., if not before. Once developed, the techniques of simple mixed farming were acquired by societies over an increasingly large area to the east and west of the original centre, and rapidly became more complex as technology advanced and the early artisans learned to work with copper and gold, and eventually bronze.

Stone-using agricultural communities, 'Neolithic' in the conventional nomenclature, were established in eastern Europe by the sixth millennium and had spread to the western Mediterranean and up the Danube into central Europe, and even to the Netherlands, by the end of the fifth, and to Britain by late in the fourth millennium B.C. Eastwards, the beginnings of farming economies in the area from Turkestan to the Indus must go back at least to the fourth millennium. In eastern Asia China presents us with an unresolved problem, for here independent invention and importation from outside are equally plausible. Further, the difficulty is heightened by the lack of any even approximately fixed dates for events before the middle of the second millennium B.C. In the New World the development of agriculture is necessarily the result of independent invention: here the cultivation of plants dates from the seventh millennium B.C., and the growing of a cereal crop (maize) from the middle of the third. But the absence of animal domestication in the prehistoric Americas led to the formation of societies of a noticeably different type from those of the Old World.

This change in the method of winning subsistence has on occasion been hailed as a Neolithic Revolution, comparable in economic and social importance to the Industrial Revolution of modern western Europe, and has been regarded as the inevitable progenitor of urban societies and civilization. Certainly it was on the basis of the prehistoric peasant economies that in certain areas – Mesopotamia, Egypt, Asia Minor, India and China, for instance – complex societies, literate and urban, permanent and technologically inventive, were to be founded, each presenting us with individual facets of the range of ancient civilizations. But their structures, when documentary sources illuminate the archaeological evidence, are seen to be various, and their emergence from the simpler societies that preceded them can hardly be attributed to the inevitable working out of any common set of social, economic and technological factors. The long and widespread persistence in the Old World of non-literate peasant communities side by side with civilizations at a higher level, at least of material achievements, cannot be interpreted in terms of 'failure' to rise to the norm set by these more complex societies. Civilizations are the exceptions, each the accidental product of innovating circumstances, as likely to be created by individuals as by impersonal and inexorable forces of technological development following on a 'revolution' in subsistence economics. To the historians the simpler peasant communities of the prehistoric Old World have significance and value, both because they represent a norm and because they were the common stock from which civilization could, and sporadically did, develop as an exotic variant.

However, before we come to discuss these early peasant communities, two underlying factors must be examined: on the one hand, the unapprehended and unconscious, but nevertheless potent, psychological patterns of hunting and food-gathering peoples, and, on the other, the natural environment in which certain of these groups found themselves in Post-glacial times with the onset of Neothermal conditions.

The life of communities whose economy is based on hunting is necessarily one of tactics rather than strategy, of short-term decisions taken, perhaps rapidly, in relation to the movement and behaviour of the larger mammals which constitute the basic food supply. It is possible that they followed the movements of herds during their seasonal migration from one pasture area to another, and indeed such rhythms are well documented for Late Glacial and Post-glacial Europe by the hunters' camps of the Meiendorf or Star Carr type, but even these patterns are essentially limited to an annual cycle. The same summer or winter camping site may be regarded as evidence for long-term planning, even in terms of a year or less. Similarly, the essentially mobile quality of a hunting economy did not foster in the minds of the hunters concepts of permanency or a perspective beyond the lifetime of the individual, or, at the most, the natural family group.

When, on the other hand, animal domestication and plant cultivation are consciously envisaged as an essential part of the economy, a long-term view is immediately inevitable. There may be, it is true, economic stages intermediate between hunting and fully settled agriculture, involving, for instance, no more than herding wholly or partially wild flocks, or sowing a cereal crop and returning to harvest it after a period of hunting or intermittent herding over a large area. We shall note probable examples of such economies, and in such circumstances the community may look ahead no further than a single year. But once a society enters upon a deliberate policy of selecting suitable strains for breeding, it is involved in a process which may extend not only beyond a year, but even beyond a lifetime. The achievement of this larger perspective is in itself a psychological advance of no mean order. The relatively slow breeding cycle in those animals and plants susceptible of development as suitable sources of food necessitates a long-term view, and it is no surprise to find a complex of ideas relative to succession and heritable property highly developed in the earliest agricultural societies for which we have written documents. Similarly, the early development in such societies of the architectural skills required for the erection of monumental and permanent buildings, such as temples and palaces, is eloquent evidence of an enlarged time perspective, for these buildings were made to last beyond a single lifespan and were intended for the conduct of ceremonies and traditions similarly conceived as permanent. While we cannot deny that some food-gathering and hunting communities may also have apprehended, however dimly, a continuity of tradition, and even a transmission of skills, beyond the time limits set by the lifespan of a single natural family, we must also recognize that the enlargement of the conceptual horizon in terms of an increased perspective in time is an achievement indissolubly linked with the beginnings of animal- and plant-breeding. Indeed, we might say that the archaeological evidence for the latter is also our tangible evidence for this advance in mental capacity.

The transition from one economy to the other cannot, therefore, have been easy or quick. The world picture of the hunter does not include the possibility of domesticating animals (with the important exception of the dog), for this activity would involve concepts of permanence, of deliberation, and indeed of patience, which are wholly alien to a mentality that evolved as the result of circumstances and stimuli quite unrelated to such factors. To adapt a phrase of R. G. Collingwood, Oxford philosopher and historian, the aims and satisfactions of the farmer are 'not contained' in those of the hunter, and they are therefore to that degree incompatible. What had been comprehended in Mesolithic societies was the advantage inherent in an association with the dog, not as a preliminary to the subjugation of animals on a more extended scale, but solely as an adjunct to the hunter. The domestication of the dog in such communities was not the beginning of a conscious process whereby an increasing command over members of the animal kingdom was envisaged, but rather the exploitation of a single situation whereby a scavenging animal could be brought to transfer its allegiance from its own pack to the human hunting group. In doing so, the initial domestication of the dog in Mesolithic communities merely intensified, and made more efficient, an existing hunting economy; nevertheless, the dog's capabilities in rounding up a herd were to have far-reaching effects in those areas of the Old World where the advantages of using the dog in this way were seen in a longer perspective than that of contemporary groups in other regions. Perhaps in domesticating the dog Mesolithic peoples, while temporarily increasing the efficiency of their own economy, did in fact unconsciously provide one of the means whereby their way of life was to be rendered obsolete and superseded throughout most of the habitable world by that of agriculture or developed pastoralism.

The second basic factor involved in the beginnings of animal husbandry and plant domestication in the Old World is the distribution, under post-Glacial climatic conditions, of the animals and plants that were suitable for the early attempts at a farming economy. The grasses that were the precursors of cultivated wheat and barley demanded favourable conditions of warmth and dryness, and their distribution at the onset of Neothermal conditions was therefore restricted to regions where such conditions obtained, notably the foothills and plains adjacent to the western Asiatic mountain ranges from Anatolia to Iran (Figure 47). Again, the natural distribution pattern in

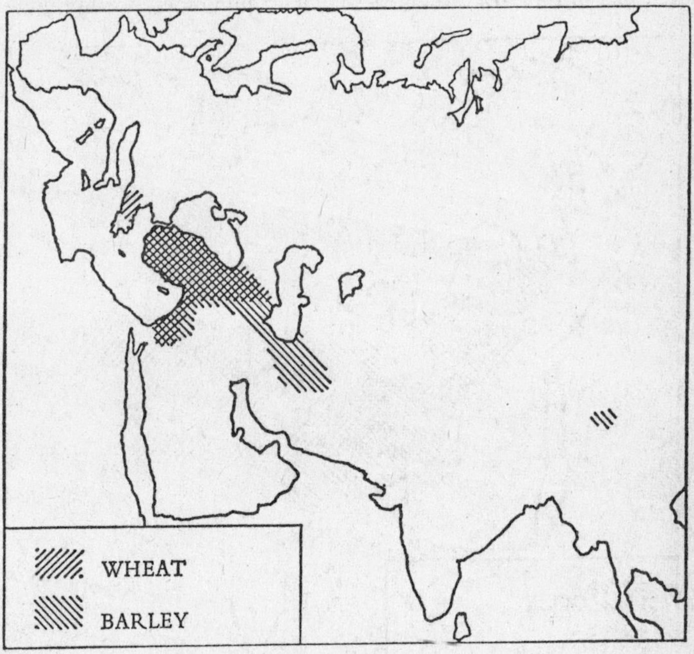


47. Distribution of wild wheat and barley

Eurasia of wild goats and sheep, which according to archaeological evidence were the earliest ruminants to be domesticated, extends over much the same area. The possible ancestors of the pig and of the wild cattle of *Bos primigenius* type had a wider distribution, but were present in the areas under discussion (Figure 48). The horse, not domesticated until relatively late in prehistoric times, in its main wild form (represented by Przewalski's horse) was a denizen of the steppelands on the northern edge of the cradle of the earliest agricultural economies. Secondary domestication of the European 'Forest' type of wild horse, a relic of Pleistocene breeds in western Europe, was to take place later, after the initial domestication of the original grassland type.

It was, therefore, in these climatically favoured regions of western Asia that the prerequisites for agricultural economies existed. We have seen that in this area certain Mesolithic communities, notably those

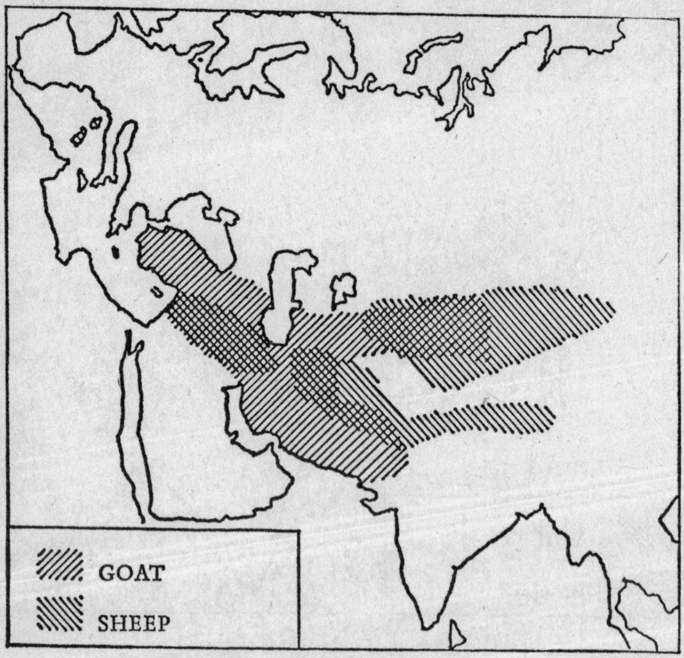


48. Distribution of wild sheep and goats

responsible for the Natufian cultures of Palestine, were in fact moving towards an economy in which, to judge from the presence of reaping-knives or straight sickles, pounders and mortars, a wild or cultivated cereal crop might have been reaped and converted to flour. There is at Jericho, in a remarkable stratified sequence, a Lower Natufian occupation, with structures and characteristic artifacts with a Carbon 14 date of around 8840 B.C.; a thousand years later there had accumulated many feet of deposits from successive settlements in which the tentative beginnings of agriculture had been pushed to a stage at which permanent occupation of a large settlement, and the erection of defensive walls and towers of stone, had been made possible.

Various attempts have been made to produce a systematic grading of basic economic developments from food-collecting to food production in Eurasian prehistoric societies as a whole. A sequence has been envisaged moving through degrees of incipient cultivation and animal domestication, settled village communities or pastoral nomadism, and the development of the complex economy immediately antecedent to the beginnings of town life and literacy. It may well be wise to postpone the construction of such systems until more abundant archaeological material is available, for though it is clear that some sort of developmental grading may be demonstrated for individual sites or restricted areas, the assumption of a general pattern to which all relevant cultures and regions should theoretically conform is, in the present state of knowledge, untenable. Such a scheme may eventually be worked out with a show of probability as a valid inference from the archaeological evidence, but since conservative cultural traditions inevitably exist side by side with those in which innovation is set at a premium, the evidence will hardly permit the devising of a time scale on more than a very generalized basis.

A note of warning concerning the archaeological evidence for early agriculture should be inserted here. The only convincing evidence for the subsistence economics of a prehistoric community is that based on what is primarily zoological or botanical data – in other words, the nature of the animal or plant refuse surviving on the site as a result of the preparation and consumption of food. With respect to animal remains, it must be determined whether the bones are those of wild or domestic breeds; similarly, the seeds of cereals or other crops must be identified as wild or cultivated, on the basis of grain actually surviving or attested by casts in the fired clay of pottery or hearths. In addition, it is possible, under certain circumstances, to demonstrate the advent of agriculturalists in a region by the evidence of significant man-made disturbances in the natural plant cover, as reflected in otherwise inexplicable alterations in the percentages of pollen, or the appearance of the pollen of cultivated plants or their concomitant weeds in the pollen spectrum. The evidence of material culture alone is less explicit. Sickles or reaping-knives need not have been used to harvest a cereal crop, but may have served other purposes, such as cutting reeds: nor must querns, mortars or pounders necessarily be associated with the production of flour.

With these provisos in mind, we may turn to the evidence for the beginnings of food production, or at least of the control of the food supply, in Eurasia. Significantly, this evidence comes from the regions we have already indicated – broadly from the Aegean to the Caspian – where climatic conditions and the pattern of plant and animal distribution would favour such developments in Post-glacial times.

An *a priori* assumption, based on the fact that the dog had been domesticated in more than one Mesolithic community (though, it seems, not in the Natufian of Palestine, a critical culture in the Near Eastern sequence), would be that the capacity of this animal to assist in rounding up herds of game for destruction might be extended to the process of corralling herds of smaller ruminants for at least temporary preservation, or restriction to a certain area. Animal domestication could proceed from such a set of circumstances, and this, in fact, appears to be confirmed by inferences from the archaeological evidence itself. In the Upper Natufian, a not very well substantiated claim for the incipient domestication of the goat has been made, at a date likely to be in the seventh millennium B.C. at least. In domestic or semi-domestic form, goats of the Bezoar or Pasang type (*Capra hircus aegagrus*) were typical of the earlier Jericho settlements of what we will distinguish as Jericho IV, with Carbon 14 dates of about 6840 and 6710 B.C.; the dog had also been domesticated by this time. Again, at Jarmo in northern Iraq, where, although Carbon 14 dates are conflicting, the economic stage of the settlement was equivalent to that of earlier Jericho (the excavator suggests a date of *c.* 6750 B.C.), goats and dogs were the earliest domesticated animals. At the Belt Cave near the southern end of the Caspian Sea, goats and dogs may have been domesticated at a rather later date. At Jarmo, goats (and some sheep) accounted for eighty per cent of the animal bones found, pigs ten per cent, dogs and probably domesticated oxen five per cent, and wild animals the final five per cent. A large land snail was also eaten. At the other end of the map, the earliest agricultural settlements in Greece, those of Thessaly, inland from the Gulf of Volos, show once again an economy based on a high proportion (eighty-three per cent) of goats with some sheep, fewer pigs, and still fewer cattle (not certainly wholly domestic). Sheep and goats are difficult to distinguish skeletally, but it is interesting to note that the identifiable sheep in the Thessalian site of Gremnos-Argissa appear to belong to the *Ovis orientalis* (cf. *vignei*) type, with a natural habitat extending today along a belt of country approximately from the southern end of the Caspian to Nepal. This species, in fact, appears to be ancestral to all domestic sheep, of prehistoric and later times, throughout Europe and Asia, the Soay sheep of St Kilda remaining nearest to the prototype. Although the Mouflon (*O. musimon*) has the most westerly habitat of the wild sheep, surviving today as far west as Corsica, it does not seem to have contributed to any ancient European breed.

The domestication of sheep, which is, of course, well attested for later times throughout all the earlier agricultural communities of western Asia and Europe, does not in the first instance imply the use of wool as a fibre and as raw material for textiles, as the wild sheep is no more woolly than the wild goat. Both must have been bred initially for meat, milk and skins, and the use of wool as a textile fibre is a relatively late prehistoric development. By the seventh millennium B.C., then, we have evidence of the domestication of dogs, sheep and goats in more than one area of the Near East, and at a date so far undetermined, but on general grounds likely to be before 5000 B.C., in eastern Europe as well. By this latter date the rapid and precocious development of human societies in western Asia, as far west as Anatolia, had resulted in the establishment there of settlements with a complex material culture and advanced agriculture which entitle them to be regarded as small towns, with all the criteria of potential civilization. We must retrace our steps and examine the earliest agricultural settlements of shepherds and goatherds in their other aspects.

Plant cultivation had gone hand in hand with animal domestication. We have seen that the archaeological evidence could be interpreted to imply that the final Mesolithic cultures of the type of the Natufian were in fact engaged in growing cereal or similar crops, but direct evidence is lacking. At Jericho agriculture can only be inferred, not demonstrated, for the earliest series of post-Natufian cultures on the site, but from the phase that may conveniently be called Jericho IV (whose Carbon 14 dates have just been cited), actual grain, as evidence of cereal cultivation, survives side by side with the remains of domestic or semi-domestic goats and those of pigs, sheep, and cattle that could be either wild or domestic. The more or less contemporary inhabitants of Jarmo in northern Iraq were cultivating a wheat, known as emmer, which comes very near to the wild *Triticum dicoccoides* that still grows in the area, and a two-row type of barley, similarly close to the wild *Hordeum spontaneum*. Mixed crops of wheat and barley were normal in prehistoric times, and indeed continued through the Middle Ages of Europe (the English 'maslin' (*mixtillum*) corn) and survive in the 'dredge' crops of today. Grain and leguminous seeds of pea or bean type are attested at the Thessalian site.

It is time to turn to the human material culture of these primitive agricultural settlements (purposely left until this point in order to stress the underlying homogeneity of their economy), and to consider the exceptional case of Jericho. In the nineteenth and the early twentieth centuries archaeologists took the use of pottery as one of the distinguishing marks of a 'Neolithic' assemblage of material culture, and thus appeared to make a technological distinction between stone-using cultures otherwise comparable save in this feature. This criterion is still employed in Russian archaeology, presumably owing to its association with Morgan's, and hence Engels's, theories of social evolution. With the recognition of other possible distinguishing factors, and with the more precise documentation made possible by cooperation with the natural sciences, western archaeological thought moved from a technological to an economic model, and made the distinction between Neolithic and other stone-using cultures in terms of subsistence economics: a Neolithic culture must of necessity be based on some form of food production, normally involving the domestication of animals and the cultivation of edible plants.

This new concept led to the recognition of the existence of prehistoric cultures that had an agricultural basis but did not manufacture pottery, and, conversely, of cultures with a hunting and food-collecting basis of Mesolithic type which, nevertheless, included pottery as a characteristic trait. For the former type of culture the phrase 'Pre-pottery Neolithic' has been coined, but this clumsy term carries with it an implication of antecedence to all pottery-using cultures, which is misleading, as such cultures were sometimes only locally without pottery as a cultural trait in areas where pottery-making existed in close proximity. The non-pottery culture in the Quetta region of Baluchistan is such an example (with a Carbon 14 date of about 3300 B.C.), and that of Khirokitia in Cyprus another (Carbon 14 dates of from about 5750 B.C. to about 5610 B.C.). 'Non-pottery' seems preferable to 'Pre-pottery', and perhaps 'aceramic' is better than both. It is clearly unwise to lay too much stress on the presence or absence of a single cultural trait, however important it may seem to the archaeologist today.

The early agricultural communities of the type of Jericho, Jarmo, Argissa, Khirokitia, and Quetta were all of aceramic type, but they exhibit a series of striking variations on the basic pattern of simple stone-using agricultural economies in which containers were made of perishable substances or were represented by stone bowls. The deeply stratified sequence at Jericho present a unique series, so far without even approximate parallels. The site, an oasis adjacent to a copious spring, was first occupied by Lower Natufian hunters, whose visits were permanent or recurrent enough to warrant the making of some form of a structure with a clay platform or floor, and stone sockets for poles which have no obvious utilitarian function and may have been 'ritual' in some sense. For this phase, which we may conveniently call Jericho I, we have a Carbon 14 date of about 8840 B.C. Above this comes Jericho II, thirteen feet of deposits consisting of successive layers of trampled floors of temporary structures; here the simple material culture in stone and bone continues the Natufian tradition.

In Jericho III, however, we have remarkable and dramatic evidence of marked advances in material culture. Agriculture cannot be directly demonstrated for this phase (though there is good evidence of gazelle-hunting), but may be inferred, if only on the grounds that we are now confronted with a settlement of an estimated area of ten acres, with dry-stone defences involving a circuit wall over six feet thick and at least one circular tower, still surviving to a height of thirty feet, with an internal stairway. The likely population has been estimated at some 2,000 persons, housed in round or curved-wall huts, slightly sunk into the ground and having walls of clay bricks or of wattle-and-daub construction. The surviving material equipment includes a stone industry continuing the traditions of phases

I and II, stone bowls of accomplished workmanship, grinding stones and small stone or flint axe blades. Carbon 14 analysis has dated a phase immediately after the building of the circuit wall at about 6935 B.C., so the main period of Jericho III must be earlier than this.

The fourth phase is separated from the third by a discontinuity of stratification, and to some extent by a change in the cultural tradition as well. The Natufian tradition of flint-working is now replaced by another, and the style of architecture changes from one-roomed huts to large rectangular houses of several small rooms, often set round a courtyard, built of mud bricks of a new type, and with floors of finely finished plaster-work. The economy of Jericho IV is now demonstrably that of agriculturalists, with domesticated dogs and goats, and cereal grain (although this has not yet been studied in detail); as before, the material culture includes stone bowls (but still no pottery), a very few axe blades, querns and rubbers, and the serrated flint blades of composite sickles or reaping-knives. One building, of an exceptional nature, has been interpreted as a shrine. Also found at Jericho IV were what are probably ancestral human skulls, their features brilliantly modelled in painted clay, which constitute the earliest known examples from the ancient Orient of a naturalistic tradition in representing the human form.

In its later stages Jericho IV was walled in, and we have Carbon 14 dates from different periods of about 6840 and 6710 B.C. Traces of a similar culture have also been found in the Levant at Abu Gosh in Judea, at Beidha in Transjordan, and in the lowest levels of Ras Shamra in Syria.

In Jericho V and VI we move into a pattern of material culture that would be common throughout the Near East for centuries to come, characterized by communities based on mixed farming, pottery-making, and the occupation of permanent villages. But for the time being we must turn to other sites where the early herding cultures of the type of Jericho IV (and probably III and II) are represented. Of those, Jarmo in northern Iraq has given us much valuable evidence for early animal husbandry and cereal cultivation. Here the settlement has been estimated to have comprised about fifteen houses, with an assumed population of some 150 persons. From the earliest, aceramic levels there seem to have been rectangular-roomed houses, probably with courtyards, built of mud walls on stone footings. The material equipment included well-made stone bowls, a blade industry in flint and obsidian (with composite sickles), clay-lined storage pits, and unbaked clay figurines of humans and animals, and there is evidence of matting and basketry. The frequency of bone awls here, as at other comparable sites, may point to skin clothing, sinew-stitched through perforations made with an awl, rather than woven textiles, which do not need such treatment.

The Thessalian site of Argissa, with rectangular timber-framed huts, has yielded a slighter assemblage, without stone bowls. At both Jarmo and Argissa obsidian was used; at Jarmo the material was probably obtained from sources in eastern Turkey, the nearest 250 miles away as the crow flies, and Argissa's source is thought to be the island of Melos in the Greek archipelago, an even greater distance away by land and sea. Such instances show that the complete economic self-sufficiency sometimes claimed as a distinctive characteristic of earlier Neolithic communities was hardly achieved even in the earliest agricultural settlements. The long-distance transmission of articles and raw materials that was carried out in the hunting and food-gathering cultures of the Old World is enough to demonstrate that a complete reliance on wholly local resources is likely to have been the exception rather than the rule.

The site of Khirokitia on Cyprus shows a comparable aceramic culture (a few ill-baked shards in the lower levels seem hardly significant) again based on the herding of goats and probably of sheep as well. It is remarkable for its circular, beehive-vaulted stone houses (later on occasion used also for burials) arranged along a metalled street, but in other respects – with its fine stone bowls, querns, sickle flints, and blade industry, its stone and clay figurines, and an economy based on the Bezoar or Pasang goat and probably sheep of the *O. orientalis* type – it conforms to the general pattern of settlement so far described. Its date, as we have seen, lies early in the sixth millennium B.C. The Baluchi site, which forms the first occupation-level in the 'tell' of Kili Gul Mohammed near Quetta, was also based on a goat-and-sheep economy, and had a chert blade industry and bone points and awls. It is interesting chiefly for its easterly position and its late date, in the later fourth millennium B.C., which show that aceramic Neolithic cultures need not be more than culturally comparable nor of the same date.

Before turning to the later developments in village economy in the Near East, we may note one important fact which these (and allied) settlements of primitive herders and grain-growers appear to demonstrate. However simple and tentative their agricultural techniques, they seem to have achieved the solution to a social problem which faced all early farming communities in antiquity, namely that of founding and continuously maintaining a settlement in one place. It is usually assumed that such settlements required an assured food supply, presumably both animal and vegetable, to enable the inhabitants to live in one spot over several generations. The problem presents itself in a more acute form in the cultivation of cereal crops than it does in animal husbandry, since the continuous croppings of plots or fields exhausts the soil and may lead (as is inferred from some prehistoric European instances we shall encounter later on) to the adoption of a shifting agricultural pattern, involving the abandonment of the settlement once exhaustion of the land necessitates travelling uneconomical distances from the village to new fields and the opening up of new territory, with a consequent moving of the village to a new site. This periodic moving about can be obviated by various techniques, the simplest being a rotation system whereby land is allowed a period of fallow for natural regeneration; others include restoring nitrogen to the fields through manuring, and the various forms of irrigation and redistribution of silt that were employed in the great river valleys.

If the land is temporarily abandoned to natural regeneration, a long-term cycle with periodic reoccupation of village sites, may in fact be possible. At a Neolithic settlement of the fifth millennium B.C. in the Rhineland it was estimated that the site, of twenty-one households, had been occupied and reoccupied seven times during a period of some 450 years, allowing ten years for each occupation and up to fifty years for scrub regeneration of the cultivated soil.

At such sites the houses were constructed of timber, which in rotting leaves no accumulation to build up a stratified heap of settlement debris, so that the sequence has had to be worked out in terms of the horizontal relationship of overlapping plans or changes in the layout and alignment of the village as a whole. But the use of mud or mud brick, with or without a dry-stone foundation course, as in the Near East and in much of prehistoric eastern Europe, results in the accumu-

1. Lower Palaeolithic hand-axe from the Kharga Oasis, North Africa

2. Advanced Palaeolithic, Gravettian art:

(a) *Limestone figurine of woman from Willendorf, Austria*

(b) *Profile of mammoth carved from mammoth ivory, Pavlov, Moravia, Czechoslovakia*

3. Advanced Palaeolithic, Magdalenian art:

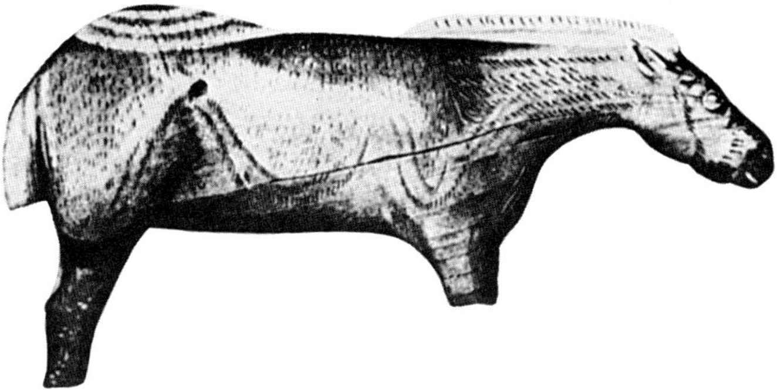

(a) *Ivory figurine of horse, Lourdes, Hautes Pyrénées, France*

(b) *Rock-engraving, Lascaux, France*

4. Arctic or Circumpolar art:

(a) *Rock-engraving of reindeer, Böla, north-west Norway*

(b) *Head of perforated stone axe carved in the shape of an elk's head, Säkkijervi, Finland*

5. Clay statuettes of woman and man, Hamangia culture, Rumania

6. Stone statuettes of women, Blagoevo and Karanovo IV, Bulgaria

7. Internal carved architectural façade, Hal Saflieni, Malta

8. Carved limestone head, La Tène, Msecke Zebrovice, Bohemia

lation of relatively bulky debris on which successive settlements are in turn built, so that the site rises on its own ruins over the centuries to form a stratified mound, or tell. At Jarmo, where there were twenty-five feet of debris (the upper layers being the products of pottery-using people whose material culture in other respects continued the tradition of the earlier aceramic settlements), the excavator distinguished sixteen main phases of rebuilding. Noting that the lifespan of a comparable mud-walled house in the region today was about fifteen years, and that its collapse produced two feet of debris, he very tentatively estimated that Jarmo was occupied for approximately 250 years.

But one question immediately comes to mind. Do these early examples of tell formation (and how many of the rather later sites) really represent a continuous cropping of fields in the immediate vicinity of a permanent settlement under some circumstances involving rotation, fallow, or manuring to avoid exhaustion of the soil? Could they not be interpreted rather in the manner of the Rhenish Neolithic site just cited, as perhaps the result of recurrent reoccupation of the sites in a cyclic rhythm that allowed for natural regeneration over perhaps a relatively large number of years? It seems scarcely credible that from the very beginning of animal and plant husbandry in the Near East a stable form of completely permanent settlement should have been achieved out of a mobile hunting-and-collecting economy virtually overnight. The archaeological evidence would appear superficially the same in the tell stratigraphy whether occupation was continuous or whether relatively long intervals elapsed between the rebuilding periods. What is needed here, and in connexion with other problems arising from the formation of tells which will be touched on later, are new investigations in which soil scientists, in close cooperation with the archaeologists, work on the actual sites and replace with precise data the empirical and sketchy observations made in the past. We are still very ignorant of tell information and of the problems which really confront us in their excavation.

Whatever may have been the situation in the earliest settlements, there seems no doubt that fairly soon the problems involved in the creation of a stable agricultural economy were faced and overcome, so as to allow the continuous cropping of fields relatively adjacent to the village or town, and before long to provide a surplus over the subsistence crop which would permit development in the size, complexity, and purchasing power of the community. This, in fact, provided the necessary basis for all subsequent peasant and non-industrial communities in the ancient and medieval world. The beginnings of the peasant world of antiquity, after these tentative foundations of a food-producing economy, can be traced over wide tracts of the Old World; in some areas they were directly ancestral to such ancient civilizations as those of Sumer, Egypt, India and China, and in other areas, such as in continental Europe and the Eurasian steppe, achieved only a limited degree of technological development and complexity.

After the initial domestication of the smaller ruminants, and of the dog and pig, several animals of outstanding importance, notably cattle, remained to be brought under human control. As we have seen, we cannot with certainty document domesticated cattle in our earliest agricultural settlements, and indeed the large size and comparative ferocity of the wild breeds of the *Bos primigenius* type might well have deterred the earliest farmers from attempting domestication. In the Near East the first certain identifications of cattle are from around 4000 B.C., but these can hardly be the first examples. Thereafter, cattle were rapidly to become one of the most important of domestic animals. They must have been bred primarily for meat, secondarily for milk, and always for hides. Their use as draught animals must have been almost wholly dependent on the knowledge of the effects of castration. With the realization that this operation could produce a docile animal of great strength, the way was open, not only to the first application of non-human power to traction, but also to a better understanding of selective breeding through the use of a minimal number of bulls to serve the cows, with the reduction of the rest of the male animals to the status of oxen. Initially, of course, the cows could be served by allowing them to run with wild bulls (a recent practice in Assam), but the more selective process must soon have followed. The Old World societies which we must next consider had all achieved the domestication of cattle, and the production of draught oxen clearly followed rapidly, for they constitute an essential part of the earliest naturalistic representations. The other animals that were domesticated, such as the onager, the horse, and the camel, may be considered in their turn as they make their appearance later.

## *2. The Legacy of Agriculture and Peasant Economies in the New World*

When we turn to the American continent we encounter an area in which situations, theoretically comparable with those of the Old World, arose in post-Pleistocene times, but were worked out in ways which offer interesting contrasts as well as comparisons with the agricultural beginnings in the latter area which we have just reviewed. These divergencies were in part the result of natural conditions of zoological and botanical distributions ranging between the two hemispheres, but partly the product of the variability inherent in the evolution of human societies, as in individuals, which we shall see operating in the Old World in a notable degree, producing here the classical antithesis of the civilized and the barbarian peoples of antiquity.

In the New World, as we have seen, hunting, fishing and food-gathering economies had been established as the result of immigration from north-east Asia, from the eleventh millennium B.C. at least: a date approximately marking the end of Late Glacial conditions in northern Europe. Henceforward, the American continent was becoming populated by its new species, man, whose material culture and subsistence-economy were equivalent to those of the Advanced Palaeolithic or Mesolithic peoples of the Old World. Climatic conditions in Central and North America in Neothermal times were such as to favour that transition from a food-gathering to a food-producing economy which we have just seen taking place in western Asia, and to some degree a similar change in economy did take place. But only to a certain extent can we really make significant parallels, for natural circumstances prevented a closer similarity in development.

The peculiar and individual quality of the beginnings of food production in prehistoric America, as compared with the Old World, was that mixed farming, involving the domestication of certain of the large mammals as well as the growing of a cereal crop, was never achieved until the modern period of European contact. The dog was already domesticated, it is true, as in Neolithic contexts in the Old

World, but we have seen that this need not be related to an extension of animal husbandry which would involve disruption of the hunting economy to which the domesticated dog primarily belongs. The New World situation was in part determined by the nature of the post-Pleistocene fauna in that hemisphere, which presented fewer animals susceptible to farmyard domestication in the areas favourable to the beginnings of cereal cultivation. But even if wild cattle were not immediately available in such areas as modern Mexico and New Mexico, where we have our earliest evidence of maize cultivation, wild sheep were indigenous to the mountain areas of the Great Basin, as well as antelope and deer, but no attempt seems to have been made to domesticate them in antiquity, nor, when agricultural techniques spread into the natural habitat of the American bison, was this bovid regarded as anything more than an animal to be slaughtered.

We have, then, to deal only with plant cultivation as a factor differentiating food-producing from food-gathering economies in prehistoric America. In many instances, we might be more accurate if we spoke of 'Early Gardeners' than 'Early Farmers', and we will notice that the adoption of cereal agriculture by tribes previously wholly dependent on a hunting and gathering economy often did not result, as appears to have been usual in the prehistoric Old World, in a wholesale adoption of farming and the virtual disappearance of the early mode of life, but in the formation of a mixed economy in which hunting continued to play a very important part. Such mixed situations could in fact be so unstable as to render a return to an almost complete hunting economy an easy and rapid process – for instance, as we shall see, when an alien stimulus such as the fur trade acted as a disruptive agent in early nineteenth-century North America, or the adoption of the horse presented an incentive to a form of nomadism.

The absence of suitable wild species, and therefore the failure to achieve by domestication an efficient draught animal as an alternative to human traction and labour, was of profound significance in the whole development of the higher prehistoric cultures of the New World, from the Andes to New Mexico. We have seen that the production of the ox by castration was an event of far-reaching importance in the ancient Near East, and the lack of domestic oxen or their counterparts in prehistoric America can hardly be dissociated from the absence there of the traction plough and of wheeled vehicles. Such civilization as could be built was necessarily founded on a wasteful expenditure of human labour for which no alternative nor amelioration had been devised.

There is another point of contrast between the Old and New Worlds in the early development and spread of agriculture. In the former area, farming economies from the first involved a complex of skills and technologies comprised in the combination of animal husbandry and cereal cultivation; and within a comparatively short space of time, when farming was being disseminated outside its original area of inception, and among hunting and food-gathering peoples, it had added further technological requirements. It had become, in fact, an economy complete in itself, and its adoption by communities hitherto not food-producers involved an almost total rejection of the previous mode of life except in so far as it could be fitted into the dominant pattern of the new economy.

In America, on the other hand, such a complex economy, capable of transmission in its vigorous entirety, was never achieved. The spread of agriculture in the New World takes the form of the acquisition by communities, who were basically hunters and food-gatherers but may also have independently come to cultivate some plant crops, of the single technique of maize-growing. Such a single skill could be added to the existing economic complex without disrupting it or rendering it immediately obsolete, doing no more than modify the original culture, and not wholly supplanting it. In consequence, this added technology of maize-growing could be dropped as easily as acquired if changing circumstances demanded it, just as pottery-making can lapse in primitive societies if the need for it ceases to be insistent. The New World agricultural picture, then, which we must now examine in more detail, is significantly different from that presented in the Old.

Among the descendants of the Palaeoindian hunter-fishers described in Chapter 5, the evidence for the earliest cultivation of a cereal crop comes from a relatively restricted area of Middle America, in which climatic and botanical factors favoured the emergence of the wild ancestors of Indian corn or maize (*Zea mays*), and *Tripsacum*. *Zea mays* is a species with a very large number of varieties, and the early history of cultivated maize in the New World is, botanically, exceedingly complex. For our purposes, however, we may note that the earliest Central and South American corns seem related to a primitive pod popcorn known, for instance, from the Bat Cave in New Mexico in contexts with Carbon 14 dates around 2500 B.C. The successive occupations at this site and elsewhere are of hunters and food-gatherers, but incipient plant-cultivation may appear before the use of maize.

The sequence has been studied in detail in a series of occupied caves in the Sierra de Tampaulipas and Sierra Madre ranges of Mexico. Here Carbon 14 dates show that the beginnings of cultivated squashes, pumpkins and peppers may go back to between 7000 and 5000 B.C., and in successive phases the subsistence economics of these stone-using peoples, based on hunting and the gathering of wild plants, show an increasing proportion of cultivated vegetable foodstuffs until around 3000 to 2200 B.C., when seventy to seventy-five per cent of the total food supply is estimated to have been provided by wild plants, and 10 to 15 per cent by cultivated species, including the first maize. This fits the Bat Cave evidence, and implies a date in the middle of the third millennium B.C. for the first effective maize cultivation in Mesoamerica. The Mexican sequence then continues to show a gradual increase of cultivated plant foods and a diminution of hunting in the subsistence economy, together with the first appearance of villages with mud-walled (adobe) houses and the establishment of permanent or semi-permanent agricultural settlements.

By 1500 B.C. we are in the so-called Early Pre-classic Maya phase with agriculture involving slash-and-burn methods of land clearance, and digging stick or hoe cultivation of maize, beans, squash, peppers and other vegetables and fruits. On this economy, with a technology still ignorant of metallurgy and of animal domestication, there developed a social pattern of farming villages, concentrated or dispersed, and ceremonial centres such as Cuicuilco in the valley of Mexico, with platform mounds, temples and other ritual structures, which in Classic Maya, in the early centuries A.D., presents us with the well-known features of monumental stone architecture, representational art in carving and painting, and a complex calendrical system recorded in the glyphic script.

There is evidence here and in related areas of a system of 'town-fields' to which communal labour was directed by a central authority or a chief, and of common granaries for storing the harvest; we shall see that some sort of an analogous situation is likely to have obtained in many of the earliest peasant and urban communities in western Asia, and probably eastern Europe as well. In the Maya civilization, as we may reasonably call it, even the primitive agricultural and technological level obtaining there enabled large ceremonial temple-cities to attain proportions such as those of Teotihuacan, with an estimated population of some 50,000 persons in the classic period. By the tenth century A.D. the Toltecs were in the ascendant; a couple of hundred years after, the Aztecs, whose dominance lasted until the Spanish arrived in 1519.

Before turning to other areas of early maize cultivation in the Americas we must touch on the question of other forms of cultivated plants. We have said that we are perhaps more justified in talking of Early Gardeners rather than Early Farmers in a New World context, for garden cultivation of a large range of non-cereal crops is a constant feature. The Chicama valley sites in Peru, for instance, show us (around 2200 B.C. on Carbon 14 evidence) primitive communities, stone-using and without pottery, hunting sea-lions and porpoises, gathering wild plants and cultivating beans, squash and peppers, beans and squash being of constant and recurrent importance in prehistoric American dietaries.

Of the beans, there were four main indigenous species of *Phaseolus* cultivated, the Chicama valley evidence just quoted being the earliest. Squashes and pumpkins were again important food plants native to the New World, and six species of *Curcurbita* were grown – mostly, it seems, originally in Mexico and South America, though the pumpkin encountered by the first European settlers on the east coast of North America, *Cucurbita pepo*, may have been independently domesticated there.

We cannot here discuss the other plants, less important in ancient American cultivation, but we must notice the problems raised by two important species, cotton (*Gossypium* sp.) and the Bottle Gourd (*Lagenaria siceraria*). Both of these appear to be not truly indigenous to the Americans, but of Old World origin. There is a wild cotton native to the New World, but the early specimens known in archaeological contexts there are not of this species, but of one best explained as a hybrid resulting from crossing with Old World cotton:

Peruvian woven textiles of dates before 1000 B.C. are our earliest known examples. The gourds, of an Old World type well known for their use as containers when dried, were widely used; the earliest are from the Tularosa cave site in Mexico in a context before the local use of maize, and probably of the second millennium B.C. These botanical indications of apparent Old World contacts in American prehistory raise fascinating problems, as do the hints of the reverse process contained in the distribution of the *Amaranthus* species (which include Pigweed and Love-lies-bleeding), New World in origin but with representatives in central Asia from Manchuria to Iran!

Central America, as we have seen, appears as one of the main centres in the New World in which a relatively complex prehistoric culture, which we may dignify with the term civilization, was developed on a basis of a stone-using technology and maize agriculture. It was not alone, however, and we may instructively turn to Peru and the central Andes, where we have already noted the early inhabitants of the Chicama valley cultivating beans and squash in the late third millennium B.C. By a period around 1400–1200 B.C. the first maize appears, together with the use of pottery, and from around 500 B.C. we have developed agriculture, adobe villages, ceremonial centres and the first use of gold. Thenceforward, from this Chavin phase we move into the developed classic period from A.D. 800, with its irrigation, its stone architecture and carving, and an increased metallurgical technology in gold, copper and silver. In the southern highlands a contemporary site is that of Tiahuanaco, near Lake Titicaca, and in the north the great mud-brick city of Chan-Chan, covering eleven square miles: later the Incas were to become dominant.

As we have seen, the highly developed Middle American cultures were formally 'Neolithic', in the Old World sense of being agriculturalists using stone or flint or obsidian for edge tools, but in the Andes non-ferrous metallurgy was being mastered in the early first millennium A.D. The first use of gold in a cold-hammered state seems in Peru to be about 300 B.C., but this is no more than the cold-hammering of copper among the North American Indians mentioned again below, and not strictly a true metallurgical process. By about A.D. 700, however, not only cold-hammering but the processes of annealing, soldering and gilding were known to the Andes, as were copper and silver in addition to gold. By A.D. 1100 the first bronze known in the New World is reported from Bolivia. In Mexico metal is hardly known before the Toltec period, in the tenth-century A.D., when competent metallurgy with such techniques as lost-wax casting was practised, though here as elsewhere in the New World before European contact the processes of smelting and casting must always have been inhibited by the absence of bellows, a device never invented in the Americas.

The ancient civilizations of Mexico, the Andes and related areas just discussed represent the summit of achievement among the prehistoric Americans. Like the early civilizations of the Old World, the background of which forms the subject-matter of subsequent chapters, they were economically based on communities whose ancestors had turned from hunters and food-gatherers to sedentary food-producers. But we have seen that, although we speak of an economic change to agriculture in both Old and New Worlds, the word does not have the same connotation in the two hemispheres. In the Old World, cereal agriculture was a part only of a complex of ideas, traditions and technologies fundamental to the emergence of what has been thought of, since classical antiquity, as civilization. But if we extend the concept of civilization to include the Maya or the Chimu as well as the Sumerians or the Greeks, we are aware of including two not wholly comparable degrees of culture. We cannot escape feeling that Mesoamerican culture, even at its highest, is no more than (to adopt a phrase of the seventeenth-century writer Roger North) 'such as an extraordinary high-spirited judicious Barbarian might be supposed originally to invent'.

Beyond these areas of higher culture in the New World, and more especially in the relatively temperate regions of North America, we are concerned with communities of hunters and food-gatherers who wholly or partially adopted agricultural techniques in antiquity. The Palaeoindian background to this situation has been reviewed in Chapter 5, and we have seen in recent pages that the cultural transmission involved was not a complex one, but the acquisition of a single trait of material culture which could to a large extent be absorbed into the indigenous economy without disrupting it or changing it beyond recognition. Indeed, from what we can perceive from the joint evidence of archaeology and ethnography, it appears that the North American Indians never experienced a complete change in economic structure from a hunting to a farming mode of life in the almost universal manner of the transition in the Old World in prehistoric times, even though maize-growing was adopted by most groups where climate permitted. We are presented, then, with a picture of communities in which hunting and food-gathering never lost an important place in their economies, even if its primacy was displaced by cereal cultivation, and perhaps only temporarily.

In large areas of northern America a complex of hunting and food-gathering cultures, grouped as 'Archaic', represent a phase following on the Palaeoindian and rather imprecisely dated between 5000 and 1000 B.C.: a Carbon 14 date for an Archaic settlement and burial site excavated in Massachusetts was about 2300 B.C. (Figure 49). In the eastern United States the ensuing cultures, classed as 'Woodland', represent the tradition which continued until the European advent, with maize, bean, pumpkin and squash cultivation, and pottery whose resemblance in form and decoration to Eurasiatic wares of the so-called Circumpolar tradition, mainly of the second millennium B.C., has raised unresolved problems of possible contact. Elsewhere notable centres of comparable cultures, though not necessarily with maize cultivation, are those occurring in the Mississippi valley, and the Plains cultures of which the Hopewell phase, dated between about the middle of the first century B.C. and that of the first century A.D., is a remarkable culmination.

In general, to simplify an excessively complex situation in which systematic research has only recently been attempted, it appears that in the first millennium B.C. a number of North American Indian cultures, with economies up to that time based on hunting and food-gathering, but with possible local cultivation of such plants as pumpkins or squash, adopted maize cultivation to a greater or lesser degree from ultimately Mesoamerican sources. In areas such as the Lower Mississippi, other cultural traits such as pottery may have been acquired from the same direction, and the cult centres with ceremonial earthworks, if not a local development, may again reflect contacts with the south.

The Hopewell culture, centred in Ohio and the Illinois valley, shows an individual and extraordinary development. The status of its basic economy has been much discussed, and it seems difficult to show

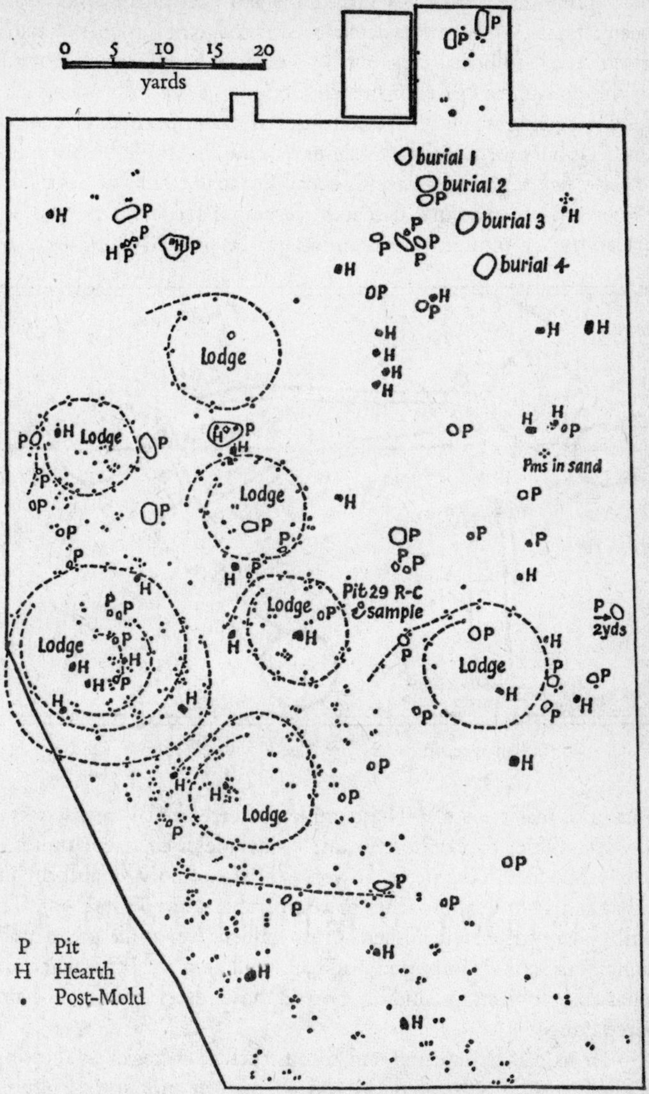


49. Archaic Indian settlement plan, Massachusetts

that agriculture played any important part in it. It may indeed have been absent. We have less detailed knowledge of settlements than of ceremonial and burial sites, but both of these bear impressive witness to the possibilities of coordinated labour in a basically hunting and food-gathering society. Tumulus-burial was practised in elaborate timber-built mortuary houses under mounds that could be from thirty to sixty feet high and curiously recall Eurasian tombs of Scythian or earlier date; earthwork defences, ceremonial enclosures, and such extraordinary monuments as the huge 'Serpent Mound' were also

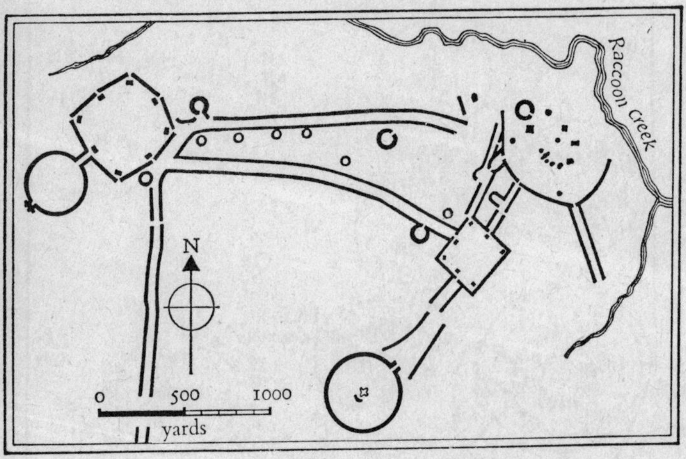


50. Indian ceremonial earthworks, Hopewell culture, Ohio

built on a massive scale. The complex of ceremonial earthworks at Newark, Ohio, to take one example, include circular enclosures of up to 1,000 feet in diameter, as well as others of polygonal form and embanked avenue approaches of comparable scale (Figure 50). The tombs, many richly furnished, show evidence of widespread trade connexions in their imported obsidian, shell or silver ornaments, and remarkable objects, including horned head dresses, in cold-hammered copper.

So far as can be inferred and reconstructed, America at the time of the first European contacts was an uneven mosaic of cultures, ranging from the relatively high achievements of the Mesoamerican and Andean areas, through varying forms of hybrid cultures, combining hunting and gathering with a greater or lesser amount of maize, bean and pumpkin cultivation, to wholly non-agricultural groups. These themselves ranged from the static and prosperous fishing communities of the north-west coast, or the Eskimos with their elaborately contrived Circumpolar economy, to the Yaghans and their neighbours in Tierra del Fuego, still preserving until the present century a Palaeoindian culture of the most primitive kind.

We may notice two factors associated with the European conquest of the New World which not only demonstrate the inherent instability of the North American semi-agricultural communities, but also provide potential parallels for analogous situations which may have existed in Old World prehistory. The first is the introduction of the horse as a domestic animal, first brought to the New World on Columbus's second voyage of 1493, then by Cortéz in 1519, and then in increasing numbers by the successive colonists in the seventeenth century and later. By 1750 the horse as a riding animal had become adopted by almost all the North American Indian tribes where the terrain permitted, particularly on the plains, with a consequent sudden resurgence of semi-nomadic hunting as the most important factor in the economy. This process was accelerated and encouraged by the second factor, the opening up of the fur trade by the Hudson's Bay Company and lesser trading organizations, so that many tribes almost completely reverted to hunting (further facilitated by imported firearms), and not only reduced agriculture to a minimal status in their economy but abandoned such crafts as now became irrelevant. Pottery-making was given up in favour of European metal cooking-pots that did not break in transit on horseback; basketry and rabbit-skin weaving were replaced by a simpler use of skins and hides as material for containers. These examples of sudden economic change, internal although resulting from outside stimuli, in no sense involved the adoption of the culture of the motivating peoples. They must be typical of many comparable sets of circumstances, undocumented by written sources, throughout antiquity.

CHAPTER NINE

# *Peasant Communities of Prehistoric Western Asia*

WE may now return to the Old World and consider the development of early peasant communities in the Near East after the initial stages of animal domestication and plant cultivation had provided a basis for them. In more than one area, such peasant communities were themselves to form the bases upon which literate civilization was built, notably in Mesopotamia and in Egypt, where the evidence of written documents and explicit representational narrative art inform us of the nature of the civilizations created in the two areas from early in the third millennium B.C. The script of the Indus civilization is as yet unread, and its art is less abundant and less susceptible of interpretation in comparable terms than that of the two former nations. The Hittite kingdom was literate from some time in the second millennium, though its culture was not transmitted in an unbroken tradition from the earlier settlements of Anatolia. At the time it becomes comprehensible as a civilization, through literacy and art, it was a mixture, rather, of indigenous and relatively intrusive elements.

In effect, then, though in many regions we shall be dealing with peasant cultures ancestral to those we may dignify with the name of civilization, it will not always be easy to relate the simpler and earlier traditions of culture to the more complex and later situations which were their outcome, save in very generalized terms of technological relationship. Without a knowledge of the 'form' of a given civilization – that is, in Frankfort's use of the term, its essential and distinguishing characteristics – it may be difficult or impossible to perceive, by inference from the archaeological evidence of the pre-literate cultures, what elements may have been transmitted as essential contributions to the developed civilization. On the other hand, lacking the information on the nature of a civilization that only literacy and narrative art can provide, we may be deterred from attempting to make a reconstruction of aspects of the pre-literate cultures not directly documented by archaeological evidence by assuming the earlier existence (in simpler form) of phenomena, such as institutions, already well established when first attested in the literary tradition. But we shall see that in certain very interesting and important instances we can in fact legitimately use evidence contained in the literary record to illuminate aspects of society and organization in the preceding prehistoric phases; such evidence is available from Mesopotamia, Anatolia and Egypt.

The purely technological and mechanistic view of the emergence of civilized societies from the barbaric peasant communities we are about to review, in which civilization becomes a phenomenon inevitably arising from recurrent circumstances of surplus food production, the development of villages and small urban settlements, metal-working and trade, and similar economic factors, is hard to sustain except strictly in terms of the limited technological evolutionary model of archaeological thought. Such a model has, in fact, to be used for much of prehistory, but its continued use as the only means of approach in historical fields in which other evidence is available, and perceptible in terms of other models, can only lead to a false picture. The evidence for prehistory may be amenable to treatment only in terms of the technological model, but in the case of historically documented societies we should count ourselves the more fortunate that we have alternative modes of approach which can be used in conjunction with it. The exclusive preoccupation with technology which characterized the work of V. G. Childe in Oriental archaeology, for instance, was such as to ignore completely the evidence of the nature and character of the literate civilizations provided by their art and writings. A deceptively uniform process of social evolution appeared to be substantiated, when prehistoric and historic societies were treated as if the latter had transmitted to posterity no evidence of their quality and character other than that of material culture in its most narrow aspect. Frankfort was able to demonstrate, in the classic instances of Egypt and Mesopotamia, that two completely differing forms of civilization were in fact based on what in purely archaeological terms seemed closely comparable peasant communities; had we knowledge of the true nature of the Indus civilization we might well find that this differed as significantly from both.

The apparent homogeneity, amounting at times almost to monotony, which we perceive in the archaeological evidence for the earlier peasant communities in the Near East, may in itself be deceptive, and at least should not lead us to expect uniform developments in civilization from all the varied regions where such settlements occurred in antiquity. The evidence we are now about to review shows us, indeed, that the emergence of civilized societies in the Near East was by no means a matter of inevitable sociological development, and that in certain regions the simpler forms of peasant and limited urban economy persisted for centuries close by those areas where exceptional and unpredictable combinations of circumstances and persons brought about one of the manifestations of human achievement which we call a civilization.

It will be convenient to take the various regions in turn, and to consider in each the developments from the simplest agricultural economies. A beginning may be made in Mesopotamia, turning then eastwards to Iran and Turkmenia, and thence to India. Asia Minor and the Levant form another area closely linked to the same world; Egypt with its highly individual and localized traditions, can then be considered as an outpost on the African continent.

The prehistoric culture sequence in Mesopotamia is the best known, and the earliest established in its main outlines. Practically all the basic elements are to be found in the later settlements of Jarmo, running without a stratigraphical break from the earliest aceramic settlements – agriculture at a level of competence sufficient to allow for continuous occupation of one site, pottery-making, villages of close-set agglomerations of rectangular-roomed houses. But the basal settlement of the tell of Hassuna, of a culture more developed than that of Jarmo, was that of nomads who made nothing more permanent than hard standings for tents, though they used the pottery characteristic of the later layers of occupation, when mud-walled houses were being built. Clay-lined storage pits for grain now appear, a large range of pottery types, plain and painted, stone blades for the hoes used to cultivate the corn plots, reed matting, sling bullets of clay or stone, and clay figurines of women. For the Hassuna culture we have Carbon 14 dates of about 5610 B.C. for a relatively early phase and around 5080 B.C. for a mature phase.

We have here certain elements of material culture which were to become recurrent throughout the peasant communities of western Asia, and it is worth-while commenting on them at this point. The making of pottery with painted designs on its surface, usually in dark brown or black on a reddish or buff background, is a technical accomplishment of a relatively high order. It necessitates baking in a kiln which prevents access of free flames to the pots, and firing to a high temperature; moreover, it demands a knowledge of the empirical chemistry involved in choosing and controlling the composition of slips and paints which will fire to the desired combination of colours or tones. In principle, a potter's kiln is closely allied to the type of smelting furnace necessary for extracting copper and other metals from the parent ore, and the coincidence of the earliest copper-working in the Old World with the Neolithic centres of production of painted wares can hardly be dismissed. Throughout the cultures now under review the first tentative beginnings of copper metallurgy soon developed into accomplished craftmanship in this metal and in bronze, so that by Early Dynastic Sumer, in the middle of the third millennium B.C., skill in bronze working had reached a level approximating to that of the Italian Renaissance.

The use of the sling in hunting and warfare, rather than the bow and arrow, was to become a western Asiatic and Aegean practice in prehistory. The bow and arrow have, as we have seen, an ancestry in Palaeolithic and Mesolithic cultures, and always remained essentially African weapons; they are typical, for instance, of Ancient Egypt. But the sling was early established as an alternative weapon in Mesopotamia and the Near East, where the bow was to return only at a somewhat later date, whereas the use of the bow, in part or wholly based on surviving Mesolithic traditions, was always characteristic of western Europe.

A third element is the prevalence of a related group of religious beliefs which find their archaeological expression in figurines of women, and to a lesser extent of domestic or, more rarely, wild animals, especially cattle. Such figurines, normally modelled in clay but on occasion carved in stone, have an almost universal distribution in the western Asiatic peasant cultures under discussion, and occur in circumstances that suggest that their place was in the household shrine rather than in any formal temple. What relation these early examples from prehistoric contexts may have had to cults which survived to be documented in the earlier literate civilizations is hardly to be determined save in the most general terms, but we may guess at variants on the theme of the earth-mother, associated with fertility, the agricultural seasons, and rebirth, or with the Lady of Beasts, the *potnia theron*, whose cult seems attested in Anatolia as early as the sixth millennium B.C. The cults represented by these figures seem primarily Asiatic, as the figures in their household context have no real counterparts in, for instance, prehistoric Egypt, with its already distinctively African type of culture; but they occur in profusion in a large number of early agricultural communities in Eastern Europe, which we have reason to regard as westerly counterparts of the cultures now under discussion.

To return to the Mesopotamian archaeological sequence, we note the development in northern Iraq and Syria of local cultures, such as at Halaf, distinguished by a very high quality of painted pottery, and at Arpachiya on the Habur river, a settlement with circular beehive-vaulted structures comparable with those in the aceramic culture of Khirolitia in Cyprus. In the subsequent Mesopotamian phase, that of Ubaid, we see for the first time the colonization of the swampy regions of the lower Tigris-Euphrates basin, around what was then the mouth of the Persian Gulf, but now some 150 miles inland. At least some trade contacts between the northern regions and the Gulf had already been established; sea-shells imported to the Habur river region are evidence of this. But the colonization of the southern Iraqi marshlands need not have taken place from the north, and indeed the evidence is against this supposition; the south-east, from the highland regions across the Tigris, seems a more likely point of origin.

Seal-shaped pendants capable of impressing a geometric design upon soft clay were known in Mesopotamia from Halaf times onwards, and could have been used in pre-literate antiquity for denoting ownership, as were their historical counterparts. Such 'stamp seals' recur throughout many of the ancient western Asiatic peasant cultures and, as we shall see, have their representatives in the early village communities of eastern Europe (Figure 51). In Mesopotamia, stamp seals were almost wholly replaced by cylinder seals, rolled on the clay to impress their designs, in Proto-Literate times, at the end of the fourth millennium B.C.

The Ubaid culture was to be of considerable importance for the whole of the subsequent prehistory and early history of Mesopotamia. In the colonization of the southern marshlands, the newcomers were forced to devise elaborate systems to separate the lands from the waters, and to utilize the surplus for irrigating the adjacent semi-desert areas. This painful and necessary acquisition of skills was to stand the colonists' descendants in good stead. Having established themselves, the creators of the Ubaid culture were able to effect colonization northwards and to spread throughout the area that was later to become the early kingdom of Sumer something of a common tradition. As we shall see, it is the anonymous creators of what appears in archaeological nomenclature as the Ubaid culture who have the best claim to be in fact ancestral Sumerians themselves. Carbon 14

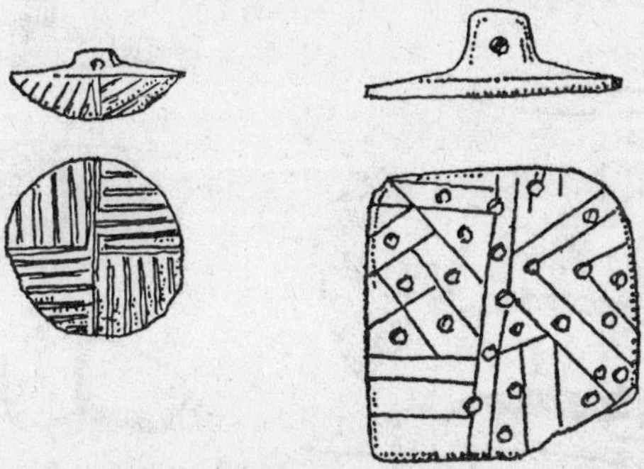

51. Stamp seals, Sialk

dates for two phases within the Ubaid culture are around 4015 B.C. and 3450 B.C.

The newcomers in the delta of the Two Rivers had to contend with many difficulties, not least with a shortage or non-existence of the material resources to which they must have been accustomed in their original homeland. They were especially handicapped by the lack of metal and stone. The archaeological evidence makes it clear that the use of copper shaft-hole axes must have been known to the Ubaid settlers at some time in their history, as these and related types are reproduced in fired clay and in forms only appropriate to metal. Not only this: pottery 'battle-axes' exist which copy stone forms which themselves reproduce types proper to cast metal, so that we are at two removes from a copper-using economy (Figure 52). And instead of sickles with a curved cutting edge made of serrated flint blades, in what was now an ancient tradition, we find sickles made entirely of hard-fired clay. However, neither the shaft-hole axes nor the battle-axes can be regarded as functional, but rather as the reproduction of unobtainable and expensive weapons of prestige in the only locally available material – mud. Similarly, building techniques were developed to deal with the prevailing situation, so that not only was mud-brick architecture brought to a high level of competence, but a number of useful tricks were devised, such as waterproofing reeds with bitumen, which seems to date from this time.

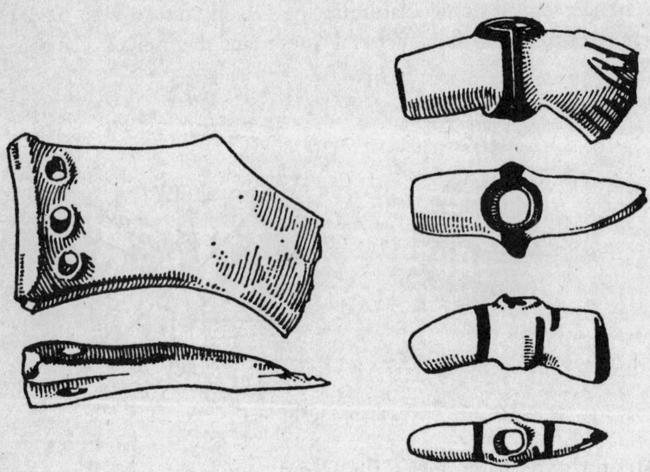

52. Clay models of copper axes, Ubaid culture, Tell Uqair

One of the most important developments within the Ubaid phase, however, was to have far-reaching effects on later Sumerian society, and affords a significant link between prehistoric and early historic Mesopotamia. This was the embodiment in monumental architectural form of what must have crystallized out of developments in Ubaid religious speculation and liturgy, the concentration of certain aspects of ritual and belief in a building which transcended the household shrine with its symbolic figurines of the goddess and her beasts. The temple, with all that it implied in the social and political structure of later Mesopotamia, can first be recognized as an architectural concept of Ubaid times. This tangible embodiment of a system of belief and thought, to be intimately bound up with the beginnings of writing and literature as well as with important social and economic aspects of the community, can first be perceived at Eridu in the earliest structure of what was to be a long-venerated site. Here, in the middle of the Ubaid phase, are already to be found the basic planning and proportions of a long series of Sumerian temples; in the north of Iraq, at Tepe Gawra, another approximately contemporary structure repeats, on a rather smaller scale, the same formal planning of a long central hall with flanking lateral chambers. Such planning, with minor modifications, was to become as traditional for the Sumerian temple as the formalized plan of church or mosque has become for the Christian or the Moslem world. Religious architecture is essentially the monumental setting for a series of prescribed ceremonies involving the position and movement of priests and celebrants; it is the three-dimensional embodiment of liturgy, and the tangible memorial to its conduct. Through the Mesopotamian religious tradition we can take the story of continuity from prehistoric Ubaid to literate Sumer a step further. In the prehistoric sanctuary at Eridu itself was found an altar six inches deep in a litter of fish bones; in historical times the city was famed for the cult of Enki, the water and fish god:

> When Enki rose, the fishes rose and adored him:
> He stood, a marvel unto the Deep.

Enki had arisen from the waters of the Gulf when the first Ubaid colonists made their brave settlements in that ambiguous territory of land and water, symbolic indeed of primeval Chaos and Old Night.

From the traditions established in the Ubaid culture were to evolve the beginnings of historical Sumer and its successor states. The succeeding Uruk and Jemdet Nasr phases are sometimes grouped as the Proto-Literate period; late in the earlier of these two phases, the first evidence of writing is contained in clay tablets inscribed with pictographic symbols. The whole period between Ubaid and the first dynasties of Sumer, by whatever name we call it, was one of growing technological competence in many fields. Temple architecture is refined and elaborated, especially at Uruk itself, where there is a notable series of buildings with polychrome surface decoration in geometric patterns built up of a mosaic of coloured pottery cones;

the ziggurat, or artificial temple-tower, is also already in being. Art, in the form of mural paintings, sculpture, and the miniature glyptic of seals, takes on a new representational and indeed narrative aspect. And most significantly, as we have seen, we encounter at this time the first written documents of Old World antiquity. The inscribed clay tablets which constitute these documents are concerned with the mundane affairs of temple accounts, which had reached a degree of complexity in which fallible human memory or simple systems of tallies could no longer provide a sufficient record. Basically pictographic, it must, almost from the start, also have employed pictograms as ideograms; signs must on occasion stand for concepts or words. In the latter instance we are approaching the more complex idea that a pure sound may be denoted by a sign, the phoneme by the grapheme, irrespective of any independent meaning that sound may have apart from its context. This concept of the arbitrary value of graphemes, significant only in combination, involves a mental process comparable to the appreciation of numerical position in mathematics: in the Proto-Literate numerical notation we note a sexagesimal system as already established (which survives even today in the compass-card and the clock-face).

We are here on the threshold of history, faced with a society complex enough to be reckoned civilized, but we may pause for a moment to consider the phenomenon of representational and narrative art (which we similarly encounter here for the first time). This we must distinguish from those elements of naturalism and narration that Advanced Palaeolithic art and later styles (as the eastern Spanish rock-shelter art) may contain, which are unrelated to the problem under discussion, and also from one startling exception in Anatolia, discussed in a later section. We note in Mesopotamia, Egypt and, to a lesser extent, India, the emergence of a representational and increasingly formal narrative art style concurrently with the first intimations of a written script. We may turn further afield to other contexts – Minoan Crete, Geometric Greece, Etruscan Italy – and suspect that we are dealing with analogous situations. Are not in fact the two modes of presenting the mental concept in visual form – writing it schematically in pictograms or ideograms, and depicting it in representational conventions of paint, line, or volume – essentially parallel concepts and performances? It should surely be no surprise that the two phenomena do in fact appear concurrently in the same context on more than one historical occasion.

We must, therefore, as throughout our study of the ancient and thus alien world, clear our minds of modern presuppositions about the nature of a work of art. 'There was no such distinction in ancient Egypt between the scribe who expressed himself in words and the artist who embodied ideas in form, as there is in modern art'; these words, written of narrative reliefs of the twelfth century B.C., are equally applicable, within Egypt or outside, at the very dawn of literacy. Up to this point in the evolution of human consciousness, and beyond it in those areas where the shift of viewpoint did not occur, we find a stylized art convention in which 'man is a stranger', and even the beasts are subject to reduction to a formalized notation, and abstract pattern is dominant. This, in the ancient Near East, is essentially the art of the painted pottery so characteristic of the prehistoric peasant cultures now under review; in Mesopotamia, on the eve of literacy in the Proto-Literate and Early Dynastic periods, there is a final phase of narrative vase-painting as exemplified in the 'Scarlet Ware' of the Diyala region, but beyond this lies a plain, utilitarian, pottery tradition, and the artist is employed elsewhere, and with a new application of his skills.

It is at this point, on the conventional boundary between prehistory and history, that we must leave the Mesopotamian scene and turn to seek parallels or divergencies in adjacent geographical areas. The boundary is, of course, more than a conventional one. History must be different from prehistory, because it involves a model of the past which must take into account a large and varied body of evidence which is not that of archaeology in the sense of the archaeological evidence used to write prehistory. But at a final stage of this chapter we must return to consider the extremely important evidence for those aspects of the social and political organization of prehistoric Mesopotamia that survived to be incorporated in later practice, and so described in historical texts. Sumer and Akkad were not alone in preserving these traditions of government and polity from a preliterate age, and we shall see that Anatolia provides us with a situation remarkably similar, Egypt with one wholly divergent. But discussion of these situations, and of their possible implications beyond the Near East, is best put aside until the evidence for communities comparable with those of prehistoric Mesopotamia in other areas has been presented.

Eastwards from the Land of the Two Rivers the country rises in mountain ridges, and beyond them are large tracts of desert that were probably not much more hospitable in antiquity. Immediately to the south-east of the kingdoms of Sumer and Akkad, between what was then the north shore of the Persian Gulf and the foot-hills of the Zagros mountains, the kingdom of Elam, with its main centre at Susa, emerged from a prehistoric background wholly comparable with that edge of the central Persian deserts of the Dasht-i-Kavir and the Dasht-i-Lut, and extending to the Elburz mountains at the southern end of the Caspian Sea, sites exist which provide evidence for the emergence of village communities in a manner similar to those of the Iraqi area. Still further to the north, across the mountains in Russian Turkmenia, a string of settlements below the northern foot-hills of the Kopet Dagh range continue the same story, and bring us to the northern frontier of the peasant village communities we are studying here. Beyond lie the Oxus river and the Aral Sea, and we enter the southern edge of another and quite dissimilar province, prehistoric Eurasia, at a notably lower technological level and in part retaining the hunting and food-gathering traditions of the Mesolithic to a late date.

The site of Tepe Sialk in Kashan is adjacent to an oasis formed by a perennial spring on the western edge of the Dasht-i-Kavir. The basal layers in the tell, though consisting of over ten feet of material, contained no recognizable remains of buildings, but above this deposit are four building levels of mud-walled houses. The material culture from the lower levels includes good painted pottery, stone hoe blades, querns, and mortars, and a blade industry with at least one piece of imported obsidian. Flint blades were mounted in bone hafts to form composite-edged knives comparable to the Natufian reaping-knives; one from Sialk has a very stylized animal's head at its butt, and another is carved to represent a kilted or skirted human figure. Sheep or goats, and perhaps cattle, were domesticated, and gazelles and other wild species hunted. Slings were used, and the presence of spindle whorls implies the spinning of fibres and presumably the weaving of textiles. No clay figurines are reported. The use of native copper, neither smelted from a parent ore nor subsequently cast, but simply hammered cold from the pure metal, is attested by a few awls and pins. Crouched burials, reddened with ochre, were found among the houses of the settlement.

Across the Kopet Dagh, at the edge of the Kara Kum desert north of Ashkabad, similar sites have been found at the mouth of streams running down from the foot-hills of the mountains. At Jeitun and Chopan Tepe, a culture with a flint-working tradition comparable to that of the early Sialk settlement has been identified; the settlement at the former site occupied an area nearly 300 by 200 yards, and at the latter the accumulated debris of mud-walled dwellings had accumulated to a height of twenty feet. Barley and probably wheat were grown, some goats or sheep were domesticated, and their wild counterparts, together with saiga and gazelle, were hunted. The flint equipment includes microlithic forms and sickle blades in bone handles; bone awls and stone mortars were used, together with a simple form of painted pottery. The houses were small, square and single-roomed (Figure 53).

Both in northern Iran and in Turkmenia we can see, then, the beginnings of agricultural settlement in a manner closely comparable to that of the Mesopotamian sequence. The material culture is slightly more complex (with pottery in both regions, and native copper in use at Sialk), but the situation is otherwise comparable to the aceramic herding settlements with which we began our survey. We need not assume a 'diffusion' of agricultural techniques from any one centre, however, though chronological priority must be given to some areas. What we appear to have, over a relatively large area of the Near East, is the independent emergence of simple agricultural economies based on herding and grain-growing, each subsequently developing a slightly divergent variant of the basic pattern. Regionalism becomes distinguishable mainly in pottery styles, which need not of course indicate anything more than local schools of craftsmen, and certainly cannot on their own be taken to imply any deep cultural separation or affiliation between comparable or contrasting groups. The growth of trade, particularly after copper and bronze metallurgy had been developed, and luxury objects such as gold, semi-precious stones, and shells were involved, was to link up the settlements of western Asia and spread a degree of basic cultural uniformity over large areas.

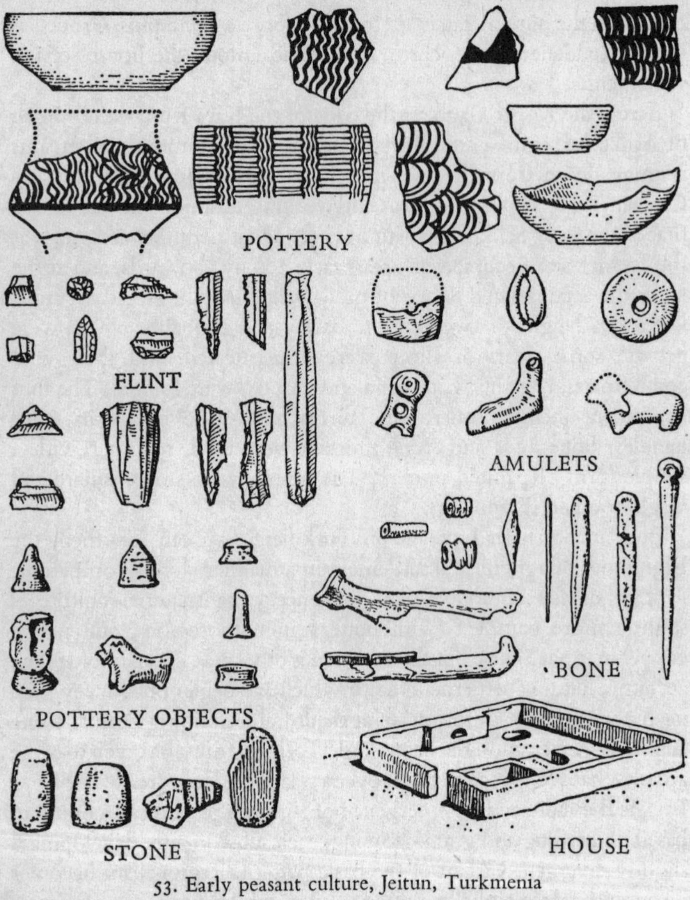


53. Early peasant culture, Jeitun, Turkmenia

The mature development of these peasant communities in prehistory can be traced in a large number of excavated sites in Persia: at Sialk itself, at Tepe Giyan, at Tepe Hissar at the foot of the Elburz, and at sites in Fars. In Turkmenia the incomplete evidence long known from the site of Anau near Ashkabad can now be augmented and better understood as the result of new work on many comparable tells, notably that of Namazga in the same district. There is, in both areas, a direct evolution from the earlier cultures: at Sialk this can be observed in direct stratigraphical succession on the same site, and in the Ashkabad region the earliest culture in the stratified sequence at Anau is closely related to that of Jeitun. The painted pottery tradition is developed to a degree of often brilliant competence, though in its first phases the wheel was not yet used; at Sialk actual kilns for firing pottery have been found, with provision for a regulated air intake whereby the temperature could be raised under controlled conditions. In the approximately contemporary settlements of Turkmenia we can see a uniform culture extending for some 500 miles south-east from the shores of the Caspian Sea; settlements of up to thirty-six acres in area, and large houses of up to eighteen rooms of mud-brick construction, have been excavated. In some of the sites the internal walls of the rooms in the houses are plastered and painted with geometric designs of the same type as those on the pots; these must antedate the earliest wall paintings in Mesopotamia – those on the walls of the Uruk period temple at Tell Uqair, which date from the end of the fourth millennium B.C. But it is interesting to see how in Turkmenia the paintings simply transfer the abstract patterning of the pots to the walls, whereas at Tell Uqair at the dawn of literacy the mural art is already representational, monumental, and probably narrative as well, whereas the contemporary pots on the site have no more than stylized and geometric ornament. Here we already have two forms of art, side by side, one deriving from the ancient non-literate tradition, and the other new and instinct with the pictorial concepts of the literate mind.

In both Persia and Turkmenia we now see a phase of technological advance and consolidation which marks the heyday of this prehistoric culture, at a date which might be estimated as the middle of the fourth millennium B.C. – at Sialk the destruction of the final settlement of this culture on the site and the establishment of a trading post from Proto-Literate Elam give us a chronological *terminus ante quem*. Copper, and probably bronze, metallurgy had now been mastered to a degree of competence which involved not only the primary processes of extracting the ore and smelting the metal but also the capacity to cast the metal in closed moulds. We have noted how in this field of primitive industry a knowledge of kilns and furnaces, of raising the temperature of burning charcoal by a forced draught, and the careful control of the whole complex of processes concerned, must have been learnt in the firing of fine painted pottery. The principles of the potter's kiln and the simple metallurgical furnace for non-ferrous metals are so basically the same that the transference of the skills learnt in the older craft to the creation of a new industrial process would make the transition easy, once the fundamental properties of ore and metal and the processes required for their separation and manipulation had been grasped.

This technological achievement – the transition, in older archaeological terminology, from a 'New Stone Age' to a 'Copper Age' or a 'Bronze Age' – could have taken place independently in more than one area where native copper and copper ores were locally present and available for potential exploitation. But so far as western Asia is concerned, a case could be made, on the available evidence, for the invention of non-ferrous metallurgy within a single limited region (though perhaps at more than one centre), where the raw metal does in fact occur naturally, with a subsequent spread of the knowledge and techniques through the movement of itinerant craftsmen and traders to adjacent communities. Broadly speaking, the Iranian highlands would be an area suited by geology and by what we know of the prehistory of the region concerned. There remains one point, however, that of the fairly advanced copper-working implied by the clay models of such tools as shaft-hole axes in Ubaid contexts, already mentioned. Actual shaft-hole adzes at least are known as products of early metallurgy in Elam and at Sialk, but only at a date slightly before or contemporary with Proto-Literate Sumer. Some of the Ubaid models (at Tell Uqair, for instance) belong to a late phase of the culture, as do the one or two actual copper objects of the Ubaid phase. If the original Ubaid colonists did in fact come from the adjacent highland regions at a time before copper metallurgy had been developed, subsequent contact with the same region could explain the acquisition of some of the first products of the new industry, and the copying of them in clay, at a time immediately before the Uruk phase of Sumer. The real development of copper and bronze-working in Mesopotamia would then be a part of the general advance in technology and other fields of human endeavour which characterizes this period and that of the Proto-Literate.

In this same culminating phase of the peasant communities of Iran and Turkmenia other technological innovations appear, including the invention (or perhaps more probably the adoption from Sumer) of the wheel. Pottery thrown on the wheel appears at Sialk at a relatively late phase, and a wheel from a model pottery cart comes from the contemporary settlement of Namazga III near Ashkabad, with a Carbon 14 date of about 2750 B.C. Wheeled (as well as sledge-type) vehicles are represented in the Proto-Literate pictographic script, vehicles, models, and representations in art become common in Sumer and Elam from Early Dynastic times. Here again we appear to have a well-documented example of invention in a restricted area, with subsequent diffusion over great tracts of Eurasia. The two standard types of vehicles, the two-wheeled cart and the four-wheeled wagon, seem to have been built from the beginning, and by Early Dynastic times the former had also been adapted into a battle car, drawn by domesticated onagers (*Equus onager*). The development of the cart and wagon is, of course, intimately bound up with the domestication of cattle and, as we have seen, with the use of castration to produce a docile draught animal. Where the animal bones have been studied, all settlements of the area and period under consideration show that cattle were fully domesticated by the middle or latter half of the fourth millennium B.C. In Namazga III we have our first evidence of the camel, which is also amenable to use as a draught animal, although it is unlikely that this was the primary reason for its domestication; the camel is also found in a comparable context at Shah Tepe in northern Persia.

The vehicles of this early period, and for centuries to come, were made with solid or virtually solid wheels, cut from a single plank or more often from three planks jointed together to make the characteristic 'tripartite disc' wheel. Such a primitive and heavy form was partly the outcome of a simple technology, which lacked the refinements in bronze tools necessary to make a spoked wheel. However, the finished cart or wagon was wholly adequate for the main purpose for which it was needed – a slow-moving but strongly built contrivance, driven by ox-power, to transport material in bulk over rough surfaces. Simplicity and strength were the desired qualities, so that the vehicles could be made or repaired in almost any village and could stand up to the rigours of use over difficult terrain. Speed was immaterial, and the added weight of the unspoked wheel was of little consequence in field or farmyard. It is significant that when vehicles with light-spoked wheels were first produced, in the middle of the second millennium B.C., they were war chariots drawn by horses, in which lightness and speed were at a premium. One need go no farther today than the Anatolian plateau to see the heavy ox-cart or wagon with its tripartite disc wheels, fulfilling its immemorial functions on the farms, while the smart merchant from the town drives a light cart, with spoked wheels constructed, incidentally, in a peculiar technique at least as ancient in Europe as the pre-Roman Celtic world. The use of ox-drawn carts or wagons must have played its part in increasing agricultural efficiency, both in the transport of harvest and in manuring, not only by virtue of the bulk of material that could

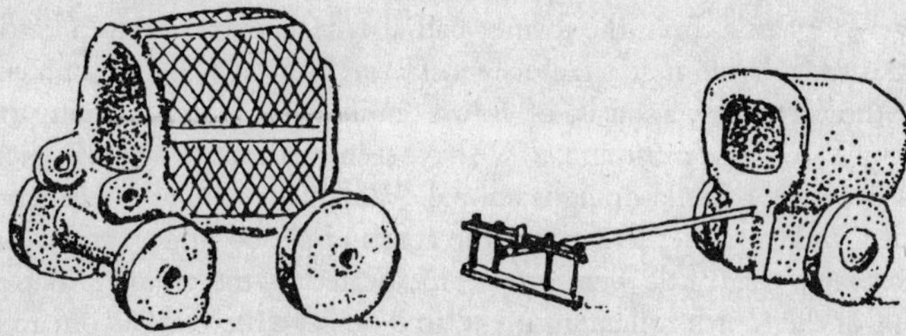

54. Model covered wagon from Tepe Gawra, and covered cart from Tri Brata, south Russia

be carried but in the relatively long distances that could be covered beyond those reasonable for human transport or even for transport by sledge. Wagons or carts are known in Proto-Literate and Early Dynastic Sumer, in the later third millennium B.C. in the Ukraine, and in the early second millennium in northern Europe (Figure 54).

Our next geographical region in this survey of related prehistoric cultures in western Asia is that of Baluchistan and north-western India, where pottery styles suggest links between the peasant communities of that area and the cultures of Persia and Turkmenia already described; indeed, we appear to see here the eastern frontiers of a group of related cultures stretching from the Caspian Sea to the Khyber Pass. Of the intervening area of Afghanistan we know little that can contribute to our knowledge of the earlier stages of development with which we are now concerned, and we take up the story again on the frontiers of the Indian sub-continent, in the region of the Bolan Pass, which gives access from the Baluchi highlands to the Indus plain. Here, as we have already seen, in the neighbourhood of Quetta an aceramic culture is basal at one tell, certainly, with a Carbon 14 date as late as around 3300 B.C. – approximately contemporary with the late Ubaid or the Uruk phase in Sumer. The subsequent settlements of mud-walled houses in this region have a restricted material culture, with painted pottery allied to that of Namazga and related sites, of which they may be provincial outposts. Further north, in the Zhob valley, the stratified sequence in the Rana-Ghundai tell shows us that it was first occupied by people who made unpainted pottery and domesticated not only sheep of the O. *vignei* type but also cattle recognizable as the distinctive type of *Bos indicus*. The essentially Indian character of Indian prehistory, so marked in many features of its more mature development, is hinted at here from the very start. We cannot tell on the available evidence how much the beginnings of these Indian peasant communities may have owed to stimuli from outside (presumably from the west), and how much to independent moves towards incipient agriculture and animal domestication from an assumed but unproven final Mesolithic population, but on the whole the spread of colonists bringing with them a simple farming economy from the Irano-Turkmenian region seems the more probable.

From such beginnings, what appear to be rather impoverished peasant cultures, differentiated by a number of vigorous styles of painted pottery, grew up in the valleys of the Baluchi mountain ranges and on the eastern foot-hills overlooking the plain of the Indus. Little is known of the details of the settlements, as excavations have been few and in the main limited to obtaining pottery sequences and establishing significant variants in pot-painting on a geographical basis. Houses of mud or mud-brick walls on stone foundations seem to be the norm, however, and clay figurines of women and domestic animals (usually recognizably the humped *Bos indicus*) are common to all areas. A few copper implements are known, but it is difficult to be sure whether any are earlier than the period of contact between these settlements and the developed civilization of the Indus basin, and the same is true of the models of carts which appear on more than one site, where styles of pot-painting as well reflect contact with Indus idioms and motifs.

The relationship of these peasant villages and small towns to the genesis of the Indus civilization is, as is well known, a much-debated question. The situation remains in a condition of great uncertainty, owing partly to the lack of purely archaeological evidence, partly to our ignorance of much of the content of the Indus civilization itself because of our inability to read its script, and partly again to the restricted range of its naturalistic art. A few points may be made, however. In the first place, it is only in a limited deep excavation at Harappa that a stratum containing material anterior to the Indus civilization itself has been discovered in stratigraphical relationship, and here only a handful of potsherds typologically related to northern Baluchi wares intervene between virgin soil and the first settlement of the mature Harappa culture. We know, in fact, the material culture of the Indus civilization only in an evolved form, notably in the script, which is clearly the product of a long period of development wholly lost to us. The features that the Indus civilization and the peasant cultures of Baluchistan or Sind have in common are best explained in terms of trading or other contacts between the two worlds, and only in the most general terms can it be said that one might represent a tradition ancestral to the other. Even in chronology there may be difficulty, for both the Carbon 14 date of Kili Gul Mohammed and the likely equations which can be made in terms of pottery styles with regions to the west hardly allow of an antiquity beyond the fourth millennium B.C., which leaves only another thousand years to contain the whole sequence up to the point at which the by then highly developed Indus civilization can be related by reciprocal imports with Mesopotamia at the end of Early Dynastic times around 2350 B.C.

Our inability to read the script and the limited nature of the art of the Indus civilization make it peculiarly difficult to appreciate its 'form', in Frankfort's sense of the term, and hence to look for antecedents which might in part determine this form in inferences from the material culture of the prehistoric periods. One may, however make a few possibly significant points. Unless they have been missed by consistently inadequate excavations, no trace of structures that can be construed either as temples or as palaces has been found in any of the Irano-Turkmenian sites, nor in the Baluchi and Sind sites that may represent their easterly outposts. There appears, therefore, nothing that could reasonably be considered architecturally antecedent to the defended citadels of Harappa or Mohenjodaro in the known layout of these earlier villages or small towns in the manner in which the early temples of Eridu and Gawra provide the simple prototypes for the later temple developments in Mesopotamia. Here discontinuity rather than persistence of tradition might be indicated. The script, pictographic in origin but, by the time we encounter it, in a state of sophisticated development, bears no relation, except in so far as it *is* a script, to those of contemporary Mesopotamia or other literate societies, and the use of stamp seals rather than cylinders seems to preclude Sumerian or Akkadian connexions.

On the other hand, the black-on-red painted pottery tradition that survived into the Indus civilization, and indeed flourished side by side with a large utilitarian output of plain wares, might be held to argue for some form of continuity from the northern Baluchi ceramic styles. Again, the prevalence of female figurines in both the peasant communities and the literate civilization suggests at least a participation in a common cult, if not an inherited religious tradition. The fact is that, on present showing, we must frankly confess our ignorance of the real origins of the Indus civilization, and can say no more than that in the simpler societies of Baluchistan and Sind the necessary technological level upon which a civilization could be built did in fact exist. In this civilization as we know it, we are confronted with a *fait accompli*; the circumstances and occasion at which the first decisive steps were taken towards its foundation still elude us. Refuge in a theory that 'ideas of civilization' were somehow prevalent in western Asia in the fourth and third millennia B.C., and were thus responsible for the genesis of the Indus civilization, seems unrealistic and at variance with what we can infer of the emergence of civilized societies elsewhere. A frank confession of our ignorance seems the wiser course.

Elsewhere on the Indian sub-continent, beyond the ambit of the Indus civilization, the emergence of simple peasant societies is hard to document, though recent excavations planned with the elucidation of this problem in mind have given us some information. In the Andrha region of south-east India, communities that used microliths and ground stone axes and domesticated goats or sheep and cattle (including *Bos indicus*) have been given a Carbon 14 date of around 2100 B.C. Of approximately the same period are the earlier settlements at

Navdatoli, on the Narmada river, sixty miles south of Indore. The inhabitants were predominantly stone-using, with a microlithic industry and ground stone axes, but they possessed a few copper objects – axe blades, fish-hooks, pins and rings, perhaps acquired by trade. Their economy was based on domesticated goats or sheep, cattle, and pigs; wheat was their staple crop in the earlier phases, but was replaced by rice at a later stage, together with peas, beans, lentils and other edible seeds. The village of Navdatoli has been estimated as comprising some fifty to seventy-five houses – of bamboo framing with clay and cow-dung plaster, both circular and rectangular in plan – with a population of about 200 persons. An accomplished pottery craft was established, but some wares seem to have been imported from Rajputana. An undated but possibly broadly contemporary site at Nevasa, 110 miles north-east of Poona, has rectangular timber-framed huts, a flint industry of 'Mesolithic' type with lunate and trapeze forms, pottery and domesticated cattle. There is no direct evidence that grain was grown.

We must now turn westwards and examine the earlier prehistoric peasant communities in an area of great fascination and complexity, those of the Levant and Asia Minor. In part, as we shall see, the geographical position of this region rendered its Mediterranean coastland more or less a single culture-province in antiquity. But in Asia Minor at least two other provinces can be perceived from at least the middle of the third millennium B.C., that of the Anatolian plateau north of the Taurus mountains, and that of the western lands with their indented coastline and archipelago of islands in the Aegean. We know little of the earlier prehistory of the northern, Pontic, coast, but there are hints that the distinctive geographical features of the region, with its forest cover and higher rainfall, may also find reflection in significant cultural distinctions in prehistory.

In Palestine we have already seen how the site of Jericho developed precociously from a shrine and camping place of hunters to a permanent walled settlement of agriculturalists. Here and elsewhere in Palestine we can trace a complex series of traditions, many apparently intrusive, that are basically those of stone-using agriculturalists but with evidence of some knowledge of copper-working by the early fourth millennium B.C. at least. A site of this date at Teleilat Ghassul has remarkable mural paintings, mainly non-representational but including a naturalistic rendering of a pheasant; and contemporary, but unrelated in other respects, is an extraordinary troglodyte settlement of copper-workers at Tell Abu Matar, with artificial rock-cut dwellings.

In Syria, settlements of the tell type, with long-continued occupation, go back at such sites as Ras Shamra (Ugarit) and Byblos to stone-using communities of the fifth millennium B.C. at least (a Carbon 14 date of around 4550 B.C. was obtained for the Byblos 'A' level), and here and in Palestine one sees a steady development of peasant communities with a knowledge of copper-working, living in villages or small towns and soon forming what on analogy must have been the equivalent of city-states. There is no evidence of literacy, however, until a date some 1,500 years later than its inception in Sumer and Egypt, around the middle of the second millennium B.C. Correlations with Egypt and Mesopotamia enable us to date these 'proto-urban' sites, as they have been called, for the most part within the third millennium B.C. It is apparent that shortly before 2000 B.C. almost all of these sites underwent dislocation or destruction, which is to be associated with the general barbarian movements in western Asia at this time, and in Palestine, at least, attributable to the Amorites, the Amurru who also attacked the now fully literate civilizations of Mesopotamia. Recovery was made, and the tradition of town and city life restored, with bronze-working and tell settlements averaging in Palestine some twenty acres in extent, but they were as formally illiterate as the contemporary Turkmenian communities already described, or those of eastern Europe to be discussed below, and so technically still 'prehistoric'.

On the Mediterranean coast near Antalya in south-western Turkey, the stratification of the Beldibi cave shows us, above Late Palaeolithic occupation levels, a microlithic industry, apparently of Natufian affinities, in two superimposed phases, in the second of which are miniature sickle flints with the characteristic gloss from cutting corn stalks or similar plant stems, and coarse burnished red or brown pottery in simple shapes. Other comparable sites are not yet identified, but the pottery would appear to be related to other, rather more accomplished, wares, plain or with fine impressed ornamentation, known from the earliest occupation levels of sites, either in Syria (such as Byblos, and those on the Amuq Plain) or in Anatolia (as at Mersin in Cilicia). At Catal Hüyük, south-east of Konya, excavations have recently begun on an enormous site of a comparable Neolithic culture, covering over thirty acres and forming a tell up to fifty feet high – dimensions indicating a settlement four times the size of early Jericho. The culture is that of stone-using agriculturalists who grew wheat and bitter vetch and possessed a rich obsidian industry and other equipment in stone and bone. Slings were used, and clay figurines of both females and animals are common. Mud-brick houses of rectangular plan, with carefully plastered and painted walls, are arranged in blocks around courts or along narrow streets. Two structures, apparently public buildings or shrines, have large-scale mural paintings of human beings and animals in a vivid naturalistic style, depicting scenes of processions and dancing and of hunting, including the capture of a huge wild bull. These wholly unexpected documents in the early history of art show us how much still remains unknown about the capabilities of the peasant communities of Anatolia at this early date, which, on the evidence of the roughly contemporary Mersin settlements referred to below, must be in the vicinity of 6000 B.C. Evidence for sites of the same culture extends, in regional variants, from Syria to the edge of the western Anatolian plateau.

At Mersin, nine building levels of this culture formed the lowest occupation of the site that could be explored above the water table. These levels contained houses on stone foundations, greenstone axes, stone bowls, and a remarkable industry in obsidian brought from central Anatolia, characterized by superbly flaked tanged arrow- and lance-heads, which has also been found at Catal Hüyük and other sites. Some of the burnished pottery is a creamy white colour, probably imitating marble or similar stone, and late in the sequence tentative painting in straggly red lines appears on this cream surface. Female figurines and stamp seals also occur.

In view of its geographical position in south-eastern Cilicia, it is not surprising that in subsequent settlements on the site connexions can be made with the Mesopotamian sequence, running from Hassuna through to Uruk and indeed well beyond; by a phase at Mersin, equivalent to that of Halaf in northern Syria, copper is relatively abundant. A Carbon 14 date of around 6070 B.C. has been obtained for the earlier settlements at Mersin, with their plain wares and fine obsidian industry, which would agree with the Mesopotamian correlations with the subsequent Hassuna phase on the site. The date is further confirmed by independent evidence from the site of Hacilar in south-western Anatolia, where a Neolithic phase comparable to that at Mersin just described was brought to an end by a fire, dated by Carbon 14 methods to about 5693 B.C. In the Hacilar Neolithic levels there occurs the most remarkable series of figurines, often of some size and of great sophistication; they include figures of women holding leopards or seated on thrones supported by two such animals – the Mother of Beasts.

We now enter a phase of Anatolian prehistory in which, whether on the southern coastal plain, the plateau, or the lands of western Turkey facing the Aegean, we find evidence for a growing command of copper (and soon bronze) metallurgy. This is coupled with a greater complexity of social organization reflected in an increase in the size of settlements and in many instances the development of fortified sites, presumably implying the emergence of independent communities of miniature city-state type, between which warfare was expected and provided for (Figure 55). Even if such fortified sites, in many instances, can hardly be regarded as more than castles, their presence is symptomatic on a small scale of social conditions comparable, for instance, to the contemporary developments on a much more grandiose scale in early historic Mesopotamia. Hacilar and Mersin enable us to follow such developments from the sixth millennium B.C. onwards. At the former site, the 'Level II' settlement, with indications of copper working and a superb painted pottery tradition, and with a Carbon 14 date of about 5506 B.C., took the form of a rectangular walled village 190 by 120 feet; the mud-brick architecture included houses comprising a main room with a hearth and an anteroom, three potters' workshops near the middle of the compound and a complex building interpreted as a shrine with a bakery and adjacent clay ovens (Figure 56). Grain-storage bins of unbaked clay were found, and approximately contemporary at Mersin was an area of clay-built circular bins on stone bases. At Hacilar, actual carbonized wheat and barley has survived, as have plum or almond stones.

By a date which must lie in the second half of the sixth millennium B.C. the settlements at both Hacilar and Mersin were turned into fortresses. Hacilar seems the earlier (with a Carbon 14 date of about 5317

B.C.), but in both the principle was the same – the building of a defensive circuit wall, with a ring of buildings forming an integral part of its internal structure in such a way as to leave a central open area. The external diameter of the Haciliar fort (Level I) was a little over 500 feet, and Mersin (Level XVI) was probably comparable in size; such

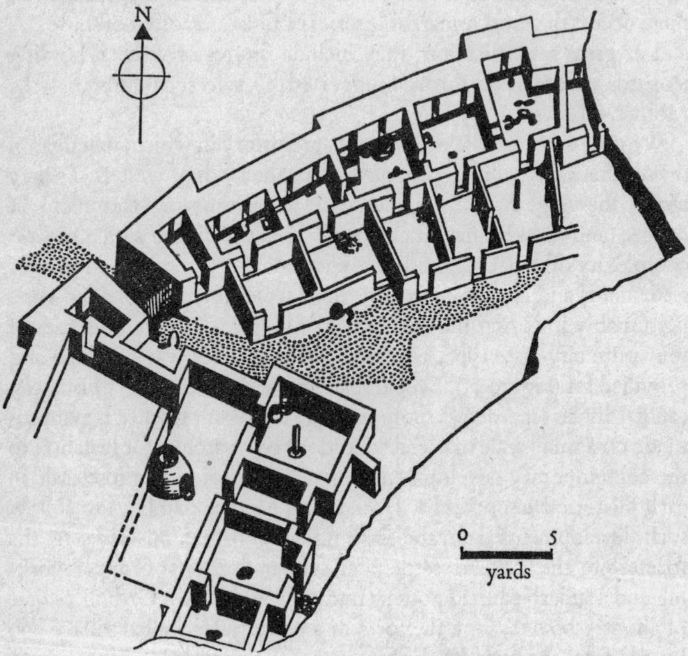


55. Defences of chalcolithic fortress, Mersin

dimensions may not seem very great in themselves, but they exceed those of the second 'city' of Troy, as we shall see. At Mersin the gateway was of a more elaborate form than that at Hacilar, and in both sites the defensive structure was of mud brick on stone foundations, with timber-work upper storeys. The strictly comparable planning of these two sites (which must surely be representative of many more yet unexcavated) bespeaks not only a common tradition of fortification technique but also authoritarian rule over the communities concerned. For we are not dealing with the addition of a defensive wall round an existing village or township but with a military work constructed in one operation: at Hacilar the whole site was cleared and levelled for the establishment of the stronghold. This must surely imply a local ruler who could command not only the initial dislocation of his community but its subsequent mobilization as a labour force

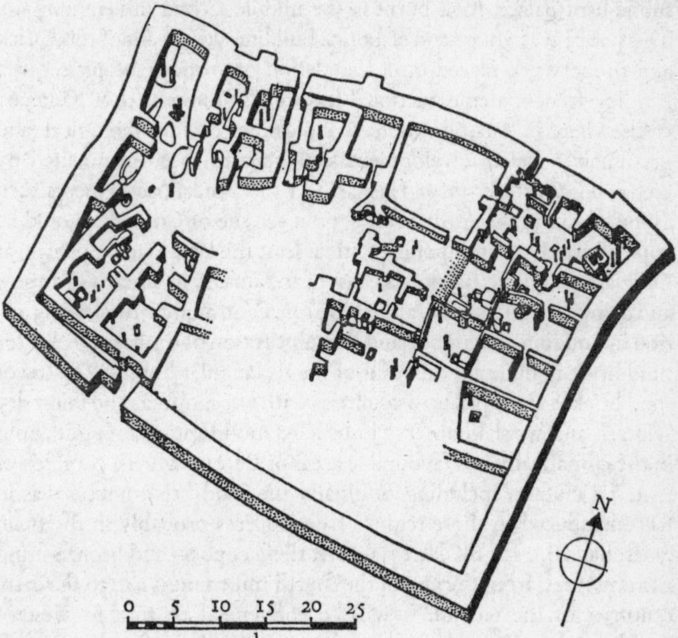


56. Plan of settlement of Hacilar II

to build the defences to a prearranged plan; it must also presuppose conditions of insecurity and emergency which would render such drastic action necessary. The tradition of fortress- or castle-building, though with different schemes of defensive works, was to continue throughout Anatolian prehistory and early history, the site of Troy, as we shall shortly see, providing a history of military architecture from the fourth millennium B.C. to the time of Priam and Agamemnon.

At Beycesultan, near the source of the Maeander river, a remarkable sequence has been established, beginning with an early copper-using culture broadly of Hacilar type, in the latest phase of which a small building of hall-and-porch, or *megaron*, type was found, in a context which should be late in the fourth millennium B.C. The occupation continues, with architecturally complex shrines and private houses (including *megara*), to a destruction level of about 2300 B.C., and a subsequent palace, itself burnt in the middle second millennium B.C. This palace was a huge and elaborate building with walls of mud brick and timberwork placed on a foundation of wooden beams set in a bedding trench, a constructional feature also known from Kültepe.

Elsewhere in Anatolia we have indications of a technological (and presumably social) development analogous to that documented by archaeology at Mersin or Hacilar. On the plateau, settlements such as the lowest in the Alishar series, or at the site of Gulucek, should be approximately contemporary with at least the later Hacilar phases; at Dundartepe on the Black Sea coast near Samsun, in an area of forests and comparatively heavy rainfall, we can see an architectural modification in building techniques, and the substitution of timber and clay for mud brick in building the walls of the rectangular houses. The use of mud brick is appropriate to countries with hot summers and fairly dry winters, and we shall observe just such a modification brought about in the climatically less favourable areas of Europe when a complex of material culture, including originally the mud-brick house, was in fact introduced to those regions from sources probably in the main Anatolian. But for the later stages of these copper- and bronze-using communities, from the end of the fourth millennium B.C. to the early centuries of the second, it will be convenient to turn to western Turkey and the Aegean coasts, and to the sequence of settlement and fortification on the best known of all prehistoric Anatolian sites, that of Troy.

Both on the plateau and in the west we are, archaeologically speaking, beyond the areas of the ancient Near Eastern painted-pottery tradition and in an area of plain, dark-surfaced wares. What this may imply in terms of cultural antecedents we do not know, for in neither area of Anatolia can we take back the story of our peasant communities beyond the fourth millennium B.C. with any confidence. It should be stressed that we are moving into regions where an absolute chronology becomes increasingly difficult to construct. Archaeological correlations with the Near East (of the type possible at Mersin, for instance) are virtually impossible at present, and we so far lack sufficient Carbon 14 dates to provide points in our time scale. Attempts have recently been made to extrapolate from the evidence of the few Carbon 14 dates that we have in eastern Europe, back to Anatolia and the Troy sequence itself, with a consequent raising of the date of the foundation of that site much beyond that in current use; on the other hand, archaeological evidence from the Minoan world has been used to lower it. We seem to have a reasonably fixed point around 2300 B.C. for the destruction of the final phase of the second 'city' of Troy, consonant, as we shall see, with evidence from other sites in other parts of Asia Minor; before that date it is prudent to suspend judgement pending further trustworthy data.

There is evidence from such sites as Kumtepe and Fikirtepe for a phase antecedent to Troy I, with continuity of cultural tradition leading up to it. A recent reassessment of the architectural remains of Troy I and II by Mellaart has led to interesting results which, while likely to remain controversial in detail, do in the main seem to illuminate a situation which has been remarkably obscure in the past. Troy was fortified when it was first founded, but there seems to have been three constructional phases, resulting in a small stronghold some 340 by 260 feet over-all, surrounded by a mud-brick wall with four monumental gates, one adorned with a low stone relief of a highly stylized human face and what looks like a baton or staff of authority. We know comparatively little of the layout within these defences, except that it included houses of the hall-and-porch, or *megaron*, type, of up to seventy by twenty feet over-all. This house type has played a confusing part in many Homeric discussions: it became the Mycenaean palace-plan, but it existed in northern Greece, at Dimini, in what must be a fourth millennium B.C. context. It is present again, in an early phase of Beycesultan, from the beginning of Troy, and has counterparts of this date on Lesbos and Lemnos. At Kültepe on the Anatolian plateau a public building featuring this plan dates from late in the third millennium B.C. At Karatepe in the Anti-Taurus a *megaron* seems to have been built in Byzantine times! Anatolia has probably the best claims as the region in which the type first originated.

The subsequent development of the Trojan defensive system is very complex, and the second settlement has been divided into seven phases, of which the last appears to have been sacked and burnt around 2300 B.C. (Figure 57). The *megaron* buildings grow in size in each successive architectural phase. In Troy II–c, two main *megara* with adjoining

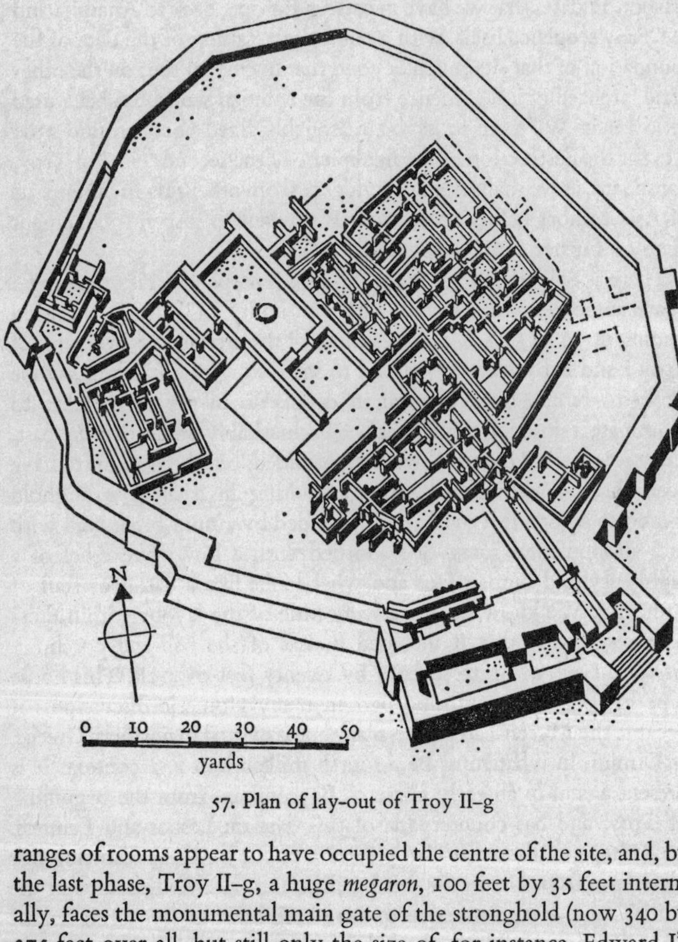


57. Plan of lay-out of Troy II–g

ranges of rooms appear to have occupied the centre of the site, and, by the last phase, Troy II–g, a huge *megaron*, 100 feet by 35 feet internally, faces the monumental main gate of the stronghold (now 340 by 375 feet over-all, but still only the size of, for instance, Edward I's castle of Beaumaris in Anglesey) and dominates the whole place. Round it are agglomerations of rooms which can be interpreted as houses comparable to contemporary structures in the undefended town of Poliochni on Lemnos, and one such house, lying near a postern gate, was that which contained the famous 'Treasures', abandoned when the site was sacked, and discovered by Heinrich Schliemann in his excavations. This evidence may be interpreted as implying that the *megaron* element, originally a simple house in itself, has now developed into a Great Hall, for public assembly and audiences, and that the residential part of the 'Palace' was the building complex that contained the treasures. The roughly contemporary public building of *megaron* plan at Kültepe would make an appropriate comparison, and another similar and contemporary hall has been identified at Poliochni.

The defences of Troy II show interesting constructional details. The walls, twelve feet thick, were basically constructed of sun-dried bricks in the immemorial tradition of western Asiatic architecture, but they were reinforced with a timber-work lacing of massive beams a foot square, laid parallel to the walls for the most part, but with some transverse members, the ends of which would have appeared flush with the outer wall face. Wilhelm Dorpfeld, Schliemann's collaborator in the later work at Troy, misinterpreted this timber-laced defence in its burnt condition (following the destruction of Troy II–g) as a deliberate device to obtain a wall of fired bricks. It is amusing to remember that a precisely similar mistaken interpretation was for long current in the comparable instance of the stone walls of similar timber-laced Scottish hill-forts of the last few centuries B.C., which were believed to have been deliberately 'vitrified' in an analogous manner, whereas their condition, as at Troy, was the result of enemy incendiarism. The timber-laced defensive wall has a long history in prehistoric Europe, and its origins there, as we shall see, may not be unrelated to Aegean prototypes.

Contemporary with Troy II on the Anatolian plateau are such sites as Polatli and Ahlatlibel, the I–b phase at Alishar, and the earliest settlements so far reached in the excavations of the town site at Kültepe. In central Anatolia, within the great bend of the Halys river, we can now, in the second half of the third millennium B.C., begin to speak in terms of peoples known from literate sources, which begin to become available in the early centuries of the second millennium, and to recognize the ancestors of the Hatti, who were to give their name to the Hittite Kingdom; their town at Kültepe was called Kanesh. But before we come to consider the exceptional evidence from that site another aspect of the ruling classes of Anatolia late in the third millennium B.C. can be considered – that provided by the evidence of material wealth already indicated by the treasures abandoned in the last phase of Troy II.

The content of these treasures, which are likely to represent the accumulation of some generations of rulers of the site, are spectacular in their implication of material wealth obtained through a far-flung network of trade and diplomatic relations. Vessels of gold and silver, the gold jewellery which looks so charmingly Victorian when worn by Sophie Schliemann in the well-known portrait, the ivory, and the weapons of prestige in the form of battle-axes wrought in lapis lazuli and other semi-precious stones – all point to the accumulation in a ruler's treasury of precious objects for display or for exchange on ceremonial occasions. This formal exchange of gifts between chieftains or kings has come down to us in the Homeric concept of *keimelion*: 'The twin uses of treasure were in possessing it and in giving it away, paradoxical as that may appear.' But it was accumulated not only for these mundane, if highly ceremonial, occasions. It was also offered to the dead, so that members of a ruling dynasty might not find themselves ill-equipped in the other world, but could display their appropriate status symbols in that land of class-conscious ghosts.

At Alaça Hüyük, within the Halys bend, not far from the eventual Hittite capital of Hattusas, and itself later to be a Hittite town, while excavation has not recovered the palatial buildings which surely must have existed, it has revealed thirteen tombs of a dynasty ruling from about 2400 to 2200 B.C. These are rectangular stone-lined grave pits originally roofed with horizontal timbers covered with clay, on which were laid offerings of the heads and feet of sacrificed cattle (representing a ritual deposit of their hides), and in at least one instance a dog, as well as other remains of funeral feasts (Figure 58). This type of tomb, incidentally, has simpler counterparts in southern Russia at about this time, and, dug to a depth greater than those of Alaça, it is represented by the Shaft Graves at Mycenae in the sixteenth century B.C. These Alaça graves contained a fantastic quantity of objects of copper, gold, silver and semi-precious stones, comparable with, though stylistically different from, the Trojan treasures. The so-called

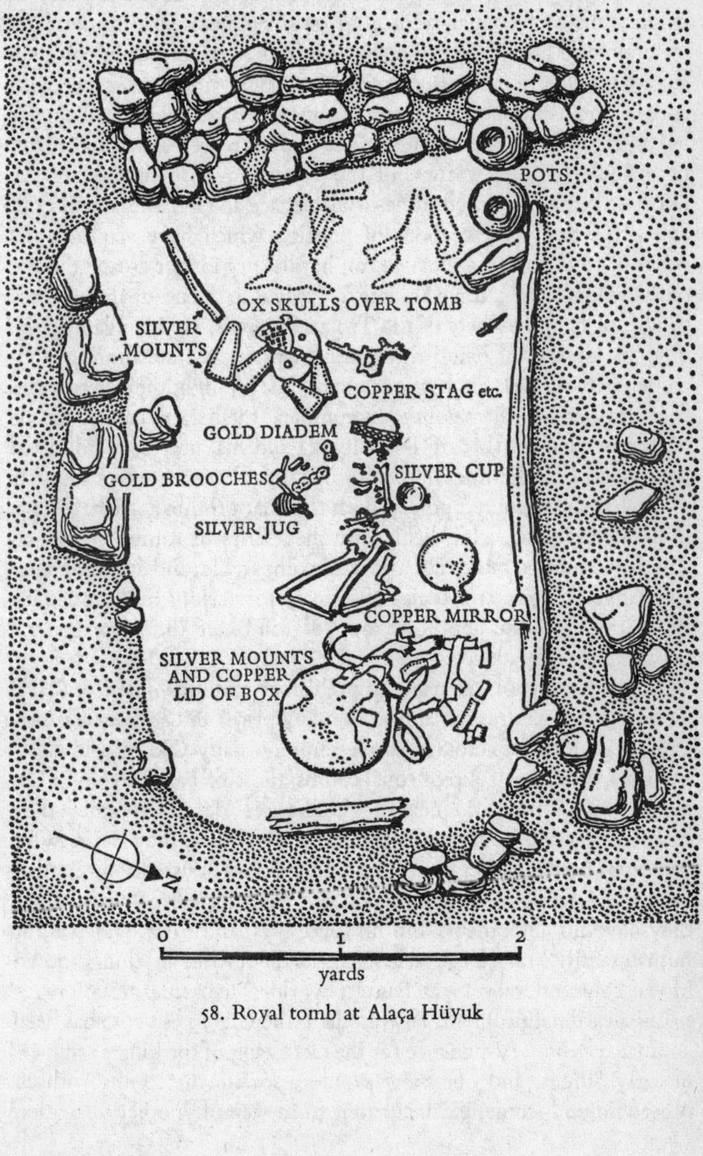


58. Royal tomb at Alaça Hüyuk

'standards', with figures of bulls and deer up to a foot and more in height, made of copper with gold or silver inlay and mounts, are technological *tours de force*. They appear to have been cast in complex closed moulds, a process extremely difficult when working with copper, and by no means easy with bronze. A large gold-hilted dagger has an iron blade, one of the earliest known pieces of wrought iron in antiquity, and an earnest of the precocious ironworking of the Hittites; a gold-mounted stone-headed mace and a battle-axe in gold and silver represent weapons of prestige which have acquired the status of royal insignia. For we can hardly any longer escape the use of the word 'royal'; if we hesitate to apply it to the occupants of these tombs, or to the owners of the Trojan treasures, we are evading the obvious for fear of being thought romantics. We are dealing with nameless dynasties, anonymous men, but though their territories were smaller and their polity less complex, their status can hardly be far removed from that of Tudhaliyas I and his successors, admitted monarchs of the Hittite Old Kingdom. A find near Amasya suggests a royal treasure contemporary with the Alaça tombs; at Horoztepe, in the same region, a less richly furnished series of tombs should on stylish grounds be rather later but still comparable; and at Dorak near lake Appolyont, 120 miles east of Troy, a mysterious find, now vanished, may indicate another group of tombs of the same general nature in the Troad.

As a phenomenon recurrent in prehistory and early history, Royal Tombs and Treasures can appear in many places and at diverse times, and we shall come across examples among many Old World communities. But one group of royal tombs, those of Early Dynastic Ur, must be mentioned in connexion with those of Alaça, with which they have on occasion been compared. Chronologically, they can now be seen to be hardly earlier than 2500 B.C., and thus not so distant in time from the Anatolian tombs as was at one time thought. But in Sumer they have no antecedents and no successors, and their evidence for human sacrifice on a large scale separates them from anything known in the contemporary Near Eastern world. Their interpretation remains a cardinal problem: an episode in the Gilgamesh epic has been construed as literary evidence for the sacrificing of the king's retainers in early Sumer, and one view would associate the tombs with an otherwise undocumented incursion, from some hypothetical region beyond Mesopotamia, of a ruling dynasty having such barbarous practices. Another view has associated the tombs with the custom of celebrating a 'sacred marriage' – the *hieros gamos* of a goddess with a temporary mock king, who was subsequently immolated – a custom which survived into later Babylonian tradition. But for the present their interpretation must remain obscure.

In Anatolia, as elsewhere, the last centuries of the third millennium B.C. were a time of disturbance and of movements of peoples. The archaeological evidence shows us that over large areas of the country the long-established traditions of the peasant communities and small kingdoms came to a violent end at this time; it has been estimated that some 350 sites in southern Anatolia show evidence of such destruction or abandonment. At Kültepe, the ancient Kanesh of the Hatti, on the central plateau, we have the first historical intimation of what in fact was taking place. Here, outside the town, merchants from the now fully literate and highly organized kingdom of Assyria had established a trading colony, or *karum*, soon after 2000 B.C., one of at least eight in the land of the Hatti which are known by name but not yet identified on the ground. These trading colonies were comparable to the European 'factories' in India in the eighteenth century, and from the archives we can not only see the complex and highly efficient trading organization which brought them into being and maintained them in prosperity but also note that, among the persons with whom mercantile operations were being conducted at Kanesh, some have names which do not belong to the indigenous Hattic language but to one of Indo-European type. We have here, in effect, the first historical documentation for members of the intrusive group of peoples who were to take command of the Anatolian plateau, and to found the kingdom which we know as that of the Hittites. With the Hittites we move from prehistory to history, for by their rapid adoption of cuneiform script they created the first literate civilization to establish itself beyond Mesopotamia to the north-west.

We shall have to concern ourselves with the speakers of the Indo-European languages in Europe in later chapters, but here we may conveniently note one point. The documents of the Hittite Kingdom use more than one Indo-European dialect, in addition to the one used mainly for diplomatic and liturgical purposes, which we call Hittite though the name given to it by its speakers is lost to us. One such variant is introduced in the texts by the adverb *luwili* – 'in the manner of the Luwi' – and has hence been named Luwian. One of its characteristics appears to be the formation of place names by the addition of a possessive adjectival termination *-sas*, 'his, its', to a noun, thus producing such forms as *Datassa(s)*, *Pitassa(s)* and *Tarhuntassa(s)*. Such place names occur in Hittite documents in reference to regions outside the Hittite Kingdom in south-western Anatolia, and they appear much later in Greek forms ending in *-assos* or *-nthos*, not only in these same regions of Asia Minor but elsewhere in the Aegean and in Greece itself – *Knossos* and *Korinthos*, for example. The significance of this linguistic connexion for Greek prehistory, in the context of the folk movements in the third or fourth millennium B.C., must be discussed in a later chapter.

We have seen how over an extensive area of western Asia there grew up, from roughly the sixth or seventh millennium B.C., a common peasant culture based on a developed system of cereal cultivation and animal husbandry, furnished with a series of accomplished traditions in craftsmanship, especially that of the potter, and in its later stages fully familiar with a relatively complex non-ferrous metallurgy. This culture was organized in village and small urban communities, linked to one another by trade contacts, and appears from the archaeological evidence to have been remarkably homogeneous over the whole area of its distribution, from the shores of the Aegean to the western edges of the Indian sub-continent. In its latter stages, this culture, in exceptional instances, provided the basis for real civilization and the emergence of literate and complex urban societies – the earliest apparently in Mesopotamia, next in India, and the latest, under conditions of cultural admixture resulting from immigration from outside, in Anatolia. In Anatolia, too, we can infer that before this time, from the fifth millennium B.C. onwards, non-literate city-states or minor kingdoms under the authoritarian rule of local dynasties were developing; and this may have happened elsewhere, though direct evidence is lacking.

Can we at this point go further, and infer anything, beyond the barest generalities, about the social and political structure of these communities? It seems that we may. The fortunate circumstances of the early emergence of literacy in Mesopotamia, and its comparatively early appearance in Anatolia, have provided us with texts that not only illuminate the contemporary world they describe but contain evidence for an order of things already old and hallowed by tradition by the time it was recorded, and therefore legitimately attributable to the non-literate societies from which these civilizations developed. What is more remarkable is that independent investigations of Mesopotamian and Hittite sources have produced concurrent results.

As we know it in its heyday, the polity of Sumer and Akkad is that of authoritarian rulers wielding undisputed power over their respective city-states. But it has been shown that almost up to the time of Hammurabi there appears to have existed a constitution calling for a general assembly with a council of elders for each city-state, to which the ruler was more or less responsible. All the evidence shows that there was no movement towards such a 'democratic' concept in early historic Mesopotamia, but that the trend was away from it, towards absolutism and autocratic rule; it is 'a last stronghold, a stubborn survival of ideas rooted in earlier ages'. This system operated in the trading posts of the type already described at Kanesh, where the highest judicial authority resided in a general assembly of all the members of the *karum*, and it is the setting given to legendary events or stories of the gods located in a mythical past. One finds it, for instance, in the Gilgamesh epic:

> Gilgamesh before the elders of the town spoke up
> After an assembly had been established, the elders of the town
> Gave answer

Not only had the king to consult with the assembly and obtain its consent for decisive actions, but it seems that in its original form it alone could grant or withdraw kingship.

This earlier stage of development of the Mesopotamian *puhrum*, or general assembly of free citizens of the town, with its governing body of elders (*sibutum*), must lie at the beginnings of Sumerian history. We have seen that the archaeological evidence demonstrates complete continuity between historic and prehistoric Mesopotamia, and it is surely permissible to attribute to the prehistoric peasant communities those circumstances in which, to quote Jacobsen, not only

> the normal run of public affairs was handled by a council of elders but ultimate sovereignty resided in a general assembly comprising all adult free men of the community. This assembly settled conflicts arising in the

community, decided on such major issues as war and peace, and could, if need arose, especially in a situation of war, grant supreme authority, kingship, to one of its members for a limited period.

The evidence from Anatolia is entirely on the same lines. Gurney, discussing the *pankus*, or Hittite general assembly, sees it as the survival of an ancient system proper to the Hatti, in connexion with a council of elders in each city. 'The Hittite state', he comments, 'was the creation of an exclusive caste superimposed on the indigenous population of the country, which had originally been loosely organized in a number of independent townships, each governed by a body of Elders.' He thinks that the historical Hittite practice whereby the king formally designated his heir to the assembled nobility, though by that time no more than a statutory ceremony, derives from a concept in which 'Hittite monarchy was originally elective'. We hear nothing of the assembly after the reign of Telepinus (1525–1500 B.C.); 'the later Empire appears to conform more closely to the pattern of absolute oriental monarchies.'

The Hittite *pankus* has more than once been cited, not, as in Gurney's view, as a survival of the original traditions of the indigenous Hatti but as a concept introduced by their Indo-European conquerors, and the institutional parallels for such an assembly and elected ruler in Celtic and Teutonic societies have been stressed. We must return to this problem in another chapter; the question of institutional origins in barbarian Europe must, of course, be considered in relation to the archaeological evidence for the derivation, and subsequent contact, of these societies in prehistory. We may say this, however: the Mesopotamian parallels are so striking as to obviate any necessity for importing the concept into Anatolia from outside, since both areas share a common cultural substratum in prehistory. The presence of comparable institutions in Sumerian, Hittite, Celtic and Teutonic societies (and probably in yet other contexts, such as that of early Israel) must be regarded either as evidence that the institution is sufficiently simple and obvious to be developed independently on more than one occasion or as an indication that the archaeological evidence for the ultimate derivation of the prehistoric European peasant communities from those of western Asia may have to be given weight in this regard.

So far as Mesopotamia and Anatolia are concerned, however, the consistent evidence in the two areas at the dawn of literacy does suggest that we can with reason extrapolate beyond the historical period into at least the later phases of the non-literate cultures which preceded it and formed its substratum. We have noted that the various prehistoric peasant communities in western Asia have a marked homogeneity in material culture, and while this appearance of uniformity may be deceptive, there is nothing in the archaeological evidence that would be inconsistent with a wide distribution of the social structure just described among the various groups of peoples represented in archaeological terms by settlements of the permanent tell type. From such a social structure, and its parallel expression in technological achievement, development towards authoritarian kingship could easily take place, and clearly did in more than one region, but it was not an inevitable outcome of the social and economic circumstances, any more than was the emergence of literate civilization from the same background. In Egypt, on the other hand, the primitive agricultural societies of the Nile valley developed in a totally different manner, and when, after the beginning of the third millennium B.C., we can, as in Sumer, use our historical evidence to suggest the type of society that lay behind it, we are in a world foreign to that of Mesopotamia or Anatolia, but recognizably an African world of the god-king.

The earliest agricultural settlements in the Nile valley cannot on present showing be dated before the middle or second half of the fifth millennium B.C. in Lower Egypt. In this region no antecedent hunting and food-gathering cultures have been identified; in the Sudan a transition from one economy to the other can be demonstrated in the Khartoum region, but here the introduction of animal domestication, which distinguishes the later from the earlier phase, is likely to have been due to Egyptian contacts from further down the river, at a date in the fourth millennium B.C.

When one comes to consider the natural prerequisites for the initiation or establishment of agricultural communities in Egypt, one must remember that there were no wild goats in Africa south of the Sahara, and that Vavilov's view that a primary centre of cereal cultivation existed in Abyssinia has not received support from archaeologists or palaeobotanists in recent years. Wild cattle existed, however, but, as we have seen, the western Asiatic evidence suggests that cattle were not among the first animals to be domesticated. There are, therefore, *a priori* grounds for assuming that agriculture was introduced into Egypt from outside, together with the initial nucleus of herds and seed corn that alone could make such economies possible in the Nile valley.

We have, of course, lost all trace of the earliest settlements in the valley itself. They have been washed away, or silted over by the river, or erased by later agriculture and exploitation, and there are left to us only the marginal sites at the desert's edge. These are grouped in two geographical units, Upper and Lower Egypt, the former mainly between Abydos and Hierakonpolis, the latter in a region more or

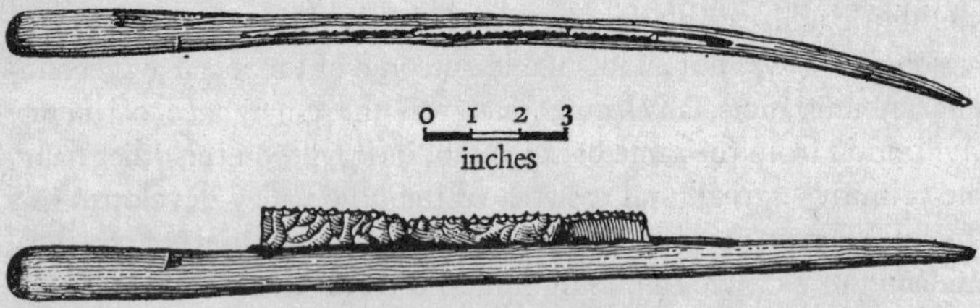


59. Wood sickle with flint teeth, Fayum, Lower Egypt

less centred on Cairo. In the Lower Egyptian area the Fayum sites are of great interest, at present representing the earliest agricultural settlements of the region, with Carbon 14 of about 4150 and 4450 B.C. Goats were almost certainly domesticated, and probably sheep, and emmer wheat cultivated, together with remarkable forms of two-row and six-row barley which have suggested to palaeobotanists a phase of vigorous mutation following the recent introduction of the plant to a new environment. Straight wooden reaping-knives with multiple flint blades (Figure 59) and a wooden flail for threshing have survived in the arid conditions of the Fayum, as have wheat and barley grains contained in mat-lined storage pits; baskets, grass and rush mats and the earliest fragment of linen fabric so far known were also found. There was an industry in stone and flint, and bone spear-points, of either barbed or simple form, and simple forms of plain pottery were made. The chronological range of this culture is uncertain, as is that of subsequent settlements at Merimde and Maadi. The cultural level was never high; windbreaks of reeds or, as at Merimde, oval huts built of rudimentary mud-lumps rather than bricks are the highest architectural achievement recorded for these sites. By the second half of the fourth millennium B.C. we enter into the final, Late Pre-Dynastic, stage, but before dealing further with this crucial phase we must consider prehistoric Upper Egypt.

Here a rather more complex sequence presents itself, but with a restricted enough material culture. For the first, Tasian, phase, domesticated cattle have been claimed but not satisfactorily verified, but, in the ensuing Badarian and Amratian stage, goats, sheep, dogs, and cattle were all certainly, or at least probably, domesticated. The evidence for dogs includes representations painted on Amratian pots, which show a greyhound or saluki type. There is virtually no architecture in these pre-Dynastic phases other than traces of huts, but cemeteries of some size imply permanent settlements. The pottery tradition is mainly that of plain, well-fired, burnished or ripple-surfaced red ware, often fired so as to obtain a black zone round the top of the vessel. A fine flint-working tradition developed, and later on working in stone for vases and other objects was brought to the stage of an accomplished art; ivory carvings including small human figures are known from the first. Sporadic copper objects, which must have been obtained by trade from outside sources, appear in the Badarian and increase in number in succeeding phases.

Higher up the Nile, in the Sudan around Khartoum, an interesting succession of prehistoric economies in the fourth millennium B.C. has been demonstrated. We have first a culture that was 'Mesolithic', in that it was economically dependent on hunting, fishing and food-gathering, but possessed a material culture in stone, bone, etc., augmented by an accomplished pottery industry, with vessels elaborately decorated with impressed and combed patterns, largely made with catfish spines. This culture is then replaced locally by one named from the site at Shaheinab; here, ninety-eight per cent of the animal bones recovered were of wild species, but incipient domestication is attested by the remaining two per cent, made up of goats (and just possibly sheep). The material culture, with some minor changes in the barbed bone points and the use of stone and bone adzes (perhaps for hollowing the soft Doleib palm into dug-out canoes), is basically that of the Khartoum Mesolithic. One presumes that we are here seeing a process of acculturation from farther north, and the presence of black-topped pots, intrusive to the local 'impressed ware' tradition, may be significant in this regard. Since, as we have seen, goats do not occur wild in Africa south of the Sahara, those at Shaheinab must have been introduced and not domesticated from wild species on the spot. There is no evidence of cereal cultivation, and the site is dated by Carbon 14 to about 3300 B.C.

These simple peasant communities of prehistoric Egypt have from the first an essentially African quality, and the physical type of the burials confirms the Hamitic nature of the population. We shall see that we may infer from the literary evidence of early dynastic Egypt that the settlements were products of a social structure with rain-making god-kings at its head, and, isolated from many essential sources of raw materials, such as hardwoods and copper, these communities of Upper and Lower Egypt had a primitive and conservative quality which contrasts with the vigorous technological developments in contemporary Mesopotamia. Without contact with that region, the emergence of the necessary conditions for the founding of a civilization might have been long delayed, but at the end of the fourth millennium B.C. such contact was established, during the last prehistoric period of Egypt, the Gerzean. This has yielded evidence that can only be interpreted as showing an infiltration of a new element into the population, which must have been Semitic and in touch with early literate Sumer.

During the later prehistoric periods in Egypt, trade increased, and not only metal but pottery was imported from the Levant (or perhaps a commodity contained in the characteristic jars was the real object of trade). And by the last phase of the Gerzean, at a time just before 3000 B.C., a whole series of innovations bespeak critical cultural contacts between the two regions. These innovations include monumental architecture in mud brick with characteristic recessed panels in the exterior walls, known elsewhere only in contemporary Sumer, the use of cylinder seals in a modified form, stylistic peculiarities in art, and above all the introduction of the concept of writing and literacy, even if a script of a wholly different character from that of Mesopotamia was devised and developed.

The transition in Egypt from prehistory to history, from barbarism to civilization, was not, however, the inevitable result of the adoption of these new technologies, though writing in particular would have been required for any such development. The transition was effected in Egypt, and probably within a comparatively few generations, by the establishment of the ascendancy of a single ruler, god on earth, as Pharaoh of Upper and Lower Egypt. With the beginning of the first dynasty we move into Egyptian history, and through the media of literature and monumental art perceive a civilization and a constitution wholly unlike that of contemporary Sumer save in its economic and technological bases – an African and not a western Asiatic world.

The emergence of what was to be the essential pattern of Egyptian civilization seems to have been remarkably rapid, and the 'form' it took appears to have been settled almost from the start. The development of writing and monumental art is technically parallel to what was happening in contemporary Mesopotamia, but it discloses to us an alien world. Here there is no trace of autonomous city-states with their assemblies, elders and mortal rulers, and their independent temple organizations; rather, from the beginning, there is the insistent fact that there is one king, and that 'the King of Egypt was a god, and that he was a god for the purposes of the Egyptian state'. He was begotten by the Sun God himself, the Lord of the Two Lands of Upper and Lower Egypt, holy and unapproachable, the divine shepherd of his people: 'He was a lonely being, this god-king of Egypt. All by himself he stood between humans and gods.' The archaeological evidence for continuity between Pre-Dynastic and Early Dynastic Egypt shows us that these circumstances must reflect, save in one respect, the prehistoric conditions in formalized and consciously elaborated form. What has changed is that, instead of having many little tribal rain-making god-kings of a kind which were to recur throughout Africa at many times and places, the country of the Nile had been brought under the rule of one supreme divine ruler. The Egyptian texts hint at the king's capacity as a rain-maker to control not only the Nile but the clouds: a Hittite ruler is made to point out the value of an alliance with Egypt, because rain is under the command of Pharaoh, and 'if the god accepts not its offering, it sees not the waters of the heavens.' So, too, there are allusions that point to a tradition in which the rulers, 'as in the Sudan in recent times, were probably killed ceremonially, perhaps by drowning or dismemberment, when their powers began to wane.'

The inferences which we may make from the evidence of early

literate Mesopotamia and Egypt about the nature of the societies which formed their prehistoric foundations demonstrate to us that two wholly divergent forms of social organization could, and did, emerge from a common technological basis of simple animal husbandry and plant cultivation in two areas of the Near East not very far from each other. The Egyptian solution to the problem gave rise to a civilization which was to achieve a remarkably ingenious and satisfactory adjustment of man to his environment within the peculiar natural conditions of the Nile valley, but could hardly be transferred elsewhere except as an integral part of the Egyptian state, still under the direct government of the god-king, who in the nature of things could have neither deputy nor rival. The creation in western Asia from Anatolia to Baluchistan of a social pattern which was individualistic and particularist, rather than with any claims to universality, provided for elasticity and adaptability even if it also had in it the seeds of potential fragmentation unless its disparate units were welded together under autocratic rule. But the essential social unit, the autonomous village or town community that could become a city-state, despite the fact that the city god and the temple formed its centre of religious and economic organization in historical times, was based on concepts of local loyalties; it was organized and ruled by men whose service to the gods of the town was direct, and not conducted through the medium of a single god who as king ruled over all such towns within a realm which existed only in terms of his own divine person.

This, then, we must account an achievement of prehistoric western Asia as distinct from both the Egyptian and the still unknown Indian solution to the problem of creating a stable civilization. The archaeological evidence to be reviewed in subsequent chapters demonstrates that the transmission of agricultural economies into a Europe hitherto populated only with hunting and food-gathering communities was largely a matter of colonization, and subsequent indirect acculturation, from western Asiatic sources. Archaeology can perceive and record only what is tangible and what is durable, but material culture is the expression of behaviour, which itself can function only within a social framework. In more than one set of circumstances, therefore, we may legitimately infer the transmission not only of commodities and techniques, modes of architecture, and types of settlement, but also the simple basic concepts of the social structure of which they were the material expression. As we said at an earlier stage, the possibility that analogous institutions were independently created can never be ruled out, but the ultimate dependence of the earlier agricultural and metal-using communities of Europe upon western Asia must be taken into consideration. We must forget modern boundaries, and realize that eastern Europe and the Aegean are no more and no less peripheral to Mesopotamia than are Turkmenia and Baluchistan. We may have to dig deeper for the foundations of certain European institutional concepts than has sometimes been thought necessary, and in regions outside that continent.

CHAPTER TEN

# The Earliest Peasant Communities of Europe

ALTHOUGH it has become almost a commonplace to recognize the ultimately Oriental origin of most, if not all, of the main elements in European Neolithic cultures, we are perhaps still inhibited in our comprehension of the relationships between eastern Europe and western Asia in antiquity by a failure to recognize that the conventional boundary between the two continents is for this purpose irrelevant and even misleading. We should rather remember how narrow is the Hellespont, and how the waters of the Aegean join rather than divide its coasts and islands; again, north of the Black Sea, not only are there no natural barriers between east and west, but the steppe and forest-steppe zones offer continuous links between the two regions. The steppe intrudes itself far into continental Europe in the Great Hungarian Plain, reaching up the Danube to the mountains of Austria and Slovakia; and across the Carpathians the North European Plain merges imperceptibly with that of southern Russia. Anatolia thrusts into the Aegean, as in complementary fashion the Mediterranean Sea stretches eastward to the Levant and the Nile Delta, and was throughout antiquity itself a unit, a pathway for sea traffic joining east to west. In considering the early development of peasant communities in eastern Europe, we do well to form a perspective in which the position of Constantinople is seen as the centre of a region with common traditions, rather than as an outpost of either an eastern or a western world.

We have seen in a previous chapter that the natural conditions in the Old World which alone made possible the first domestication of animals and the cultivation of food plants existed in post-Glacial times in a relatively restricted area of what is now the Near East. The most enterprising and inventive Mesolithic community could not have changed its basic economy from hunting and food-gathering to one of farming and food production in areas of Europe where neither suitable wild ruminants nor grasses existed. These were necessary to offer the potentialities of such a shift in the subsistence pattern, though the possibility of the independent domestication of such wild fauna as pigs and cattle, which were to be found in Europe in post-Pleistocene times, cannot be wholly ruled out. The dog, as we have seen, had been domesticated in Mesolithic northern Europe, but as an adjunct to the hunter, not as an initial step towards an agricultural economy. We must, in fact, accept the evidence set out in an earlier section of this book for the genesis of agricultural economies in western Asia, perhaps in several areas within the general natural region, with a spread therefrom to adjacent territories both east and west. Its spread to the west and north-west constitutes the first founding of agricultural societies in ancient Europe.

The western Asiatic development of the agricultural community produced a characteristic type of settlement behind which we can infer a simple but efficient social organization. At first stone-using, these peasant societies soon learnt to exploit copper; the use of mud-walled architecture, well suited to the natural conditions of climate and vegetation, led to the tell type of settlement in which successive rebuilding on one site caused the village or town to rise up on the ruins of its predecessors. These circumstances, repeated from Baluchistan to Anatolia, gave rise to a common social and economic pattern which in some regions could develop into small or large city-states, and in still fewer could provide the basis for the emergence of true civilization.

In its simplest and earliest forms, with a technology still pre-metallic, this economy – and, by inference, the accompanying social order – was extended also into eastern Europe and, once established there, continued in some areas into the second half of the second millennium B.C., developing its technology to the level of full bronze-using cultures but showing no evidence of achieving any social or political development beyond the peasant village. Outside the limits of this economy, we encounter other adaptations of agricultural techniques to climatic and botanical conditions very different from those obtaining in the western Asiatic regions in which such economies had their genesis. Much of the prehistory of European agriculture must be seen in terms of the extension of cereal crops further and further beyond the bounds of the climatic conditions of their origins, with the consequent modification of the original staple grains and the development of resistant and hardy cereal types which had originated as weeds in the primitive mixed wheat and barley crops of more favoured climates.

So, too, modifications of social patterns can be inferred, as the traditions of ultimately Oriental agriculture were eventually introduced into regions where the indigenous hunter-fisher communities had developed highly complex economies which enjoyed a deeply entrenched survival value in the ecological conditions in which they had been evolved. Here a fusion of cultural traits, each contributing to the eventual amalgam, took place, producing new patterns of behaviour which, from the archaeological evidence, imply profound modifications of the primary types of wholly agricultural economies. To this mingling of traditions, beginning in eastern Europe at least in the sixth, and already reaching to the north-west by the fifth and fourth, millennia B.C., were to be added to the end of the third millennium further contributions, suggesting a more pastoral element, of remote steppe origin. These three components – the indigenous hunter-fisher element, the settled mixed farming of western Asiatic derivation, and the more mobile pastoralism of the Eurasian grasslands – were to form in combination the essential fabric of later prehistoric Europe.

The end of the third millennium B.C. was, as we have seen, a period of crisis in Anatolia, Mesopotamia, the Levant and Egypt, and the repercussions of these events are reflected in European prehistory. In terms of the technological model used in the past, this is the beginning of the Bronze Age cultures of Europe. It is that, and more; it is a phase of a realignment of powers and a movement of peoples which make it a natural dividing line between an early and a middle phase in barbarian Europe. Our present survey of the earliest peasant communities of Europe may then be conveniently taken, in chronological terms, up to a date just before or around 2000 B.C., from an uncertain point in time which should, however, lie in south-eastern Europe before 5000 B.C. at least.

We saw in a previous chapter that agricultural communities without a knowledge of pottery were established in northern Greece at a date probably in the sixth millennium B.C. Thereafter a sequence of cultures differentiated mainly by pottery styles can be followed here and elsewhere in Greece, all before the conventional date for the beginning of the Early Helladic period early in the third millennium B.C. (A Carbon 14 date of about 2670 B.C. has been obtained for this phase at Eutresis.) The settlements with their mud-walled houses form accumulations of the tell type and so presuppose a degree of competence in settled agriculture. A fine-burnished pottery with mottled surfaces recalls Anatolian types, such as the wares from the early settlements at Mersin, and the specimens at Drakhmani have a Carbon 14 date of about 5480 B.C. This is then followed by rusticated, fingernail-ornamented and comb-impressed pottery which, as we shall see later, has affinities with that of a widespread series of agricultural settlements in south-eastern Europe, with Carbon 14 dates of about 5000 B.C. Throughout the early phases, goats and sheep were the predominant domestic animals, as in the aceramic phase. There follow two phases characterized by fine-painted pottery, the earlier, that of Sesklo, having some similarities with that from the late Neolithic settlements of Hacilar in Anatolia, and with a Carbon 14 date (again at Drakhmani) of about 5360 B.C. Domesticated pigs are now attested, as is barley as a cereal crop. Settlements are known from Thessaly to the Haliakmon river, in central Greece, the Peloponnese, and Leukas, with tell accumulations of up to nearly twenty feet in thickness. The settlements were small, usually around 300 by 250 feet, though this is almost twice the size of the sixth-millennium phase at Hacilar and approximately the same as the first settlement of Troy.

With the Sesklo houses we are introduced to an interesting difference between the European and the western Asiatic architectural modes which is found throughout prehistory (Figure 60). The Oriental house, from an antiquity extending back to Hassuna and even to Jarmo, was an agglomeration of small, approximately rectangular, chambers united in a small or large complex that might include one or more open courts. In Anatolia the *megaron* form appears at an early date either as a free-standing structure or as a hall associated with groups of smaller rooms, and the site of Dundartepe on the Black Sea coast may have contained rectangular one-roomed houses. In such instances, as we know from reliable excavations in Europe, however, all settlements of the earliest agricultural communities (and their later successors in many regions) are made up of

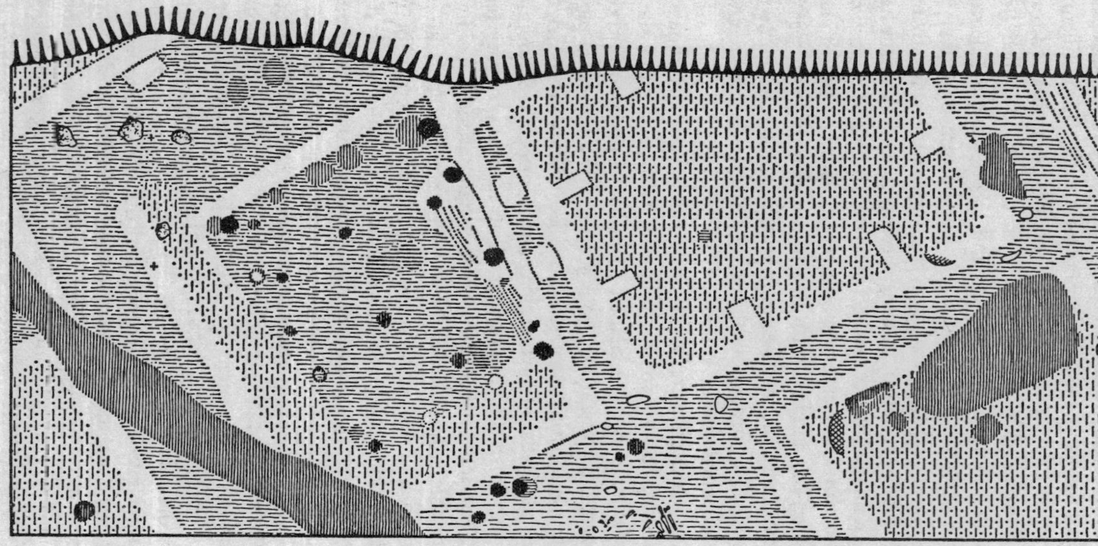

60. Plans of Sesklo culture houses

individual houses, rectangular in plan in the east and centre of the continent and largely circular in the west. Even if there are simple internal subdivisions, each is a free-standing unit. In many areas we have single-room houses without permanent subdivisions. The Sesklo sites exhibit a method of providing internal buttresses for rectangular or nearly square houses that has parallels at Hacilar, but in other areas and cultures we shall see types of houses and patterns of settlement that mark a complete break from Oriental tradition, except in such areas as the Aegean, where proximity to and contact with Asia led to an early adoption of its architectural tradition. From a very early stage, the ancient peasant communities of western Asia built villages of closely packed many-roomed houses, with party walls and narrow alleys between, which were directly ancestral to the similar closely planned towns and cities that were to develop from them – a type of settlement well adapted for defence, once it was surrounded by a town wall.

The European settlements, however, as we see them from the sixth to the fourth millennium B.C. in Greece, on the Bulgarian plain, in the western Ukraine and up the Danube and Rhine as far to the north-west as Belgium, normally display a looser planning with rectangular houses standing free of each other, often with comparatively large spaces between. In some cultures, as we shall see, we are dealing with dwellings no larger than would house a natural or nuclear family averaging, say, five persons; in others, with large buildings, sometimes with evidence of internal subdivisions, which on anthropological analogies would be likely to house a family of the extended type of up to twenty or thirty individuals under a single roof. Here differences of social structure are presumably implied, even if we cannot perceive their precise nature. Differences are also seen in the actual mode of construction, perhaps hinted at in Anatolia by the use of wattle and daub rather than mud, or mud brick, at Dundartepe. The Oriental mode of mud construction continues in Greece and probably elsewhere in the Balkans, but in Bulgaria, at least, a variant appears using a light timber framework and a thinner wall. In the Ukraine, timber and mud are again employed, though in a different technique, but when we come to the early agricultural settlements in the Danube valley beyond the Bakony mountains in central and west-central Europe, we find, appropriate to the heavy forest and wetter climate, an architecture of massive woodwork with no more than mud plaster. The roof type also changes; contemporary house models in Greece, Bulgaria, the Ukraine and central Europe show that the Oriental flat roof has been abandoned in favour of a gabled ridge roof more suited to the climatic conditions of temperate Europe (Figure 61).

Nevertheless, the general complexion of the material culture of these early Greek peasant settlements implies an origin in western Asia – the grain, and domesticated animals themselves, mud architecture with resultant tell formation, stamp seals, painted pottery, female figurines, and the use of the sling. There is nothing specifically

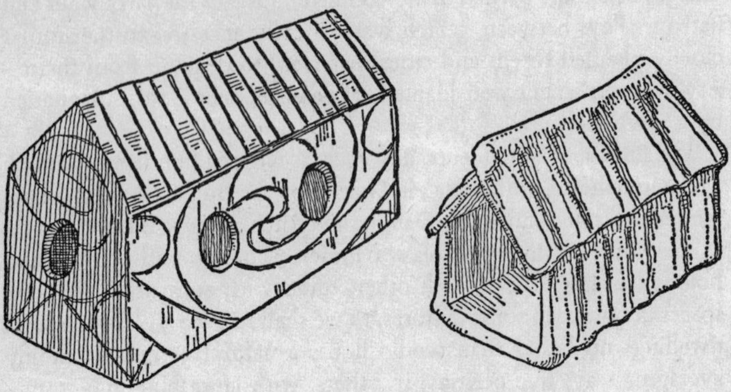

61. House models, Bulgaria and Czechoslovakia

Anatolian in the tradition, and the northern Levant might be a more likely point of contact. But the succeeding phase, named from the site of Dimini, near the Gulf of Volos, seems to show contacts with the Troad, for the stone-walled fortress of Dimini is a rustic Troy. It must belong to more than one constructional phase, as its arrangement of multiple walls and gates is meaningless as a unitary building. An outer wall (now incomplete) took in an oval area of some 80 by 70 metres, a little smaller than the first defences at Troy, and within is a sub-rectangular citadel, 30 by 23 metres, with a main gate at one end and, facing it across the defended area, a *megaron* building 15 by 7 metres over-all with a postern gate nearby (Figure 62). The formal planning and the use of the *megaron* echo, in fact, the final layout of

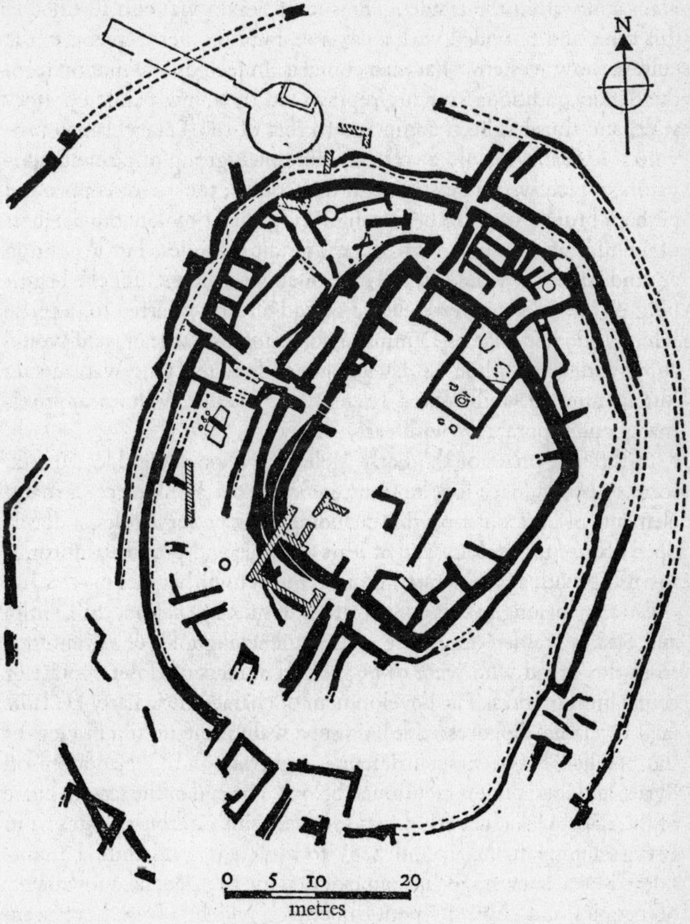


62. Plan of Dimini

Troy II rather than the earliest fortress there; fragmentary walls show that other structures and clusters of rooms lay between the walls and within the citadel. The site of Sesklo was also fortified at this time, and provided with a *megaron*, but no other elements in the culture show western Anatolian contacts. In fact, differentiation from the Sesklo tradition is mainly represented by a new painted pottery style, and thus has been compared to that of the Transylvanian province of what is mainly a western Ukrainian group of peasant cultivators, which we will examine in due course; the use of copper and perhaps bronze was also beginning. It is difficult to date the defences of Dimini and Sesklo, with their Troadic affinities, but a position around 3000 B.C. would fit the date of about 2700 B.C. for the beginning of the Greek Early Helladic period already referred to, a phase which followed that of Dimini in some regions at least, and would agree with the Carbon 14 dates obtained for the Transylvanian sites just mentioned (and quoted later on), as well as with an approximate contemporaneity with early Troy.

In the first phase of the Early Helladic period there does, in fact, seem to be evidence for the transference to parts of Greece of many elements of Anatolian origin, including new pottery styles, a developed bronze technology and at least a simple and provincial form of township with agglomerated houses; the 'Luwili' names in *-ssos* and *-nthos* may belong to this context, too. In such a situation, the Dimini and Sesklo 'castles' might be seen as the strongholds of adventurers from the Troad who were to be the forerunners of closer contact or actual immigration. The development of characteristic Early Helladic (and Cycladic) defences with bastioned walls is interesting in view of the parallels between such defences at Lerna, and Chalandriani on Syros, and Iberian sites mentioned below. The end of the second phase of the Early Helladic period was sudden, with Carbon 14 dates from Lerna ranging from around 2283 to 2041 B.C., and must be considered at a later stage in connexion with the general movements of peoples and shifts in political power which, as we have seen, affected large areas of western Asia late in the third millennium B.C. Europe too, was involved in these events, and their onset has been taken as a convenient point for breaking our narrative in this chapter. We must turn from Greece and the Aegean to consider the primary agricultural settlements of other regions of continental eastern Europe.

We saw that in certain Thessalian tells the Sesklo settlements were stratigraphically later than others characterized by pottery with surface roughening and impressed patterns. Such pottery is also found in a series of sites in eastern Europe, from Yugoslavia to Hungary and the Bulgarian plain, with the earliest evidence of agriculture in those regions, and at the basal occupation in many tell sites, such as Vinča on the Danube near Belgrade, and Karanovo near Nova Zagora in Bulgaria. A Carbon 14 date for this culture in Yugoslavia is around 4690 B.C. The surface rustication of pottery with the finger-nails or other instruments, or the impression of designs with the edge of a shell or similar serrated object, is perhaps too simple and obvious

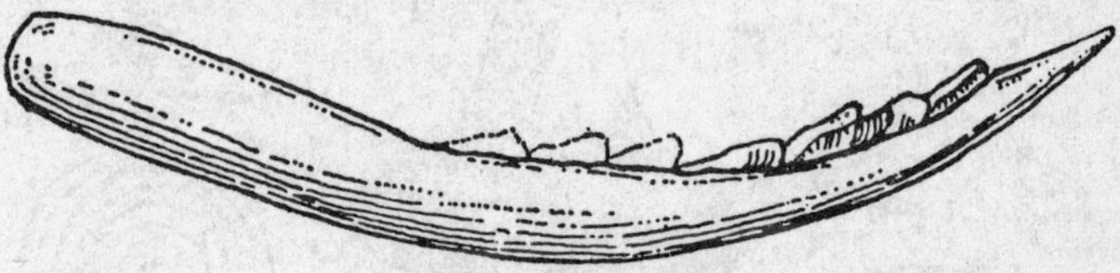

63. Sickle, Karanovo I culture

a device to be used entirely on its own as an index of cultural contact, but it may be noted that a specialized form of such ornament does occur, for instance, in the pottery of the earliest Mersin settlements and in comparable contexts in Syria. Its presence again in Thessaly and the Balkans may show relationships between the two areas, and in the latter region it is found on occasion with good white-on-red painted wares, as at Starčevo in Yugoslavia and Karanovo in Bulgaria. In Karanovo, the houses of the basal settlement of the tell are small, square, single-roomed huts with mud walls reinforced with internal wattle work; the site measures about 800 by 600 feet and it is estimated to have comprised some fifty or sixty houses in each of the main phases of its occupation. As the small houses imply occupation by nuclear or natural families, a population of some 300 persons is indicated.

Goats, sheep, pigs and cattle were domesticated in these settlements; corn was grown and reaped with composite flint sickles in bone hafts (Figure 63); whorls and loom weights show that animal or plant fibres were being spun and woven; figurines and stamp seals

(Figure 64) suggest links with Asia Minor; and external trade relations are indicated by obsidian imported from northern Hungary and shells from the Mediterranean coasts. We have in these sites the beginnings of agriculture in the Balkans and adjoining areas, and the route from northern Greece, up the valley of the Vardar and down that of the Morava to the Danube above the Iron Gates near Belgrade, provided a natural means of contact between the two areas. On the basis of a technologically simple agricultural economy, as found at Starčevo or Vinča in Yugoslavia, Körös in Hungary, and Karanovo I

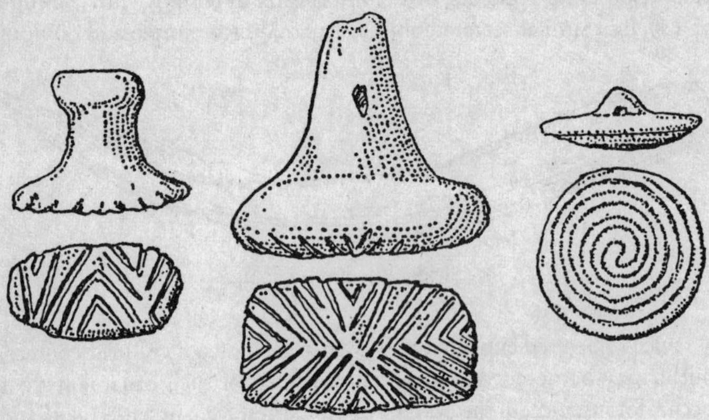

64. Clay copies of stamp seals, Körös culture

in Bulgaria, local cultures grew up, differentiated usually by pottery styles in which painting was abandoned or little used by comparison with incised or burnished techniques. Technologically, the economy remained Neolithic in that stone was used for edge tools, but in certain regions, notably the Bulgarian plain, copper objects, probably of Anatolian origin, began to be imported and copied, perhaps from the beginning of the third millennium B.C.

From the start, the economy was a provincial version of those which in western Asia produced the tell type of settlements – Vinča accumulated thirty feet of deposits and Karanovo over forty by the end of the third millennium. The end of the first (A) phase at Vinča has a Carbon 14 date of about 4240, the D phase a date of about 3895 B.C. The architecture at Karanovo, the best-documented site, changed from the small square houses of the first phase to larger rectangular buildings with an entrance and sometimes a porch at one end in *megaron* fashion; they were still built in the wattle-and-clay technique and were no bigger than would be appropriate for a nuclear family: the population does not seem to have increased materially during the long history of the site. The houses were ornamented inside with wall plaster painted white and maroon in horizontal bands and carrying oval motifs linked with S-curves. Decorated models suggest that the

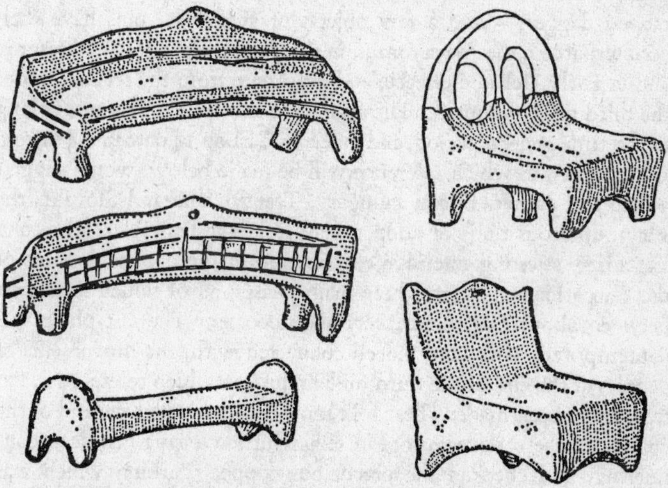

65. Model furniture, Yassa Tepe, Bulgaria

exterior walls might also have been gaily painted. Clay models of chairs, benches and couches contemporary with the fifth settlement of Karanovo show remarkably sophisticated forms and appear to represent padded or upholstered seats and wooden frames (Figure 65). The female figurines from the earlier Karanovo levels include forms again vaguely reminiscent of Greek or Anatolian types, and in a Rumanian site near the Black Sea, contemporary with Karanovo III, most remarkable stylized but naturalistic figurines of seated men and women show us that works of art capable of making a profound aesthetic impression on us today were then being produced in eastern Europe.

The sixth settlement of Karanovo illustrates a phase well represented on other sites, not only in Bulgaria but across the Danube in south-eastern Rumania as far as the Bucharest region, and marks the culmination of the culture of the early peasant communities in those regions. With it, too, must go the first exploitation of Transylvanian copper deposits and the parallel phases of developing peasant economies there and on the Hungarian plain. In the Karanovo VI phase there appear, as we have seen, copper objects likely to be of Anatolian origin – shaft-hole axes and adzes, pins with double spiral heads, and tanged daggers – and a few objects of gold. The pins have their counterparts in the Alaça tombs, in the Troy and Poliochni treasures, and in Early Helladic Greece, and must date from the second half of the third millennium B.C. The shaft-hole axes and adzes must belong to the same general period, and indeed a Carbon 14 date in the eastern Carpathians, to which reference will be made below, would suggest a date still earlier. But in Hungary, Transylvania and Slovakia the very numerous finds of copper shaft-hole axe-hammers, adzes and axe-adzes, attesting intensive exploitation of the copper deposits of the Carpathians, fall into three main phases, all of which should lie between about 2500 (or earlier) and 2000 B.C. The last phase was contemporary with, and indeed connected with, the movements of peoples at the end of the third millennium, to which reference has so frequently been made. These folk movements marked the end of the culture of the eastern European tells which we have just been considering, and checked the precocious copper working which was beginning in Transylvania. When copper and bronze metallurgy was again taken up, on the Hungarian plain, it was again a product of a tell type of economy but owed its inspiration to new trade connexions with central Europe.

North-east of the mouth of the Danube and the Carpathians we enter, for the first time in this survey, a world which is immediately recognizable as alien to the culture of the tell type of settlements. It represents an individual response to the problem of establishing agricultural communities in regions beyond those climatically and geographically closely allied to the western Asiatic homeland. Beyond the Dnieper river on the north-east, and the Sereth, a tributary of the Danube, on the south-west, is a belt of country intermediate between the true steppe to the south-east and the deciduous-forest zone to the north-west. In this forest-steppe region, both in the Ukraine and in eastern Rumania, a large number of settlements of stone-using agriculturalists have been identified and excavated. A few sites from an early phase are known, with houses partly sunk in the ground, and evidence of the domestication of goats, pigs, cattle, dogs and perhaps horses, and of the cultivation of millet. Pottery with incised decoration, figurines of women and domestic animals, and a few copper objects have been found. Dating is almost guesswork, and it seems

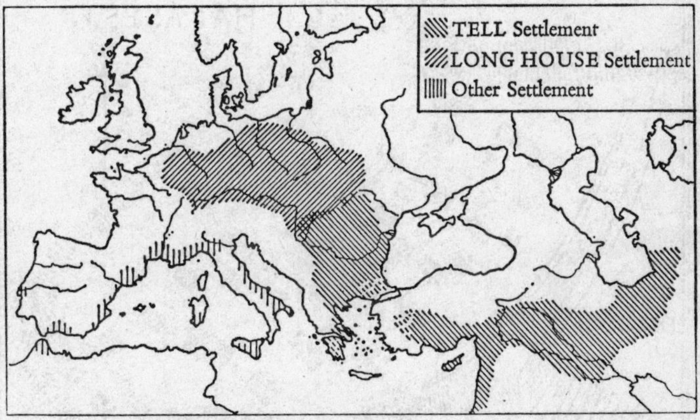


66. Distribution of 'tell' settlements and 'long-house' settlements

difficult to place the culture much before 300 B.C., if as early, although Carbon 14 dates for allegedly successive phases would push it back into the fourth millennium B.C., unless we could allow an overlap between this and the main manifestation of what is called the Tripolye culture, from a site near Kiev.

We have at least four completely excavated settlements of this mature phase. All show large timber-and-clay-built houses of consistent and curious construction. The floors were of split logs, laid transverse to the long axis of the building, and covered with a thick layer of clay which was hardened by means of a fire built on its surface: this provided a substantial platform insulated from damp and cold (as well as from mice). The walls were of mud or mud-plastered timber and, as models show, covered over with gabled ridge roofs. In the Russian sites the houses were up to 100 by 28 feet in size. At Vladimirovka 162 such buildings were set in five roughly concentric ovals; at Kolomiishchina there were two rings of thirty-nine houses. Subdivisions and internal hearths, from two to five in each house, imply occupation by extended families of up to twenty or thirty persons, so that the former settlement might have had a population of 4,000 persons if all the houses were occupied at one

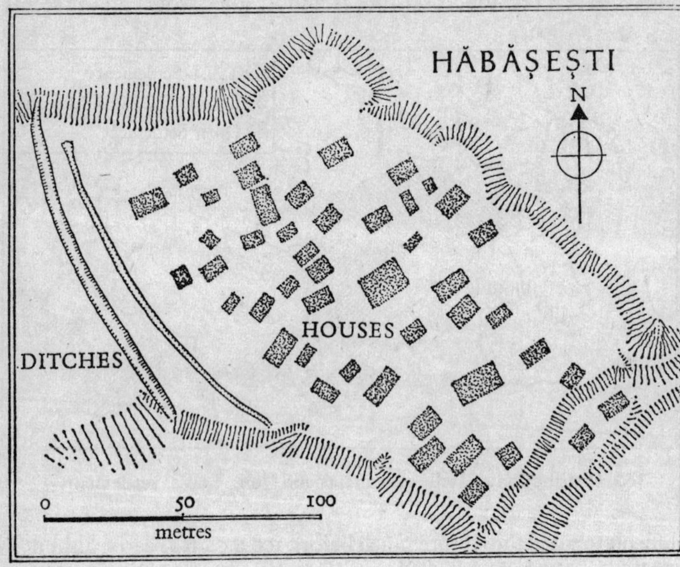


67. Plan of Tripolye settlement, Habaşeşti, Rumania

time, the latter about 1,000. Two Rumanian sites have closely comparable plans, with villages set on low promontories defended by a bank and ditch at the base of the spur; Habaşeşti (Figure 67) has forty-four houses and Truşeşti fifty-five. But they are smaller than the Russian houses, averaging about fifty by twenty-five feet, so that population estimates should at least be halved, giving a rough figure of 500 and 700 persons for the two settlements, about twice that estimated for Karanovo. None of these figures can be regarded as more than hypothetical approximations, and with the Tripolye sites we must be on our guard against necessarily accepting the total plan as excavated as representing a one-period settlement in which all houses were in use at one time. The evidence from analogous settlements of the early Danubian agriculturalists, which we shall shortly consider, shows that such plans may actually represent the final pattern resulting from periodic resettlement and rebuilding on the site, after temporary desertion following exhaustion of the land, and that therefore the population at any one time may have been far less than the total number of houses might imply at first glance.

The circular or oval plans of Vladimirovka and Kolomiishchina are curious, and should reflect some aspect of the economy that differentiates such settlements from others that were laid out in what would seem a more normal manner. The herding and corralling of cattle or other flocks and herds within the area would seem a possibility, or some possibly pre-agricultural tradition in which camps were set up in circles in the manner, for instance, of certain North American Indians on the Plains: the concentric planning of the British Neolithic causewayed camps in a cultural context which may have had a large pastoral content should not be forgotten.

Tripolye agriculture was based on the growing of wheat, barley and millet, with hoe cultivation and reaping with flint-bladed sickles; bones of domesticated animals amounted to seventy per cent at Vladimirovka, with the remainder made up of deer, elk and wild boars; the remains of river molluscs also were found. A fine-painted pottery was manufactured, and female figurines and clay stamp seals provide links with the south-west rather than directly with Asia Minor. Clay models of sledges on log runners give an interesting glimpse of transport methods (Figure 68). In the later phases in the Ukraine and in Rumania, copper objects appear, including mid-rib daggers in the former area and shaft-hole axes in the latter, both indicative of dates within the third or fourth millennium B.C. In Rumania Carbon 14 dates of about 3380 and 3000 B.C. for the two main phases have been obtained, the former contemporary with the Salcuța phase, just antecedent to the appearance of local metallurgy, dated to about 3500 B.C. The lack of evidence for continuous occupation with several phases of rebuilding on Tripolye sites has been taken as an indication that their agricultural techniques may have been of the primitive slash-and-burn type, with movement of population from one site to another following local exhaustion of the land, in a manner comparable with the Danubian settlements described below.

The Tripolye settlements show us, for the first time in our study of the European region, the adaptation of the western Asiatic agricultural methods to a new type of terrain and climate. The painted pottery, the stamp seals, and the religious cults attested by the figurines all suggest links with the early Oriental peasant economies, but the large, free-standing subdivided houses, with their implication of a society in which the extended family normally lived in a single rectangular building, and the construction of these houses with relatively heavy timbering, show something new and un-Asiatic. Nor is there evidence of continuous settlement on one site in the tell

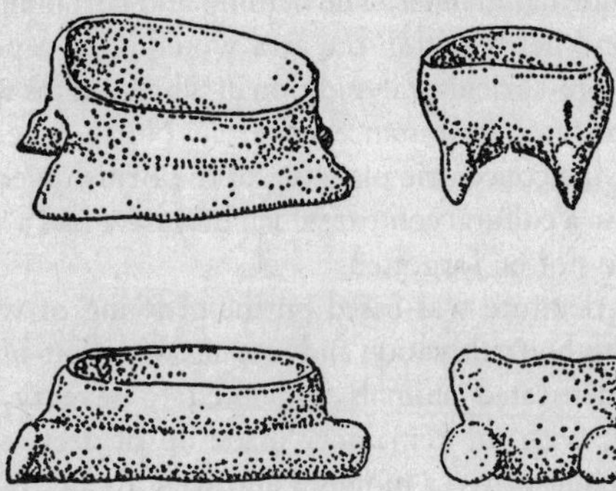

68. Model sledges, Tripolye culture

tradition. When we turn now to the next major area of early agricultural settlement in Europe we find more links with Tripolye than with the ancient East, a still more specialized development of a peculiarly European pattern, and one earlier than the Tripolye culture itself.

From a point in the Danube basin around Belgrade, northwards and westwards over the loess country of central Europe to Poland, the Rhineland, Holland, Belgium and even eastern France, there are abundant traces of a remarkably uniform pattern of settlement with a homogeneous material culture to which the name 'Danubian I' has been given – an unsatisfactory form of nomenclature in which a chronological phase has been given a cultural connotation. The evidence comes mainly from settlements extensively excavated in Germany, Czechoslovakia and southern Holland, and a series of consistent Carbon 14 dates has been obtained. Danubian I pottery occurs in Vinča A, a phase which came to an end before about 4240 B.C.; in Germany sites have been given dates ranging from about 4580 to 3890 B.C.; dates from settlements in southern Holland run from about 4470 to about 4060 B.C. To recall for a moment Near Eastern dates, this means that stone-using agriculturalists were established in north-western Europe at a time contemporary with the earlier part of the Ubaid period of Mesopotamia and with the Fayum settlements in Egypt. The Oriental progenitors of such European cultures as Starčevo-Körös must date from the sixth millennium B.C. at least, approximately contemporary with the earliest settlements found at Mersin, or those of Matarrah, and not so distant from Jericho 'Pre-Pottery Neolithic B'. The peculiarly European version of Neolithic agricultural settlement represented by the Early Danubian sites had already evolved at a date relatively high even for the Orient.

These sites show a remarkable degree of uniformity in house type and layout, as does the material culture from Belgrade to Brussels. This should argue for a rapid spread of the peoples who brought this culture into central and northern Europe, as would the importation, all over the area eventually colonized, of the Mediterranean shell *Spondylus gaederopus* as raw material for ornaments (Figure 69). This maritime contact, together with the fact that the pottery types suggest that they are derived from copies of vessels made from hardened gourds, indicates that the population originally spread out from the south-eastern end of its known distribution, for such gourds do not ripen north of the Bakony mountains in Hungary. The agricultural economy was based on the cultivation of barley, einkorn and, at least in the northern areas of its distribution, emmer and bread wheat, as well as beans, peas, lentils and flax; sheep, cattle and pigs were domesticated, but wild-animal bones are virtually lacking in the settlement debris. The pottery whose forms suggest gourd prototypes is incised in rectilinear and curved band-like motifs; there is a flint industry including sickle blades, and small stone axes and adzes of peculiar forms, none of which would seem very effective for heavy forestry. Neither stamp seals nor figurines appear – we have moved out of the sphere of the cultures to which they belong.

A few burials and small cemeteries are known, with the crouched burials in some instances within a setting of four posts, that suggest a small mortuary house. But the most abundant and interesting information on the culture is afforded by the settlements and their structures. The houses were massive rectangular structures averaging about 100 by 25 feet, with a timber framing carried on large upright posts, normally set in individual holes for about two-thirds of the building and in a bedding trench for the remainder, a recurrent

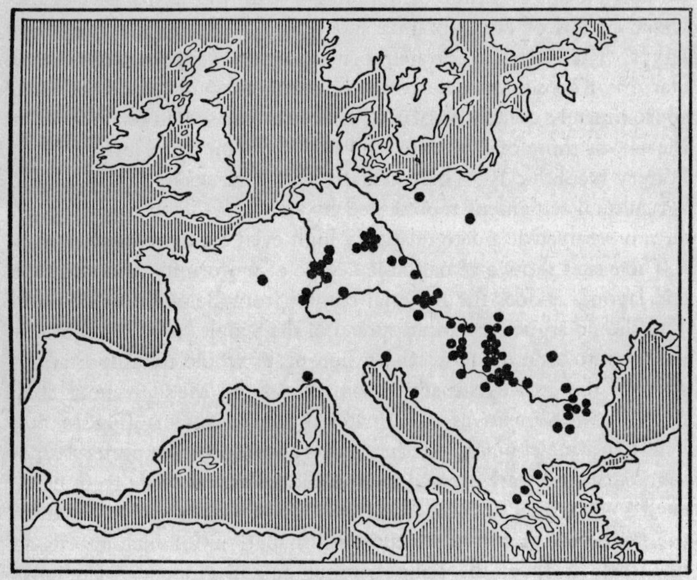

69. Distribution of *Spondylus* ornaments

feature which should reflect some difference in above-ground construction and function between the two ends of the house. This, it has been suggested, might relate to some such circumstance as keeping farmyard stock, or the harvest, under the same roof as the family. But this differentiation of structure is not wholly constant, and in the later phases of the cultures the house plan is often modified to a trapeze form, wider at one end, and the whole post structure is set in a continuous bedding trench. Within the walls of the houses are up to three rows of posts, presumably to support a ridge roof structure with aisles, and other post-supported features of doubtful function. Hearths are not normally present inside the houses, though in Czechoslovakia one such building did in fact contain a row of four hearths down the middle, and in other instances the severe erosion and solution to which the surface of the loess is subject appears to have led to the disappearance of these and other features (Figure 70).

Between the scattered houses in the settlements are numerous shallow pits, sometimes following the outline of the houses; these are to be interpreted as borrow pits for mud daubing of the timber-and-wattle walls. They were at one time thought to be huts, and the

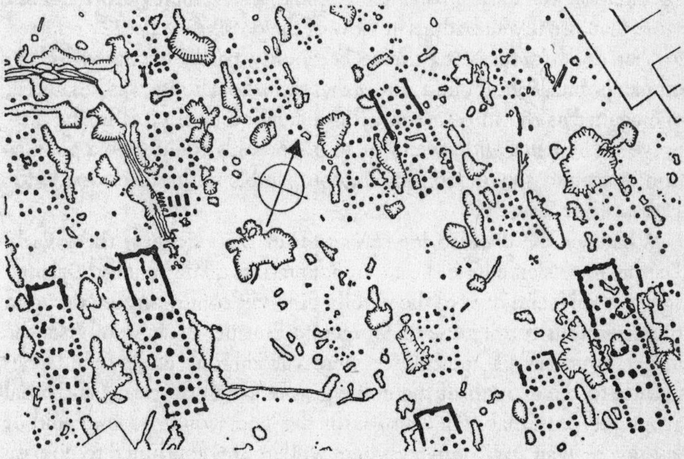

70. Part of Danubian I settlement, Sittard

houses barns, but the small stake holes round some of the pits are better explicable as designed for holding light fences to keep children out of, or pigs in, the hollows rather than the walls of flimsy huts. What were also claimed as square post settings supporting raised granaries in the earlier excavations now seem better explained as fragments of half-eroded house plans.

The intersecting house plans on a completely excavated site in suburbs of Cologne can be disentangled to show a village of some twenty-one houses rebuilt seven times, implying that the site was successively abandoned and reoccupied owing to temporary exhaustion of the land after the soil was deprived of its nitrogen content by continuous cropping with cereals. Allowing ten years for each occupation, and fifty for regeneration, the total duration of the Köln-Lindenthal site has been put at some 430 years. This may well be a questionable estimate, and the point is further discussed below. At present this is the only site that offers information on the total number of houses and phases of building – at Sittard in Holland the twenty-two houses excavated formed only a part of the whole site (Figure 70), although the great Bylany sites in Czechoslovakia show larger settlement units and will eventually give us a mass of new information on these problems. Population estimates are rendered more than usually hazardous in view of the possibility already referred to that the structures may have been only partly occupied by the human population: if one assumes that the whole house was inhabited, one again has the implication of an extended family, as in the Tripolye settlements, and twenty or so households could give a population of around 500 to 700 persons, comparable with our estimates for Habaşeşti or Truşeşti.

Whatever the detailed interpretation of the evidence, these Early Danubian settlements indicate an adaptation of ultimately Oriental agricultural techniques to the wholly different conditions obtaining in the deciduous forest zone of temperate Europe. In western Asia the initial processes of agriculture were carried out under conditions natural to the growth of the noble grasses ancestral to the cultivated crops and presumably exhaustion of the land would be less rapid or less severe in an environment where wild grasses continued to flourish and maintain permanent natural growth. Along the Danube, and still more in north-western Europe, the cereal crop was transferred to a habitat alien to that of its ancestors, and the emergence of barley, a type resistant to damp and cold, as an important element in early European crops may be significant. It is usually assumed that, in the absence of any knowledge of rotation and fallowing (other than that obtained by total abandonment of the site), shifting agriculture would be an uncontrollable necessity forced upon the early agriculturalists of temperate Europe, but this does not seem altogether inevitable. Some knowledge of a simple rotation had presumably been current in the eastern European tell settlements, adjacent to the original homeland of the Danubian culture, to ensure their permanency.

There is another point, that of the characteristics of leguminous plants, which feed back nitrogen into the soil and so prevent exhaustion. The presence of such plants (peas, beans, lentils, etc.) in early agricultural assemblages, including the Danubian, could presumably imply either that they were grown separately, and so would produce regenerated plots which could revert to cereals in a simple rotation, or even that they were grown with cereals as a mixed crop, ripening before the corn harvest, and so slowing down nitrogenous exhaustion or even maintaining it in approximate equilibrium. It seems possible that the primitive character of Danubian and similar Neolithic agriculture in Europe has been overestimated, and that settlement was more permanent than has been supposed. Certainly, if local exhaustion of the land was controlled to some degree, the massive timber architecture of the settlements would in itself have a far longer survival value than the ten years suggested above. It is well up to, or exceeds, the standard of house-building in later prehistoric Europe, when settled plough agriculture was fully mastered, and indeed compares favourably with much of the early medieval period: the elaborately fired-clay hard standings of the Tripolye houses again suggest more than transient occupation. Perhaps the permanency that such construction implies should be taken in itself as a hint that the builders of the Danubian villages were contemplating something more than a very temporary occupation when they erected their substantial timber halls on newly cleared sites.

It may be permissible at this stage to make some very tentative inquiries into the size of the areas of cultivation necessary to support the type of community we have been describing in eastern and central-western Europe. It can hardly be dignified with the title of more than reasoned guesswork, but provided it is not given too much weight, it is worth-while to make the attempt. The simple formula is that the consumption-yield of grain per acre, multiplied by the population and divided by the consumption per head, will give the acreage necessary to support that population unit. Unfortunately, in prehistory all three factors must be assumptions. We have already made such assumptions for certain population units, and for the other two, figures originally used for Early Iron Age farming in Britain may be adopted as reasonable: a consumption-yield of seven bushels of corn per acre and a human cereal consumption of ten bushels per head per year.

Applying these hypothetical factors, we would have as a start, using Braidwood's estimated population for Jarmo as 150 persons, a requirement of about 200 to 220 acres of cereal cultivation in each year to provide corn for that village. In Europe, Karanovo, with an estimated population of about twice that of Jarmo, would therefore need something over 400 acres under crop. If the houses in the enormous Tripolye site of Vladimirovka are all indeed of one period, the proportionally large figure of some 6,000 acres would be needed to feed the extended families we have assumed to have lived in the houses there. Kolomiishchina and Truşeşti and Habaşeşti would, respectively, need about 1,400, 1,000 and 700 acres, and finally the Köln-Lindenthal village, of some twenty extended families, around 600 to 800 acres.

If one thinks of cultivation in terms of the responsibility of a family, these undivided Danubian family units could each be responsible for some twenty-four acres, whereas to apply the same principle to Karanovo would be to allot to each nuclear family responsibility for about fourteen acres. The Danubian figure is a perfectly possible one, but for the tell type of settlements such as Karanovo, cultivation could be organized only through some form of social structure in which cooperation between family groups was involved, through the medium of 'town fields' or some alternative system.

However uncertain the assumptions for corn-production and -consumption may be, the relative proportions among the sites will be the same, as we are left with the assumption that our different house-types imply different social structures in terms of types of family. If this can be considered valid, we may be seeing a correlation between the transference of agricultural techniques beyond the eastern European nuclear area of tell settlements and a change in social structure. This change would be, among other things, from a social situation demanding the relatively complex and static social organization of some form of shared obligations in farming for the whole village or township, to one more mobile and adjustable, in terms of social units comprised within extended families, each capable of producing its own cereal supplies and so perhaps better adapted to advancing the frontiers of early agriculture into the virgin lands of Europe.

The concentration of Danubian settlements on the loess soils is presumably related to the presence of natural plant cover which would permit of agriculture with digging stick or hoe. Prairie or steppe, with its tough grass-sod cover, is so difficult to break up with primitive agricultural implements that the soft soil of woodlands is preferred, even though this involves felling trees or at least the elimination of as much of the tree canopy as possible to allow access of light to the cleared soil and growing crop. In this connexion we may note the situation of the Tripolye settlements in the forest-steppe belt but not on the steppe itself, and recall that, in comparable conditions in North America, Indian agriculture was inadequate for cultivating such grasslands as the potentially rich prairie regions of Iowa, and was normally carried out in cleared woodland. Here again we may appositely note that clearance was by burning, and large trees were killed by ringing, so that the foliage died and admitted the sun; the ash from the burning, of course, provided a rich fertilizer for the new crops.

The Indian situation, important because the natural conditions of environment on the North American continent approximated closely enough to those of Europe, may be used here in another context. The Iroquois of New York State lived in extended families in settlements of long houses averaging 60 by 18 feet in size, with light pole framing and walls, and barrel roofs made of layers of elm bark. It was a matriarchal society, and each of the cultivated plots for growing maize was owned and worked by a long-house extended family. The villages or townships (which could comprise up to 3,000 persons) were shifted about twice a generation owing to exhaustion of the soil, scarcity of firewood and building timber, and depletion of game. Here is a situation closely comparable with those suggested by the archaeological evidence for Tripolye and Early Danubian cultures, except that the population units in America may have exceeded the norm of Neolithic Europe and the houses were certainly of much lighter and less permanent construction in the New World. In terms of basic economics, however, the comparison would appear valid enough.

The next region of Europe to be examined must be that of the Mediterranean coasts and the western world from the Rhine to the Atlantic coasts of the Iberian peninsula. Here, unfortunately, we are sadly lacking in evidence for settlement patterns and house types in much of the area concerned, and for the earliest agricultural colonization west of the Aegean we rely almost wholly on potsherds. From the central Mediterranean region, which includes Malta, Sicily and southern Italy, westwards along the Ligurian and southern French coasts, and to eastern and southern Spain, there are sites yielding versions of impressed or rusticated wares which bear a general resemblance to those we have already encountered in Thessaly, and less specifically to those of the earliest agricultural settlements of the Balkans. Similar wares are again known from sites along the North African coast. In two stratified cave sites, one in Liguria and the other in the south of France, occupation layers containing such pottery and the bones of domestic animals, or animals presumed domesticated, occur immediately over strata of final Mesolithic Sauveterrian or Tardenoisian tradition. At the Ligurian site of Arene Candide the Mesolithic flint industry, with 'trapezes', continues into the layers containing the impressed pottery, but bones of presumed domestic animals do not appear earlier. At Châteauneuf-les-Martigues, near Marseilles, the bones of sheep, pigs and cattle are already present in the Mesolithic stratum and continue (as do the flint types) into the layers in which pottery is also present. In terms of absolute chronology we have seen that such final Mesolithic cultures may be relatively late, but Carbon 14 dates for Ligurian impressed pottery sites of about 4618 and 4284 B.C. imply that such pottery, either as a single cultural component or as a concomitant of the earliest agriculture in the region, was being made in the western Mediterranean at a time not far removed from the Starčevo-Körös wares to which it may be related. In Iberia the impressed wares are again found in cave sites; here and elsewhere in the Mediterranean a specialized version with impressions made with the edge of a cockle shell ('cardial ware') also appears.

In Sicily and southern Italy similar pottery appears in settlement sites on the limestone. Stentinello in Sicily, with a highly individual form of the impressed ware, was surrounded by a rock-cut ditch enclosing an oval area some 700 by 600 feet, but we know nothing of the type or number of houses which may have been within the enclosure; the flint industry here retains the Mesolithic blade and trapeze forms. In Apulia and in the Lipari Islands versions of impressed ware, and analogous incised and scratched types, are associated with painted pottery of more than one style which seems generically to be connected with or derived from that of Sesklo or Dimini in Greece. On the Lipari Acropolis, painted wares, with some black scratch-patterned types, begin a long stratified sequence of occupation on the site, and elsewhere in the Aeolian Islands are comparable settlements which must be connected with the exploitation of the local obsidian, which can be flaked to produce fine blades with extremely sharp but fragile edges; it is a reasonable supposition that such blades were used for shaving, and were like modern safety-razor blades, an expendable commodity of which recurrent supplies were needed. The Apulian sites include ditched enclosures, sometimes containing settlements but perhaps sometimes used for penning flocks or herds, as those near Matera, or such sites as Passo di Corvo on the Foggia Plain, where a great circuit of double-ditches with annexe, 2,400 by 1,500 feet over-all, contained 100 circular enclosures, from 45 to 150 feet in diameter, containing house sites (Figure 71). The material from these sites includes bones of domestic animals, sickle flints and stone or flint axes, but no such objects as figurines or stamp seals to show connexions with more easterly traditions.

The date of these settlements should lie within the fourth millennium B.C., though direct evidence is lacking. But stratified sequences such as those in Lipari and Arene Candide show that they must be earlier than other cultures for which Carbon 14 dates early in, or near the middle of, the third millennium B.C. have been obtained, and certainly we must suppose that, by 3000 B.C. at least, a whole series of agricultural settlements had been established in the central and western Mediterranean. Of these, the earlier would be those with impressed wares, though this style survived for a long time in France and Spain (to the end of the third millennium at least), and in North Africa such pottery seems to have been made until Roman times. Even though this style, and the painted wares which followed it, may have had origins in the Aegean world, the evidence (such as it is) yet implies that at an early stage a specifically western version of peasant economy was being evolved, which was to be transmitted in variant forms northwards across France, to Switzerland and the Rhineland, and to the British Isles. Subsequent connexions between the eastern and western Mediterranean areas are not those of a general movement within an area of common traditions of culture, but specific contacts of trade or colonization coming from the Aegean – by now, developing its own highly

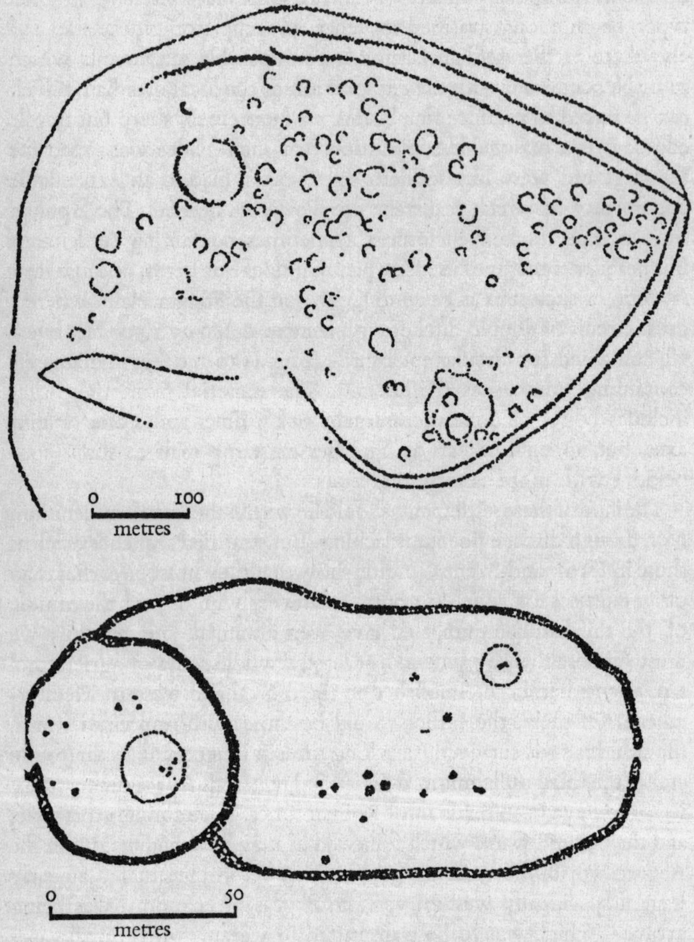


71. Neolithic enclosed settlements, south Italy

characteristic individuality, in which Minoan contributions played an increasing part – into a perceptibly more barbarian world to the west and north-west.

This 'western Neolithic' area shows an increasing spread of farming economies inland from the Mediterranean coasts, attested largely by a simple material culture with stone and flint edge tools and pottery styles based on a limited repertoire of normally undecorated, bag-shaped pots, bowls and cups. Very little is known of settlement plans. Caves were occupied in southern France; and in the French Jura, and still more in Switzerland, the well-known lake-side settlements of these cultures, as a result of the survival of organic materials, have greatly amplified our knowledge of the material equipment. In north-western France many ditch-enclosed sites are known – for instance, in the Charente at Peu Richard and Les Matignons. At the latter site the occupation comes before a Carbon 14 date of about 2615 B.C., and in Brittany an occupation layer in a peat bog at Curnic in Finistère, with pottery, stone axes and transverse flint arrowheads in a Mesolithic tradition, is dated to about 3390 B.C. We shall see too that a collective chambered tomb in the same part of France has a Carbon 14 date around 3280 B.C. These latter dates are not incompatible with those of around 2750 and 2350 B.C. from what appears to be a comparable phase of the French Neolithic in the south of France, and about 2940 B.C. for the earliest agricultural economy in Switzerland.

The Swiss sites have been famous for over a century as the earliest phase of the 'Lake Dwellings'. There is now general agreement that the older view, enshrined in countless restored drawings and museum models, that these settlements were on platforms raised on piles above the open water of the lake, must be abandoned in favour of constructions on the damp ground between strand scrub and lake reeds, when the lakes were at a lower level than they are today. What was needed was an efficient insulating layer of timber and bark, held in place by wooden stakes that were in part elements in the framing of the houses which stood on this platform. The plans of the houses are not easy to disentangle, but they seem certainly to be rectangular, and post settings suggest that dimensions around 24 by 16 feet would be likely: there is no evidence of long houses of the Danubian type. Wheat of the einkorn, emmer and *compactum* types was grown, as well as peas, beans and lentils; wild plums and apples were eaten and the latter split and dried for keeping. Flax was grown for its oil-rich seeds, and also for the fibre, the earliest linen textiles in Europe being those surviving from these contexts. Fine, complex basketry was also made. The animal bones were 70 per cent domesticated, and two assessments give 50 and 39 per cent cattle, 18 and 21 per cent pigs, 10 and 11 per cent sheep and goats, and, in one count, 21 per cent dogs; the high figures for cattle and pigs as against sheep and goats are interesting. Lake fish were also netted and speared. There was an adequate industry in stone and flint, including axes and arrowheads, as well as reaping-knives of a peculiar form with a long flint blade projecting obliquely from the straight haft. Wooden self-bows survive from several sites and bowls, ladles and troughs of wood are relatively common.

In France we have evidence for the survival of Mesolithic flint industries into contexts associated with evidence of the domestication of sheep and goats, contemporary with early agriculture, as at Cuzoul de Gramat in Guyenne. At Belloy-sur-Somme a flint industry of Tardenoisian type was found with sickle flints, bones of domestic animals, and pottery containing impressions of barley grains. There is much collateral evidence to suggest such a position for allegedly Mesolithic industries of this type, and it is possible that the occurrence of cereal pollen in certain central and west-central European peat deposits of Early Atlantic date (earlier than Danubian colonization, which seems to be of Middle Atlantic date) may be related to aceramic cultures with such flint industries.

Spain appears to have shared in the spread of Neolithic cultures with the exception of those associated with impressed wares. Cemeteries in Catalonia contain material that is similar to that from Arene Candide in its Middle Neolithic phase, which can be dated by Swiss and French correlations to before 3000 B.C. In Almeria, settlements of round or oval houses and collective circular or cist graves should be more or less contemporary in the first of its two phases; the origins of this culture have variously been sought in Egypt and in the Cyclades.

The initial implantation of agriculture in the British Isles must in the main have resulted from cross-Channel emigration from areas of Neolithic cultures in France and perhaps Belgium, of the general family of those just described, though there may, as we shall see, have been some contacts with regions of the North European Plain. A group of Carbon 14 dates now shows us that this event must have occurred around or before 3000 B.C.; this date must approximate to the alteration in the plant cover perceptible in peat stratigraphy which indicates a corresponding climatic change, that from Zone VII–a to Zone VII–b in the British forest sequence, or from Atlantic to sub-Boreal in climatic terms. This point needs further comment. In northern Europe this change in the composition of the natural plant cover so often coincides with evidence for the first agricultural settlement of the region as to raise doubts whether in fact the change was wholly natural or whether, in part at least, it was produced by man. In discussions of the decline of the elm – one of the criteria of the change – much has been made of the hypothetical feeding of cattle on lopped elm branches, but it is difficult to assume that so large and so decisive an attack on the elms of the northern deciduous forests could have been made by what must after all have been small and migratory bands of farmers and pastoralists. There appears to be no evidence, incidentally, to show that the advent of the Early Danubian agriculturalists in central Europe had any perceptible effect on the pollen percentage in the Atlantic phase to which they would belong.

The earliest British agricultural communities seem to have been established in southern England as the result of cross-Channel migration which radio-carbon dates show to have been as early as about 3400 B.C. Similar movements may have been responsible for an independent but parallel introduction of agriculture to Ireland, where Carbon 14 dates such as that of about 3060 B.C. for an Ulster site suggest an early continental contact not necessarily connected with the broadly contemporary English events. The English culture included large earthwork enclosures often of more than one concentric ring of discontinuous ditches; they do not seem to have enclosed permanent settlements, but were certainly occupied intermittently, perhaps in connexion with some form of cattle corralling. At the type site of Windmill Hill in Wiltshire, the earthworks were found to have been constructed on a site already occupied and in part cultivated, with a Carbon 14 date of about 2950 B.C. for this initial settlement, and about 2570 for the earlier silting of the main ditch of the enclosure. The agricultural economy was based on domesticated cattle, pigs, sheep, goats and dogs; of the cultivated plants, einkorn and emmer wheat predominated over barley in the proportions of 91·6 to 8·4 of the grain impressions in the pottery. Flax was also grown and wild apples collected, as in the Swiss lake-side settlements. The material culture included excellent pottery, mainly plain dark wares but also a high-quality burnished type, made within reach of the Devon or Cornish rocks (which contributed to its grit) and traded into southern and eastern England from the west. Similarly, stone was used for axe blades in the west, and flint in the chalk areas, where it was mined extensively. By the middle of the third millennium B.C., systematic exploitation of stone for axe blades was taking place in Cornwall, North Wales, Cumberland, Northern Ireland and other localities, the products of the 'factories' being traded widely over the British Isles. An axe of North Welsh stone was found in a context in Somerset with a Carbon 14 date of about 2580 B.C., and a lake-side settlement of people in Cumberland who used axes from the not very distant Great Langdale screes is similarly dated to around 2165 B.C. We need not suppose that these mining and stone-working activities necessitated specialized full-time labour, but the trading system whereby the products were distributed must have been on a level of efficiency comparable with that usually associated with similar activities in early metallurgy, though over shorter distances.

We shall touch on the general question of the stone-built collective chamber tombs of western Europe at a later stage in this chapter, but at this point we may note that the Windmill Hill culture in the south of England (and in a variant form as far up the east coast of Britain as Aberdeenshire) seems to be characterized by a type of collective burial beneath elongated mounds of earth or stone, frequently of trapezoid plan. In these long barrows various forms of timber structure are incorporated, including mortuary chambers which could not, however, have been used for successive burials once they had been buried under the mound, but which seem to have served as ossuaries up to this phase of construction. Carbon 14 dates for such barrows in south England range from about 3200 to 2720 B.C., so that the type appears to be primary to the culture. The continental origins of such monuments remain obscure, but possible analogues are mentioned below.

In the areas occupied since at least the fourth millennium B.C. by the earlier peasant cultures, we can observe a fragmentation of the original large, homogeneous culture-areas into local individual versions with divergent pottery styles and, though less often, differentiation in other traits of material culture as well. The long-house, tentatively associated with the social phenomenon of the extended family, persists in some areas, notably in the north-eastern regions such as Poland, where houses with trapezoid plans up to 100 feet long have the entire post-structure of the walls set in a continuous bedding trench, but otherwise resemble the Early Danubian houses already described. Elements in the material culture, such as antler mattocks and the use of boar tusk for ornaments, suggest a mixture with Mesolithic traditions, but eastern Mediterranean contacts are also apparent in the imported sea shells and copper ornaments of double spiral form, implying a date in the second half of the third millennium B.C.

In the descendants of the earlier Danubian cultures in some areas, such as southern Germany, we see the abandonment of the long-house in favour of two-roomed houses about 20 by 12 feet over-all, with a smaller room in front containing a clay oven. The lake-side village of Aichbühl consisted of twenty-four houses, and its population, based on a single nuclear family per house, would thus amount to some 120 persons, whose grain consumption on the estimates previously used would demand about 170 acres of corn plots (Figure 72). Larger villages of up to seventy-five houses are known, with evidence of frequent re-flooring, implying a long-continuing settlement.

Over a large area of the North European Plain, from the basins of the Vistula and Oder to north-western Germany, Holland and Scandinavia, we encounter an early agricultural economy of obscure origin but perhaps derived in part from Danubian and in part from 'western' sources. The earliest of the four main phases distinguished on the grounds of pottery types has Carbon 14 dates of about 3185 and 3075 B.C. in northern Germany, and about 2820 B.C. in Denmark, not far from the dates of the early Swiss (Cortaillod) culture or that of Windmill Hill in England. In Denmark we can see the interaction between this intrusive agricultural economy and the surviving indigenous coastal hunting-and-fishing groups, who acquired at this time the techniques of making coarse pottery. In the fourth phase of the culture, long barrows were being built in western Poland similar in plan and construction to the earlier English examples just mentioned but containing individual extended burials; copper ornaments link the third phase in Denmark with Poland and Rumania. In Scandinavia, Holland and much of northern Germany, the pottery styles of this agricultural economy, basic for the northern European world, show a continuance into the second millennium B.C. in various regional groups.

In Denmark, at Barkaer in Jutland, an extraordinary settlement, probably of the third phase of the culture, has been excavated, consisting of two parallel buildings each 300 by 200 feet over-all, with a cobbled pathway 10 feet wide between them. Both buildings were

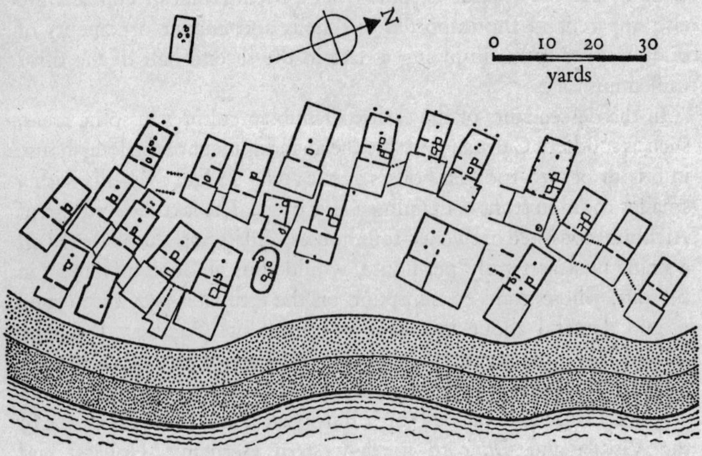


72. Late Neolithic settlement at Aichbühl

subdivided into twenty-six identical single-room elements, each 12 feet wide and containing a hearth; 'foundation offerings' in pits under the houses contained amber beads, pottery and copper ornaments. This settlement would appear to imply a population of some 250 persons if each room is construed as a house for a nuclear family, but the regularity of planning and the regimented coordination of the whole are without parallel elsewhere. Similar 'offerings' of amber and copper objects, contained in pots of the second and third phase, have been found elsewhere in Jutland, and the copper types (flat axe-blades, a dagger and spiral ornaments) are presumably to be derived from some East European area where copper metallurgy had been established at or before the middle of the third millennium B.C.

In Scandinavia and northern Germany, in the latter phase of this first northern agricultural economy, individual burial within a massive stone-built cist, or 'dolmen', becomes frequent, and these dolmens may be contained in long mounds flanked with a boulder kerb. In the early study of Scandinavian prehistory, these large structures were placed at the beginning of a continuous typological series, which the pottery sequence as represented in the grave offerings confirmed, and which continued from the dolmens into varying forms of collective megalithic tombs with chamber-and-passage plan. The whole was envisaged as a self-contained Nordic evolution. We can now see that, while the development of the pottery and other elements in material culture is a valid local sequence, confusion has arisen between the single-burial dolmens and the collective chamber tombs, stemming from the fact that both series of structures of necessity use the only available stone of the region, the clumsy and massive glacial boulders which render any building inevitably 'megalithic' in the literal sense. The collective chamber tombs (Figure 73) are, as a ritual architectural

73. Collective tomb at West Kennet, Wiltshire, England

type, intrusive into the north, and an assessment of the general problems posed by such monuments must form the concluding section of this chapter.

The tradition of the rock-cut tomb for single or collective burial goes back in the eastern Mediterranean at least to the beginning of the third millennium B.C. At a date not much later than that it can be traced (probably initially as a single-grave burial) in the west-central Mediterranean in Sicily and southern Italy. In that region and further west, in areas including Malta and perhaps southern Spain, an architectural development took place whereby the ritual necessities of a tomb chamber, with an entrance and approach, which could be used for successive burials and blocked when necessary, were translated into architectural form in an above-ground structure that retained the planning of the rock-cut version. In Malta the development took the unique form of the creation of monuments which can only be called temples, in which burial was no longer the primary function. Elsewhere, either rock-cut tombs for collective burial continued to be made or (as in Iberia) above-ground chamber tombs for multiple and successive burials developed into characteristic architectural modes during the third millennium B.C.

The early stages of the development of the above-ground tomb and its later rock-cut counterparts in the western Mediterranean are complex and obscure. But in Iberia this development must in part be associated with the establishment in the middle of the third millennium B.C. of what have been called the 'colonies' of eastern Mediterranean and perhaps mainly Cycladic origin. At several sites in the south and south-west of the peninsula, from Almeria to the Tagus estuary, copper-using communities whose material culture included exotic elements of eastern Mediterranean derivation or inspiration seem to have been established within a comparatively short period of time. At Los Millares in Almeria and Vila Nova de San Pedro near Lisbon the settlements were fortified with stone walls having a series of external semicircular bastions, for which the only parallels are at such sites as Chalandriani on Syros or in the Early Helladic phase at Lerna on the Greek mainland: we may recall the Carbon 14 date of about 2670 B.C. for Early Helladic I and 2431 B.C. for Early Helladic II (Figure 74). Bone pins at Vila Nova include bird-headed forms that were at home in the Aegean in the third millennium, pottery types and ornament recall Cycladic styles, and at Los Millares are what may be miniature copies in bone of Egyptian types of semi-circular axe blades of types current around 2000 B.C. The copper technology of these 'colonists' included the capacity to cast in closed moulds, and it is possible that the establishment of these small exotic settlements was connected with a trade in metals, including perhaps the silver deposits in such localities as Herrerias: silver appears in the Aegean at this time and could be of westerly origin. The modern sailing distance from the Piraeus to Gibraltar is about 1,800 miles, but

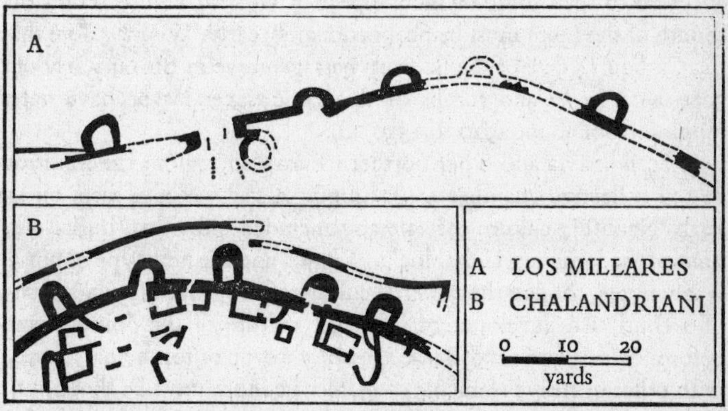


74. Bastioned defences at Los Millares and Chalandriani

any contacts would obviously be maintained by short coasting journeys. A Carbon 14 date for a mature phase of the Los Millares settlement is around 2345 B.C.

The chamber tombs of 'passage grave' type immediately outside the bastioned wall of the settlement at Los Millares, and other similar tombs containing characteristic objects of the culture of the 'colonists' at Alcala in Portugal, show that this type of sepulchral architecture must have been current in the western Mediterranean by the middle of the third millennium B.C. at least. Beyond the Strait of Gibraltar and along the Atlantic coasts of Europe to western France, the British Isles and ultimately Scandinavia, the distribution pattern of collective stone-built chamber tombs shows that the architectural type, presumably embodying concomitant ritual and beliefs, was spread into areas where Neolithic cultures had already been established, so that the grave-goods in the tombs represent the contemporary material culture of the region, and not a set of new traits introduced with the concept of the tombs themselves. Similarly, movements eastwards in the western and central Mediterranean brought various collective-tomb forms, rock-cut or stone-built, into such areas as southern France and Sardinia. In the northern world, the building of collective chamber tombs within the area of the southern English Windmill Hill culture must have begun by at least the middle of the third millennium B.C., if not before, and the characteristic architectural forms ancestral to such tombs which appear in western France round the mouth of the Loire must be proportionately early. We may note that the Carbon 14 date of the Île Carn passage grave in Brittany is about 3280 B.C.; in Ireland tombs of this same general type have dates ranging from about 1920 to 1520 B.C.

In Scandinavia and other northern European regions the tradition of the collective chamber tomb impinged, as we have seen, on an Early Neolithic culture that already included individual burial cists built of the local unwieldy blocks of stone, and the new type of burial was adopted, though the material culture of the grave offerings is that of a continued development from the culture of the dolmens and before. This Atlantic and Baltic spread of a type of tomb unassociated with other intrusive elements of material culture must be thought of as analogous to the spread of early Christianity or Islam, in which a stereotyped form of ritual building is duplicated in all areas where the new religion is adopted, though not necessarily with the adoption of any other cultural traits from the region of proximal origin. Once established in western Europe, the collective chamber tomb and the ritual that brought it into being had a long life, producing such eccentricities and deviations from the original tomb form in, for instance, the British Isles that one wonders whether architectural divergencies were accompanied by equally curious vagaries in basic concepts and beliefs.

It will have become clear that considerable diversity is apparent in the different areas of Europe to which agriculture was introduced or in which it was acquired through culture contact. As might be expected from their geographical situation, the settlements of tell type in the south-east, dating probably from the sixth millennium B.C. onwards, come closest to the Near Eastern norm of settled peasant economy, and indeed represent a provincial western outpost of such communities. If we are right in thinking that the Near Eastern evidence suggests that these settlements are to be associated with a social order involving some sort of general assembly, a council of elders and an elected ruler, such a social structure might have been brought into Europe in the context of the tell settlements of the south-east.

Beyond the area of the settlements, however, in the Ukraine and the Carpathians on the one hand and in the Danube basin on the other, profound modifications of the original economic pattern seem to have been made, as territory geographically and climatically increasingly divergent from that of western Asia was colonized at the end of the fifth and in the fourth millennium B.C. Some form of shifting agriculture, perhaps of the slash-and-burn type, seems demonstrated in both the forest-steppe and the full deciduous forest zones, and the accompanying modification in house types suggests that forms of social structure embodying extended family systems had come into being in both areas. The long-house, and so presumably the social unit that it sheltered, persisted in the north-east (e.g. in Poland) until late in the third millennium B.C. at least, and a curiously formalized version appears in Jutland.

In the west our information is far less amenable to interpretation, in part owing to the lack of adequate excavation. An initial colonization of the Mediterranean coasts seems indicated, with a subsequent spread to the north across France to Switzerland, Britain and the Rhineland of some form or forms of simple stone-using agricultural economy at the end of the fourth millennium B.C. There is no evidence for the long-house in these western cultures, and there are hints that their economy may have had an increased pastoral content. The long-house also disappears in central Europe, and villages of houses appropriate to nuclear families appear in its stead. Contacts between the eastern and western Mediterranean appear to have led to the development of copper metallurgy at points in the latter area by the middle of the third millennium, contemporary with, but deriving from traditions different from, that of the early metallurgy of the Carpathians. From the third millennium, too, evidence is found for the spread, first in the Mediterranean and subsequently along the Atlantic littoral, of a mortuary cult involving the construction of rock-cut or stone-chambered tombs for collective burial.

By the end of the third millennium B.C., stone-using agricultural economies had become established over virtually the whole of Europe south of the Arctic or near-Arctic regions. The situation in extreme eastern Europe and the adjacent steppe regions of Asia, to the north of the long-established agricultural traditions of the ancient Near East, must be examined in another chapter, where the long survival of hunting-and-fishing economies in these areas will also be discussed. We have already indicated that the centuries around 2000 B.C. were, in western Asia and in Europe, a momentous period in the realignment of powers and the movements of peoples. In such a context the intrusion into central and northern Europe of peoples of steppe ancestry and the developments in non-ferrous metallurgy, which in technological terms move us from a Neolithic to a Bronze Age world, both play a part. For the moment, we may conveniently end this chapter, which has described the primary establishment of agriculture on the European continent, and later turn to its sequel, the middle, formative phase of later prehistory.

CHAPTER ELEVEN

# *The Later Prehistoric Settlement of Northern Eurasia and China*

A FIRM limit was set to the northward expansion of farming economy – and so of the Neolithic way of life – by ecological circumstances. The feeding of livestock and the cultivation of cereals could hardly have been carried on beyond the range of temperate conditions as these were defined by the northern frontier of the deciduous forest. Although this may locally have extended beyond the existing limit, the evidence of fossil pollen suggests that, broadly speaking, the position in Neolithic times was much as it is today; and this is confirmed by the pattern of Neolithic settlement. Whereas the whole of the British Isles, including even the Shetland Islands, was colonized by Neolithic farmers, vast tracts of the northern hemisphere could only be occupied by peoples able to support themselves by hunting, fishing, fowling and gathering. The frontier between the two ways of life, which it is important to emphasize was never precisely drawn and which fluctuated in the course of time, may be summarily traced: from the coastal zone of south-west Norway it looped round the head of Oslo fjord and across middle Sweden to include the province of Uppsala; across southern Finland it ran from the province of Turku along the north shore of the Gulf of Finland; and from thence across European Russia to the head-waters of the Volga.

Although the circumpolar zone, comprising extensive tracts of coniferous and birch forests, and in the far north open tundra extending to the shores of the Arctic Ocean, was not suitable for primitive farming, it was capable of providing a rich living for people able to exploit its vast resources of wild life. Indeed, as we shall see, the northern hunter-fishers lived a life in no obvious way inferior to that of the rather low-grade peasants of the North European Plain with whom, in the area of overlap from Denmark to middle Sweden, they lived in particularly close relationship.

On the score that they borrowed the art of potting from their peasant neighbours to the south – they made characteristic egg-shaped vessels decorated more or less lavishly with comb-imprints and pits (Figure 75) – the circumpolar peoples of the period can rightfully be classified as sub-Neolithic in the sense that they appropriated one of the main Neolithic crafts without practising a Neolithic economy. Yet this must not be taken to mean that they were in any sense inferior: on the contrary, their economy represents what was in the conditions of the day the most effective use of the potentialities of

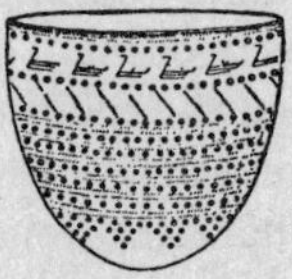

75. Pot with water birds, lake Onega

their territory; and to judge from their art, as seen both in rock-engravings and in small artifacts, their spiritual life was at least as lively. It seems unlikely that, apart from various kinds of berry in the tundra zone, the northern territories provided much in the way of wild plant food. As during the earlier part of the Boreal period in Denmark, when the forests were likewise mainly of pine and birch, elk were among the most prized victims, though sea mammals like seals and porpoises played an important part in the Baltic and on the Atlantic and Arctic coasts; in addition to meat and blood, the former yielded hides for clothing, boats and possibly tents, sinews for lines and sewing thread, bones for harpoon-heads, and fat for lighting and heating. The territory was also well adapted to fishing: great rivers like those of the Soviet Union, inland lakes and, in the case of the Baltic, the Atlantic and the Arctic, the sea itself provided ample opportunities, particularly for line-fishing. Again, fowling made its own contribution both on inland waters, notably on lake Onega, and on the sea coasts.

In the intermediate territories of south Scandinavia a mixed economy was practised, and the various catching activities were fitted into the farming year: for instance, the farmers of the Bergen-Stavanger region of south-west Norway took time off for the fishing season, when they occupied caves and rock-shelters and took cod, ling, whiting and other fine fish that must, in conjunction with other forms of catching, have added richly to the sources of food provided by herds and corn-plots; again, there is evidence for intensive seal-hunting from Gotland and round the south coast of Sweden, and this was carried on by people who spent much of their time farming. To judge from recent practice, and from the youth of many of the seals represented on prehistoric sites, it seems likely that the young were attacked while still on the ice or the rocks, immediately prior to taking the water; but we also know that harp and ringed seals were harpooned because bone and antler harpoon-heads have been found with skeletons at various points round the coasts of Finland and Sweden.

To aid them in traversing their vast hunting grounds, the Arctic peoples used sledges and skis and turned to account one of the very factors that inhibited farming, namely the length and severity of the winter and the duration of snow cover. Heavy sledges twelve feet or more long, with runners hollowed out for much of their length and holes in the side flanges for securing the superstructure, had already been invented by the Mesolithic pioneers. The sledges used in the area from Scandinavia to the Urals, and possibly beyond, by the sub-Neolithic hunter-fishers, with whom we are now concerned, were more refined in construction, and the cords needed for bracing were threaded through holes in the upper surface on either side of the median groove in which the uprights supporting the platform were set (Figure 76). Although a little lighter and smaller, these sledges were still big enough to carry the tents and belongings of a hunter and his family and can hardly have been drawn by manpower alone. Since there is no sign that reindeer had been domesticated at this time, it seems almost certain that dogs, at least two varieties of which were kept, served as sledge teams. The skis used by the sub-Neolithic hunter-fishers were of the Arctic type, still used in one form or another, over a vast territory from Norway to the Bering Strait – broad and short, tapered at one end, squared at the other, and having the under-surface covered with hide. From actual finds preserved in old lake-beds and from the Carelian rock-engravings, we know that such skis were used in conjunction with steering sticks to bring the hunter and his bow within shooting distance of his intended prey. Conversely, for hunting and fishing at sea or on inland waters,

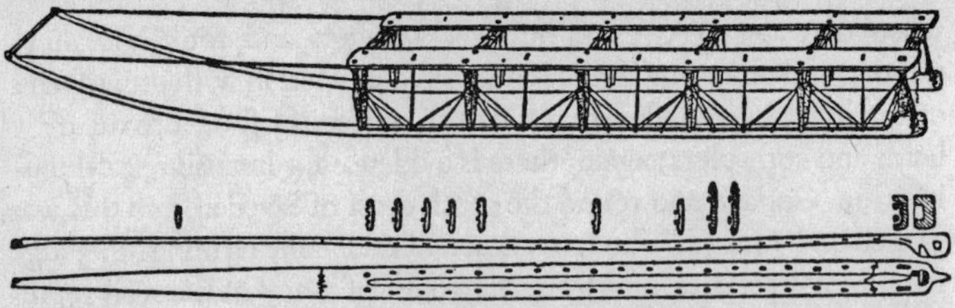

76. Reconstructed sledge, Finland

the Arctic people developed light, easily manoeuvrable boats, made from animal skins stretched over light wooden frames. It is significant that, when depicted on the Norwegian rock-engravings, these boats are shown in more or less close association with seals, porpoises or large fish (Figure 77).

Although in due course they acquired bronze, the circumpolar people were for long dependent entirely on flint, stone and various organic substances for tools and weapons. By contrast with their southern neighbours they made extensive use of slate, which by means of sawing and polishing they shaped into a variety of single-edged

77. Skin boat, whale and seal

knives, daggers, spearheads and arrowheads (Figure 78). Equally, they made a variety of wood-working tools, notably adzes with gouged or hollow-ground working edge, from different kinds of stone and even imported flint ones from Denmark. Where flint could be obtained fairly easily, as in Carelia or southernmost Scandinavia, it was used to make a particular type of flake-arrow, which might be finished by delicate scale-flaking. The same technique was applied to a wide range of materials from flint to quartz for finishing arrowheads of leaf, lozenge or hollow-based form, as well as knives, spearheads and even representations of animal forms. The microlithic technique, on the other hand, had vanished almost completely, save for the production of the regular microflakes needed for inserting into slotted

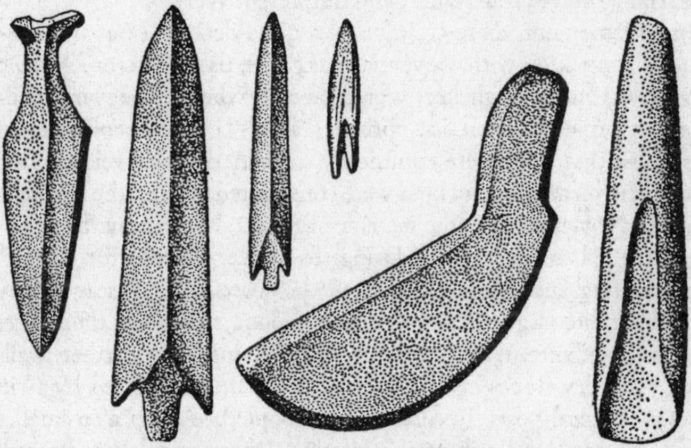

78. Slate and stone forms, Arctic Stone Age

bone points, a type widely distributed in Eurasia and itself of Mesolithic origin. Another Mesolithic bone form, the fish-hook, underwent considerable development: although barbless hooks continued in use, barbed ones became common: and over broad tracts of Eurasia as far west as Norway a composite form was used in which the shank and point were made from separate pieces bound together.

A notable feature of circumpolar culture was the extent to which raw materials were traded. This was in some measure due to the mobility inherent in a hunting way of life, but it was facilitated in this case by the possibilities of snow transport. Much of the trade took place within the confines of the circumpolar zone itself. For instance, the green slate of Olonetz in Carelia was traded over much of Finland as well as to the east Baltic states, the red slate of Ångermanland in Sweden was carried across the Gulf of Bothnia to Finland, and east

Baltic amber passed through the Trondheim gap to the west coast of Norway. On the other hand, the trade in axe and adze blades and later in dagger blades made of Danish flint, a trade that reached the mouths of the great Swedish rivers by way of the Baltic and spread as far as the Lofoten Islands, traversed the divide between the two provinces, presumably in return for the products of trapping in the far north, another indication of the complementary nature of economies based on farming and hunting-and-gathering respectively.

As to settlement, there are signs of a good deal of seasonal movement in connexion with movements of game, fish and so on. At such times caves and rock-shelters would be used where these were available, but numerous open sites with no features beyond fireplaces seem to suggest that tents were commonly used. Artificial dwellings of a more permanent and solid kind were constructed both on the northern coasts of Norway and in the interior of Russia. In Norway the population tended to concentrate during the winter months for cooperative hunting and fishing on and off the coasts. At this season they occupied quite large villages strung out along the shore: the houses were semi-subterranean, oblong in plan, having thick earthen walls faced with dry stones and turf roofs on a frame supported by twin rows of vertical posts. In summer the people broke up into smaller groups to hunt and fish in the interior. Rivers and lakes attracted settlement in the Russian taiga and timber provided the main material for buildings. In Russia the settlements were commonly on river-banks or on peninsulas projecting into lakes.

A further indication that despite seasonal mobility there was a basic stability in social life is provided by the size of cemeteries and by the wealth of objects buried with the dead. The best explored sites are those on Olen Ostrov, an island in the northern part of lake Onega (Figure 79), Karelia and Västerbjers on the Baltic island of Gotland. In both, the graves are numerous – over 170 were examined at the former, and at least 49 survived at the latter, despite extensive quarrying. The dead were buried in an extended position, fully clothed and accompanied by ornaments and other personal possessions; red ochre was scattered over the bodies as a general rule at Olen (a practice that seems to have originated among Advanced Palaeolithic peoples), but only rarely at Västerbjers. Analysis of the grave goods found in graves of the two sexes gives a useful insight into the basic division of labour. The importance of hunting among both communities – and it must be remembered that the Gotlanders relied to some degree on farming – is reflected in the lavish use of the teeth of wild animals for personal ornament by both sexes: at Olen elk, bear and beaver were especially favoured, and at Västerbjers wild boar and seal. At Västerbjers it was observed that whereas hunting seems to

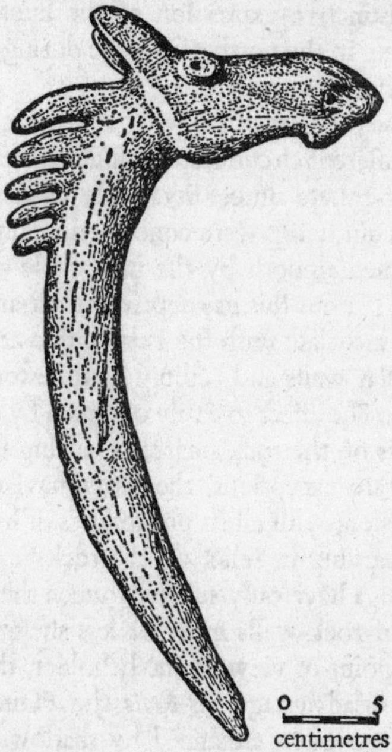

79. Ceremonial object, Olen Island cemetery

have been the responsibility of men, with whom were buried flint flake and slate arrowheads and the barbed antler and bone heads of harpoons and spears, line-fishing was practised by men and women alike. Much of the women's work, like the preparation of skins, the making of clothes, the gathering of plant food and cooking, was of a routine character, far removed from exploit and not associated with equipment to which the user felt the same attachment as a hunter to his arrows or harpoon.

A most vivid and penetrating insight into their life is provided by graphic art. Like the much older Franco-Cantabric art with which it challenges comparison, the Arctic group is mainly devoted to the representation of animal forms, in varying degrees of naturalism, both on small movable objects and on the surface of the living rock. Despite a number of other points of resemblance, and the possibility that there may even prove to be some element of continuity, the Arctic art is a distinctive expression of the hunting and catching mentality prevailing in the north of Europe during some parts of the second and third millennia B.C.

In comparing the rock-art of the two groups it is important to take note of the very different circumstances under which it was executed. The Arctic hunter-fishers almost invariably worked in the open air and, so far as the engravings were concerned, mainly on the surfaces of hard rocks planed smooth by the inexorable movement of ice-sheets. For several reasons this has deprived their art of something of the animation we associate with the Palaeolithic art, executed as this was on the irregular walls and ceilings of limestone caves often far from the entrance. The effect so easily obtained by exploiting natural bosses and hollows on the rock surface is lacking from the northern art; again, with rare exceptions, the Scandinavian rocks were too hard to allow incision, with all its possibilities of liveliness and spontaneity, still less carving in relief on the rock-face; and, with few exceptions, paintings have only survived when these were applied to the vertical face of rock-walls more or less sheltered from the elements. From the point of view of the beholder, the Arctic rock-art suffers a further disadvantage *vis-à-vis* the Franco-Cantabric, the effect of which is so often enhanced by shadows cast by artificial light in the mysterious ambience of the caverns: we must beware of underestimating either the technical skill or the magic of the Arctic art merely because we view it in the common light of day.

The distribution of movable works of art in the Arctic style shows that this extended at least as far east as Sverdlovsk, the territory immediately east of the mid-Ural gap, but so far as we know at present the rock-art did not reach beyond Karelia. The most numerous finds have been made in the western half of the Scandinavian peninsula, distributed at intervals round the whole Norwegian coast from either side of Oslo fjord up to the uppermost province of Finnmark, with an eastward intrusion from the Trondelag into central Sweden. In view of this pattern it seems reasonable to view the isolated finds in Finland and the much richer but still localized occurrences in Karelia, on the lower Vyg as this approaches the White Sea, and on the east side of lake Onega, as extensions from the Scandinavian province, either from central Sweden across the Gulf of Bothnia or from Finnmark round the White Sea. It is worth emphasizing that paintings are almost as widely distributed as engravings, occurring in south and south-west Norway, in the Trondelag, on the north-west coast as far north as *c.* 69° N., in central Sweden and in south Finland. They must surely be considered an integral part of the art group, and it seems probable that they were once commoner than the engravings. Apart from the single locality of Hell in the Trondelag, where the rock was soft enough for incision, designs were either pecked out of the surface or ground into it so as to form a smooth U-sectioned line. This ground technique is restricted to the coastal region of Norway between Trondheim fjord and Vestfjord and the engravings made by it in themselves comprise a distinct group, life-sized and naturalistic in feel though depicted only in profile. The cortical situation of this group, its archaic treatment and the height of the engravings above modern sea-level combine to suggest that it is the earliest in the Arctic rock-art. By comparison, the rock-engravings to the north, south and east, and all the paintings, are smaller in size and more schematic in treatment.

Among the animals most commonly represented in the engravings and paintings of all styles are elk, reindeer and bear, with porpoises, seals, halibut and water-birds as well in coastal areas. Unlike the Franco-Cantabric group, in which women are commonly shown, these appear to be quite absent from the Arctic art, whereas men are featured rather frequently. More often than not, the men are distinctly phallic, and on several occasions they are depicted in hunting scenes, in skin boats, mounted on skis (Figure 80) or, as in a notable instance at Garde in central Sweden, linked by footprints to an elk (Figure 81). It is evident that in a general sense the Arctic, like the Franco-Cantabric art, was an outcome of anxiety about the chase and about the continuance of game and of men. Enigmatic patterns, frequently with lozenge-like motives, recall in the most general way similar features in the cave art and, like these, may well have some magical significance. The close juxtaposition of the rock-art with water, whether lakes, rivers, waterfalls or inlets of the sea, would also seem to call for some magical explanation; either water was thought to be linked in some way with the game animals that drank it or even lived in it, or conceivably its capacity to flow was in some way associated with renewal of life or reproduction.

The same preoccupation with animals and men is reflected in the movable art. More or less schematic figures of human beings, again masculine where the sex was indicated, were carved from a variety of

80. Skiing scene

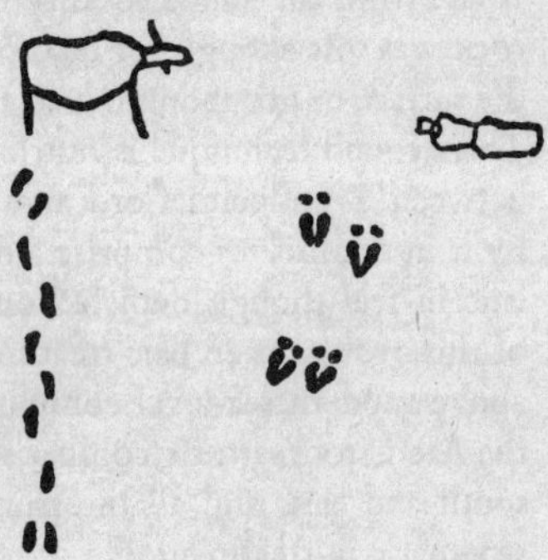

81. Hunting-magic scene

materials, including amber, bone and wood, as well as modelled in clay and chipped in flint, along with animals, birds and fish. A favourite trick was to carve the heads of various implements and weapons into the shapes of elk- and bear-heads. Some of the perforated stone axes and maceheads treated in this manner display a very high order of workmanship. Other objects with animal-head terminals were slate daggers, bone combs and wooden ladles, closely similar examples of these latter occurring as far apart as Finland and the mid-Ural region. Again, elk and swimming birds were imprinted by combs on the surface of clay pots found in the same area, a symbol of the vitality of hunter-fisher mentality even in the face of borrowings from the peasant world to the south. The whole phenomenon of the Arctic art is an indication, if one were needed, that it was possible to live well, even abundantly, in territories where for ecological reasons farming could either not be practised at all at that time or, as in the marginal zone of south Scandinavia, could only be carried on as a part-time activity.

The acquisition of the techniques of agriculture was a late feature in the development of the Eurasian hunting-and-fishing communities described in Chapter 5. We have seen that the craft of pottery-making was acquired by some of these groups, from the Baltic to lake Baikal, but without any accompanying culture traits involving a change in their subsistence economy. At many points in eastern Europe and western Asia these peoples preserved for centuries their basically Mesolithic traditions, on the fringes of the long-established peasant cultures, and only latterly and sporadically modified their economy.

The adoption of pottery-making itself among such communities appears to have occurred relatively late in their history, not before the end of the third millennium B.C., in a great area characterized by related forms of pit-ornamented and comb-impressed wares, stretching from the Vistula eastwards beyond the Volga and the Middle Urals northwards to the White Sea, and southwards to the northern edges of the territory of peasant communities in the north Pontic and adjacent steppe area. In Turkmenia, allied communities in the Oxus Delta lay adjacent to the developed tell culture of the lands north of the Kopet Dagh already described and eastwards again to lake Baikal. Throughout this great tract of Eurasia there is nothing to suggest a much earlier dating for these pottery-using communities, whose basic subsistence of fishing, with ancillary hunting, was able to support a more static society than a wholly hunting economy; at the western end of their distribution this late-third-millennium date is fairly well fixed in terms of other chronological sequences.

At the European end the introduction of agriculture into this sub-Mesolithic world resulted from the incorporation of their territories, early in the second millennium B.C., into those of the Steppe peoples, with their corded ware and battle-axes, who will be described in the next chapter. Further east, the first appearance of agriculture beyond the Pontic culture area is marked by a widely scattered series of related sites extending from the Oka river and the lower Volga to the Yenesei valley in southern Siberia, the upper Ob valley, and the northern Altai. This Afanasievo culture, with comb-stamped pottery, a stone-and-bone industry, and a few copper ornaments, is based on agriculture or pastoralism (cereal crops are not directly attested), with domesticated cattle, sheep and horses; wild oxen of some kind and deer were hunted. Relations with the Oxus Delta to the south are indicated by imported shells of *Corbicularia fluminalis*, obtainable only from this point, and equations with Pontic cultures indicate a date early in the second millennium B.C. In the delta of the Oxus (Amu Darya), related settlements of hunting-and-fishing peoples with pottery probably date from late in the third millennium, and the subsequent phases of this Kel'taminar culture (and comparable southern Ural sites) have domesticated animals, with sheep predominating over cattle by eighty to twenty per cent. In the Urals the horse is present as well. The Kel'taminar pottery is broadly in the northern stamped tradition, though a few pieces of imported painted wares from the tell settlements of the type of Namazga Tepe, only some 300 miles to the south-west, appear in the first (non-agricultural) phase. East of the Yenesei, in the region of lake Baikal, retarded pottery-using sub-Mesolithic cultures continued, in several places, until the beginning of the second millennium B.C. or even later, when a fully bronze-using culture, that of Karasuk, introduced the first agricultural economy into the area, at a period which may not be long before that of the Shang Dynasty of China, from the middle of the second millennium B.C.

Throughout this great stretch of country, then, the hunting-and-fishing traditions of Mesolithic and Advanced Palaeolithic derivation had a long survival. They appear to be first translated into agricultural economies in the west, and a millennium or more later in their eastern territories. Throughout, the techniques of pottery-making had been acquired, or were independently invented, before any alteration in the basic economy had occurred, and there is nothing in the archaeological evidence to suggest that when the change took place it was accompanied by any form of nomadism. It is true that direct evidence of the growing of a cereal or allied crop is not available and we have only the evidence of domesticated animals, but there is nothing in the assemblage of material culture to differentiate it from that of any normal, static, agricultural community. The continued manufacture of a pottery of not very high quality – heavy and fragile and most unsuitable for transport under nomadic conditions – may well be significant in this regard, and there is again no direct evidence that the horse was used as a riding or draught animal among these peoples. A claim for nomadism at this stage could be supported only by *ex silentio* arguments, though pastoralism, with the more restricted amount of mobility inherent in such an economy, is of course not excluded. It may be noted, too, that there is evidence that in many of the pottery-using non-agricultural communities of the Eurasian steppe, fishing played a very important part, and these societies may have been more static than those upon which the constant and exclusive pursuit of game enforced a more mobile existence.

Returning to southern Russia, we have seen that an important centre of metallurgical development had come into existence in the Caucasus late in the third millennium B.C., as the finds from the royal tombs of Maikop and other tumuli show. Fine workmanship in copper, gold, and silver was achieved here, and the Caucasus soon became an active and inventive centre for working in bronze, which through the second and early first millennia B.C. exerted a great technical and stylistic influence, and created brilliant schools of metal-working not only in the Caucasus but beyond into Persia. The fantastic and artistically exciting products of these related ateliers form an important chapter in the history of the Eurasian animal-art style and must in part lie behind the later Scythian development. By the end of the second millennium an independent bronze-working centre was also established further to the west, in the lower valleys of the Dniester and Dnieper.

In the north Pontic region, and closely connected with the development of the Caucasian bronze industry in the second millennium, a distinctive culture known from settlements and stone-slabbed cist graves can be defined. The rectangular houses were mud-built on stone foundations, measuring around 25 by 12 feet; barley and millet were grown, and cattle and other animals domesticated. On a decorated tomb slab is a representation of a two-wheeled vehicle; there is no evidence to suggest nomadism.

North of the area of this culture, and spreading over a vast tract of country from the Volga to the Yenesei, we can trace a uniform cultural tradition beginning in the middle of the second millennium

B.C., mainly represented by graves. Settlements have also been identified, however, with groups of up to ten roughly rectangular houses partly sunk in the ground and ranging in size from 60 by 30 to 30 by 20 feet, their walls of timber beams or planks in a 'log cabin' construction. Wheat and millet were cultivated, and cattle bones predominate in the food refuse, with sheep and horses next and pigs last; the camel, also, was known. The evidence suggests that young horses were eaten, but they were also used for traction or riding as the side-pieces for bits in the graves show.

The use of wooden burial chambers under tumuli has given the name Timber Grave culture to this complex in the western (Volga) area; further east, in southern Siberia, it is named from a cemetery at Andronovo. The mortuary houses are of sturdy 'log cabin' construction and up to eight feet or so in length, with jointed corners and gabled roofs. There are also ceremonial horse burials and cattle sacrifices represented by the skull and fore parts of the legs only, presumably indicating the original presence of an ox hide retaining these parts, in a manner comparable with horse sacrifices in the Eurasian post-Roman Dark Ages and among the recent Buryat shamans (Figure 82).

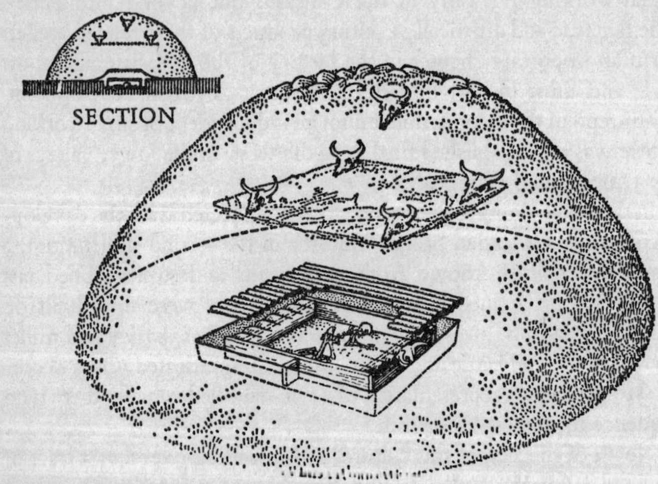


82. Timber grave, south Russia

The recent suggestion by Gimbutas that in the north Pontic and Timber Grave cultures we have the ancestors, respectively, of the Cimmerians and the Scythians of ancient history carries conviction. The Homeric tradition knew of Cimmerians 'around the Ocean', and Greek and Assyrian historical sources show that the Scythians attacked the Cimmerians around 720 B.C., driving them through the Caucasus into the Urartian area, while the Scythians themselves, known in antiquity only to have come from 'Asia' – i.e. east of the river Don – would in all aspects of their known material culture fit the picture given by the archaeology of the Timber Grave culture. Their nomadism could well be a quick change in economy brought about perhaps by a sudden development in their management of horses which gave them increased mobility and military superiority; such a change in economy could be brought about in a few centuries at the most, as is shown by the comparable cultural revolution which took place so quickly when the horse was introduced to the North American continent. There is evidence that the attack on the Cimmerians in the eighth century B.C. was part of a general expansion of Scythian peoples, the repercussion of which can be traced into central and western Europe.

The Scythians appear in recognizable form, archaeologically and historically, from the seventh century B.C. or a little before. The descriptions given by Herodotus of their barbaric and opulent funeral rites, in which the sacrifices of humans and horses are accompanied by the deposition of treasures in the timber mortuary houses under the burial mounds, are abundantly confirmed by excavated tombs from southern Russia to the Altai mountains. Even the ritual intoxication of their shamans by inhaling the smoke of burning hemp seeds is illustrated by actual finds from Pazyryk, where also evidence of trade with China in the last few centuries B.C. is provided by imported silks and bronzes.

The Scythian version of the animal-art style constitutes one of the major achievements of ancient Eurasia. As we know it from the seventh century B.C., it is already distinctively Scythian, however much it may share with other more or less related styles, such as the Minusinsk bronzes from the wooden-chambered tombs in the Yenesei valley, or even with the later Chou bronzes of China. If we are correct in thinking that the Timber Grave people of the Volga basin (and their eastern counterparts in the Andronovo culture) are ancestral to the Scythians, we have to admit that there is no trace of the animal-art style, or anything comparable with it, in these phases; nor does it appear in southern Siberia until well after the end of the Andronovo culture, when it is found in the Minusinsk kurgans, which hardly date from before the seventh century and the art of which is usually thought to have been derived from outside the Yenesei area.

On the other hand, we have seen that in the Caucasus a vigorous and inventive animal-art style had been practised since the second millenium B.C. Its roots, in fact, strike even deeper, into the late third millennium ambit of the animal-art and related metal-work of the Trojan and Poliochni treasures, the Alaça Royal Tombs and that of Maikop. This represents the Early Kuban phase; in the middle period,

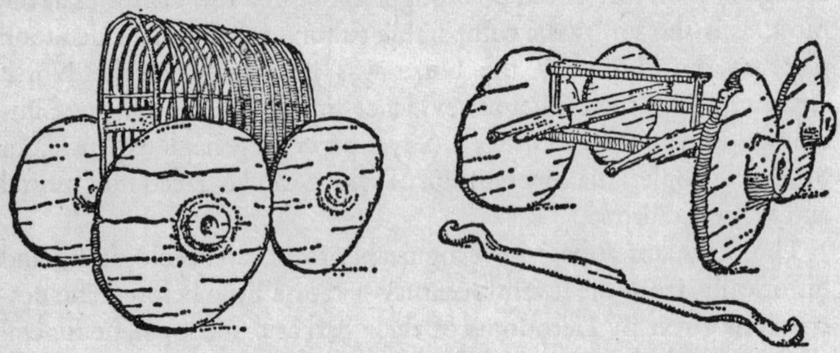

83. Reconstructed wagons, Lchashen and Trialeti

covering the first half of the second millennium, the characteristic Caucasian forms develop. The Late Kuban phase, continuing until the eighth century B.C., includes finds such as the Borodino Treasure and those from timber-chambered tumuli in the Caucasus such as Trialeti, which have Mycenaean connexions of the fifteenth and fourteenth centuries B.C. and recall the Argonauts. Later in the phase come the southwards connexions with Armenia, Azerbaijan, and the Luristan area of Persia, where a notable animal-art style is known from a large series of bronzes. Here are found the wagon and chariot burials from the lake Sevan region of Russian Armenia and the Helendorf tumulus in Azerbaijan, with its timber-roofed grave with burials of men and horses accompanied by bronze swords, battle-axes, and other objects of about the thirteenth century B.C., as well as, from a later date, the

B Cemetery of Tepe Sialk as far away as Kashan (Figure 83). In its final, Koban, aspect we are on the eve of the Scythian invasion of *c.* 720 B.C., and here might be found prototypes for certain eastern and central European bronzes discussed in Chapter 13, which were transmitted, it seems, by early Scythian movements of migration and trade.

With the annexation of the north Pontic homeland of the Cimmerians, the Scythians were in a position to profit from the bronze-working traditions of the northern Caucasus, and to act as new patrons

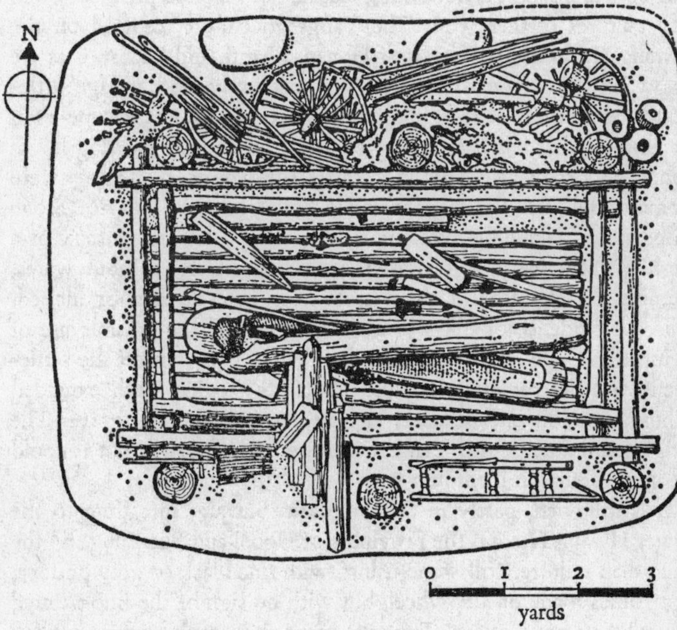


84. Grave under Kurgan V, Pazyryk

to artists and craftsmen with a long history not only of technical excellence but of work in animal styles. Scythian art is something original and individual, it is true, but not wholly without roots; these, we may plausibly suggest, lay partly in the ancient Caucasian tradition which was taken over by new masters in the eighth century B.C. and partly in the ultimately Mesolithic animal art of Eurasia (Figure 84).

There remains for brief discussion the emergence of peasant economies in China. Here, it must be confessed, the situation is rendered unsatisfactory from the start by the complete absence of a reliable chronology for the period before the Shang Dynasty and the historical foundation of Anyang by P'am Keng in 1384 B.C. The two main cultural phases before the Early Shang period, those of Yangshao and Lungshan, are thus wholly undated except in so far as they precede the middle of the second millennium B.C., for no satisfactory contacts can be established between these periods of Chinese prehistory and any cultures further west. The Yangshao culture, centred on the Hwang Ho in the provinces of Honan, Shansi, and Shensi, is as we know it an already mature agricultural economy, with village settlements of a dozen or so houses, and on occasion (as at Pan-po-t'sun in Shensi) what has been interpreted as a communal meeting house some 70 by 40 feet over-all. Pigs, cattle, sheep or goats and dogs were domesticated, and the crops included millet, kaoliang and rice. Stone implements, including axes and sickles, were used, and pottery of a high quality was manufactured, including superb painted wares, though the majority of the vessels were cord-marked or incised. There is evidence of silk-worm cultivation, and the possible use of hemp fibre. Children were buried, often in pots, within the settlement, but the cemeteries of the adults lay outside, with extended inhumations, in one instance, at least, in a plank-lined grave. The origins and date of this Yanshao culture are unknown, but it could lie in the fourth millennium B.C.

It is followed, partly in the same area but also spreading to the lower Hwang Ho and the provinces of Hopei and Shantung, by the Lungshan culture, still stone-using, with fine black or grey pottery, sometimes made on the wheel, but with no sign of the fine-painted wares of its predecessor. The settlement sites, with circular sunken houses and storage pits, were sometimes defended with town walls of rammed earth and stones – at Ch'eng-tzu-yai, for instance, enclosing a rectangular area 1,500 by 1,300 feet. Millet, wheat and rice were grown, and the horse may now have been domesticated in addition to the farmyard stock kept by the Yangshao people. An interesting feature now perceptible is evidence for the practice of scapulimancy, or divination by fire-cracked shoulder blades, a widespread practice known in the New World as well as the Old, and here in prehistoric

China antecedent to the more regularized divining of Shang times. The lower limits, at least, of the Lungshan culture can be fixed, as it comes down to the time of the earliest Shang phase in the fifteenth century B.C.

With the Shang Dynasty we not only enter early historic China but

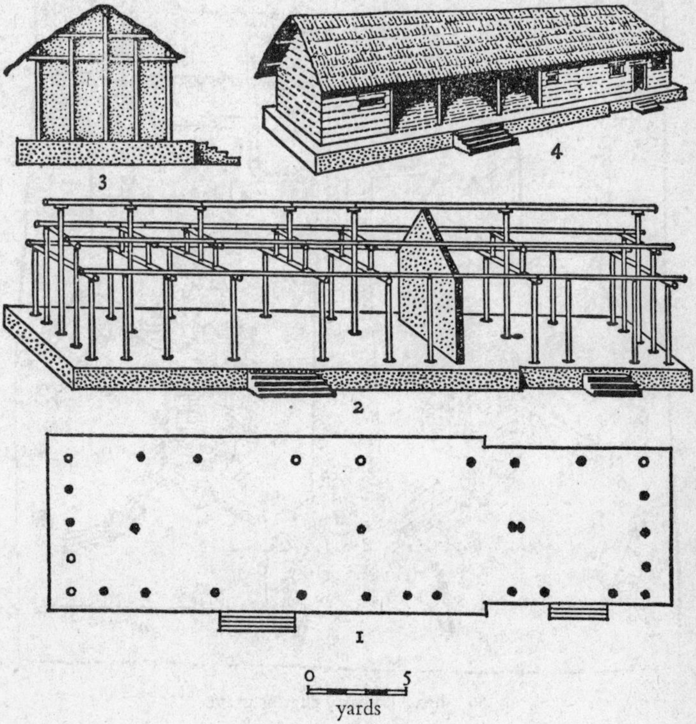


85. Shang Dynasty building

also encounter a series of innovations and changes that cannot be attributed to any indigenous evolution from Lungshan traditions unaffected by outside stimuli (Figure 85). To some extent continuity can be demonstrated – at Early Shang sites such as Cheng-chou in Honan, probably before 1384 B.C. – but even here the city walls enclose an approximate square with sides a mile long, specialized crafts including accomplished bronze founding are in evidence, and writing is

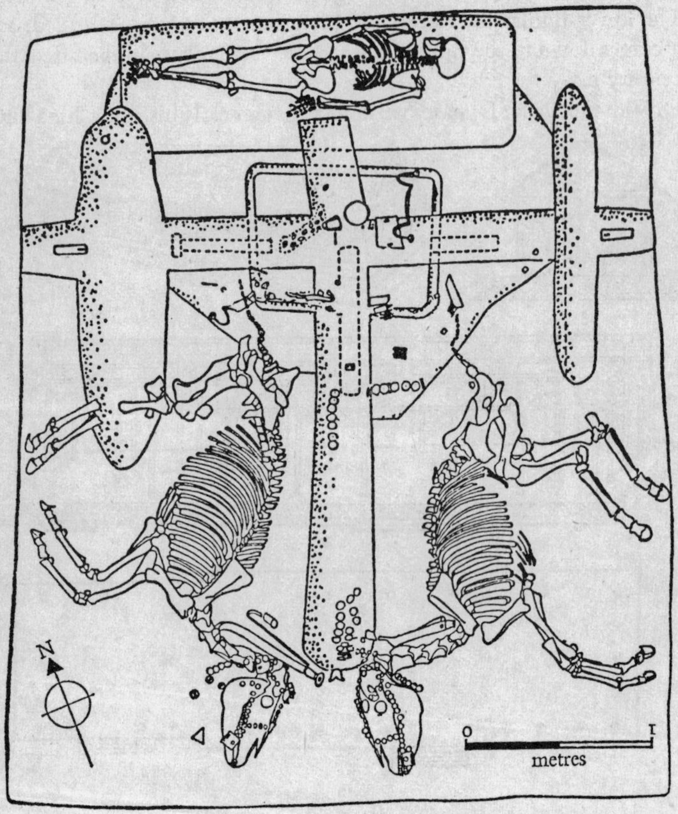


86. Shang Dynasty chariot grave

already present on the scapulae and tortoise shells used in divination. By the fourteenth century or so at Anyang, we are confronted with a large city with a literate civilization and an exquisite refinement in art matched by technical virtuosity in craftsmanship; the royal tombs contain in the wooden mortuary houses evidence of human sacrifice and chariot burials in which the vehicle and the sacrificed horses have been buried with their aristocratic owners (Figure 86).

The circumstances whereby the Lungshan stone-using peasant communities or their equivalents were suddenly transformed into a high and sophisticated civilization elude us, but some outside stimulus must have come into China from the west. The royal chariot burials can hardly be dissociated from the comparatively sudden and wholly successful development of the horse-drawn chariot as an engine of war and an ornament in parade in western Asia around the middle of the second millennium B.C. Some time in the second half of that millennium the Sanskrit-speaking Aryans carried the technique of chariot warfare and manufacture as far east as the Indian subcontinent, and the Shang evidence ought to be connected in some way with other contacts, such as perhaps the transmission of the Tocharian language eastward to the Takla Makan from its Indo-European homeland. The distances are immense and the terrain difficult, but both were surmounted in antiquity once the silk trade with the west was established, and we should not be much surprised if we were to find that the routes of access had been explored in some now unexplained context in the middle of the second millennium B.C.

We have seen how civilization developed from simple peasant communities in Mesopotamia and in Egypt into completely different forms, and we suspect that in India yet another variant emerged. In China we have a fourth, individual and characteristic from the earliest form in which we so far know it, essentially Chinese and as unexplained in its genesis as any.

CHAPTER TWELVE

# *Barbarian Europe: The Middle Phase*

BEFORE taking up the tale again in barbarian Europe it is important to recall what was happening in the civilized Near East late in the third millennium B.C., since our European story subsequent to that date cannot be separated from the general picture of events elsewhere. In Chapter 9 we saw how in certain restricted areas of the Near East literate civilizations had emerged by the end of the fourth millennium B.C. Both in Mesopotamia and in Egypt complex communities, with not only an advanced technology but correspondingly developed forms of social organization, were established from soon after 3000 B.C., and in the centuries following, building on the foundations of the ancient peasant economies, civilization was extended and consolidated in these two great kingdoms of antiquity. In Egypt the Old Kingdom under the first five dynasties enjoyed continuous peace and mounting prosperity. In Mesopotamia the Early Dynastic period, from *c.* 3000 to *c.* 2340 B.C., was a phase of great technical advances: we may instance the development of wheeled vehicles and the achievement of a full bronze industry by the last phase of the period. There follows the beginning of the Kingdom of Akkad under Sargon, with the transference of Sumerian cuneiform script to the Semitic Akkadian language, and the beginning of a long historical and literary tradition. Outside Egypt and Mesopotamia, in regions such as Palestine and Anatolia, communities which remained non-literate nevertheless fell little short of their literate neighbours in technological, agricultural and artistic achievement in towns or little city-states under efficient systems of social organization.

The end of the third millennium B.C. and the beginning of the second marked, however, a time of trouble and disruption among all these peoples. After 600 or 700 years of ordered rule and high artistic and architectural achievement, Egypt fell prey simultaneously to internal dissension and the attacks of Asiatics upon the Delta. With the death of Pepi II in *c.* 2265 there was a weakening of central authority, and the hereditary governors of the provinces competed for power; the Delta was temporarily lost to the Asiatic war bands. 'Behold,' wrote a bewildered contemporary, 'it has come to a point where the land is robbed of kingship by a few irresponsible men ... no office at all is in its place. It is like a stampeded herd without its herdsman.' Recovery was, in fact, effected by about 2000 B.C., but it had been a severe dislocation of what must have seemed for all Egyptians an immutable order of things.

In Mesopotamia, attacks from barbarian raiders from the mountains were received almost simultaneously with the Asiatic raids on the Nile Delta; the Guti were plundering in the last phase of the Kingdom of Akkad, *c.* 2150 B.C., and within a century the kingdom itself came to an end in civil wars when people asked who was king, who was not king. The Third Dynasty of Ur achieved temporary stability, but only before the onset of new raids, around 1950 B.C., from tribes including the Elamites and the Amorites – the Amurru, that 'host whose onslaught was like a hurricane, a people who had never known a city', and whose destructive progress can be traced in the archaeological evidence for sack and pillage in the townships of Palestine around 2000 B.C.

In Anatolia, too, the last centuries of the third millennium are marked in the archaeological record by evidence of violence and destruction. Troy II was sacked and burnt probably around 2300 B.C.; there is similar evidence from the contemporary settlements at Beycesultan, Kusura, Tarsus, and probably at least three hundred more sites in south-western Anatolia. Documentary sources show us that at least some of the raiders here were speakers of Indo-European languages. The place names ending in *-nthos* and *-ssos* in Anatolia and Greece, if not of Early Helladic date in the latter country, may be related to the break in continuity in Greece that marks the end of the second phase of the Early Helladic period, dated by Carbon 14 methods to about 2136 B.C. at Lerna. The Hittites were now establishing themselves within the bend of the Halys river as rulers over the subject Hatti, and perhaps burning the second of the Assyrian trading colonies at Kanesh, *c.* 1900 B.C.

It is clear from the concordant evidence of history, philology and archaeology that the period from about 2300 to 1900 B.C. was marked not only by internal shifts of power within the great kingdoms of Egypt and Mesopotamia but also widespread movements of barbarian tribes on the fringes of civilized western Asia, including some who spoke languages within the Indo-European family. The accidental and almost simultaneous weakening of political power in Egypt and Mesopotamia following the deaths of Pepi II and Naram-sin respectively, may well have given some of the barbarians an opportunity and an excuse for plunder, and so inclusion in the historical records of the time, but outside the literate world archaeology picks up consistent evidence of anonymous folk movements not only in Anatolia but in Europe as well. What we have called the middle phase of later European prehistory has its beginnings in the political and social disturbances just summarized.

The chain of philological reasoning that supports the hypothesis of an original area of closely related dialects which were subsequently dispersed to form the progenitors of the Indo-European languages, as we know them in extinct or extant form, is well established and need not be repeated here. For our immediate purpose we need consider only three main problems: the likely date of the assumed linguistic unity, the possible region as indicated by a common vocabulary for features which might limit the geographical possibilities and the elements of material culture which such linguistic evidence would imply for the speakers of the dialect before their dispersal as independent tongues.

The first question can be answered in some measure by using the evidence from the Assurian documents from the Kanesh Karum, referred to in Chapter 9. Indo-European speakers including Hittites had reached the Anatolian plateau by the middle of the twentieth century B.C., so that some dispersal and language differentiation must have taken place before *c.* 2000 B.C. Into this group would come all the Indo-European languages known from Hittite cuneiform and hieroglyphic texts. Philologically, the likelihood is that, in a second phase, languages including Celtic, Italic and Germanic were dispersed, and in a third, a group comprising Greek, Indo-Iranian and the Balto-Slavic languages; but it must be stressed that this is a sequence to which dates cannot be given.

The problem of an Indo-European homeland has been much discussed since the concept was first framed in the last century. Despite a minority view favouring the North European Plain, there is a general consensus that the common vocabulary of words denoting trees (e.g. birch, beech, oak and willow) and animals (wolf, bear, goose, wasp, salmon or a similar large river fish, and bees, implied by a common word for honey) would be appropriate to an area west of the Urals, and in view of other factors, a region not too far distant from the northern fringes of the civilized area of western Asia and Asia Minor. A belt of country north of the Black Sea, between the Carpathians and the Caucasus, would fit all significant factors.

The material culture implied by the common vocabulary is that of agriculturalists, growing grain, domesticating cattle, pigs and probably sheep, and knowing of the wild or domesticated horse; there is, curiously enough, no common word for the goat. A metal that could be either copper or bronze is known, and wheeled transport is well attested by common words for wheels, axles, hubs and yokes, but not for the spokes of a wheel. In archaeological terms, a late-third-millennium copper-using or bronze-using culture with a knowledge of the horse and of wagons or carts should be indicated.

Some philologists have claimed that in addition to the patriarchal society that the linguistic evidence also demands, we should recognize the existence of common institutional patterns in societies speaking Indo-European languages, involving on the one hand the social organization of the assembly and council, and on the other the details of land tenure and allocation, which appear to be implicit in the early Greek documents in the Linear B script, of the second half of the second millennium B.C. If this were so, our choice would be further limited, always provided that one can recognize such factors in the archaeological evidence of non-literate societies. But we have seen that the first factor need not be exclusively Indo-European at all, since its earliest documented manifestation is in Mesopotamia in a Sumerian context, and its Hittite counterpart could as well or better derive from an indigenous Hattic source rather than from the Indo-European Hittites. Similarly, the bureaucratic tradition within which the Linear B tablets were written is that of the ancient Oriental and presumably Minoan world, and despite their language they can hardly be used as evidence for a pure Indo-European system. Both features could well find their archaeological expression in settlements of tell type, as we have seen, of ultimately Asiatic origin.

In the steppe zone of the eastern Ukraine and southern Russia, from the middle of the third millennium B.C., we find a group of inter-related cultures known mainly from tombs under tumuli but also from settlements such as that of Mikhailovka near Kherson, with rectangular timber-built houses up to 55 by 15 feet over-all, and in some instances subdivided into two or three rooms and possibly accommodating small extended families. Copper knives and awls were in use, querns and flint sickles imply agriculture, and bones of cattle, sheep or goats, pigs and horses are present. The contemporary 'Pit Graves' contained burials in shafts under flat roofs like those of Alaça or the Mycenae Shaft Graves, and in the 'Hut Graves', with wooden mortuary houses of a slightly later phase, two finds of solid-wheeled carts have been made.

This culture is usually hought to be broadly contemporary with a series of richly furnished burials under large tumuli in the northern Caucasus, where we have burials in wooden or stone mortuary houses. At Maikop, the mortuary house had three chambers, one containing a richly equipped burial of a man and the others less splendidly arrayed burials of a man and a woman. The main burial had worn a robe decorated with eighty-seven gold plaques representing lions and bulls, and lay under a baldaquin, the supports of which were threaded through the figures of massive gold bulls. Turquoise and carnelian beads, stone and gold vessels, two silver vases with repoussé ornament including a representation of the wild steppe horse, and an equipment of copper axes, axe-adzes, chisels and knives had also been placed in this royal tomb. Indeed, this burial, and the other similar if less splendid tombs of the same series, must be thought of beside the royal tombs in the Alaça cemetery or at Ur. They must in their way be expressions of similar circumstances, with their suggestion of a stratified society and the accumulation of treasures in the manner of those of Troy II. Like the Alaça tombs, too, those of the Caucasus show the first flowering of an animal-art style and a high tradition of metallurgy which was to stretch from the Troad to the Caucasus and to continue in varying forms until the time of the Scythians and Sarmatians.

From the general matrix of these southern Russian cultures (as exemplified by the Pit Graves) and their successors (the Hut Graves containing a mortuary house), and so from a setting presumptively

Indo-European in speech, came the third main contribution to barbarian Europe within the last few centuries before 2000 B.C., to join the descendants of the early Danubian colonists and those who first implanted the techniques of agriculture in the western Mediterranean and thence in north-western Europe. The details are not clear, but in more than one move and by more than one route, eastern and northern Europe received increasingly important immigrations of steppe origin at the turn of the second millennium B.C. In the south-east, tumulus graves of southern Russian type appear in Rumania, one with a Carbon 14 date of about 2580 B.C.; and we can recognize contributions again from the steppes, in the movements of peoples with a knowledge of the horse who appear as the likely destroyers of the long tradition of tell settlements in Bulgaria and Rumania. In the final phase of the Hungarian Copper Age, at the beginning of the second millennium B.C., a hybrid culture shows just this mixture of eastern and indigenous elements, with a knowledge of the horse and the solid-wheeled wagon. The pottery of this Baden culture has been compared to the Greek Middle Helladic Minyan wares, and significantly such pottery appears in the Troy sequence for the first time in the sixth settlement, together with the first evidence for the horse on that site. And in all these instances we should not be going beyond the bounds of legitimate inference to associate language and archaeology, and see them as evidence of part of the Indo-European language dispersal.

In northern and central Europe the steppe contribution can be equally well traced, in part associated with intrusive pottery forms and the single-grave burial beneath a tumulus, in part with the introduction of the horse and the use of stone battle-axes, derived in form from copper prototypes, as weapons of prestige. These Single Grave, or Corded Ware, cultures, known mainly from graves, spread widely into Scandinavia, Germany, Switzerland and Holland, and graves have Carbon 14 dates ranging from about 2500 to 2200 B.C. in Holland and Germany. Here again we should be dealing with the presumptive speakers of some Indo-European tongue, and in noticing these archaeological hints of folk movements from the assumed homeland we must remember that 'lost' Indo-European languages may well have existed: the relatively recent discovery of Hittite and Tocharian as members of the family shows how this may happen. We will have to return to the question of early Indo-European languages in north-western Europe; a case has been made for a pre-Celtic Indo-European substrate language largely preserved in river names, and the immigrant groups we have just been describing could be considered among those most likely to have spoken it.

Meanwhile, in those areas of Europe where agricultural economies had been implanted from late in the fourth millennium or before, instances can be observed in which mixed cultural traditions eventuated, characterized by a recrudescence of elements derived from the earlier hunter-fisher population. Such Secondary Neolithic cultures are naturally best observed in northern Europe, where the earlier population had developed cultures peculiarly suited to the difficult conditions of terrain and climate, and especially on the southern fringes of the Circumpolar Zone. It is in such a context that we must see the remarkable sites of the early second millennium B.C. in the Shetlands and the Orkneys. In the former islands agriculture was introduced, necessarily from the south, and maintained in the teeth of adverse climatic conditions, with settlements of individual thick-walled stone-and-sod houses, roofed on a framing of drift timber, which on occasion was of North American origin. Irregular cultivation plots of about one-tenth acre per house were cleared of field stones and tilled, the crop being a resistant strain of barley, but the consumption yield of such a plot would be less than a bushel of grain. In Orkney, villages of small semi-subterranean stone-built houses, roofed perhaps with whale-bones or drift-timber framing, reproduce in startling detail recent Eskimo types, sub-rectangular with a bed on each side of a square central hearth, and with a 'dresser' facing the door; all these details were executed in stone, owing to the absence of wood and the convenient supply of easily split flagstone. There is no evidence here of the cultivation of a cereal crop, but domesticated animals included a polled breed of cattle without parallels elsewhere but clearly the result of careful selective breeding. The stone and bone types from Skara Brae have Mesolithic affinities and represent characteristic forms within the general Circumpolar tradition.

The use and construction of collective stone-built chamber tombs continued in the British Isles and Scandinavia well into the second millennium B.C. In the latter region at this time there were several strains in the make-up of the population: the builders of the passage graves, otherwise belonging to the traditions of the earliest agriculturalists in the north; the intrusive peoples of ultimately steppe origin with their single graves and battle-axes; surviving relics of Mesolithic coastal hunter-fishers, and other similar groups with a marginal agricultural economy based to a large degree on pig-keeping, but also actively engaged in such activities as sealing, and making pottery of the types so surprisingly recurrent through the Circumpolar Zone in the Old and New Worlds. Traces of similar hybrid Sub-Neolithic cultures, largely traced from cemeteries of extended burials, are known from an enormous area of Eurasia, from Gotland and the Elbe to the White Sea and ultimately to lake Baikal; these have already been described.

In the British Isles the individual quality of the later Neolithic cultures is well seen in the circular ceremonial monuments with enclosing banks and ditches and uprights of wood or stone, sometimes associated with cremation cemeteries. To this class of open sanctuary the first of the main structural phases at Stonehenge belongs, as well as that at Avebury and many other sites scattered from Cornwall to the Orkneys. We seem to have here a product peculiarly British, related to some set of beliefs involving the concept of the sky-directed open temple rather than the deities of an other-world beneath the ground. The circular plan was already implicit in the tombs of passage-grave type, but perhaps more significantly in the recurrent circular burial mound, with fences and curbs of wood or stone uprights, within the Corded Ware and allied traditions.

We saw in an earlier chapter that a knowledge of working copper had been introduced, from ultimately Oriental sources, into Transylvania and Iberia around the beginning of the third millennium B.C. From such an easterly source must have come the copper objects imported into otherwise Neolithic contexts in northern Europe, which we have also noted, and the same is true of comparable imports in such west-central European Neolithic cultures as that of Altheim. We must now turn once again to Iberia, and trace the curious and complex situation which followed the installation of the 'colonies', one which is closely bound up with the beginnings of metallurgy in much of western and central Europe. The colonies do not seem to have had long lives, and the end of Vila Nova de San Pedro at least was sudden and violent. Subsequently this site was occupied by people who made a highly distinctive form of pottery known as a Bell Beaker, and such pottery appears elsewhere in Iberia in contexts which show it to be subsequent to, but probably also overlapping with, the duration of the colonies. There has been much discussion about the origin of this pottery and the status of the culture it represents in Iberia, but the general likelihood is that we are seeing a development in the third millennium B.C., outside the very limited territories occupied by the colonies, of an indigenous culture whose pottery traditions are derived from the impressed and 'cardial' ware, of which the Bell Beaker pottery is a refined and sophisticated version. It is presumably from the colonists that the makers of this pottery acquired their knowledge of copper metallurgy, but at a slightly reduced level of technological achievement, in that they do not seem to have mastered closed-mould casting and used only the simple open mould for the axe blades and tanged daggers which are their most distinctive products.

Within Iberia, we can recognize two regional variants of the pottery of this culture – a 'maritime' type along the coasts and a 'Meseta' group on the central plateau. There would be little remarkable about this early copper-working group of peoples if they had confined their activities to the peninsula, but at the turn of the second millennium, there occurred the most astonishing dispersal of the peoples who made this highly individual pottery – not only in western Europe, but as far as the Vistula and even the Hungarian Plain to the east, north-west to Britain and southern Scandinavia, in the Mediterranean to Sardinia and Sicily, and sporadically even to North Africa. And in almost every area not only the characteristic pottery appears, but evidence of working in copper and gold as well. This dispersal took place over an area in Europe between a thousand and fifteen hundred miles from the Iberian peninsula, as the crow flies, and considerably more by any of the sea and land routes which could in fact have been used. It is a phenomenon without a real parallel in European prehistory – though it was approached by the spread of Early Danubian culture from the Balkans to Belgium – and for analogues one has to turn to early historical events, such as the dispersal of the Celts from central Europe to Ireland and to Anatolia in the first few centuries B.C., or the barbarian folk movements of post-Roman times. The distribution pattern of Bell Beakers and their accompanying metal-

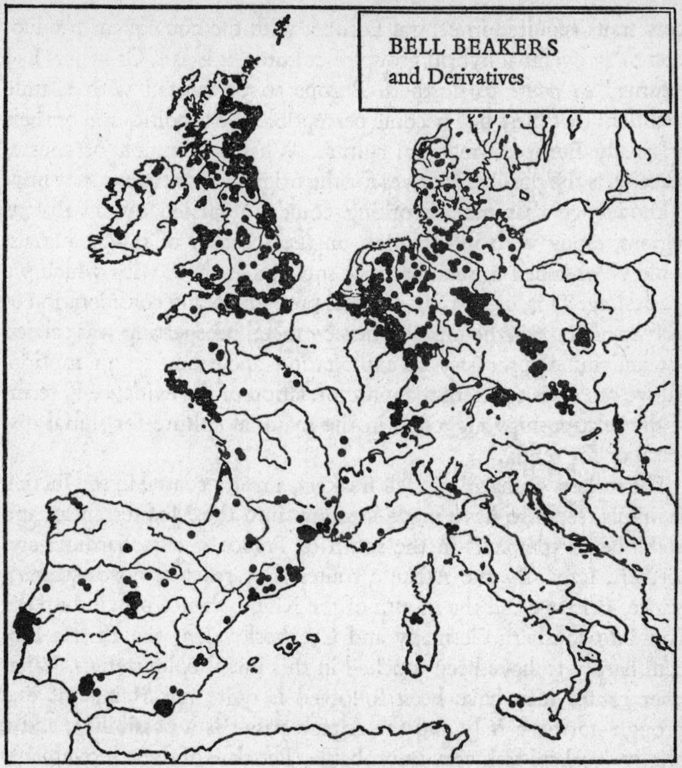


87. Distribution of Bell Beakers

work and other elements of culture poses in acute terms a problem of archaeological interpretation. In an attempt to explain the pattern, the suggestion of a central European origin has been put forward on more than one occasion, but in the absence of any perceptible progenitors of the pottery style in that area it is difficult to sustain, and the Iberian origin of this remarkable *diaspora* seems inevitable (Figure 87).

The most recent studies of the problem agree in regarding the final distribution pattern as the product, not of a single migration from west to east, but of a complex of initial emigrations from the Iberian coasts towards central Europe, followed by a secondary movement of reflux from that area, also complex and involving the importation of new traits acquired in central Europe, with the consequent production of an eventual hybrid group of cultures. It is as if Crusaders had returned *en masse* to northern Europe so permeated with Islamic traditions that these had become perceptible as a modification of their originally European material culture. What we cannot, of course, perceive is the possible motives for the original movements, nor how a knowledge that metal-working could be carried out in distant regions, along with information on the location of raw materials, could be obtained in such barbaric societies as those with which we are dealing. This, indeed, is a cardinal problem in any consideration of early metallurgy – the means whereby metal prospecting was carried out and initial processes of exploitation and trade set in motion. All we can do is to attempt an interpretation of the evidence in terms of the relationships suggested in the material culture for initial dispersal or for reflux.

The makers of maritime Bell Beakers, already coastal in the Iberian peninsula, seem to have made journeys into the Mediterranean and established settlements in the south of France, Sicily, Sardinia and northern Italy. By the Atlantic routes they reached north-western France, Brittany and the mouth of the Rhine, thence moving up the river into southern Germany and Czechoslovakia; the British Isles seem hardly to have been touched in this initial colonization. What other routes may have been followed is quite uncertain, but one through northern Italy and the Alpine passes is a possibility, and a wholly overland trek very improbable. The date of these movements of colonization can be approximately fixed, in the first place by the chronological position of the parent cultures in Iberia after the 'colonial' episode, with a Carbon 14 date of about 2345 B.C. in its mature phase, and by correlations with Sicily implying the introduction of Bell Beakers there at a point in the local sequence which should roughly equate with the end of the Early Helladic period in Greece. Both factors would indicate a date sometime before 2000 B.C.

In central and west-central Europe the makers of Bell Beakers found themselves in a region in which long-standing traditions of Danubian and allied ancestry were now mixed with, and in some areas dominated by, the steppe-derived cultures archaeologically denoted by vessels of Corded Ware, stone battle-axes and such other features as individual burial under a tumulus. Corded Ware vessels are, in fact, similar in form to the Bell Beakers themselves, but their characteristic ornament is normally cord-impressed. Hybrid forms of pottery were soon being made, with decorative techniques and motifs from Corded Ware being transferred to Bell Beakers, and it is such vessels that mainly document the reflux movement. In a grave in Saxony one such vessel was found with a copper knife and awl of Bell Beaker type, and a bone pin of a peculiar hammer-headed type which belongs to the Early Bronze Age cultures of southern Russia, thus stressing the complex components which were now being brought together in central Europe. Carbon 14 dates show, as we have seen, that Corded Wares were being made in the Netherlands by late in the third millennium B.C., and early Bell Beaker forms are there dated to about 2000, in northern Germany to around 1900 and in England to around 1800 B.C. All these dates are consistent with those estimated for Iberia and Sicily, and we must visualize the whole dispersal and return as a rapid process centred on *c.* 2000 B.C. The extremely uniform and consistent standard and quality of the pottery involved throughout the whole area of its dispersal would also argue a short duration for its manufacture in the earlier stages of advance and return. It is in the context of the reflux movement that Britain received her Beaker immigration early in the second millennium B.C. The newcomers to Britain were of a clearly defined ethnic type, tall and short-headed and contrasting strongly with those of the Danubian, Mediterranean and northern worlds; they were also present in central Europe and perhaps in the initial Bell Beaker stock of Iberia. The reflux movement extended into western and southern France and even across the Pyrenees into eastern Spain, and, as it did so, it established contacts between central and western Europe along a number of lines of communication which were to be those of the early metal trade.

There is another point to remember, and that is the possible linguistic contribution which the Corded Ware element in the mixed Beaker cultures could have made. The reflux movement may well have also spread Indo-European dialects into western Europe, and, so far as the British Isles are concerned, the distribution of river names belonging to the non-Celtic but Indo-European substrate language already mentioned, present not only in continental Europe but also in Britain and Ireland, would be best explained by referring them to the folk movements involved in the Bell Beaker reflux.

The comprehensive spectrographic analysis of the earliest copper and bronze artifacts in western and central Europe is still in progress, but already certain significant trends have emerged. Centres of manufacture, using both westerly (Iberian) ones and those of eastern (Transylvanian) types, can be defined, as well as others including a Hiberno-British group and east Alpine sources of material. It can be seen that certain cultures and certain chronological phases can be equated with the use of specific metal resources, and the existence of a period of working in copper, before the discovery of the tin alloy of bronze, is now confirmed. The linking up of Europe through the metal trade is a demonstrable reality from the moment of the inception of copper metallurgy, and further work will certainly extend the picture in detailed and convincing form. These long-range contacts are something new, even if the less extensive trade in stone for axe blades may be thought to have been their precursors. Copper is not a common metal in Europe; tin is actually rare, and the economic necessities enforced on communities entering into non-ferrous metallurgy involved a breaking down of the traditions of relative self-sufficiency within which the stone-using cultures could exist and the building up of trade relationships over long distances. From the beginning of the second millennium B.C., Europe was caught up in a network of trade which extended eastwards into Asia and in which the Aegean, now one of the centres of ancient civilization, played an active part.

The introduction of copper metallurgy to western and central Europe by the Bell Beaker movements was not, however, to remain an isolated episode, for even by the time of the reflux there is evidence for the increased use of new metal types which owe nothing to Bell Beaker traditions – first by makers of Bell Beakers themselves, and then as the dominant forms in a new cultural tradition that was to be the foundation of a central European culture which in variant forms came to achieve a dominant position in mid-second-millennium Europe. The new copper types, which include riveted rather than tanged knives, dress pins implying a sartorial contrast to the buttoned clothes previously in vogue, neck torcs and armlets and ingots of copper made in the shape of these objects, appear in an area from the middle Rhine to lake Constance and thence to Austria and the Danube into central and east-central Europe, including Czechoslovakia. They have no immediately local antecedents, but their quantity and wide distribution implies metal-working on a scale larger than that initiated by the makers of Bell Beakers, and in quite a different tradition. In the early stages of the industry the types in question do not show a distribution south-eastwards down the Danube, so that links with the early copper metallurgy of that area cannot be claimed.

On the other hand, the prototypes of the critical forms are indeed eastern, and of the ancient Orient. The pin types are ultimately derived from Sumerian and Early Akkadian styles current from the middle of the third millennium B.C.; more comparable and geographically less remote examples were common in the Levant and Anatolia shortly before and around 2000 B.C. Here, too, it should be mentioned parenthetically, are the counterparts of other dress pins of a later phase in Europe; the earlier and later forms have not always been distinguished in discussions of the problem, and confusion has therefore arisen. The characteristic torc and its ingot version can also be shown to be a Levantine type of the same period, from the late third to the early second millennium B.C. It is hard to escape the conclusion that the two groups of metal types are in some way related; one could suggest that the central European copper and earlier bronze technology may owe its origins and initial stimulus to contacts established between the Levant and the sources of copper and tin in the Tyrol or the Erzgebirge. The rapid development of bronze technology in the Near East from the beginning of the third millennium must have led to an active search for accessible deposits of ore, and once trade concessions had been obtained by one or another power, political control of the distribution of, and access to, raw materials could be exercised. There must, therefore, have followed an eager watchfulness for new sources of supply which had not already been secured for exploitation by the great powers, and barbarian Europe would have presented itself as a Far West of promise to the miner and prospector, a 'desart yet unclaimed by Spain', not only as a source of copper and tin but as an Eldorado with gold in Transylvania and the British Isles. The Aegean was on its way towards opening up the West and doing what it could to exploit its natural resources, and the beginnings may be archaeologically expressed in the novel types of tools, weapons and ornaments that now, early in the second millennium B.C., were first being made in copper, and soon in bronze, in south-central Europe.

In view of the distribution pattern of these types in their earliest phase, the only likely route of contact seems to have been across the Alpine passes to the head of the Adriatic and thence by sea to the Levantine coast. It has long been thought probable that such trade routes were in use rather later, towards the middle of the second millennium, in connexion with the dispersal of a northern European commodity of some value, amber from the Baltic region. This amber trade plays an important part in the connexions between the Aegean and central and north-western Europe. It becomes well documented from about the sixteenth century B.C., but by this time we are dealing less with a Levantine world than a Greek one, and increasingly one in which the Mycenaeans were playing a dominant role.

We noted in a previous chapter that, in the Aegean, Anatolian connexions (late in the fourth millennium B.C. or at the very beginning of the third) were apparent in such features as the defended citadels with *megara* at Dimini and Sesklo, and perhaps names ending in *-nthos* and *-ssos* and other elements of culture shared with Anatolia at the beginning of the Early Helladic period. An alternative view, as we have seen, is that the distribution of the critical place-names reflects circumstances of a millennium later, at the end of the Middle and not of the Early Helladic II period, about 2100 B.C. and in the context of the general folk movements of that time: the date is confirmed by radio-carbon tests. But it is usually held that the archaeological discontinuity which marks this change must, in view of the subsequent continuity into a period when the language is known, be associated with the coming of the first Greeks. If so, there is no agreement about the place of origin of the Greeks before their arrival in their eventual homeland late in the third millennium B.C., nor, of course, about any routes they may have taken. To some archaeologists, pottery correlations in grey 'Minyan' wares have suggested an Anatolian origin for the Greeks, or a substitution of hypothetical 'Luwians' for the peoples coming into Greece at the end of Early Helladic II times: all philologists do not find this acceptable. The question must remain unanswered in our present state of knowledge.

There is, however, no doubt about the break nor about the evidence of violence and destruction in most areas. New towns were built and fortifications soon added at, for instance, Aegina, Tiryns, Mycenae and Malthi (Dorion). At the last-named site the Early Helladic town had been burnt, and in Middle Helladic times a defended palace-city was built, rather larger than Troy II, about 515 by 300 feet over-all (Troy II was 375 by 340 feet), with five gates in its massive circuit walls. No *megaron* structures appear, but a building identified as a palace lay in an inner citadel, with workshops for metal smiths, potters, etc., around it, and houses in the outer town, backed on to the defences in a ring. The planning of the site, with this ring of houses inside the walls (as also in the fragment excavated at Aegina), is unlike the early Trojan plans, and the absence of a *megaron* is striking; but if Anatolian parallels are sought, the fortresses at Mersin and Hacilar in the fifth millennium, of comparable size and with a similar layout of the peripheral buildings, would perhaps come nearest.

In Crete the Minoan civilization was mounting to its climax during the early second millennium B.C., and the Knossos palace bears eloquent testimony to the height of Minoan power in Late Minoan I, for a century or so from 1600 B.C. The final phase of the Middle Helladic culture of the Greek mainland was heavily 'Minoanized'; the products of Cretan ateliers, whether imported or created by resident craftsmen, dominate the scene, and we encounter a new phase, documented by the material from the Mycenae Shaft Graves, that of Late Helladic I or the first Mycenaean period, again covering the century of Minoan ascendancy of *c.* 1500. But, despite the predominance of Minoan influence, the dynasties buried in the Shaft Graves show, even in burials from the earlier (Grave Circle B) group of tombs, evidence of contacts with other and alien regions.

Some indeed have suggested that the first Mycenaean dynasties themselves came from outside, but at all events the type of their tombs, with the rectangular-walled and flat-roofed burial chamber at the bottom of the grave shaft, recalls the royal tombs at Alaça Hüyük and the less splendid southern Russian Pit Graves. The circular enclosure within which the earlier tombs (Circle B) were set, and its more sophisticated counterpart later built over the A tombs, are without parallels in the Middle Helladic world, or indeed in early Anatolia. These people also seem to have been the first in Greece to use the horse-drawn war chariot, depicting it in low-relief stone carving which is also the first of its kind on the mainland. The chariot as an engine of war had been developed, probably among the Mitanni or the Hittites, late in the first half of the second millennium, as the result of combining the knowledge of the horse as a domestic draught animal with the technological skill needed to make a light, strong, spoked-wheeled vehicle. It was now on its way to becoming a decisive element in Near Eastern and Aegean warfare. Also in the Shaft Graves were gold and silver objects in barbarian art styles harking back to the treasures of Troy II, the Alaça tombs, Maikop and the Caucasus; so, too, ornaments not only made of a northern substance, amber, but in styles current in north-western Europe. A famous gold mask and other portrait representations show men with trimmed beards and moustaches in a manner quite foreign to the clean-shaven tradition of the more ancient Aegean and Minoan world.

The Mycenaeans, over the next couple of centuries, were to increase in power and apparently gain command of Crete and Minoan Knossos. They would acquire and develop conditional literacy and a framework of bureaucracy, by means of the Linear B script, in the general tradition of the literate civilizations of the ancient Orient. The *megaron* house plan, known in Middle Helladic contexts (there is one at Korakou and another at Lerna), appears again as a Mycenaean palace form in Late Helladic times.

In the second half of the second millennium B.C. the Mycenaeans were the great Aegean power, displaying their strength not only in sacking and violence (for which archaeology provides the only clue) but in one episode which, by way of the oral epics, got caught up into written literature, the attack on the seventh settlement on the site of Troy around 1240 B.C. Within a generation, however, the barbarians were on the move again, and, partly under their attacks, the Mycenaeans and other kingdoms fell in the few years around 1200–1150. These circumstances we will discuss in the next chapter; for the present we are concerned with the earlier days of the Mycenaean dynasties. 'It was the start which was difficult,' a classical scholar has recently written; 'the resources of Mykenai are altogether unknown to us: how was procured the gold of the Shaft Graves and the wherewithal to build a fleet.' We shall shortly suggest that a partial explanation may lie in those northern and north-eastern barbarian contacts which are implicit in some of the non-Minoan aspects of Mycenaean civilization.

Meanwhile, in central Europe, a vigorous if barbarian culture had grown up, with a highly competent and technologically adventurous tradition in working true bronze. The natural occurrence of both copper and tin in the Erzegebirge of Czechoslovakia – the 'Ore Mountains' – led to the initial development of a bronze industry in this region, and it spread rapidly south-eastwards to Transylvania and the Hungarian Plain, southwards to the valley of the Po and that of the Rhône, northwards to Saxo-Thuringia, western Poland and the Baltic, westwards to Brittany and the British Isles, with ultimate repercussions in Iberia. By the middle of the second millennium B.C. this huge area formed a common market for the bronze work of armourers and craftsmen in ornaments, for the trade in gold and amber, and for the circulation, as we shall see, of exotic objects, ornamental motifs and ideas from the Aegean world. It was a period when prehistoric Europe was first achieving something of a unity, however loosely knit, over large tracts of country which up to then had held scattered, self-sufficing communities, with variant traditions and apparently no element of cohesion. Behind the widespread distribution of common or closely related types of tools and weapons, ornaments and burial customs, decorative motifs and technical processes, we may perhaps infer not only trading activities between different tribes, but an element of political unity – rudimentary and tenuous but not dissimilar in degree to the unity which at the dawn of history in continental Europe permits us to talk of the Celtic peoples, or on the steppe to perceive the basic unity of Scythians. And the parallel with the later Celts may well carry further implications, for the authors of the second-millennium cultures under discussion occupied in their central homeland the region which was to be that of the Celts, and must have contributed to the eventual emergence of that people.

On the Hungarian Plain and in the adjacent areas of Rumania and Slovakia at the beginning of the second millennium B.C., the establishment of settlements which mark the transference of the tell tradition to its furthest north-western limits can be perceived. It is perhaps significant that the Hungarian settlements of this type seem to begin at approximately the same time as, or just after, the abandonment of the Bulgarian tells already commented upon, after the period of disruption which may be associated with the appearance there of peoples from the steppes of south-eastern Europe. At all events, the permanent settlements which the tells imply now spread further into Europe. If we are correct in inferring that such settlements also represent a social structure similar to that obtaining in the peasant economies of western Asia, which produced similar archaeological phenomena, it would mean that such a structure also was now, early in the second millennium, brought into the heart of temperate Europe. Timber-framed clay-daubed houses are found in such sites, with dimensions of from 25 by 20 to 40 by 20 feet, but entire plans of settlements have not been recovered. Clay models show that solid-wheeled wagons and carts were in use.

At Barca in Slovakia, a village of the same general culture contained twenty-three close-set houses, arranged to a very regular plan, in the uneroded area of the defended promontory on which it was sited. If the layout was originally symmetrically planned, as the surviving remains strongly suggest, the village could have comprised a total of about thirty-three houses, some of one room, others of two or three; the three-room houses would have measured about 40 by 15 feet, with a wooden floor, perhaps for grain storage, in the central compartment. Population estimates here are very hazardous, but if the single-room houses imply nuclear families, and the additional rooms in the larger houses are for storage or stabling, one might guess at an estimated total of about 150 persons, with a required corn yield of something over 200 acres. Our main knowledge of the period derives from cemeteries, with the burials probably all originally under low tumuli. In Saxo-Thuringia and western Poland, richly equipped graves under very large mounds, some with large wooden mortuary houses, show not only a local version of the royal-tomb concept, with its implications of a stratified society and a warrior aristocracy, but also the still-surviving traditions of the steppe and of such burials as that of Maikop in the northern Caucasus.

In the south of England, before the middle of the sixteenth century B.C., a society with a comparable warrior aristocracy, known from richly furnished tumulus burials of men and women, had emerged and had trade relationships both with Ireland and with central Europe. The position of the Wessex downland in relation to the river system made it a natural site for an entrepôt between the Atlantic sea-routes and those of the English Channel and the North Sea. In Brittany, comparable tumulus burials, with a Carbon 14 date of about 1350 B.C. for their later phase, again show central European contacts and, as in Britain, the use of east Alpine copper, though the copper resources of the British Isles were certainly also exploited at this time, and probably those of Brittany; slightly later the high tin percentages imply that Cornish sources had been discovered and worked. Silver objects in the Breton tombs may indicate contacts with Spain, as the metal was being used there in the Argar phase following the Bell Beaker reflux, which again shows traces of direct influence from central Europe. Scandinavia, without natural resources of copper or tin, remained a technological backwater at this time; a few bronzes were imported from Europe, and more particularly from the British Isles, and the metal-hafted bronze daggers of the territories to the south were laboriously imitated in flint, while pendants in the form of whetstones accompany the flint daggers for which they were irrelevant.

The trade network of middle-second-millennium Europe extended virtually from the Black Sea to the Atlantic and from the Mediterranean to the Orkneys. Through central Europe, from Jutland to the head of the Adriatic, the natural routes followed by the traders of amber can be traced, and we have seen how at the beginning of the second millennium there may have been Levantine connexions already established by similar sea- and land-ways. The links between the Aegean and Sicily seen at an earlier date were maintained and intensified during the Middle Helladic period, for which at least one imported cup of Greek painted ware and numerous local copies of the style can be recognized. And from the end of this period, about 1550 B.C., we have evidence in the Aeolian Islands and in sites on the southern Italian coasts of the establishment of Mycenaean trading posts, in the form of imported painted pottery, which continued to be brought in up to the Late Mycenaean phase of *c.* 1230 B.C. In eastern Sicily, too, a tentative precursor of Greek Syracuse is suggested by similar imports from *c.* 1400, for tiny and primitive as these little 'colonies' and trade stations must have been, they do represent the first Greeks in the west. In such legends as that of Odysseus, a faint tradition was handed down into historical times, when the first western Greek colonies were founded from the middle of the eighth century B.C. To this same period of Mycenaean exploration and trade belongs the story of the Argonauts, and although imported Mycenaean pottery has not yet been found on the Pontic coasts, there is good archaeological evidence for trading ventures up the Danube and into central and northern Europe.

The evidence for an Aegean (and largely Mycenaean) interest in barbarian Europe beyond the Mediterranean coasts falls into two groups, one related to the Danube thoroughfare and the other to the north-westerly Atlantic coasts and especially the British Isles. To anticipate, the contacts began in late Middle Helladic times around 1600 B.C. and continued for about a couple of centuries, with sporadic finds suggesting at least intermittent continuance up to the end of the Mycenaean period in the thirteenth century.

The eastern and central European contacts are probably to be related to that strain in Mycenaean tradition on which we have already commented, perceptible in the material from the Shaft Graves, in which metalwork, including examples of an animal-art style, derives from a world outside the Aegean and Minoan *koinè*, and relates rather to the tradition established at the time of the Troy II treasures and the Alaça and Maikop tombs. Such metal-work implies an inherent interest in a world north of the Aegean, including its western extremity in the Danube basin. In remembering the Golden Fleece and Cholcis we must not forget that at the other end of the Argonauts' world lay the copper and gold deposits of Transylvania and, beyond, Bohemian tin.

The most striking evidence of contact comes in the form of a series of objects in bone and antler with designs based on compass-drawn patterns involving ring-and-dot ornament and, in the more elaborate examples, spirals, triskeles and a looped band of running omega-motifs (Figure 88). Such patterns were in use in the Mycenaean world from Argos to Syria, and again sporadically in Anatolia, from the sixteenth to the fourteenth century B.C. In eastern Europe, north of the Rhodope, these patterns appear suddenly in the mature bronze-using cultures from the Carpathians to the Hungarian Plain, and also into Czechoslovakia, on the antler cheek-pieces of horse bits and on bone discs and tubular mounts that could have decorated the shafts of weapons of prestige or wands of office. Once adopted, the ornament was enthusiastically used on pottery and metal-work, including magnificent bronze battle-axes, now a characteristic parade weapon in the Hungarian and Transylvanian region, and as a result of the spread of the metal trade northwards was taken to Scandinavia and used extensively in variant forms on the fine bronzes of that area in the second half of the second millennium B.C.

With it, too, comes other evidence of Aegean contacts, such as a bronze helmet from Brandenburg, whose closest parallel is from a Late Minoan II grave at Knossos, or a pottery cup from the same part of the world copying in clay a metal handle of the well-known Mycenaean type seen on the Vapheio cups, for instance. In the same general context would fit the numerous beads of faience, of eastern Mediterranean or Egyptian origin, widely scattered at this time in central and north-eastern Europe. We have seen how the war chariot

88. Bone objects with Mycenaean-derived ornament, central Europe

had been developed in the mid-second millennium in the North Syrian/Anatolian area, and introduced into Greece at the beginning of Late Helladic times; and the clay spoked wheels from model vehicles which appear in Czechoslovakia in the same setting should once again be connected with technological developments in the wheelwright's craft deriving from an Aegean, and probably Mycenaean, source. Scattered finds of bronze rapiers, from Germany to Transylvania, suggest local copies of Aegean originals, and a small group from Bulgaria, two with Mycenaean spears, are locally made copies of characteristic Mycenaean 'horned' rapiers or swords. Mycenaean or Minoan bronze double-axes have also been found in Bulgaria and further east along the Black Sea coast. The cumulative body of evidence is impressive enough for us to infer with some confidence that in a period based on the century *c.* 1550–1450 B.C. there was a distinct interest in barbarian Europe on the part of the Aegean world, and that Mycenae played a predominant part in whatever traffic was involved. One is tempted to think that, with local or Oriental metal resources largely in the hands of the long-established civilizations of Mesopotamia, Anatolia, the Levant, Cyprus, Egypt and Crete, the necessity for supplies to support the Mycenaean bid for power led to their exploiting the areas to the north for copper, tin, gold and other commodities less apparent in the archaeological record.

In the west a similar but different body of evidence is available. We have seen how the distribution of Mycenaean trading posts in Lipari, Sicily and southern Italy, with their imported pottery, implies some fairly permanent interest in that region; faience beads were also reaching these places. But the main volume of evidence for western connexions with the Mycenaean world comes, surprisingly enough, from the British Isles. There are, for instance, four widely scattered finds of bronze double-axes, and faience beads occur in some numbers. The concentration of exotic objects is in the south-west of England, particularly in the tumulus burials of the rich bronze-using culture of Wessex, which we have already noted in connexion with its central European contacts. A set of zig-zag bone shaft-mounts from one of these tombs has an exact parallel in one of the Shaft Graves of Circle B at Mycenae, of Middle Helladic date of *c.* 1600 B.C.; gold-mounted discs, gold-studded dagger hafts and gold cups, such as those from Cornwall, Brittany and the Rhineland, all copy or reflect Aegean and Mycenaean craftsmanship. But a more specific link is in the amber beads, for here we may be able to perceive both ends of a story.

In both groups of the Mycenae Shaft Graves, Circles A and B, and in a later Mycenaean tomb at Kakovatos, there occur not only amber beads of simple globular forms, but spacer beads – rectangular plaques of amber bored transversely to keep the strings of a multiple necklace separate. The basic type is simple and was widely used in antiquity, and we need not invoke diffusion in the case of so simple a device. But some of the Shaft Grave spacers, and that from Kakovatos, have complicated V-perforations of cross-borings which can hardly be utilitarian and were presumably decorative, for the threads they contained could be seen through the translucent amber. Precisely similar spacers occur in Britain and, less closely parallel, in southern Germany. The north-western European, and probably actually British, manufacture of these Mycenaean amber ornaments seems likely in view of the close correspondence in meaningless detail, and the proximity of the northern European amber, much used for other Bronze Age ornaments in Britain, makes Mycenaean manufacture less probable. So far as chemical analysis can determine, amber in the Aegean at this time seems to be of northern type.

The question of the routes used between Mycenae and Wessex is not easy of resolution. The main amber routes of continental Europe at this time, though not studied comprehensively for forty years, are generally held to indicate a main Mediterranean outlet at the head of the Adriatic Sea and the use of the east Alpine passes. We have suggested that Aegean and Levantine contacts with south-central Europe might have been established by such routes early in the second millennium B.C. But the presence of the Lipari and Sicilian sites suggests that we should look rather to the Tyrrhenian Sea and the Gulf of Lions for western European routes of contact, and the distribution of faience beads and other factors incline one to the view that the connexions with the British Isles were effected by the well-known natural land-route from Narbonne, through the Carcassonne Gap, and so to the mouth of the Loire, Brittany and Britain. We may have to recognize that some of the Mycenaean amber was transported by this westerly route, and certainly the reciprocal contact with Britain appears to have been made in this manner, and not via central Europe.

It is in this context of relationships between the Aegean and Britain at the middle of the second millennium that we must place the final building phases of Stonehenge. Here we have an architectural composition in exactly proportioned and finely tooled stonework, achieved in a manner without parallel in Europe beyond the eastern Mediterranean at this time. Among the prehistoric carvings on the stones is a dagger which can be interpreted as a Mycenaean type: if accurately rendered, it is unlike forms current locally in northern Europe at the time. But, apart from this, the skill and sophistication of the monument itself bespeak an architectural tradition of a different and more civilized kind than that of the up-ended boulders of its British contemporaries. Chronologically, it must have been built about the middle of the second millennium, and it is ringed round with the tumulus cemeteries of the local dynasties, whose grave goods show that they traded not only with central Europe but with the Mycenaean world as well. In some way we must visualize the transmission of techniques, and of the command of labour necessary to execute the task, combined in a fusion of exotic and indigenous stimuli of sufficient power to cause this monument of immense and laborious craftsmanship to be planned, its component stones to be transported and assembled, and the final structure to be dressed to shape and erected.

Stonehenge raises the question of the likely social conditions under which such a monument could be constructed in a situation of relatively simple technological and economic resources, and beyond this immediate and local problem is that of the socio-economic structure of societies in second-millennium Europe as a whole. While any inference of social phenomena from archaeological evidence is infinitely hazardous, we should not feel entirely debarred from making the attempt from time to time, provided always that we realize that such inferences are of an order of reliability and validity far lower than those we make, for instance, on matters of prehistoric technology and the trade in material products.

We have seen that one feature of the set of changes which seem to have occurred at the end of the third millennium, in large areas of eastern and central Europe, is the shift in house plan from a long rectangular building of 100 feet or so in length, to smaller structures of less than half that size. The evidence of comparative ethnography, and to some degree the archaeological evidence, such as subdivisions, multiple hearths and so on, would suggest that the long-house is appropriate to a social structure embodying families not of the natural or nuclear type, which consists of parents and offspring, but rather of the undivided or extended family, an aggregate of two or more nuclear families of three or more generations of relatives. In the former type of family, the unit would normally amount to some five persons; in the latter, from twenty-five to thirty or even more. The extended family survived sporadically in Eurasia down to modern times, but for our prehistoric material the most apposite comparisons may be with the North American Indians, whose societies developed from a stock common to both North America and Eurasia, and in climatic and geographical circumstances not dissimilar to those of Europe. Using this evidence with all reserve, we have already compared the Early Danubian or Tripolye settlements with those of the Iroquois, whose social system embodied matrilinear extended families living in long-houses; the archaeological evidence would permit us to suggest that Early Danubian society was also matriarchal, if we wished to push the comparison to or beyond its reasonable limits.

The change in house-type noted in the late third millennium would, on this thesis, be the archaeological expression of the break-up or modification of the social systems that embodied the extended family, and their replacement by others in which the natural or nuclear family was the socially accepted unit. In western Europe, the evidence, scanty though it is, suggests that long-houses which could be equated with extended-family systems hardly occur west of the Rhine, and that the 'Western Neolithic' cultures had houses, rectangular or circular, appropriate to nuclear families and presumably derived from earlier Mesolithic traditions of small hunting units. The Indo-European social system has been patrilinear from its beginnings, as the common vocabulary shows, and such settlements as are known of Corded Ware and allied groups of late third or early second millennium date, and the mortuary houses in the graves, show no sign of the long-house type, but only of structures appropriate to the nuclear-family group. If we are correct in our estimate, the permeation of central Europe from both west and east by societies that were probably based on the nuclear family during the third millennium would have contributed to changing any dissimilar pattern which had been established there before.

At all events, by the time of the middle of the second millennium B.C., we are in a Europe which must have been becoming increasingly affected linguistically and socially by Indo-European speakers, and in which archaeology shows no surviving trace of the long-house and its assumed extended-family correlate. If we are correct in thinking that the tell settlements of Neolithic eastern Europe could be expressions of the social organization, which we have reason to believe lay behind their Oriental prototypes, we should now have as far to the north-west as Slovakia the village system of patrilinear nuclear families organized under an assembly, with a council and an elected chieftain: the known house and settlement plans would not conflict with this picture. Furthermore, this institutional pattern is later recorded for Indo-European societies in central and western Europe, such as the Celts and the Germanic peoples. However transmitted, some version of this primitive ancestor of Oriental and later Mediterranean city-states and townships, of *polis* and *civitas*, must have now begun to spread through even barbarian societies all over Europe.

The background of Bronze Age Europe provides the setting for a scene which suddenly takes on a familiar aspect, for we are, in the early second millennium, at the prologue of a play whose main action is set in the world of Homer. However squalid and barbarous the material culture with which we are concerned may appear at first sight, it is recognizably the product of societies differing in degree rather than in kind from those of the Iliad and the Odyssey, or of the Argonauts. It is a world that has its roots in the earliest orally transmitted strata of the Homeric poems, but which continues to Cuchulainn and the Mabinogion, to Beowulf and the Sagas, and the dawn of the Middle Ages. Agricultural and pastoral in basic economy, a pattern of farmsteads and villages and rustic princelings' courts, set in open country or in the assarts of the forests, it is perceptibly a stratified society, with farmers and field labourers, and a warrior aristocracy which provides the patronage for the fine craftsmanship in wood or metal, in textiles or in poetry; perhaps, too, a rudimentary merchant class was developing, dealing in trade exchanges and long-range trafficking by land and sea.

It is a Heroic Society, with all the barbarity and insecurity that such a condition involves, the antithesis of the corporate civic life which out of Oriental seed was now striking new roots in the Aegean, but it is one in which the craftsman and the artist have their valued place, and, though unlettered, may nevertheless foster a great tradition in oral poetry and prose. It is something which was to be peculiarly European, and was to perpetuate its simple patterns for centuries beyond the confines of the city-states and the eventual empires of the Mediterranean world. We are the heirs of the one way of life as much as we are of the other.

In the next chapter we shall examine this form of society in its demonstrably Celtic version. But its formation must have taken place during the second millennium B.C., in the context we are now discussing. The stratified society within a tribal entity may involve kings or chiefs, great or small, along with a warrior aristocracy, perhaps a separate priesthood, and a foundation of *plebes*, who may include craftsmen as well as farmers; all are united in a system of obligations and privileges. The main features of this ancient European type of society – visible in a modified form in the Homeric epics, implicit in the contemporary continental Europe we are now discussing, and later displayed among the early Celtic and Germanic peoples – were those which lay behind the elaborate formulation of medieval feudalism, in which the obligations of society were recognized and given formal legal status. In these codes, obligations of service in labour no less than in warfare are prominent; the Saxon *burh-work* made provision for the construction of military earthworks. In the context of such social patterns the organization of the labour force for the building of such a monument as Stonehenge becomes a reasonable possibility, though without in any sense minimizing the greatness of the whole operation. In general, we see the formation in Europe of communities of an increasingly familiar pattern. The comparison with feudalism may be valid in more than one respect, for it may not be extravagant to see an origin for much of medieval Europe in the prehistoric societies which developed in the second millennium B.C.

In the second half of this millennium there followed in Europe a period of consolidation or, in some areas, of stagnation. The Iberian peninsula now moves into obscurity from the final phase of the Argar culture, and in the British Isles there is a period of insular development marked mainly by the growth of a native bronze industry and by the universal adoption of cremation as a burial rite. This changeover was already starting in the middle of the rich Wessex culture, and seems to owe nothing to outside influences. Cremation had been known as an alternative rite to inhumation since Neolithic times, and although the immigrants of the Bell Beaker reflux brought in a solid tradition of inhumation, the earlier trend now seems to have developed into an accepted rite.

The main European development stems from the earlier series of bronze-using cultures in central Europe and its periphery which we have been considering. Tumulus burial, once thought to be a peculiar characteristic of this later development, seems not to have been equally well established in the earlier phase, and the bronze types are in the main modifications of those which went before. By *c.* 1400 B.C. the

Nordic area of northern Germany and southern Scandinavia was not only importing bronzes, but developing individual and highly skilled workshops of its own, with craftsmanship at a level of great excellence and a free use of ornament, in part inspired by the Mycenaean motifs already discussed. Here and elsewhere in this general area of culture, extended rather than flexed burial was becoming widespread, perhaps a northern trait of Neolithic and even Mesolithic origin, and comparable in its resurgence with the contemporary adoption of an earlier burial rite in Britain.

Scandinavian burials of this period, between *c.* 1400 and 1200 B.C., were frequently made in hollowed tree-trunk coffins under large tumuli, and chemical conditions, probably including tanning from the oak wood used and the sealing of the burials by the clay mound, have combined to bring about an unusual degree of preservation of organic material, such as the hair of the dead and the woollen clothes in which they were buried. It is worth-while reviewing at this point the necessarily scanty evidence for early European clothing, in order to see how the Scandinavian material takes its place.

In the broadest terms, there are two basic types of clothing in the northern hemisphere – the tailored clothing which normally consists of trousers and a jacket, based on skin prototypes, and the single-piece wrapped garment, which is a product of a woven length of textile. Tailored clothing goes back to the Advanced Palaeolithic societies at least, and survives on the one hand in the skin clothes of the Eskimo, and on the other in the derivative tailored garments of the civilized western world. The single-piece garment was represented in antiquity by the toga, and today includes the burnous and the derivative forms of sarong or kilt. Within these major divisions we can also see in prehistoric Europe another dichotomy, between fastening garments with toggles or buttons and fastening them with pins. The former is adapted to skin clothing, the latter to textiles, particularly the looser weaves of antiquity. As the materials of buttons and pins are normally more durable than the garments they fasten, they alone provide evidence for much of our inquiry.

At the beginning of the second millennium B.C., button-fastened garments seem to have been developed in north-central Europe, and then adopted and dispersed as one of the components of the Bell Beaker reflux movements. Almost certainly, we are here dealing with tailored skin clothing, and we know that, in some instances at least, the buttons fastened some form of jerkin down the front from neck to waist. The beginnings of early metallurgy in south-central Europe, however, are marked from the first by the production of a large range of garment pins with typological antecedents in the Ancient East, where they are, of course, related to textile clothing in various forms. It looks, therefore, as if we are seeing not only a metallurgical revolution, but a sartorial innovation as well, connected with the new use of textile-manufactured, pin-fastened garments. Furthermore, from the positions of pins in women's graves we know that in the second half of the second millennium they were worn singly or in pairs, below the neck or the shoulders; the second mode is that familiar in the early Greek world as the fastening of the *peplos*, which takes its place as a European pattern of dress distinct from the Minoan-Mycenaean styles which preceded it in Greece. From other graves we have evidence of caps with elaborate metal studding, and similarly studded shoulder-capes (Figure 89) a splendid ceremonial version of which in gold plate was found in a British tomb of this period. The British Isles, incidentally, remained almost outside this world of pin-fastened garments during this period, and, although we have evidence of woollen textiles, the form of the garments eludes us.

The Scandinavian evidence shows a most interesting mixture of traditions. In the first place, the only durable parts of the clothes were occasional bronze cloak pins for the men, and an ornamental bronze belt-disc for women. All clothing was in natural brown woollen cloth, and the men wore a skirt or kilt, in some instances partly covering the body above the waist as well, and an oval cloak over the shoulders. Hats or caps of fabric were also worn, some with a pile imitating fur. The women's dress comprised a knee length skirt of multiple braided cords, held by a tasselled belt, and a short-sleeved jerkin with a neck opening. The pattern to which these jerkins were made is most curious: they were cut from one piece of cloth, and made up with seams under the arms and down the back, but the lower part, which in the finished garment came down to the waist, was made of a series of small strips sewn on. This was not imposed by any limitations in the size of available cloth – huge sheets of textile have survived – but it has been demonstrated that if one tries to cut a jerkin to this pattern from half a doeskin (the remainder being used for

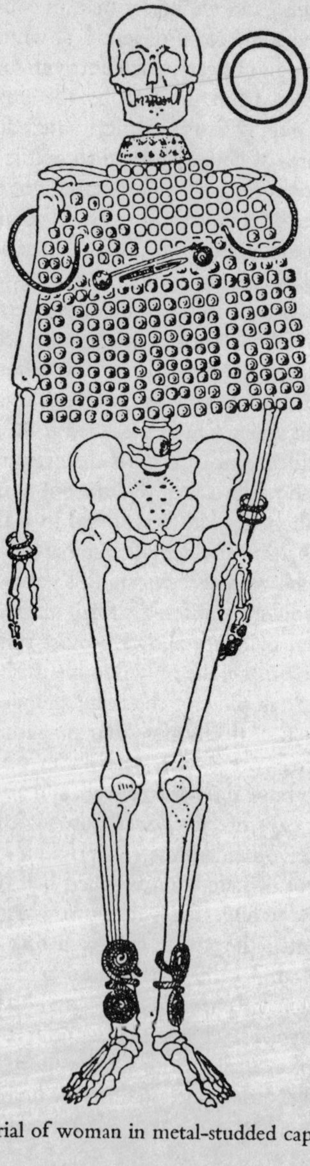

89. Bronze Age burial of woman in metal-studded cape, north Germany

trousers or a skirt) there is never enough skin to make the full length in one piece, but the scraps left over can be joined, to use up the whole skin and lengthen the garment. We have, in fact, a textile-made garment still preserving, in its anomalies of pattern, complications necessary only in the skin prototype.

The second millennium B.C. in Europe has a certain homogeneity, and during the course of it a coherent culture area was created over a large region, connected throughout its various provinces by trade within its own world and also with that of the Aegean and of Mycenae. But, by an odd coincidence of chronology, the years centred on 1200–1000 B.C. are as fraught with change, the movements of peoples and the redistribution of power, as were those of a millennium before, about 2200–2000 B.C. Here, then, we may pause, and in the next chapter consider the evidence of history and archaeology for these events.

CHAPTER THIRTEEN

# Later Barbarian Europe and the Celtic World

The islands were restless, disturbed among themselves: they poured out their people all together. No land stood before them, beginning from the land of the Hittites. ... They marched towards Egypt with fire prepared before them. ... These peoples were united, they laid their hands upon the countries as far as the circle of the world, the people which came from the islands in the midst of the sea.

So in 1186 B.C., the Egyptian scribe summarized the terrifying events which had culminated in the destruction of the Hittite Empire and other powers. The barbarians, turning southwards through Cyprus and Palestine, were repulsed by the Egyptians in a sea battle under Rameses III, a victory commemorated in monumental art and the record just quoted.

These barbarian raids against the ancient civilizations, though they reached their climax early in the twelfth century B.C., had begun over a century and a half earlier. By about 1400 B.C. Egypt had become the supreme power in western Asia, in treaty correspondence with the Hittites and the Mitanni. Of the latter power, with its Indo-European rulers, Assyria was now a client kingdom; in Babylonia the Indo-European Kassite Dynasty ruled. The Armana correspondence shows, however, that in the reign of that well-known figure Akhenaton (1370–1344), trouble was beginning, as the ruler of Alasia (probably Cyprus) complains of raids by barbarians known as the Lukki; the same pirates are soon raiding Egyptian territory.

The historical records are then silent until the end of the nineteenth Egyptian Dynasty, when the Pharaoh Merenptah, about the year 1230 B.C., was confronted with an attack from the Western desert by a mixed force of Libyans and 'Sea People' – 'all peoples of the north, coming from every country', including the Lukki, and others whose names we will consider later. They were defeated (hence the laudatory Egyptian inscriptions recording the engagement) and booty captured, including, it is alleged, 9,000 bronze swords: the raiders were swordsmen.

There then followed, as we have seen, some forty-five years later, the last and greatest of this series of barbarian raids of which we have precise information, and again the opponents are listed by the names of their territories. By 1186 the Lukki, usually equated with the Lycians of south-western Asia Minor, are no longer mentioned, and the only peoples common to the two major raids of 1230 and 1186 are the Shekerlesh and the Shardana, who may be Sicilians and Sardinians. In the war band of 1230 there were also the Aqawasha and the Tursha; the former may be the Achaean Greeks (the Hittite Ahhiyawa) and the second, less surely, Tyrrhenians or Etruscans. In the naval engagement of 1186 there also fought the Peleset, almost certainly Philistines; the Danuna, who may have come from Cilicia; and the unidentified Washasha.

Whatever the detailed interpretation, the general picture is clear enough. Between the middle of the thirteenth and the early twelfth centuries B.C. the centres of higher civilization in the Near East were repeatedly attacked by barbarian war bands, mixed and unstable coalitions of tribes whose raiding bases were in the Mediterranean islands and in whose armies fought some from European lands. When we now turn to the archaeological evidence from Europe itself, we shall not, therefore, be surprised to see signs of change and folk movements at precisely this time, nor to find a subsequent spread into continental Europe of techniques and trade goods that hark back to the period of disruption in the western Asiatic and Aegean kingdoms.

By the beginning of the thirteenth century B.C. the bronze-using cultures of central and west-central Europe were developing their technologies, partly no doubt under the indirect stimulus of trade contacts with the Mediterranean, but also along original lines. The copper-mining areas in the eastern Alps were now developing from simple open-cast working to elaborate deep mining with timbered adits and galleries, and production was accordingly increased enormously. It has been plausibly suggested that the advanced technology now apparent was the result of Aegean or Mycenaean interests in the region during the last phase of Mycenaean power before its collapse.

In the general context of the barbarian raids just mentioned, this was around 1200 B.C. (a date attested not only archaeologically, but by Carbon 14 determinations from Pylos). It will be remembered that we have suggested that the eastern Mediterranean interest in these copper resources reached via the Adriatic seaways may have existed since early in the second millennium B.C., and continued with the trade in amber. At all events, developments in metal-working in relation to an emergent warrior aristocracy, along with the production of new types of slashing swords and of body armour such as helmets and cuirasses, were clearly taking place in central Europe before their known development in the Mediterranean world; so, too, with brooches derived from dress pins, of types which were later to be adopted in the Aegean.

More or less simultaneously, there was a technological development in the making of bronze vessels, parallel with the manufacture of bronze armour and necessitating the same use of annealing techniques. These techniques, known in the Ancient East since the third millennium B.C., appear in central Europe in the thirteenth and twelfth centuries, partly in the context of the Late Mycenaean contacts suggested above, partly perhaps as the result of displaced craftsmen from the eastern Mediterranean finding their way to Europe in the disturbed conditions brought about by the raids of the Sea People. The recurrence of three main forms of this bronze ware – buckets or situlae, drinking cups and finely perforated strainers – has suggested that we have here the equipment appropriate to the serving and drinking of wine, with the situla used as a crater or stamnos. With the importation of Mediterranean wine and its necessary equipment, we shall see a parallel situation in central and northern Europe in the fifth century B.C., and it is also perceptible in the trade in bronze vessels beyond the bounds of the later Roman Empire to northern Europe and Scandinavia.

From the thirteenth century B.C. in continental Europe, we are also confronted with a change in the burial rite, a complete swing-over from inhumation to cremation, with the burial of the dead, their ashes contained in pots, in cemeteries or urn-fields. The circumstances and genesis of this change have been a matter of active and complicated discussion. Here we may note that cremation cemeteries had been common in Hungary, for instance, since the early second millennium, and that Britain provides an instance of a similar and more or less contemporary change of rite in circumstances where external stimuli are virtually ruled out. In passing, too, it is well to remember that the opposite change, from cremation to inhumation, took place in the historical Roman world in the early centuries A.D. as a wholly internal phenomenon. It is, therefore, clearly not necessary to invoke massive influences from without to explain the initial appearance of the central European urn-fields, though in subsequent phases their appearance elsewhere in Europe can be seen, through accompanying innovations in material culture, to be the products of the actual movements of peoples from the original homeland of the rite.

Such movements can be documented archaeologically from the middle of the thirteenth century onwards. In the Hungarian Plain, the flourishing tell culture is brought to a violent end by the incursions of new peoples using the characteristic bronzes of the phase immediately before the earliest urn-fields in the north-west, and the movements thus originated can be seen to have had their repercussions further to the south-east. The Achaean siege of Troy cannot have taken place at the traditional date in the twelfth century, for by then Mycenaean power was extinct, and *c.* 1240–1230 for the destruction of Troy VII–a, the Homeric town, is a date now usually agreed upon. The pottery in the subsequent barbarian settlement of Troy VII–b points to an eastern European origin for those who squatted on the ruins of Priam's capital. Similarly, the swordsmen among the Sea Peoples are not without their archaeological witnesses. A series of bronze swords from the Aegean, in contexts of *c.* 1225–1125, are of central European types, and can hardly be dissociated from the historical events of the period; one from Egypt is stamped with the name of the Pharaoh Seti II, *c.* 1200, and suggests booty earmarked for the royal armouries. Some swords have close counterparts in Europe north of the Alps, and between the Seine and Oder, and prompt one to wonder whether, if Sardinians were indeed involved in the raids, they obtained weapons or auxiliaries from that region. Probably as early as this time, Sardinia was beginning to develop a flourishing culture of which the defended stone castles, or nuraghi, and the superb bronze statuettes, often of sword-bearing warriors, are the later and best-known representatives (the bronzes hardly before the eighth century B.C.). Piracy organized from the strongly fortified Sardinian bases would not be surprising. The swords of the same type from the London area would seem to show that some peoples were prepared to raid northwards as well as into the rich Mediterranean world!

Into this general context of movements of peoples would also come the destruction of the Mycenaean centres of power around 1200, the subsequent Dorian movements in Greece and the immigration of the Phrygians into north-western Anatolia at the end of the thirteenth century. In Italy the earliest Urnfield immigrants appear to arrive in the early eleventh century, and Hencken has suggested that the earliest beginnings of what was to become Etruscan civilization are to be seen in these land and sea movements from this time onward, with eastern European and south-western Anatolian contributions mingling with an Urnfield substratum. In the Lipari Islands the local Bronze Age culture comes to a violent end, with evidence of newcomers from the southern Italian mainland, around 1200; there follow cremation cemeteries in Lipari and adjacent Sicily that can be dated between the eleventh and ninth centuries. Later we see the general expansion of the Urnfield cultures north-eastwards and also west into France: in the Yonne Valley and the Marne by the eleventh century, in the south of France by the eighth, and thence into Spain. Linguistically, this expansion has been variously linked with the Illyrian and the Celtic languages, and certainly a Celtic component must have existed.

The large cremation cemeteries of the Urnfield cultures in Europe, from the beginning of the twelfth to the end of the eighth century B.C., bespeak sedentary agricultural populations of some size, with competent cereal production based by now on the traction plough rather than on hoe or digging-stick. Such cultivation techniques must have been achieved by the middle of the second millennium B.C., as surviving areas of cross-ploughing preserved under burial mounds indicate; in Britain, actual fields have survived in connexion with a settlement, as at Gwithian in Cornwall, of early Urnfield date but of the local Bronze Age culture. Our fullest evidence of a settlement site comes from southern Germany: the Wasserburg at Buchau in the Federsee, a defended island-village in a lake, surrounded by timber palisades (Figure 90). In its first phase, probably eleventh or tenth century, there were thirty-eight wooden houses about 15 feet square, one of which was larger than the rest and suggests a chief's dwelling. In the second phase, probably of the ninth century, there were eight large wooden houses, each constructed of a central block with flanking wings; some rectangular structures, probably

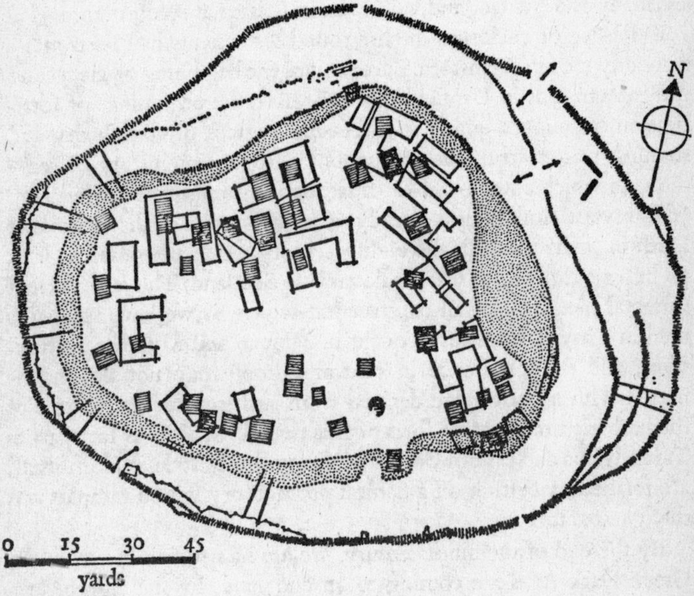


90. Plan of the Wasserburg

barns; and a larger E-shaped house, with flanking wings and a central hall, 30 by 15 feet, which had an entrance porch central to one side. This house, subdivided into six rooms, can hardly be other than a chief's residence, and its proportions and size are those of a smallish manor house of the English Middle Ages. One may reasonably guess at a population of 120 to 150 persons, with an accompanying arable of some 200 acres. The equipment of the village included dugout canoes and carts or wagons with tripartite disc wheels.

The horse seems to have been used throughout Europe in Urnfield times and later. It had by then become a part of the farmyard scene, not as a substitute for the slow but powerful ox but rather as a traction animal for light vehicles of ceremony or warfare. The local wild horses of the forest type were being domesticated, but the eastern origin of the practice can be traced in the types of bone and antler cheek-pieces for bits, derived from those of middle-second-millennium Hungary and Transylvania, appearing in Urnfield contexts in Germany and Switzerland, and even in Britain at second remove.

Defensive or enclosure ditches round settlements had been intermittently used in prehistoric Europe since the beginning of the second millennium, but in Urnfield times we have the beginnings of fortification techniques which in increasing degrees of complexity and strength were to continue throughout European prehistory. A technique in which a stone-and-earth rampart is strengthened by a lacing of transverse timbering is already seen for instance at the Wittnauer Horn in Switzerland in the eighth century B.C., and is used in later prehistoric times from Czechoslovakia to Scotland. This is an ancient Oriental method of wall construction which, as we have seen, was used in Troy II, and was frequent in Minoan and Mycenaean structures, and its appearance in central Europe may not be unconnected with a knowledge derived from such sources at the time of the barbarian raids. Most forts of this period, in areas as far apart as Transylvania and eastern Germany, and in the Wittnauer Horn itself, are formed by cutting off a natural promontory with a rampart and ditch across its base.

By the end of the ninth century, we are in a period in which the Greek Dark Ages are coming to an end; and, by the eighth, in a familiar historical situation, with the development of the Ionian Greek settlements (in which the Iliad and Odyssey must have been composed before about 700 B.C.) and the founding of the Western Greek colonies in Cumae and elsewhere from *c.* 750 B.C. onwards. Etruscan civilization was mounting to its height and about to enter its phase of intense Orientalization. Europe north of the Alps was beginning to take on its familiar aspect as the territory of barbarians outside the bounds of the civilized Mediterranean world, and much of its ensuing story is told in terms of the commercial and political relationships inherent in such a situation. But from the eighth century new cultural influences can be seen to be affecting barbarian Europe from the east, and these are best understood in relation to what was taking place on the Eurasian steppe early in the first millennium B.C.

In Chapter 11 we saw how the prehistoric cultures of the Timber Graves around the Volga and at Andronovo in southern Siberia are likely to have been ancestral to the historical Scythians, who around 720 B.C. drove the Cimmerians from the north Pontic region across the Caucasus. The appearance of bronze work in eastern and central Europe at about this time, mostly in the form of horse trappings and related to Caucasian styles, has been vaguely attributed in the past to the Cimmerians themselves, but the proto-Scythian Timber Grave culture, which shared the same metallurgical tradition and took over the Caucasian workshops from the Cimmerians, is an alternative claimant, in view of the Cimmerian territory lying east of the Crimea and the documented early Scythian expansion. Furthermore, the earlier evidence for horsemen with new forms of bits and harness mounts is followed chronologically, not only by the continuance and development of such bronze types but also by princely inhumation burials in timber mortuary houses, often under tumuli and not infrequently with a four-wheeled wagon buried with the dead. There is, furthermore, the first major use of iron, in the form of large slashing swords of novel types. Such burials are earliest in Czechoslovakia (Figure 91), but later the custom spreads westwards to Germany, Switzerland and France. Sporadic occurrences of a vehicle burnt with the dead are known from even early Urnfield times, but the concurrence of easterly types of horse trappings and the use of the wooden mortuary house with the frequent burial of wagons in the steppe manner strongly suggest that it is to those regions that we should look for these innovations, in the context of the late Timber Graves with their likely proto-Scythian affiliations (Figure 92). In some way, the first transmission of iron technology to central Europe should be connected with these movements of peoples and ideas, but in the present state of knowledge we can do little more than point to Anatolia as the ancient centre of ironworking in the Near East, and to the use of the metal in Greece before the ninth century B.C.

By the early seventh century, then, continental Europe moves technologically into the first phase of the Iron Age, and into a world which in central Europe east of the Rhine is now recognizably the homeland of the historical Celts. Settlements, fortifications and richly furnished graves, including those of the famous Austrian cemetery at

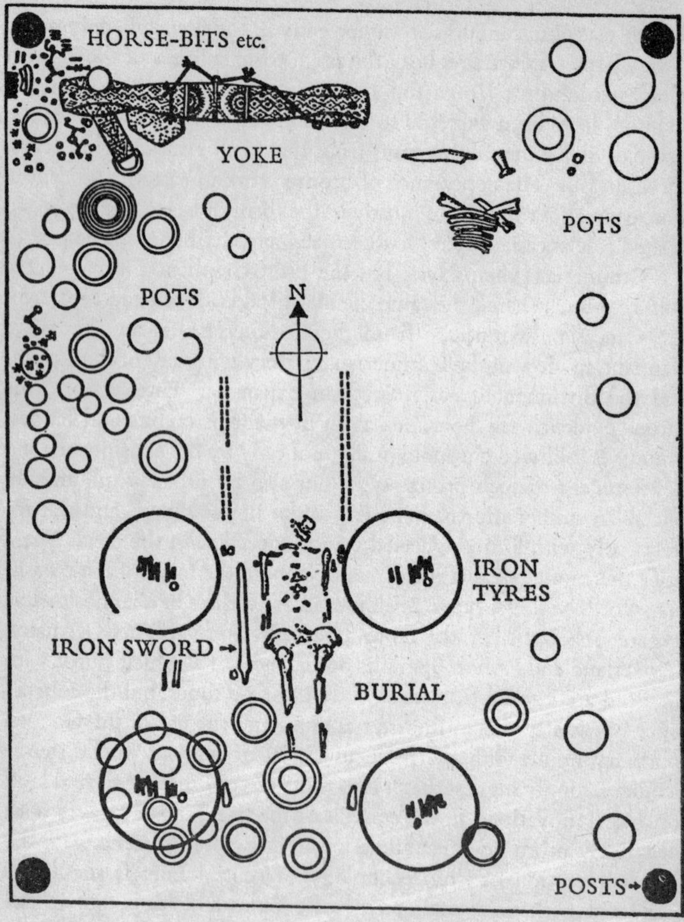


91. Grave 24, Hradenin, Czechoslovakia

Hallstatt (which gives its name to this culture), show us a stratified society in which, on a secure agricultural basis, the warrior aristocracy intermittently glimpsed from the middle of the second millennium B.C onwards now becomes a demonstrable and insistent feature. It is a phase in which contacts with the civilized Mediterranean world become numerous, partly with the Etruscans and partly with the western Greeks. Adriatic and trans-Alpine trade contributed fine metalwork to Hallstatt communities in Yugoslavia, Austria and beyond; westwards the founding of the Greek colony of Massilia about 600 B.C. provided an entrepôt near the mouth of the Rhône, so that this river became a route of access into France and ultimately to southern Germany and the Rhineland. Hallstatt reminds us, in its

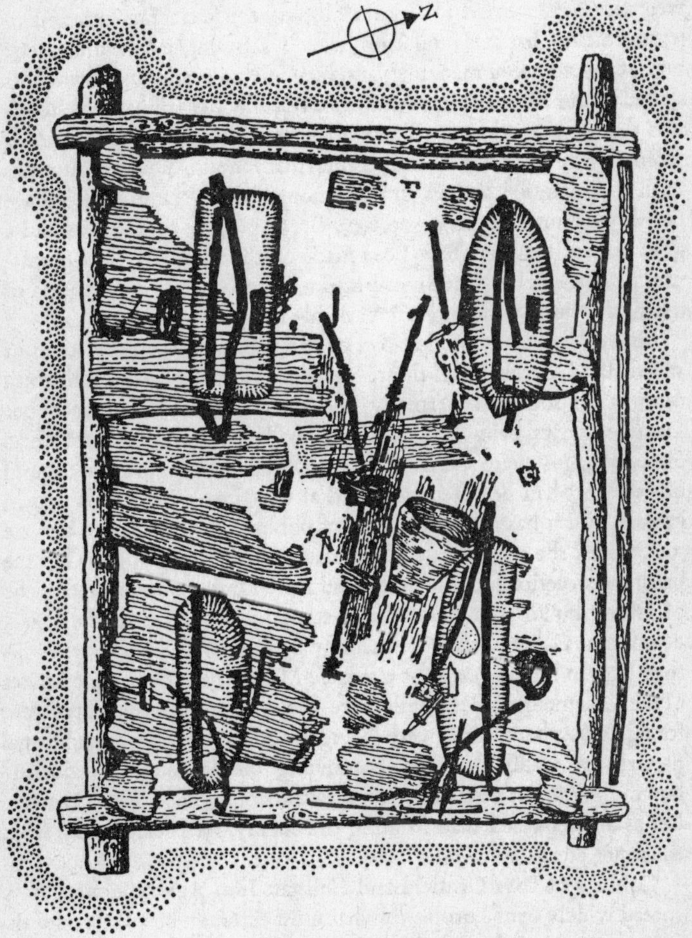

92. Wagon grave at Bell, Rhineland

very name, that there were salt deposits worked there at this time, and elsewhere the trade in salt must have been a potent factor.

Some large and spectacular pieces of craftsmanship were transmitted by this active trade in the sixth century. At Sainte Colombe in the Côte d'Or a bronze tripod of Greek workmanship was found in a tomb with its appropriate griffin-headed cauldron, and at Strettweg near Graz was found a local Hallstatt bronze cinerary urn and an extraordinary bronze model on wheels showing a religious scene with statuettes of women, stags and men, including mounted warriors armed with helmets, shields and axes. But the most remarkable tomb was that of Vix near Chatillon-sur-Seine in the Côte d'Or, where a woman was buried in a timber mortuary house under a tumulus with a dismantled wagon, an enormous bronze crater of the finest Greek workmanship of *c.* 500 B.C., Greek pottery of the 520s and a gold diadem that may have been made on the fringes of the Oriental world. At Graichwyl in Switzerland a large Greek bronze hydria of the sixth century is another remarkable imported piece.

Above Vix stands the hill-fort of Mont Lassois, the inhabitants of which used Greek black-figure vases of the middle and late sixth century. In southern Germany, the Heuneburg fort on the upper Danube shows even more striking evidence of Greek influence. Here, not only were sherds of sixth century black-figure ware found but the fort had been reconstructed at this time with a wall which, in part, was a bastioned structure of unburnt clay bricks on a stone socle; both the planning, with regular rectangular bastions, and the brick construction are foreign to continental Europe but characteristic of Greek building methods, well seen, for instance, in the (later) defences at Gela in Sicily. Its use may be suspected elsewhere in hill-forts (e.g. in the Jura), and at Cayla de Maillac near Narbonne houses of the settlements were so built: here, too, imported Greek wares were found. Elsewhere forts were being built to the more traditional patterns of Urnfield origin, continuing the technique of timber-lace ramparts, but now built not with the sloping face of earlier times but as a sheer-faced wall fronting the enemy, set back slightly from the inner edge of a ditch.

Cultures of Late Urnfield and Hallstatt Iron Age type were now spread widely over Europe, in what must certainly be a Celtic-speaking context. Local variants with strongly marked individual characteristics are perceptible, as in Spain, where at Cortes de Navarra we find a tell settlement of superimposed strata of mud-walled houses laid out in organized contiguous rows with streets between the blocks (Figure 93). In Britain the first iron-using immigrants of Hallstatt derivation are traced to the middle of the sixth century. But the strength of the indigenous tradition of the circular-house plan

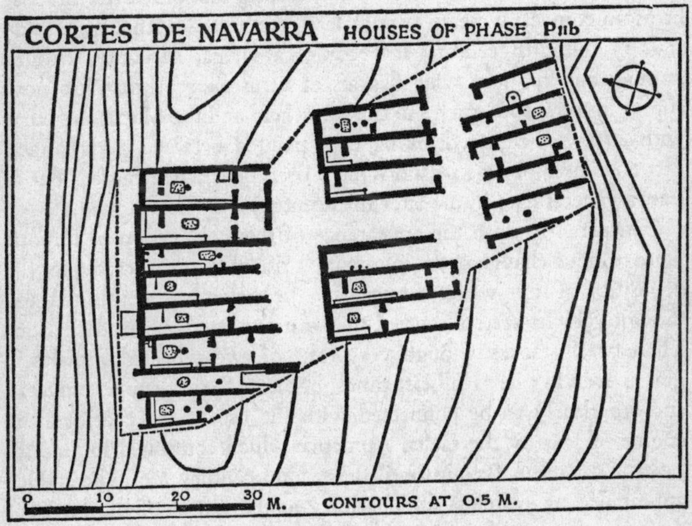


93. Settlement plan, Cortes de Navarra, Spain

is apparent even in the earliest sites, and the continental tradition of the rectangular house was never adopted in pre-Roman Britain. Britain had been in active trade contact with the Continent since earlier Urnfield times; and in the seventh century Irish bronze-smiths, in particular, were not only copying central European types of situlae, but also manufacturing cauldrons whose prototypes go back to the Greek world, and indeed beyond that to Phrygian and Urartian metal-working traditions. Full-bronze shields are again developed into distinctively Hiberno-British types, and some of the northern European shield types are derived from the Aegean.

In the middle Rhine and the Marne, from the fifth century B.C., we see new developments which, owing to continued Greek and Etruscan imports, can be dated accurately, and which in archaeological terms mark the opening of the La Tène phase of Celtic culture. Shortly before 500 B.C. the eastern Etruscan settlements from Milan to Bologna and Este were founded, providing an Adriatic outlet for trade with the barbarian north across the Alpine passes, probably mainly the Little St Bernard. We may suspect that the earlier Graeco-Etruscan contacts were, in part at least, connected with a wine trade and by the fifth century it becomes a virtual certainty. Bronze stamnoi and spouted wine flagons of Etruscan workmanship now appear in numerous graves in the Rhineland and the Marne, together with Attic red-figure drinking cups painted between *c.* 450 and *c.* 430–20. These objects may not have been new when buried, but at least a general date in the later fifth century may be assumed.

Concurrently with the appearance of this new group of imports there comes a change in the inhumation rite of the aristocracy, for the deposition of four-wheeled wagons in the graves is discontinued, and though vehicles are still buried they are now two-wheeled chariots. There are instances, though very few, of two-wheeled vehicles in graves even in early Hallstatt times, but now they become universal and are clearly to be connected with the use of the chariot as an engine of war by the Celts, a practice which continued in Gaul to *c.* 100 B.C. and in Britain until the second century A.D. The sudden appearance of evidence for chariotry at the outset of the La Tène period poses a problem not easy of resolution: from what source does it derive? The Etruscans and Greeks used chariots, but by this time largely as parade vehicles and not as fighting equipment, and their appearance in early La Tène culture implies not only the vehicle itself but also the military tactics in which it functioned. Perhaps we may tentatively look eastwards again, and remember that Herodotus knew of the chariot-driving Sigynnae on the lower Danube in the fifth century, while the chariot burials of the Roman period in Bulgaria hint at a long-standing native tradition behind them in Thrace. In one aspect, as we shall see, the La Tène Celts seem to have had contacts with such areas of Europe, if not with more easterly regions.

The introduction into the Celtic world of Greek and Etruscan works of art and craftsmanship, even if not always of the highest class, brought about one of the most extraordinary sudden flowerings of a new art style that we know of in ancient Europe. From Urnfield and Hallstatt times we have no works of art of a level higher than attractive peasant craftsmanship, but, beginning in the fifth century B.C. and continuing in various forms to the dawn of the European Middle Ages in the British Isles, we have a new, essentially Celtic, art style. It is largely one of pattern and ornament, linear and plastic but rarely sculptural, a non-representational convention in which 'man is a stranger', but with an animal world of fantasy and magic. Its roots are triple – in the immediate local Hallstatt past, in the Graeco-Etruscan use of plant ornament and in an animal-art style which shares elements with that of the steppe and the Northern Nomads, including the Scythians.

The first two sources present no problem, but the third, though undoubtedly present, raises great difficulties. By the sixth century B.C. the Scythians were indeed in eastern Europe, and were the object of Darius's campaign there in about 512 B.C. But the earliest flowering of La Tène art seems to have occurred in the Rhineland, and intermediate links are absent; it was not until the fourth or third century B.C. that characteristic objects of La Tène art are seen in, for instance, Transylvania and Hungary. To some extent Oriental animal fantasies could have come to the Celtic world from Etruscan sources, but these do not seem to supply all the necessary elements. The question must therefore remain unresolved at present.

Among the settlement sites are undefended villages and (especially in Britain) scattered farmsteads, appropriate to individual families. An element of pastoralism, probably present since the early second millennium, side by side with mixed farming, appears to have developed in later La Tène times, with a concentration of wealth in flocks and herds and in some areas (for instance, in northern Britain and probably in Ireland) with only a minimal cereal crop. With this may be connected the increasing size of hill-forts, many of which may have served as defended cattle compounds in time of war: the incorporation of a water supply within the defences, already seen in later Hallstatt times, may be significant in this connexion (Figure 94). An evolved form of timber-laced wall was frequently used from the third century B.C. onwards, on the Continent and in Britain, but it could be subjected to incendiary attack, producing the so-called

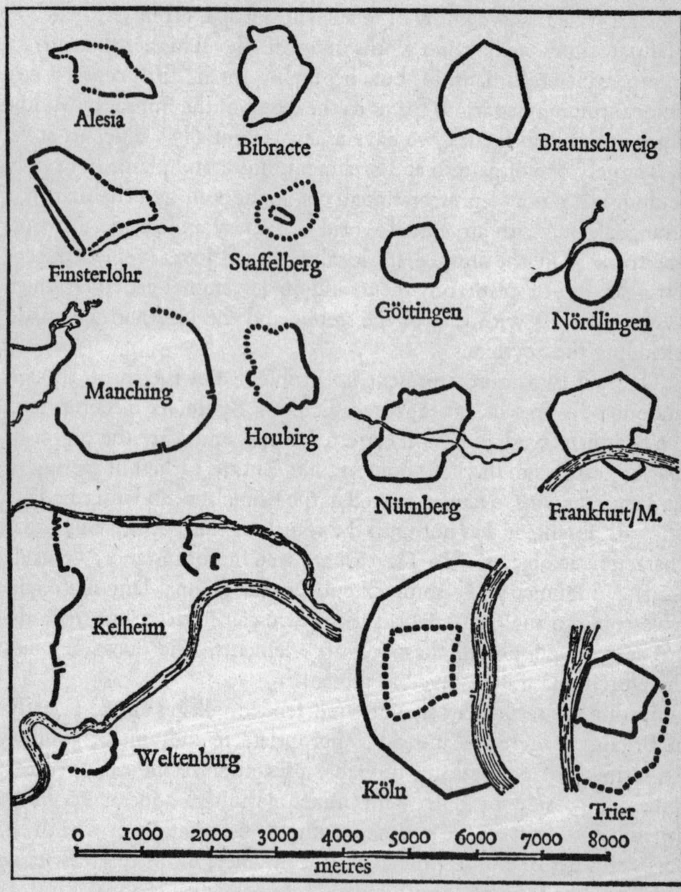


94. Comparative plans of German and French hill-forts

'vitrified' forts known in western France and in Scotland. Still later, from the time of Caesar's campaigns in 58–51 B.C., a specialized form of this construction was produced in answer to Roman attacks by fire and battering-ram – the 'Gallic Wall', in which surface timber was minimized and iron nails used to hold the wooden structure together. Large quantities of raw materials were needed for such constructions:

a tiny Scottish fort, no more than a chieftain's castle, required some 6,400 linear feet of nine-inch-square timber, the product of an estimated 640 young trees scattered through sixty acres of natural woodland. Some forts were enormous, such as Kelheim in the Saar, forty-five acres with an annexe of another 1,400 acres (perhaps for cattle), or Manching in Bavaria, with Gallic Wall defences enclosing a lowland site of 1,000 acres largely occupied by timber buildings, and requiring thirty tons of iron nails for the making of only one

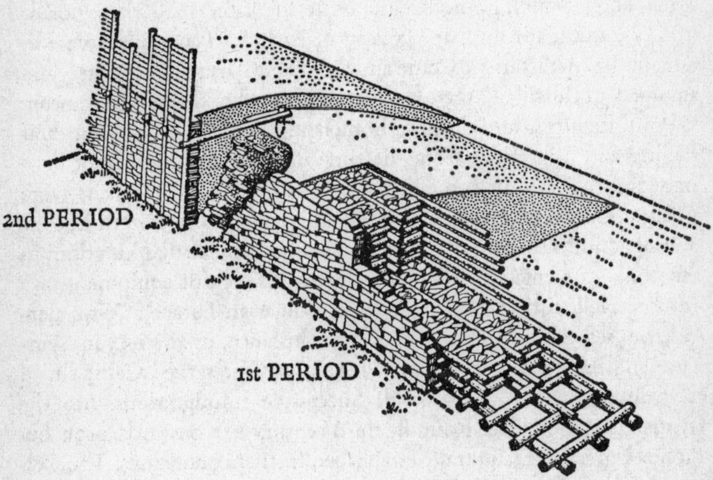


95. Timber-laced defences, Manching, Bavaria

course of its wall (Figure 95). These Celtic *oppida* of the first century B.C., and others such as Elesia and Bibracte in Gaul, represent the nearest approach to real townships achieved in the pre-Roman Celtic world.

Religious sanctuaries of what can now be recognized as the Druid priesthood include many places of votive offerings in lakes and pools, as well as temple sites, often in a rectilinear *temenos* or, as that under London Airport, with a timber building of double-square plan foreshadowing the Romano-Celtic temple plan of the early centuries A.D. La Tène on lake Neuchâtel in Switzerland, which has given its name to this phase of Celtic culture, was a votive site notable for its number of fine iron swords and bronze scabbards, and one can trace the dispersal of the products of the Swiss armourers' workshops of the second century B.C. from Hungary to Britain. Iron-working was at a high level of excellence, and the ancestors of most of the essential iron tools of pre-industrial Europe were developed by the first century B.C., while steel was used at least on occasion for chariot tyres. One is, in fact, in a world in which the similarities with medieval Europe are more striking than the differences. A change in clothing had also come about, linking the Celtic with the later barbarian world; trousers, attested from Late Hallstatt or Early La Tène times, were to remain the characteristic Celtic and Germanic garment, of course, and an object of ridicule to the toga-wearing world of the Mediterranean.

From their central European homeland, the Celts carried out their raiding and migrations from the time of their invasion of northern Italy and the sack of Rome in 400–390 B.C. By 279 B.C., Celts were making for the sanctuary of Delphi and driving into eastern Europe and beyond to set up what was to become the Galatian kingdom in Anatolia (one chieftain was buried with his chariot equipment in a re-used Hellenistic chamber tomb in Bulgarian Thrace). Celtic mercenaries served in foreign armies – for instance, in 368 B.C. in Syracuse and in 274 B.C. in Egypt, where a well-preserved Celtic shield was found in the desert sand. Successive immigrations into the British Isles took place from the third century B.C. onwards, probably none of great size, and trade established further connexions. The Celtic threat to Massilia led to the Roman annexation of the southern Gaulish province in 121 B.C., and the uncertainty and impermanence of Celtic coalitions and alliances, coupled with the mobility inherent in populations in which pastoralism was gaining ascendancy, made them uneasy neighbours for the Romans. The circumstances of the movement southwards of the Cimbri and Teutons from the Baltic area soon after 120 B.C., the subsequent move of the southern German Helvetii into Switzerland and their threatened mass migration thence in 58 B.C., and the move of the northern Suebi south-east to the Rhine, are all well known as the prelude to Caesar's Gallic campaigns and the final extension of Roman rule into barbarian Europe. The events of the late second century B.C. also precipitated the emigration of Belgic tribes from northern Gaul to south-eastern Britain at this time, there to settle and later, under Cassivellaunus, to oppose Caesar (map 4).

The accident of history documents these European population movements of the late first millennium B.C., supplying dates and naming the protagonists, as with the Sea Peoples of a thousand years before, and again with the migrations of the northern peoples of the

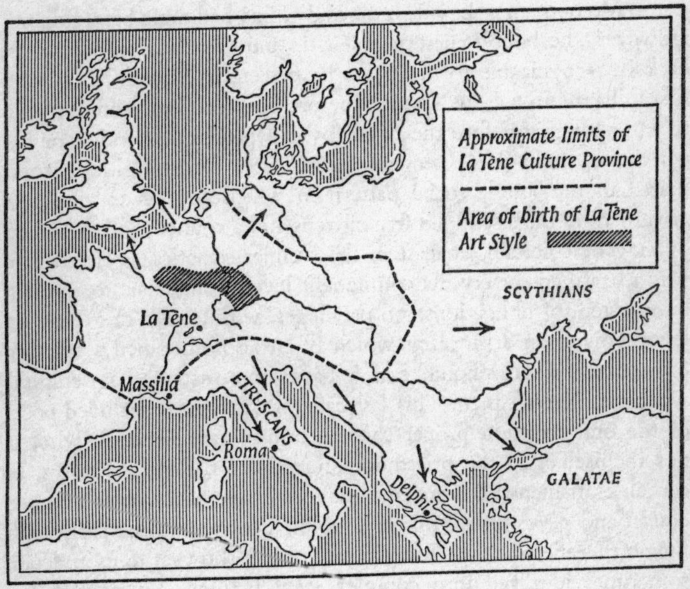


Map 4. The La Tène culture and its expansion (After Powell)

post-Roman world that began some 500 years later. They are historically recorded incidents among a mass of anonymous movements of peoples, who in prehistory can be identified only in terms of archaeological cultures. Yet they are important, for they indicate that the state of flux and shifting populations that the archaeological evidence so often implies was a reality in the ancient barbarian world of Europe and Asia. So far as Europe is concerned, temporary stability was achieved over parts of the Continent through the imposition of

Roman rule, only to relapse into the ancient pattern of barbarian folk-movements upon the relaxation of this alien authority.

For the prehistoric communities of continental Europe, north of the Alps and the Mediterranean, never achieved a true civilization, whereas the peasant communities of Greece and Rome had created their own individual versions of this infinitely variable phenomenon, just as Mesopotamia, Egypt, India and China had done before them. However, the basic structure of Celtic and Germanic society goes back in recognizable form, as we have seen, to Greece before the first millennium B.C., to Anatolia before the second millennium, and to Mesopotamia before the third. By independent invention or by derivation, Indo-European and (in its later form) Celtic Europe shared in the simple social pattern in which a tribe or village is governed by the assembled free citizens and a council, and the office of king or chieftain, at least in the simpler societies, is elective. It was a stratified society, its component levels bound one to another by a system of obligations and privileges, with a ruler of greater or lesser power, an aristocracy which often also embodied a warrior *corps d'élite*, a priesthood, and a basic population of agricultural workers and craftsmen. This last category may have included poets of the oral tradition proper to such non-literate societies, who, if not themselves in the priesthood, may have had special status, as certain craftsmen and merchants may also have had. Caesar's *equites*, *druides* and *plebes* reflect this in simplified form, and the early Irish literature, reflecting a prehistoric way of life, shows it to us in detail, sometimes idealized into complex legal fictions, but nevertheless recognizably a social structure which would have been familiar to Agamemnon or to a Sumerian of the fourth millennium B.C.

But whatever Celtic Europe achieved, it did not achieve civilization. On its pattern of society, and that of the contemporary Germanic peoples, the civilization of post-Roman Europe was to be built, and a stability of government and population effected which was strange and alien to the Celtic mind. The circumstances in which the early medieval achievement of Europe was brought about is the subject-matter of history, but its basic structure lies in the prehistoric past.

# *Selected References*

*With the exception of chapters 1–7 the references cited below were those available to the authors up to completion of the manuscript in 1963.*

## CHAPTER ONE

*Biological evolution*

Brain, C. K. 'The Transvaal Ape-man-bearing Cave Deposits', *Transvaal Mus. Mem.*, no. II, 1958.

Campbell, Bernard G. *Human Evolution: an Introduction to Man's Adaptation*. London, 1966.

Clark, W. E. Le Gros. *The Antecedents of Man*. Edinburgh, 1959.

Dobzhansky, T. *Genetics and the Origins of Species*. 3rd ed., New York, 1951.

Howell, F. Clark. 'The Age of the Australopithecines of Southern Africa', *Am. J. Phys. Anthrop.*, N.S.13 (1955), 635–62.

Koenigswald, G. H. R. von (ed.). *Hundert Jahre Neanderthaler*. Wenner-Gren Foundation, New York, 1958.

Simpson, G. C. *The Meaning of Evolution*. Oxford, 1950.

Weidenreich, F. 'The Skull of Sinanthropus pekinensis', *Pal. Sinica*, no. 127. Pekin, 1943.

*Primate behaviour*

Carpenter, C. R. 'Tentative generalizations of the grouping behaviour of non-human primates', in J. A. Gavan, 91–8.

Chance, M. R. A. and Mead, A. P. 'Social behaviour and Primate Evolution', *Symposia of the Society for Experimental Biology, VII, Evolution*, pp. 395–439. Cambridge, 1953.

De Vore, I. *Primate Behaviour. Field studies of Monkeys and Apes*. New York, 1965.

Gavan, J. A. (ed.). *The Non-human Primates and Human Evolution*. Wayne Univ. Press, Detroit, 1955.

Hayes, C. *The Ape in our House*. London, 1952.

Hooton, E. *Man's Poor Relations*. New York, 1942.

Köhler, W. *The Mentality of Apes*. Pelican, London, 1952.

Schaller, G. B. *The Mountain Gorilla*. Chicago, 1963.
Schultz, Adolph. H. *The Life of the Primates*. London, 1969.
Spuhler, J. N. *The Evolution of Man's Capacity for Culture*. Wayne Univ. Press, Detroit, 1959.
Thorpe, W. H. *Learning and Instinct in Animals*. Cambridge, 1956.
Yerkes, R. M. *Chimpanzees. A Laboratory Colony*. New Haven, 1943.

## CHAPTERS TWO AND THREE

Arkell, A. J. *The Old Stone Age in the Anglo-Egyptian Sudan*. Khartoum, 1949.
Balout, L. *Préhistoire de l'Afrique du Nord*. Paris, 1955.
Biberson, B. 'Le Cadre Paléogéographique de la Préhistoire du Maroc Atlantique', *Publ. d. serv. d. ant. d. Maroc*, Fasc. 16 (1961a).
Biberson, B. 'Le Paléolithique interieure du Maroc', *Publ. d. serv. d. ant. d. Maroc*, Fasc. 17 (1961b).
Bishop, Walter W. and Clark, J. Desmond. *Background to Evolution in Africa*. Chicago, 1967.
Black, D. *et al.* 'Fossil Man in China', *Mem. Geol. Survey China*, Ser. A, vol. II. Pekin, 1955.
Bordes, F. 'Les Limons Quaternaires du Bassin de la Seine', *Arch. Inst. d. pal. hum.* Paris, Mém. 26. 1954.
Breuil, H. 'Le Paléolithique au Congo Belge d'apres les recherches du Docteur Cabu', *Trans. Roy. Soc. S. Africa*, XXX (1944), 143–60. London, 1959.
Clark, J. D. *The Prehistory of Southern Africa*. Pelican, London, 1959.
Cole, S. *The Prehistory of East Africa*. Pelican, London, 1954.
Emiliani, C. 'Pleistocene Temperatures', *J. Geol.*, 63 (1955), 538.
Flint, R. F. *Glacial Geology and the Pleistocene Epoch*. 4th reprint. New York, 1953.
Garrod, D. A. E. and Bate, D. M. *The Stone Age of Mount Carmel*. Oxford, 1937.
Golomshtok, E. A. 'The Old Stone Age in European Russia', *Trans. Am. Phil. Soc.* n.s. XXIX, pt 2, Philadelphia, 1938.
Koenigswald, G. H. R. von. 'Das Pleistocäne Javas', *Quartär*, 2 (1939), 28–53.
Leakey, L. S. B. *Olduvai Gorge*. Cambridge, 1951.
McBurney, C. B. M. 'The Geographical Study of the Older Palaeolithic Stages in Europe', *Proceedings of the Prehistoric Society*, XVI (1950), 163–83.
McBurney, C. B. M. *The Stone-Age of Northern Africa*. Pelican, London, 1960.

Movius, H. L. 'The Lower Palaeolithic Cultures of Southern and Eastern Asia', *Trans. Am. Phil. Soc.*, n.s. XXXVIII, pt 4. Philadelphia, 1948.

Movius, H. L. 'Palaeolithic and Mesolithic Sites in Soviet Central Asia', *Proc. Am. Phil. Soc.*, XCVII (1953), 383–421.

Movius, H. L. 'The Mousterian Cave of Teshik-Tash, South-eastern Uzbekistan, Central Asia', *American School of Prehistoric Research Bulletin*, XVII (1953), 11–71.

Movius, H. L. 'Palaeolithic Archaeology in Southern & Eastern Asia, exclusive of India', *J. World History*, II (1955), 257–82, 525–53.

Oakley, K. P. *Frameworks for Dating Fossil Man.* Third Edition. Weidenfeld & Nicholson, London, 1969.

Sankalia, H. D. *Prehistory and Protohistory in India and Pakistan.* Bombay, 1962.

Solecki, R. 'Shanidar Cave, a Palaeolithic site in Northern Iraq', *Smithsonian Annual Report*, 1954, 389–452.

Zeuner, F. E. *Dating the Past.* 3rd ed., London, 1953.

## CHAPTER FOUR

Boriskovski, P. I. 'Palaeolithic of the Ukraine', *Mat. i Issled po Arkheologii S.S.R*, no. 40, Moscow, 1953.

Breuil, H. *Four Hundred Centuries of Cave Art.* Montignac, Dordogne, 1952.

de Sonneville-Bordes, D. *Le Paléolithique supérieur en Périgord.* Bordeaux, 1960.

Garrod, D. A. E. 'The relations between South-west Asia and Europe in the Later Palaeolithic Age', *J. World History*, I (1953), 13–37.

Garrod, D. A. E. and Kirkbride, D. 'Excavation of the Abri Zumoffen, a Palaeolithic rock-shelter near Adlun, South Lebanon, 1958', *Bull. de Musée de Beyrouth*, t. XVI (1961), 7–45.

Golomshtok, E. A. 'The Old Stone Age in European Russia', *Trans. Am. Phil. Soc.* n.s. XXIX, pt 2. Philadelphia, 1938.

Graziosi, P. *The Art of the Old Stone Age.* London.

Howell, F. C. 'Upper Pleistocene stratigraphy and early man in the Levant', *Proc. Am. Philosoph. Soc.*, vol. 103 (1959), 1–65.

Klima, B. 'Übersicht über die jüngsten paläolithischen Forschungen in Mähren', *Quartär*, IX (1957), 85–136.

Leroi-Gourhan, A. *Préhistoire de L'art Occidental.* Mazenod, Paris, 1965.

McBurney, C. B. M. *The Haua Fteah (Cyrenaica).* Cambridge, 1967.

Mongait, A. L. *Archaeology in the U.S.S.R.* (transl. M. W. Thompson), chap. 2. Pelican, London, 1961.
Movius, H. L. 'Radiocarbon Dates and Upper Palaeolithic Archaeology', *Current Anthropology*, I (1960), 355–91. Chicago.
Okladnikov, A. P. 'Palaeolithic and Neolithic in the USSR', *Mat. i Issled po Arkheologii S.S.R.* no. 59, Moscow, 1957.
Pericot y Garcia, L. *La Cueva del Parpalló*. Madrid, 1942.
Rust, A. *Die jungpaläolithischen Zeltanlagen von Ahrensburg*. Neumünster, 1958.
Solecki, R. S. 'Three adult Neanderthal skeletons from Shanidar Cave, Northern Iraq', *Smithsonian Annual Report for 1959*, 603–35. Washington, 1960.
Vértes, L. *et al. Die Höhle von Istállóskö*. Acta Arch. Hung. v. Budapest, 1955.

## CHAPTER FIVE

Befu, H. and Chard, C. S. 'Preceramic cultures in Japan', *American Anthropologist*, vol. 62 (1960), 815–49.
Bird, J. B. 'Antiquity and migrations of the early inhabitants of Patagonia', *Georg. Rev.* XXVIII (1938), 250–75.
Bird, J. B. 'Preceramic Cultures in Chicama and Viru', *Mem. Soc. Am. Arch.* no. 4 (1948), 21–8.
Clark, G. *World Prehistory – a New Outline*, chap. 10. Cambridge, 1969.
Giddings, J. Louis. *Ancient Men of the Arctic*. New York, 1967.
Gjessing, G. *Nordenfjelske Ristninger og Malinger av den artiske gruppe*. See esp. p. 197. Oslo, 1936.
Griffin, J. B. *Archaeology of Eastern United States*. Chicago, 1952.
Kidder, J. E. *Ancient Peoples and Places. Japan*. London, 1959.
MacNeish, R. S. 'Preliminary Archaeological Investigations in the Sierra de Tamaulipas, Mexico', *Trans. Am. Phil. Soc.*, XLVIII (1958), pt 6.
Mulvaney, John. *The Prehistory of Australia*. London, 1969.
Okladnikov, A. P. *The Soviet Far East in Antiquity*. Toronto, 1965.
Sugihara, S. *The Stone Age Remains found at Iwajuku, Gumma Pref., Japan*. Tokyo, 1956.
Willey, Gordon, R. *An Introduction to American Archaeology. Vol. 1: North and Middle America*. Englewood, 1966.
Wormington, H. M. *Ancient Man in North America*. Denver, 1957.
Wormington, H. N. and Forbis, Richard, D. *An Introduction to the Archaeology of Alberta, Canada*. Denver, 1967.

## CHAPTER SIX

The most useful general work is C. Daryll Forde's *Habitat, Economy and Society*. 8th ed. London, 1963.

Other works providing source material include:

Basedow, H. *The Australian Aboriginal*. Adelaide, 1925.

Birket Smith, K. *The Eskimos*. London, 1936.

Boas, F. 'Ethnology of the Kwakuitl', *Ann. Rep. Bur. Am. Ethn.*, 35. Washington, 1921.

*Handbook of South American Indians*. Smithsonian Inst., Bur. Am. Ethn., *Bulletin* 143. Washington, 1946.

Kroeber, A. L. *Cultural and Natural Areas of Native North America*. Berkeley, 1939.

Lothrop, S. K. *The Indians of Tierra del Fuego*. New York, 1928.

Man, H. T. *The Andaman Islands*. Roy. Anthrop. Inst. London, 1932.

Roth, L. H. *The Aborigines of Tasmania*. London, 1890.

Schapera, I. *The Khoisan Peoples of South Africa*. London, 1930.

Skeat, W. W. and Blagden, C. O. *Pagan Races of the Malay Peninsula*. 2 vols. London, 1906.

Spencer, B. and Gillen, F. J. *The Native Tribes of Central Australia*. London, 1899.

Thomson, D. F. *Economics Structure and the Ceremonial Exchange Cycle in Arnhem Land*. Melbourne, 1949.

Wissler, C. *The North American Indians of the Plains*. Am. Mus. Nat. Hist. Handbook Ser. no. I. New York, 1927.

## CHAPTER SEVEN

Brøndsted, J. *Danmarks Oldtid. I. Stenalderen*. See pp. 11–136. Copenhagen, 1957.

Clark, J. G. D. *The Mesolithic Settlement of Northern Europe*. Cambridge, 1936.

Clark, J. G. D. *et al. Excavations at Star Carr: an Early Mesolithic Site at Seamer, near Scarborough, Yorkshire*. Cambridge, 1954.

Clark, J. G. D. 'Blade & trapeze industries of the European Stone Age', *Proc. Prehist. Soc.*, XXIV (1958), 24–42.

Coulonges, L. 'Les gisements préhistoriques de Sauveterre-la-Lémance', *Arch. Inst. de pal. hum.*, Mém. 14, 1935.

Donner, J. J. and Kurten, B. 'The floral and faunal succession of "Cueva de Toll", Spain', *Eiszeitalter und Gegenwart*, bd. 91 (1958), 72–82.

Firbas, F. *Spät- und nacheiszeitliche Waldegeschichte Mittel-europas nordlich der Alpen*. Jena, 1949.

Garrod, D. A. E. 'The Natufian Culture: the Life and Economy of a Mesolithic People in the Near East', *Proc. Brit. Acad.*, XLII (1957), 211–27.

Godwin, H. *The History of the British Flora*. Cambridge, 1956.

Godwin, H. 'Radiocarbon dating of the Late-glacial Period in Britain', *Proceeding of the Royal Society* B, vol. 150 (1959), 199–215.

Higgs, E. S. 'Some Pleistocene Faunas of the Mediterranean Coastal Areas', *Proc. Prehist. Soc.*, XXVII (1961), 144–54.

Jorgensen, S., 'Kongemosen. Endnu en Asmosen-Boplads fra Aeldre Stenalder', *Kuml*, 1956, 23–40.

Kenyon, K. M. *Digging up Jericho*. London, 1957.

Kenyon, K. M. 'Earliest Jericho', *Antiquity*, XXXIII (1959), 5–9.

Lacam, R. *et al.* 'Le Gisement Mésolithique du Cuzoul de Gramat', *Arch. Inst. de pal. hum.*, Paris, Mém. 21, 1944.

Matthiassen, T. *et al. Dyrholmen, en Stenalderboplads paa Djursland.* Copenhagen, 1942.

Obermaier, H. *Fossil Man in Spain*, chap. X. New Haven, 1925.

Troels-Smith, J. 'Ertebøllekultur-Bondekultur', *Aarboger*, 1953.

## CHAPTER EIGHT

Braidwood, R. J., Howe, B. *et al. Prehistoric Investigations in Iraqi Kurdistan*. Chicago, 1960.

Braidwood, R. J., and Willey, G. R. *Courses toward Urban Life*. Edinburgh, 1962.

Bushnell, G. S. H. 'The Birth and Growth of New World Civilization'. In S. Piggott (ed.). *The Dawn of Civilization*. London, 1961, Ch. XIII.

Cole, S. *The Neolithic Revolution*. London, 1959.

Driver, H. E. and Massey, W. C. 'Comparative Studies of North American Indians'. *Trans. Am. Phil. Soc.*, XLVII, 1957.

Herre, W. 'The Science and History of Domestic Animals', in Brothwell, D. and Higgs, E., *Science in Archaeology*. London, 1963.

Kenyon, K. *Archaeology in the Holy Land*. London, 1960.

Mellaart, J. 'The Beginnings of Village and Urban Life'. In S. Piggott (ed.). *The Dawn of Civilization*. London, 1961, Ch. II.

Zeuner, F. E. *A History of Domesticated Animals*. London, 1963.

## CHAPTER NINE

Aldred, C. *The Egyptians*. London, 1961.
Braidwood, R. J. *The Near East and the Foundations for Civilization*. Eugene, Ore., 1952.
Childe, V. G. *New Light on the Most Ancient East*. London, 1952.
Frankfort, H. *The Birth of Civilization in the Near East*. London, 1951.
Ghirshman, R. *Fouilles de Sialk*, Paris, 1937–9.
Gurney, O. R. *The Hittites*. London, 1952.
Jacobsen, T. 'Primitive Democracy in Ancient Mesopotamia', *Journal of Near Eastern Studies*, II (1943), 159.
Lloyd, S. *Early Anatolia*. London, 1956.
Lloyd, S. and Safar, F. 'Tell Uqair: Excavations by the Iraq Government. Inspectorate of Antiquities in 1940 and 1941', *Journal Near Eastern Studies* II, (1943), 132.
Masson, V. M. 'The First Farmers in Turkmenia', *Antiquity*, XXV (1961), 203.
Nagel, W. *Die Bauern-und Stadtkulturen im vordenastischen Vorderasien*. Berlin, 1964.
Piggott, S. *Prehistoric India to 1000 B.C.* London, 1961.
Wheeler, R. E. M. *The Indus Civilization*. London, 1960.
Woolley, C. L. *Ur Excavations II: The Royal Cemetery*. London, 1934.

## CHAPTER TEN

Almagro, M. and Arribas, A. *El Poblado y la Necrópolis Megaliticos de Los Millares*. Madrid, 1963.
Berciu, D. *Contributii la problemele neoliticului în Romînia in lumina noilor cercetâri*, Bucharest, 1961.
Blance, B. 'Early Bronze Age Colonists in Iberia', *Antiquity*, XXXV (1961), 192.
Böhm, J. and de Laet, S. *L'Europe à la Fin de l'Age de la Pierre*, Prague, 1961.
Brea, L. Bernabo. *Sicily Before the Greeks*. London, 1957.
Childe, V. G. *The Dawn of European Civilization*. London, 1957.
Clark, J. G. D. *Prehistoric Europe: The Economic Basis*. New York, 1952.
Daniel. G. E. *Megalith Builders of Western Europe*. London, 1958.
Evans, J. D. *Malta*. London, 1959.
Gimbutas, M. *Prehistory of Eastern Europe*. Vol. I. Harvard, 1956.
Piggott, S. *Neolithic Cultures of the British Isles*. Cambridge, 1954.
'Neolithic and Bronze Age in East Europe', *Antiquity*, XXXIV (1960), 285.

Piggott, S. *The West Kennet Long Barrow: Excavations 1955–6*. London, 1962.

## CHAPTER ELEVEN

Cheng Te-k'un. *Archaeology in China*. Vols. I–II. Cambridge, 1959–60.
Dewall, M. von. *Pferd und Wagen im fruhen China*. Bonn, 1964.
Gimbutas, M. *Prehistory of Eastern Europe*. Vol. I. 1956.
Gjessing, G. *Norges Steinalder*. Oslo, 1945.
Hallström, G. *Monumental Art of Northern Europe*. Stockholm, 1938, 1960.
Jettmar, K. *Die fruhen Steppenvolker*. Baden-Baden, 1964.
Phillips, E. D. 'Nomad Peoples of the Steppes'. In S. Piggot (ed.). *The Dawn of Civilization*. London, 1961, Ch. XI.
Watson, W. *China*. London, 1961.

## CHAPTER TWELVE

Atkinson, R. J. C. *Stonehenge*. London, 1960.
Broholm, H. C. and Hald, M. *Costumes of the Bronze Age in Denmark*. London, 1940.
Childe, V. C. *The Dawn of European Civilization*. London, 1957.
Clark, J. G. D. *Prehistoric Europe: The Economic Basis*. New York, 1952.
Crossland, R. 'Indo-European Origins: The Linguistic Evidence', *Past and Present*, XII (1957), 16.
Filip, J. *Celtic Civilization and its Heritage*, Prague, 1962.
Giot, P. R. *Brittany*. London, 1960.
Hachmann, R. *Die frühe Bronzezeit im westlichen Ostseegebiet* . . . Hamburg, 1957.
Piggott, S. 'The Early Bronze Age in Wessex', *Proceeding of the Prehistoric Society*, IV (1938), 52.
Powell, T. G. E. *The Celts*. London, 1958.
Powell, T. G. E. 'Barbarian Europe'. In S. Piggott (ed.). *The Dawn of Civilization*. London, 1961, Ch. XII.

## CHAPTER THIRTEEN

Catling, H. 'A New Bronze Sword from Cyprus'. *Antiquity*, XXXV (1961), 115.
Clark, J. G. D. *Prehistoric Europe: The Economic Basis*. New York, 1952.
Jacobsthal, P. *Early Celtic Art*. Oxford, 1943.
Powell, T. G. E. *The Celts*. London, 1958.
Rice, T. T. *The Scythians*. London, 1957.
Sandars, N. K. *Bronze Age Cultures in France*. Cambridge, 1957.
Wheeler, R. E. M. and Richardson, K. M. *Hill-Forts of Northern France*. London, 1957.

# Index